A. Toomer Porter

LED ON!

STEP BY STEP

.

SCENES FROM CLERICAL, MILITARY,
EDUCATIONAL, AND PLANTATION
LIFE IN THE SOUTH
1828–1898

AN AUTOBIOGRAPHY
BY
A. TOOMER PORTER, D.D.

HOME
HOUSE
PRESS

CHARLESTON, SOUTH CAROLINA

Led On! Step by Step: Life in the South, 1828-1898
By A. Toomer Porter
First published in 1898
Introduction and Index © 2010 Thomas Tisdale

Published by Home House Press
109 Broad Street
Charleston, South Carolina 29401

Manufactured in the United States of America

ISBN: 978-0-9845580-0-1

Cover portrait: Courtesy of Porter-Gaud School,
Charleston, S.C.

Cover background photo: © Paula Stephens/Dreamstime.com

CHARLESTON, S. C., *October 5, 1896.*

The Rev. CHARLES FREDERICK HOFFMAN, D.D., LL.D., D.C.L., President of the Association for Promoting the Interests of Church Schools, Colleges, and Seminaries in the United States :

At your kind and sympathetic suggestion, I have written some reminiscences of my life. You seemed to think some of the incidents of that life, which I have from time to time related to you, were of interest and might do some good. Appreciating your judgment and opinion, I have endeavored to make this sketch of my life, neither sparing my faults nor magnifying my virtues, but have tried to show how the Divine Love and Hand have led me all these years. I have brought out how all one's life is often turned by some incident which, perhaps, at the time, seemed trifling, but was fraught with marked results.

I ask the favor to inscribe these pages to your honored self, wishing that the record of my life were more worthy of your acceptance. But you will receive it, I trust, as a small token of the warm attachment I have for you.

With my love, I am

Yours,

A. TOOMER PORTER.

The above dedication was written before the decease of my lamented friend ; I now therefore gratefully dedicate my autobiography to his memory.

A. T. P.

CONTENTS

Contents.

Contents.

INTRODUCTION

"O Lord, save Thy people, and bless Thine heritage." [1]

The author of this book, Anthony Toomer Porter (1828-1902), was a priest and educator; today he would also be called a community organizer. Dr. Porter, as he came to be known in his time and ours, began his long life on the banks of the Sampit River in Georgetown County, South Carolina on November 16, 1828. He has told the story of his life with passion and determination in this autobiography, originally entitled *Led On!: Step By Step, Scenes From Clerical, Military, Educational, and Plantation Life in the South, 1828-1898* when it was first published by G. P. Putnam's Sons in 1898. It is a story of one who made great contributions to the restoration of civilization in what was likely the most tumultuous span of the history of the South. This new edition of his autobiography gives a rebirth to his vision and ideals for the spiritual, educational, and societal development of South Carolina and this country.

The son of John Porter Jr. and Esther Toomer Porter, the author was the youngest of five children. His father died at age thirty-three when the infant Anthony Toomer was only nine months old. The family lived on a rice plantation named Mauricena that was acquired by Porter's grandfather in the late eighteenth century. Mauricena comprised about 1250 acres and was located just inland enough from the Atlantic Ocean to support the cultivation of rice, which required fresh water. It was typical of the South Carolina coastal rice plantations that produced fortunes for their owners in the eighteenth-century Lowcountry of South Carolina and were still quite profitable a century later. The Porter plantation on the west side of the Sampit River was bordered by other rice plantations: Woodstock, Northampton, and Harmony.[2] The lands of Mauricena, like many of its neighbors, are now occupied by a mid-twentieth-century suburban housing development. In 1850 Mauricena

---

1 Psalm 28:11, and the last words of John Toomer Porter, October 23, 1864.

2 Suzanne Cameron Linder and Marta Leslie Thacker, *Historical Atlas of the Rice Plantations of Georgetown County and the Santee River* (Columbia: South Carolina Department of Archives and History, 2001), 550-552.

produced forty-five tons of rice, thanks largely to the efforts of ninety-eight enslaved men, women, and children.[3] (In 1860, at nearby Friendfield plantation, where the ancestors of Michelle Obama lived in slavery, 273 slaves tended 629 acres of land, about half that of Mauricena, and served the family that owned the property.[4])

Anthony Toomer Porter spent most—but not all—of his formative years at Mauricena. About two years after the death of his father in 1829, his mother, a widow burdened by a large family of young children, a working rice plantation, and evidently living a complicated domestic life, took her family to Connecticut. It was there that her forebears and those of her late husband had settled in the early eighteenth century when they immigrated from England. After spending two years in the North, Esther Toomer Porter and the children returned to Mauricena.

One reason for the family's two-year sojourn in Connecticut may be explained by an unsettling and unverified contemporary story. Georgetown native Thomas Peter Smith wrote that Esther, after her husband's death, was inexplicably consumed by a jealous rage directed at one of his law partners and the lawyer's two successive wives.[5] These events, if they occurred, were never mentioned in any of the known writings of Anthony Toomer Porter.

Toomer Porter, as he was known to his family and friends, left Mauricena in 1844 at age sixteen to attend Mt. Zion Academy in Winnsboro, South Carolina. He studied there for a year and a half before taking a position with the rice, cotton, and mercantile firm of Robertson and Blacklock in Charleston. The company was the largest rice house in the world in 1845 when young Porter arrived to work as a merchant. There, he first came to grips with his deep repugnance to the institution of

---

3   Slave Schedule, 1850 U.S. Census, Prince George Winyaw District: 125-127.
4   Linder, *Historical Atlas of the Rice Plantations of Georgetown County,* 545.
5   George Cuttino, "The Merry Widow of Georgetown; OR The Fire Story," *Proceedings and Papers of the Georgia Association of Historians* 10 (1989): 93-99 (http://archives.colstate.edu/GAH/1989/93-99.pdf; accessed April 6, 2010).

slavery and the slave trade that was still in full force in South Carolina.

Anthony Toomer Porter came into a world marked by slavery. His life and those of most of his contemporaries were shaped by their experiences with slavery and their reactions to it. Through the inspiration of his writings and how he responded to the social issues of his time, including slavery, we can better understand how we too might better address the societal issues of our day.

The introduction of a system of slavery to Carolina in 1670 led to the development of a social and economic institution that stripped the enslaved men and women of most of their human rights and dignity, rights which every enlightened civilization acknowledges were endowed on all living persons by God. By its very nature, slavery obliterated the humanity of the enslaved. It converted human beings into mere property—chattel, as they were legally described, like a horse or a house. By America's modern standards, the enslavement of one human being by another is a criminal act; it is impossible for us now to see how it could ever have been justified by our forefathers, much less for the reason of mere economic gain. But, slavery has deeply influenced and directed much of the history of the United States for over 300 years.

The Carolina colony was founded for the purpose of providing products—rice, indigo, and forest-related resources, at first—to the mother country of England. The colonial venture was primarily meant to benefit those few men, the Lords Proprietors, who received Royal charters to exploit the land and its resources. The success of the colony depended upon the availability of cheap human labor. Most of the first settlers—and the first African slaves—came from and through the Atlantic island of Barbados, another English colony which by 1670 was crowded with settlers growing crops for export. Later, slaves were imported directly from Africa in large numbers by slave traders on both sides of the Atlantic. In the early eighteenth century the slave population in South Carolina exceeded the number of whites by a ratio of ten to one. By the time of the founding of the United States in 1776, the black population exceeded the white in South Carolina by about three to two. There was also, of course, a prolific propagation of the slave community within itself in the years following the first settlement. Charles Towne, about sixty miles south of the Porter plantation, was the center of much of the importation of slaves to the southern colonies; about 40 per cent of all the slaves taken to North America came though the harbor at Charleston. They were generally put in holding pens on Sullivan's Island pending their sale to plantation owners and businessmen. Slavery was undeniably the key to the economic success of the colony as well as to a multitude of social problems that it engendered throughout its history.

The control of those slaves was, for civil harmony and for sheer survival, a necessary and paramount goal of the white slave owners. The system that was put in place prohibited the free movement of enslaved people from one place to another. It is also clear to us now, in the twenty-first century, that the obvious inequality of the power of slave owners and the enslaved inevitably led to violence. Laws were enacted in South Carolina that prohibited the education of slaves to prevent the slave population from achieving the ability to make informed decisions for their own betterment.

Some slaves lived and worked in the cities and towns of South Carolina, but the large majority of them were plantation workers, first to cultivate rice and indigo, and later to work in the cotton fields of the Lowcountry and in the backcountry when short-staple cotton was introduced. The effects of the institution of human bondage in South Carolina are most graphically and intimately illustrated in *Slaves in the Family,* a book by Edward Ball, a direct descendant of Dr. Porter.[6] Ball's book tells the story of the lives of thousands of those human beings who were "possessed" by the author's ancestors, including the Porter family, in the Carolina Lowcountry.

By 1828, the year of Porter's birth, a mere fifty-two years after the founding of the country, there were already signs of serious

---

6 Edward Ball, *Slaves in the Family* (New York: Farrar, Straus, and Giroux, 1998.

and controversial political and social division in the United States. The strength of the union of states steadily deteriorated in the forty years leading to the beginning of the Civil War in 1860, to a great extent because of slavery. As the Rev. James Thornwell, an antebellum Presbyterian clergyman, wrote, "slavery is implicated in every fibre of southern society."[7]

Serious political issues arose as to whether new states joining the union would be allowed to maintain the institution of slavery within their borders. Some Southerners engaged in the battle to abolish slavery. Perhaps the most notable was Angelina Grimké (1805-1879), who left her family in Charleston as a young woman, moved to the North, and fought for the elimination of slavery.

In the midst of this conflict, Anthony Toomer Porter began his life. As he reached adulthood, the hallmarks of his life were: a spiritual destiny that he first recognized as a young man; the recognition that social justice and education for all people in society was vital to the success of civilization; and an unflagging effort to serve God and man in every possible way without any limitation.

The first glimpse of Porter's spiritual life was revealed in a visit to his father's grave at Prince George, Winyah Church in Georgetown in 1838 at the age of ten years. He went alone to the gravesite and fervently prayed to be able to grow to manhood and contribute his life to the accomplishment of good works as his father had done until his untimely death. Later, writing about this event, he commented without elaboration, "The spiritual world is much nearer to us than we can possibly conceive."[8]

Porter first revealed his penchant for social justice when he was required to handle the sale of some of his mother's slaves while employed at Robertson and Blacklock. The experience was so unnerving, distasteful, and wrenching for him that he said to Mr. Robertson, one of the owners of the business, that if he had to do such a thing again he would have to resign his position.

---

7 Quoted in Walter Edgar, *South Carolina, A History* (Columbia: University of South Carolina Press, 1998), 288.

8 A. Toomer Porter, *Led On! Step by Step, Scenes from Clerical, Military, Educational and Plantation Life in the South, 1828-1898* (New York: G. P. Putnam's Sons, 1898), 12.

Porter decided to leave the mercantile world in Charleston when he turned twenty-one in 1849, declining an offer of a partnership at Robertson and Blacklock. He returned to Mauricena to take over the family land, becoming a slave-owning rice planter. He successfully ran the plantation for about two years until one day in 1851 while riding on horseback he asked God's guidance to lead him to a life that would be more fulfilling. The young man evidently realized that he was profoundly unhappy living the life of a rice planter. This feeling, perhaps an answer to his prayer, led him to a serious self-examination, trying to figure out what he should do with his life.

A month later, in the middle of a sleepless night, Porter arose, knelt beside his bed, and prayed, "Lord, if Thou dost wish me, here I am. I give myself to the ministry of Thy Word."[9] He then, at 4 a.m., awoke his mother and informed her that he had been called by God and would immediately do whatever was necessary to seek admission into holy orders. He promptly began studying for the priesthood under the direction of the Rev. Alexander Glennie, the rector of All Saint's Parish at Pawley's Island, near Georgetown. The sale of the plantation lands gave him enough financial resources to take care of his mother and others in the family who needed it. However when he sold his family's slaves as he prepared to enter the priesthood, he reduced the sale price by the hefty sum for that time of $16,500 to obtain an agreement from the purchaser not to separate them. His actions were completely consistent with the mandate of the Gospel to give up everything to follow the Savior, and that he did, never turning back for the remainder of his long life.

During the time of his preparation for a career in the ministry, on December 6, 1852, he married Susan Magdalene Atkinson, with whom he would live until her death on June 19, 1891. She was the daughter of another Georgetown County rice planter. A year later, they were blessed with the birth of their first of five children, a son they named John Toomer Porter.

In January 1854, even before he was officially ordained,

---

9 Ibid., 77.

Porter was assigned by the bishop, Thomas F. Davis of the Diocese of South Carolina, to work with the small congregation of the Church of the Holy Communion in Charleton. He wouldn't know how small it was until he visited and found only eight communicants meeting for worship at the United States Arsenal on Ashley Avenue, a site now a part of the campus of the Medical University of South Carolina.

The Civil War is, of course, the watershed event of the nineteenth century in America, perhaps even in its entire history. Although he did not enthusiastically support South Carolina's secession from the Union, once the decision to secede was made, Porter characteristically supported his fellow countrymen. He engaged the controversy as an officer and chaplain of the Washington Light Infantry in Charleston, a position that he held for over thirty-seven years in times of war and peace. The infantry unit was formed in 1807 and named to honor President George Washington. It was chosen to escort the marquis de Lafayette into the City of Charleston upon the occasion of his visit in 1824. The WLI has served in every major war entered into by this country, and has provided valuable service to both the United States and the Confederacy as those situations presented themselves. Three of its companies served with the Confederate Army. It has sometimes been designated in major military campaigns as Company B of the 118th Infantry Regiment.

Porter recounts an often-told story, but with a different twist than the versions generally reported in the histories of the state, about the reactions of the prominent Charleston lawyer James Louis Petigru to the developing plans of the state to secede from the Union. As Porter tells it, Petigru was walking up Main Street in Columbia (not on Meeting Street in Charleston as is usually recounted), when a countryman asked, "Mister, can you tell me where is the lunatic asylum?" "Yes, my man," Petigru replied. "Yonder," pointing to the State House where the Legislature was in session, "is the asylum, and it is full of lunatics."[10] (This story, of course, begs the question of what

---

10   Ibid., 116.

Petigru's opinion might be today.) After the war, Porter, while visiting in the office of C. C. Memminger, an early proponent of a public-school system for South Carolina and the Secretary of the Treasury of the Confederacy, asked, "Mr. Memminger, I am now as old as you were when this city and State went wild; why did not you older men take all of us young enthusiasts and hold us down?" "Oh!" he replied, "it was a whirlwind, and all we could do was to try to guide it."[11]

Near the end of the war, Porter tried to take his family to Anderson, South Carolina, to escape the worsening conditions in Charleston, and to avoid what was thought to be an almost certain attack on the city by the army led by Gen. William T. Sherman. The train in which the Porter family was traveling could not make it past Columbia, so they were forced to take up temporary residence in the state capital. As matters developed, during his march through the South, Sherman bypassed Charleston and stormed Columbia. The city surrendered to General Sherman on February 17, 1865, and soon after that much of the city was pillaged and torched while the residents were evacuating. Amidst the chaos, Porter personally confronted General Sherman. He recounts that Sherman said, "This is terrible," to which Porter replied, "Yes, when you remember that women and children are your victims."[12] Sherman, according to Porter, blamed the fires, pillage, and deaths on the governor of the state, Andrew Gordon McGrath, who evacuated the population without destroying the city's large supply of alcohol. The Union troops who found the supply of alcohol quickly became a drunken mob that could not be controlled. Many public buildings and over 1,300 houses were destroyed.

Porter and his family remained in Columbia until the evacuation of the city was complete. The resulting mayhem was almost unimaginable. But, as in many of the important events in Porter's life, the adversity which he faced contained seeds of future success as endurance and lessons of hardship would become staples of his character.

---

11 Ibid., 117.
12 Ibid., 164.

During the destruction of Columbia, on February 18, Porter encountered John A. McQueen, a native of Elgin, Ohio, and a lieutenant in Company F of the 15th Illinois Cavalry. McQueen, a member of the victorious enemy force, single-handedly, courageously, and without any personal motive saved Porter's family from the ravaging mob. The house in which the entire Porter family was living was the only one within ten blocks that was not burned to the ground. Lieutenant McQueen, who was unfamiliar with Porter and his family, ordered all of his fellow Union soldiers off the premises, arranged to extinguish the burning fires nearby and in the Porter home, and posted sentinels and guards to protect the Porter family inside. Skeptical at first of the protective appearances of McQueen's behavior but quickly recognizing his heroic efforts on their behalf, Porter embraced the young lieutenant. McQueen lingered behind the departing troops to assure the safety of the Porters, and Reverend Porter arranged for his safety during the days and months ahead. Porter himself described McQueen's protection of his family as an act of "gentle tenderness" and said, "It was God's Providence that brought us together."[13]

Porter gave McQueen a letter of "safe passage" through Confederate lines as he left Columbia to rejoin his unit in Sherman's army as it marched north. Ultimately, Porter's letter saved McQueen's life. The relationship that developed on the field of battle led to a life-long friendship of immense substance. The touching encounter with McQueen strangely affected the success of Porter's life and his later post-war reconstructive work in South Carolina. The remarkably unlikely connection of events in Porter's life reveals what is perhaps a godly intervention and support for what he believed was his mission in life. His encounter with Lieutenant McQueen and what followed in their relationship guided Porter's work to restore civilization in South Carolina following the Civil War.

Another central event in Porter's life was the 1864 death of his son John Toomer Porter, his firstborn, who died at the age of eleven years. The death was a pivotal moment in Porter's

---

13   Ibid., 168.

life. The young boy on his deathbed, holding his father's hand, recited a passage from Psalm 28, *"O Lord, save Thy people, and bless Thine heritage."*[14] The boy then died almost immediately. This event helped shape Porter's actions for the rest of his life.

After the Civil War, Porter felt compelled to lead his devastated state to recovery, and he realized that the recovery required provisions for a sound education for everyone, black and white, in order to preserve any semblance of civilization. But he was destitute, spiritually and financially, and with the rest of the population, had no idea what to do to begin to rise from the ashes.

In the aftermath of the Civil War in 1866, Bishop Thomas F. Davis sent Dr. Porter to New York as a first emissary from the church in the South to raise funds for the prostrate diocese in South Carolina. (The Episcopal Church in the North and the Diocese of South Carolina never formally separated, as did the northern and southern governments. When the voice of the South Carolina delegation was silent during the roll call at national meetings during the war, it was simply noted that the representatives were "absent.") Porter, at first resistant to the task assigned to him owing to a feeling of inadequacy, launched his mission with a visit to New York where he requested money for the restoration of the church and schools in South Carolina. Porter's personality ideally fit the task he was given. The simplicity, timeliness, and earnestness of his mission along with his ability as a strong preacher and adept fundraiser led to success. And, as the reader of this book will learn, he was unusually well suited for the task.

Porter had grown up a son of privilege; he was obviously not impressed by wealth, as he had given up all he had to serve God; and he was not afraid to ask the wealthy for what he needed. His financial requirements were not personal, but for the benefit of others. In one instance he rebuked a prominent gentleman in New York for treating him discourteously when he approached him for a contribution. He told the prospective contributor, "Now, sir, if my personal appearance and my manners do not

---

14   Ibid., 150.

indicate the gentleman I belie my ancestry. But I have a message to you. I am a clergyman of the Church of which you are a member; my social position is as good as yours. I have been the rector of a prominent church for eighteen years, a member of the General Convention, and of the Standing Committee of my diocese, a trustee of the University of the South, and of the General Theological Seminary and Board of Missions. . . . [M]y position is established. It is an apostolic injunction, 'Be courteous.' You may be that, if you cannot be generous." As the reader might suspect, Porter's stern rebuke was followed a few days later by a generous contribution from the grumpy gentleman.[15]

His work was endowed by contributions from church institutions, individuals, and parishes in which he was invited to speak at Sunday services. On one occasion he preached at Grace Church in New York City, a parish where one of Bishop Davis's successors as bishop of South Carolina, Christopher FitzSimons Allison, served as rector in the mid-twentieth century. Among those from whom Porter received contributions were Cornelius and William Vanderbilt and J. Pierpont Morgan.

In was also on this northern trip that Porter visited Washington, D.C. There he went to see General O. O. Howard, who had been told of Dr. Porter by Lieutenant McQueen. Howard was now the head of the Bureau of Refugees, Freedmen, and Abandoned Lands, and Porter sought him out hoping to retain the use of the Marine Hospital in Charleston as a school for African-American children. General Howard, so impressed by Porter's commitment to his mission, took Porter the same day to see President Andrew Johnson at the White House. The president, likewise moved by the quality of the project proposed by Porter, agreed to allow him the use of the building in Charleston as a school for the children of former slaves, and made a personal contribution to the effort. In later years, this institution became the Jenkins Orphanage, an institution that has had a profoundly

---

15   Ibid., 266-268. At first Porter refused the money, telling a mutual friend, "Some things cost too much, Doctor, and this is one of them." Ibid., 268. Finally, he was convinced to accept the funds, though he still would not allow them to be used for his own school.

positive influence in the social and cultural life of the African-American community in South Carolina. It is, as we shall see, one of many lasting influences that the divinely inspired and devoted work of Anthony Toomer Porter had on the development of the post-war life of South Carolina.

Porter realized that in addition to the contributions he was receiving for his ministry from the North, he needed financial support from friends in Charleston. However some of those who wanted to assist him were limited in what they could do because they had participated in Confederate activities during the War. Unless they were pardoned by the United States they would be unable to conduct normal business and banking activities. Porter again needed the president's assistance. He went to the White House one morning and informed President Andrew Johnson that he hoped to receive a pardon for George Alfred Trenholm, the Confederacy's former secretary of the treasury, a parishioner at Porter's church, and one of his financial supporters. The president, completely understanding and supporting Porter's mission, told him to come back early the next morning when the pardon would be ready for him to pick up for delivery to Mr. Trenholm. The pardon was delivered to Dr. Porter as promised, and Mr. Trenholm continued as one of Dr. Porter's strongest financial supporters during Reconstruction.

In the midst of the desperate circumstances of the so-called Reconstruction Era in the South, Porter on October 25, 1867, almost devoid of hope, decided to visit his son's grave at Magnolia Cemetery in Charleston. There he spent four hours alone with God, as he later explained, and he clearly heard his son's dying words. Porter, at the grave, asked God to "give me wisdom, give me zeal, give me continuity of purpose, and open the hearts of the people to me...."[16] This event led to Porter's steadfast purpose and devoted lifetime work to the benefit of all South Carolinians then and now. He knew then that he was called to organize schools for children, and so strong was his

16 Ibid., 232. The child's body was later moved by his father to the churchyard at Prince George, Winyah, in Georgetown. A Porter family plot can still be found there, including the graves of Dr. Porter and his wife and other family members.

recognition of his mission that he rose from his knees at his son's grave and ran a good part of the way home to begin the work of educating the children of South Carolina.

It is impossible to single out any of Porter's achievements as his greatest, but certainly one of the most remarkable was his ability to acquire the United States Arsenal property on Ashley Avenue in Charleston for use as a school for white children, most of them from destitute backgrounds. The influence of Gen. William T. Sherman was largely responsible for the agreement of the federal government to give the property to Porter to use as a school that became the Holy Communion Church Institute. Later the name was changed to the Porter Academy and even later the Porter Military Academy.

Sherman immediately supported the idea when Porter told him of his interest in using the Arsenal as a school. When Porter asked why he would endorse such a plan, Sherman replied, "Why, you saved the life of a valuable officer [Lieutenant McQueen] at the risk of your own in the war, and now the government has a piece of abandoned property that it does not know what to do with, and here you are with this noble use to put it to. You do not think a man like you can hide himself? I have watched your career. I know about your colored school, and how you have struggled to educate the children of the impoverished white people there in Charleston. You ought to have a vote of thanks for taking it."[17] With the assistance of President and Mrs. Rutherford B. Hayes, and with the intervention and support of General Sherman undergirding the powerful and unswerving willpower of Anthony Toomer Porter, Congress adopted a Joint Resolution that allowed the Holy Communion Church Institute to use the Arsenal as a school for the children of South Carolina. And so it was.

The extensive activities of Porter are powerfully revealed in his autobiography, one of at least three books written by him that give us a glimpse of the trials and tribulations of South Carolinians in the second half of the nineteenth century. The central theme that emerges is one man's response to the painful

---

17   Ibid., 344.

endemic injustice and inevitable societal destruction that arose after the Civil War. Porter's life spanned seventy of the most difficult years in the history of the state, a period during which society was always on the edge of anarchy and chaos. His actions as a private man, as a public figure, and as a priest in times of social and economic deprivation were those of a hero.

This book, *Led On! Step By Step*, modestly and powerfully portrays the remarkable accomplishments of its author to restore South Carolina and the South to a place of civility in the wake of unimaginable social dislocation wrought by the then-recent civil conflict brought on by the institution of slavery in America. Porter's life began as a son of privilege in the rice planters' social structure of South Carolina. Following the command of the Gospel, he gave up everything to preach the Word and to administer the sacraments of the Church. Within his ministry Porter saw himself called to fulfill the Gospel of Jesus Christ to improve the life of everyone in everything that he did; his every act enforced that. Anthony Toomer Porter understood his mission and the mission of his Church to be directed toward the whole community, excluding no one. He saw human need wherever he looked, and recognized the necesity to alleviate it regardless of divisions of race, ideology, financial or social standing. The Church was for Porter an extension of God and it was required to treat every person the same according to need. In the wake of the Civil War, many whites saw blacks, mostly former slaves, as a threat to society and civilization. Porter saw them simply as people in need, and he believed that the Church should do all it could to help put their lives back together.

What is the legacy of Anthony Toomer Porter that we see around us now, over a hundred years after his death?

The reader of *Led On! Step By Step* cannot escape the clear reality of Porter's vision that any community of human beings must be grounded on two indispensable foundations. The first is the spiritual development of every person based upon the teachings of Holy Scripture that are contained in the Old and New Testaments; his own faith was guided by the Book of Common Prayer of the Episcopal Church. The second foundation Porter recognized was the necessity of providing an education for every person in the community. He understood that based on these two premises social justice and equality are human rights given by God to every person. As he relates in the strong and clear writing in this book, God called him personally and directly to work tirelessly to construct both these foundations, a spiritual life and an education for everyone, in the difficult times in which he lived. His calling was abundantly fulfilled as we in our time continue to be beneficiaries of the fruits of his labor.

Much of his extraordinary ministry was exercised in the years following the Civil War. A crisis existed particularly in the vanquished South, but the ravages of war were destructive across the entire nation. Porter summed up his mission during the time of recovery as: "My effort ever since General Johnson surrendered has been to make peace between the people of the North and the South; and by the blessing of God on my humble efforts, I have been the means of bringing many on both sides to a better understanding."[18] His message by word and act was one of unity—unity of the community, unity of the Church, and the unity of all people regardless of race, economic condition, or social status.

As a young priest, Porter continued to minister to the small group of people who were informally worshipping at the United States Arsenal on Ashley Avenue in Charleston. Under his leadership that endured for over forty years, the Church of the Holy Communion thrived. On January 8,1894, Porter preached a sermon there celebrating the fortieth anniversary of his tenure in the parish. Holy Communion is now, as it was also in his time, a beautifully adorned church at the corner of Ashley Avenue and Cannon Street in Charleston. There he and his son Theodore Atkinson Porter, also a rector of the parish, are memorialized; the cross on the high altar of the church was a gift of Lieutenant John McQueen. It is a parish of the Episcopal Church in the Diocese of South Carolina, and it is a place where the faith and practice of the Catholic Church are followed and upheld by the

---

18   Ibid., 155.

clergy who serve there and by the faithful congregation. And it is there now, in 2010 A.D., that the sacraments of the Church are dispensed and the Word of God is faithfully preached in the unflagging spirit of Anthony Toomer Porter.

St. Mark's Church, now at 18 Thomas Street in Charleston, was founded in 1865 by and for the use of African Americans, some of whom were free before freedom and some of whom were enslaved. Porter's ministry at St. Mark's began in 1878 when he was asked by Bishop W. B. W. Howe to serve as rector of the parish, an assignment that was added to his responsibilities at the Church of the Holy Communion. In his tenure of ten years at St. Mark's, Porter, by his typically hard work, lovingly nurtured a vibrant parish that endures and flourishes today in the same traditions and faith as the Church of the Holy Communion. Porter believed that all parishes of the Episcopal Church in South Carolina, both black and white, should be united in one body. However, against his wishes the Convention of the diocese in the 1870s allowed the admission of only white parishes into its membership.[19] The parishes of the diocese remained racially divided until 1965, when, under the leadership of Bishop Gray Temple, St. Mark's and other predominantly African-American parishes in the Diocese were allowed to join the convention as full participants in the life of the Church. Until then, the work among African-American parishes was directed by a priest known as the archdeacon for colored work, who was directed by the bishop of the diocese.

Porter believed that civilization in South Carolina could not be restored in the wake of the ravages of the Civil War unless all children, both black and white, were provided with sound educations. His efforts to create schools for all children in South Carolina was Herculean. During one of his early visits to the North after the War, Porter raised sufficient funds to organize a school for 1,800 African-American children, most the children of former slaves.

The Holy Communion Church Institute was founded by

19 For more on this battle within the church, see Lyon G. Tyler, "Drawing the Color Line in the Episcopal Diocese of South Carolina, 1876 to 1890: The Role of Edward McCrady, Father and Son," *South Carolina Historical Magazine* 91 (April 1990): 107-124.

Porter in 1867 to provide an education for the white children of the region. At first operated under the auspices of the parish church, its name was changed to Porter Academy in 1886, and then later to Porter Military Academy.

In 1879, Porter decided to try to acquire the United States Arsenal on Ashley Avenue, the same site where the parish had begun some years earlier, to house the school. He again went to Washington and, with typical hard work and stamina, was successful. The bill to affect this transfer was shepherded through the U.S. Senate by Senators Matthew Butler and Wade Hampton, both former Confederate generals, with the support of Joseph E. Johnston and William T. Sherman, both former Union generals, and was quickly signed by President Rutherford B. Hayes (with the careful prodding of Mrs. Hayes). Thus, on January 9, 1880, the United States Arsenal at Charleston was conveyed by the U.S. government to Porter to use for his school. According to the *New York Times*, Porter called the transfer "practical reconstruction, honorable alike to both political parties, to North and South, to President and people."[20]

The site served as the school until 1964 when the Old Arsenal property became a part of the campus of the Medical College of South Carolina (now the Medical University of South Carolina). It was then that Bishop Gray Temple arranged the merger of the Porter Military Academy with two smaller schools (Gaud School and Miss Watts's School), to establish the Porter-Gaud School at Albemarle Point, just west of the Ashley River in Charleston. Bishop Temple obtained a generous gift of the land where the school is now located from the CSX Corporation. The school continues today as a real example of Dr. Porter's legacy, a vibrant and high-quality educational institution exemplifying the core tenets of Dr. Porter's faith and practice. It is yet another wonderful example of the fruit of his hard work and determination that began in the depths of Reconstruction in the South. Porter's school and its successor institutions have educated many young men and women who have become leaders of their church and state. In Porter's spirit,

---

20 "Transfer of the Charleston Arsenal," *New York Times*, January 12, 1880.

many have made important contributions to the advancement of his lifetime goals.

Just one example of a leader of the Episcopal Church who was educated at the Holy Communion Church Institute was Bishop William Alexander Guerry, who was sent there from Clarendon County, South Carolina, where his family resided. At Dr. Porter's school Guerry received his first real education outside the home. Porter then sent him to study at the University of the South where he received a sound undergraduate education and, in the School of Theology, where he studied under the great theologian William Porcher DuBose, another South Carolinian. Guerry became bishop of South Carolina in 1907. Three of his five children, four sons and a daughter, served as priests in South Carolina, and the fourth became vice chancellor (president) of the University of the South.

Guerry, like his teachers Porter and DuBose, was a great advocate of social justice and church unity. Early in his episcopacy he advocated for the appointment of an African-American suffragan bishop for South Carolina particularly to minister to the black communicants of the diocese and to help bring them into the full life of the Church. His efforts were unsuccessful, but he continued to lead the way for the future progress of racial unification. Like Porter, recognizing the need of education for all, he arranged for the affiliation of Voorhees College in Denmark, South Carolina, with the Episcopal Church, and obtained financial support for it from the diocese. In 1928 Bishop Guerry gave his life for his beliefs when he was assassinated by a priest who was enraged by his plan to appoint a black bishop for the diocese. Nonetheless, he led South Carolinians to a better understanding of the need for the advancement of social justice, education, and church unity in our time.

Others who benefited from Dr. Porter's generosity were less famous, but they are around us still. The Charleston *Post and Courier* reported in 2010 the death of Olive Massie Kinard LaRoche, the widow of Toomer Porter LaRoche Jr.[21] Mrs.

---

21 "Obituaries," Charleston *Post and Courier*, March 13, 2010.

LaRoche's late husband's uncle was said to have been sent by his mother to the Holy Communion Church Institute with a note to Dr. Porter asking him to educate her son. The note also explained that the family had no money to pay tuition (the amount of tuition was set by Porter at fifty cents per month per child[22]), but that if he educated her son she would send him a sack of sweet potatoes when the crop came in. The son was educated at the school, and the boy's mother gave her next son the name Toomer Porter LaRoche. There is no further report about the arrival of the sweet potatoes.

The depth of Porter's contribution to our generation and those beyond our time is impossible to measure, but it continues to be felt on the surface and beneath the surface of our lives every day, and it will be the same for millions yet unborn. Its depth and strength is reflected in what he has written in *Led On! Step By Step*. He died on Easter Day, 1902.

"We have drunk from wells we did not dig, and we have warmed ourselves by fires we did not light."

—Thomas Tisdale
Charleston, S.C.
Easter 2010

---

22 Anthony Toomer Porter, *History of the Holy Communion Church Institute, of Charleston, South Carolina* (New York: D. Appleton, 1876), 5.

A. Toomer Porter from *Cyclopedia of Eminent and Representative Men of the Carolinas in the Nineteenth Century* (1892)

Church of the Holy Communion, Charleston, circa 1920.
Photo courtesy of the Church of the Holy Communion.

Church of the Holy Communion, Charleston, 2008.
Photo by Vincent L. Duffy, courtesy of the Church of the Holy Communion.

Rev. Theodore Atkinson Porter, son of A. Toomer Porter and Susan Magdalene Atkinson Porter, who served the Church of the Holy Communion from 1885 to 1899. Photo courtesy of the Church of the Holy Communion.

U. S. Arsenal, Charleston, future home of the Holy Communion Church Institute.
Photo courtesy of the Waring Historical Library,
Medical University of South Carolina.

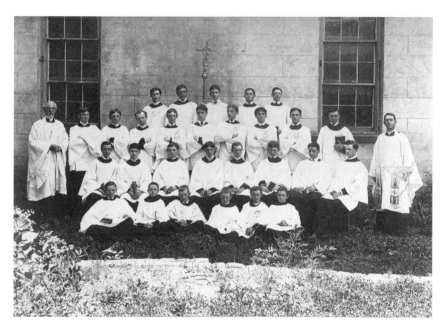

Reverends A. Toomer Porter (far left) and Theodore A. Porter (far right) with their school choir. Photo courtesy of Porter-Gaud School.

CHARLESTON, S. C. - PORTER MILITARY ACADEMY

Porter Military Academy, from a 1908 postcard. Photo courtesy of the Waring Historical Library, Medical University of South Carolina.

LED ON!

CHAPTER I

THE PORTER PEDIGREE

*My pedigree—John Porter of England, and his descendants
—My grandfather and his estate—Cotton and potatoes,
an incident of boyish travel—General Waddy Thompson
—From Georgetown to New Haven, Conn.—Yale students
—Return to Georgetown—A strange presentiment comes
true—My sister Charlotte's fate—My mother asserts her
authority—I suffer from bad teaching.*

IN compliance with the frequent suggestion of my friend,
the late Rev. Charles Frederick Hoffman, D.D.,
LL.D., D.C.L., of New York, I began, Oct. 5, 1896, to write
some reminiscences of my life. All of the older members of
my family having died while I was very young, my knowledge of my progenitors I derived from my mother, and
from an aged grand-aunt on my mother's side. The following is my family tree, as far as known :—

My grandfather, John Porter, was born in 1759, in
Connecticut, and was descended from John Porter of
England, the founder of the American family, who settled

in Dorchester, Massachusetts, some time in the seventeenth century. To him is to be traced the ancestry of A. A. Low, Bishop Huntington, of Western New York, and other men of note.

When quite a youth, fifteen or sixteen years old, my grandfather, with two brothers, took horse and travelled South. There is a tradition, for which I cannot vouch, that on their journey the three young men came across the persons who had begun the Dismal Swamp Canal. My grandfather, after watching the methods of the constructors, remarked that it could not be dug in that way. He was approached to know if he had a better plan to suggest. An agreement was entered into, and he undertook the work. He remained long enough to make twenty thousand dollars. He then resumed his journey South, and settled in Georgetown District, South Carolina. Be this as it may, he had sufficient money when he reached Georgetown to purchase a quantity of land, and began the cultivation of indigo. He continued at this until rice was introduced, and he then undertook the cultivation of rice. He purchased two plantations on Sampit River and was successful, amassing what was a fortune in those days. He died in April, 1829, aged seventy, just six months after the death of my father. He left, by will, his estate to my brother, three sisters, and myself; my father having bequeathed his estate to my mother at the request of my grandfather, who had told my father that he would provide for his children. The estate consisted of rice plantations and negro slaves, some of whom he purchased from slave-ships, which were owned in Newport, Rhode Island. In 1849, I came into possession of five of these Africans, then very old. They had been, in fact, supported for many years on the plantation without earning a dollar. The five were tattooed, and I never could understand their language, and could only communicate with them through some of their race who had become familiar with their speech. They were all dead by the year 1851. The bill of sale of some of these people was in my possession, and was lost with other valuable papers at the burning of Columbia by General Sherman's army, in 1865. Some time in 1866, I told Mr. Peter Cooper of New York of these facts, and suggested that our Northern friends should not hold up their hands in holy horror on the slavery question. If we got the slaves those who owned the ships received the money and incurred by far the least trouble in the matter.

When I was a boy I often heard that my grandfather was a Tory, and this charge was a source of great annoyance to me. For those days were not so far from the Revolutionary War that the hatred of England had all passed away. As, however, grandfather was only seventeen years old in 1776, he could not have been a very dangerous Tory, though I remember one of the stories told about him was that he had set fire to Georgetown ; and a certain corner where a house belonging to one of the Alstons had been burned, was tauntingly pointed out to me as the house he had fired. I was too young then to put two and two together. It did not occur to me that as he was then only a boy there could have been no truth in these fables. Nevertheless, I had many a good cry over my grandfather's supposed iniquity. Many good deeds and charitable acts that the old gentleman did were kept in memory by the family. One of these deeds was the education of a deserving lad named Thomas House Taylor, who afterwards became the distinguished Reverend Doctor Taylor, Rector of Grace Church, New York, who was my godfather.

My father, John Porter, was born in 1795. He graduated with distinction from the South Carolina College and studied law. On the 16th of December, 1819, he married

Esther Ann Toomer, daughter of Anthony Toomer, and from them were born two sons and three daughters— Charlotte, who died February 15, 1835 ; John, who died September 9, 1841; Eliza Cheesborough, who married Dr. E. B. Brown, and afterwards Robert E. Fraser, and died in 1861 ; Hannah, who married Dr. John F. Lessesne ; and myself, whom God has spared to outlive them all. I was only nine months old when my father died. His death occurred on October 25, 1828, at the early age of thirty-three years. My father was a man of very marked character. He was elected a member of the Legislature of South Carolina, at the age of twenty-one, and served for several years. He was a member of the Episcopal Diocesan Convention at the time of his death.

Fourteen years after my father's death, while travelling to Columbia by the railroad, we came to the section of country where cotton is grown, and I mistook the cotton for fields of Irish potatoes. Being surprised at the extent of the planting, I observed that someone seemed to be- lieve in potatoes. I was then a boy in my fifteenth year. A gentleman on the seat before me turned and said :

" My young friend, where were you brought up ? "

Perceiving my mistake, I replied, " Had you, sir, never seen a rice field, and mistook the first you ever saw for oats, I should correct your error. I see now that this is cotton, not Irish potatoes."

" May I ask your name ? "

" Certainly ; my name is Anthony Toomer Porter."

" And where is your home ? " he asked.

" Georgetown, South Carolina."

" Are you any relation to Col. John Porter, who died in 1828 ? "

" His son, sir," I replied.

Rising from his seat, and taking off his hat, he extended his hand, saying, " I am Gen. Waddy Thompson " [at one time Minister to Mexico] " let me take the hand of the son of John Porter. To your father I am indebted more than to any other man ; we were in the South Carolina College together, and to his interposition and influence I owe all I have ever been."

He then told me much of my father's college life, and of the influence he exercised in college. He was the referee and umpire in every dispute and difficulty, and the beloved of every student and professor.

This conversation and others like it, which I had with many persons, have had a great deal to do with the make-up of my life.

My ancestors on my mother's side came from Wales and from England. Like my paternal grandfather, my mother's grandfather had come South, from New England ; his forefathers having settled in Massachusetts some time in the seventeenth century. My great-grandfather, Anthony Toomer, migrated with two brothers when quite young. One settled in North Carolina, and became a distinguished jurist. From him are descended some of the chief families of that State. Another branch went to Georgia, or Alabama. Of that branch I have no knowledge. In 1767, my great-grandfather married Ann Warham, who was a lineal descendant of William Warham, the brother of Archbishop Warham, of Canterbury. While serving as an officer in the Continental army of the Revolution, he was captured after the surrender of Charleston on the 12th of May, 1780, and with other prominent citizens was sent to St. Augustine. There, for some cause, he with others was imprisoned in one of the vessels, and after much suffering was sent to Philadelphia, and not exchanged or released until the war was over. A daughter was born to him on the day of his capture, but she was four years old before he ever saw her. From him are descended a number of families, residing principally in Charleston. My maternal grandfather married Charlotte Cheesborough,

whose ancestor was a clergyman of the Church of England. They had several children, but my mother and
Mrs. Mary Ford alone married and left children.

I was born on the 31st of January, 1828, in Georgetown,
South Carolina, and was baptized by Rev. P. T. Keith,
November 16, 1828. My mother had been educated in
Elizabeth, New Jersey, and retained to her death a great
attachment for the North and her Northern friends.
Left a widow at the age of twenty-five, with five children,
the oldest eight years, and the youngest nine months,
with a handsome estate left to her by my father, she determined, four years after my father's death, to take her
children to New Haven, Connecticut, where she believed
she could educate them to greater advantage.

My mother was considered a strikingly handsome woman, and retained her beauty to over her seventieth year.
She was highly educated, and of fascinating manners,
with brilliant conversational powers. With these attractions, and the reputation of being a rich Southern widow,
of course she had many suitors. But my father's last
words to her were, " Train our children as you know I
would have done," and she determined to live for them.

There were a number of Southern students at Yale
College, and her home was their constant resort. Being
very young, I remember very little of our sojourn there.
But I recollect that several of the students kept riding
horses, and would put a pillow in front and ride me about,
a curly-headed imp. There was a young Frenchman who
was very fond of me, but he often made use of language
not fitted for a Sunday-school. One day I said to him,
" If you don't stop using those bad words, do you know
where you will go when you die ? "

" Where will I go ? " he said.

" To a place too bad for me to tell you," was my reply.
My childish rebuke had a wonderful effect upon him,

for he was never heard to utter an oath afterwards. I had
another friend, Mr. Ligon. He was afterwards Governor
of Maryland. This gentleman's name will appear later
on in my story.

Eventually my mother returned South. I have a dim
recollection of our voyage home in a sailing vessel, and our
arrival in Georgetown. I remember how much alarmed I
was at the appearance of the black people who came around
us. I had a white nurse, an Irish woman, who had gone
with us to New Haven and returned, and remained until
I was nine years old. My father had left his town residence to my mother, with his plantation and some eighty
slaves. After taking up her residence in Georgetown, my
mother retained her wish that her children should be educated in the North, and in 1836 she sent my brother John
to the Rev. Mr. Chester at Morristown, New Jersey, to
school. He remained there some years, and there was a
remarkable circumstance connected with his return. Mr.
Chester wrote mother that her son would return on the
steamer *Home*, to sail from New York. This was a pioneer
steamer, being a North River boat which had been cut in
two and lengthened. From a dream, or a presentiment,
my mother became possessed with the idea that her son
had better not come home in that boat, and she wrote at
once to Mr. Chester. It required six or seven days then
to get a letter to New Jersey, and John had been sent to
New York. After he left, Mr. Chester received the per-
emptory letter. He hastened to New York, and arrived
at the steamer after the planks had been drawn in, and
just before the ropes had been thrown off. He managed
to get to the captain, and told him to put John Porter on
shore. It was with some difficulty that he succeeded, but
at last the trunk was put out, the passenger came on shore,
and started home by land. The *Home* encountered a gale
off Hatteras, and quickly went to pieces. If I remember

rightly, only one passenger, a French milliner of Charleston, saved herself by floating ashore on a sofa. I remember the agony of my mother ; she was certain her son was on the steamer. She had not heard from Mr. Chester. The same storm had played havoc on land ; all communication by stage had been interrupted. The first information we had, was from brother John's arrival home on one of the stage horses. The stage had been wrecked, as well as the steamer, and the driver had cut his horses loose and mounted his passengers on them. It seems but as yesterday. I remember my brother's forlorn look as he rode up to the house, and my mother's rapturous joy as she recognized her son whom she had given up as lost.

I remember one other circumstance in those early years, which made a deep impression on me.

My oldest sister Charlotte, not quite fifteen years old, had always been a great sufferer from headaches. We were spending the summer of 1834 on North Island, our summer retreat on the Atlantic Ocean, at the mouth of Winyah Bay. My sister never went to school after our return from New Haven, but she was a great reader. The last book she read was *The Last Days of Pompeii*. As she finished the book, she remarked to my mother, " I will be like that blind girl." Mother, to divert her, ordered the carriage for a ride on the beach. Only those two were in the carriage, and after riding some time, my sister asked mother if she had not better order the coachman to return, as it was getting dark. " Oh, no," mother said, " it is still quite early, the sun has not gone down yet." Then my sister said, " If it is not night, I am blind, for I see nothing." And she was blind ; she never saw again. She lived until February 15, 1835, then died. It was the first time I ever saw anyone die. But the peace, the joy, of that departing spirit, going, as she said, to see all the beauties of heaven, where there is no more pain ; the absolute rapture of the young saint, have never passed from my memory. I was then in my eighth year.

At that time the remaining children, save my brother John, were attending the school of a maiden lady, Miss Betsey Taylor, who was very frequently a visitor at our home. My mother was a most sensible woman who did all she could to let her children enjoy their young life. We had a room to play in, and in that room she provided every kind of game that she could procure—cards and puzzles, lotto and backgammon, checkers and chess, picture books, and dancing ropes, dominoes, and games too numerous to mention. Friday afternoon and evening, and Saturday, we had the privilege of having as many children friends as we wished, and a rollicking good time we had, joyous without being boisterous ; still it certainly was not a silent crowd.

One evening Miss Taylor was spending the time at our house, and being somewhat annoyed at the romping going on in the children's room, she left the sitting room for ours, and bringing her school-room discipline into exercise, very peremptorily ordered us to bed, saying she did not propose to be annoyed by the noise of children. My mother perceived the sudden cessation of laughter, and the solemn silence which followed, for we all stood in mortal dread of the spinster. She quickly followed Miss Taylor, and heard her giving us her orders. Mother was a woman of considerable positiveness herself, and having the sole control and rearing of her children, it was not safe to intrude upon her prerogatives. I remember the quiet dignity of her manner on that occasion. She was severely polite as she begged pardon of Miss Taylor, and told us to resume our play, and to go to bed when she gave the direction. Then turning to Miss Taylor, she said.

" In your school-room my children are under your direction ; in my house, they are under mine. Your action is a reflection upon the manners of my children. They are never allowed to disturb my guests, and had it been necessary I would have anticipated you, by stopping their hilarity ; but with their innocent enjoyment in my own house, I permit no interference of any kind.''

It was many years ago, but I recall the rage into which the school mistress worked herself. She turned on mother, who was many years her junior, and seemed to think she was one of her pupils. Mother calmly stood it a little while, when, placing herself between the children and the open door, she pointed to it, and suggested it was about time for both of them to retire. Miss Taylor gathered up her bonnet and shawl, and it was a very long time before she crossed our threshold again.

This incident made a change in our school life. We were all withdrawn the next day, and sent to school to Dr. W. R. T. Prior. I was soon advanced in my studies, and began Latin. Being somewhat quick at my lessons, I was pushed on very rapidly, though very superficially, and found myself in Virgil in an incredibly short time, without the slightest comprehension of the language. To this day, I feel the evil effects of this injudicious method. A study which was not understood became the object of contempt. I long retained possession of my old Virgil, all spotted with tear drops, for many a hearty cry did I have over the book, with no one at home to help me, and when I went to recite, few explanations. So I hobbled along through those school-boy years, really knowing nothing.

CHAPTER II

*I visit my father's grave and vow to follow his good example
—My life is saved by a negro—My brother's death—I seek
comfort in the Bible for my mother's absence—The good
beginning of a life-long habit—I am catechised by Bishop
Gadsden in my fourteenth year and am confirmed.*

I VIVIDLY remember the 31st of January, 1838, my
tenth birthday, and how it was observed by me. I
celebrated the day by going to the graveyard where my
father was buried, in the cemetery attached to the old
church of " Prince George Winyah," Georgetown, South
Carolina, a church built of bricks brought from London.
Climbing over the brick wall that encloses the graveyard,
and going to the plot where my father's grave is, I knelt
beside it, and putting my hands on the tombstone, thanked
God for having given me such a father. In childish language I asked my Heavenly Father to spare my life so
that I might grow up to be a man, and be able at my
death to leave behind me a name as good as my father's.
I asked that I might never do anything to bring a stain
of dishonor upon that name. I was only a little boy, and no
one told me to do it, but I seemed to be led to that hallowed spot, and to draw inspiration from it. The incident
left an indelible impression on my mind. I believe that

even a child's prayer is heard, and I can venture to hope that my father would not be ashamed of his son, could he know what has been the manner of my life. Who can say that he does not know ? If it would add anything to the joys of Paradise, why may not our Heavenly Father let our dear dead know of the life of those whom they surely have not forgotten, and in whom they would delight if they were still on earth ? The spiritual world is much nearer to us than we can possibly conceive.

Another incident in my early life seemed to give the colored people of the South a claim on my life service. My life indeed was actually saved by a negro who risked his own for my safety. I felt I had incurred a debt which I was bound, and afterwards endeavored, to repay. The facts are as follows :

During the summer of 1839 I was taken in a small sail-boat, by a party of young men, to fish on the banks between North and South Islands. In a sudden squall, the boat was capsized, and I was to all appearances drowned. I remember the side of the boat I was sitting on, gradually sunk into the water, as the boat turned over, but remember no more, until I found myself in the arms of a colored man, being carried from the beach to our house. When I came to consciousness he told me it was all right, not to be scared, that I was safe. We learned some time after that all the occupants of the boat got on the bottom, except myself. When this colored man missed me, he exclaimed, " O my God, where Miss Porter child ? " Where ? Under the deep water being swept out to sea. Just then one of my little hands was seen stretched above the water. The colored man swam off from the boat, dived down, and came up with me in his arms, unconscious of course. I was held by him in his arms on the bottom of the boat until the party was rescued by some of the fishermen in other boats.

It was somewhere in the same year that my brother John returned from Morristown, of which I have already spoken. He went to Charleston, and entered the counting-house of Mr. George Y. Davis. He was then in his eighteenth year, and old enough to look into the affairs of my grandfather's estate. He found serious evidences of mismanagement, and in the fall of 1840 he left the counting-house and went to the two plantations to take charge of the interests of the estate. In August of 1841 there was a severe storm and heavy freshet, causing a large break in the river bank. The rice was at that stage that the broken bank had to be mended, or the crop would be lost. My brother, full of energy and resolve, took it in hand, and with all the force of slaves worked day and night, and succeeded in his efforts. His clothes were wet for many hours. When he had put the fields in order, he came down to North Island, at the mouth of Winyah Bay, to the family summer resort. But the deadly climate had done its work. Nine days after his wetting, he was taken with high bilious fever, or country fever, as it is known in this latitude, and on the fifth day he died, in his twentieth year. My mother was herself very sick at the same time and never saw him. I was standing by his bedside, and just before he died, he clasped his hands and said, " Conduct us, Heavenly Father, to Thy throne, and there kneeling let us praise Thee, through Jesus Christ our Lord."

We took his body, on the 10th of September, to Georgetown, and laid him beside our father, and the sister who had died in 1835. There were then left only two daughters and myself.

In the spring of 1839, my mother, still appreciating her own school experience in Elizabeth City, New Jersey, and being very fond of the North, and of Northern people, had taken my sister Eliza to New York and placed her at school at Bordentown, New Jersey, under the charge of Madam Murat, the wife of Achille Murat, the son of Napoleon's Marshal. Madam Murat was a Miss Fraser, of Charleston. There were no steamers running between Southern ports and New York in those days. The fate of the *Home*, which had been lost in a storm, and of the *Pulaski*, which had been burnt at sea with almost a total loss of passengers and crew, had put a temporary setback on steam navigation, and mother and my sister had sailed from Georgetown in a large brig. It was the first time I had ever been separated from my mother. Only nine months old when my father died, and a delicate child, I had been brought up with great tenderness, and was indeed very near to my mother. I recall to-day the anguish with which I watched that receding vessel, and my desolation when I went back home with my other sister, and a maiden aunt who was left in charge. She did all she could to comfort me, but I went supperless and sobbing to bed. I was only eleven years old. The next day I thought I must do something that would make God have pity on us, and carry our mother and sister safe, and bring them back. Going by sea to New York then seemed an awful thing. It certainly took longer to get there than it does now to get from here to London, and there were no telegraphs, and only partial railroads, and it took a week to get a letter (postage twenty-five cents), so we knew it would be nearly a month before we could hear. To childish fancy it seemed an endless age. I had said my prayers, but it seemed I ought to do something more, and it occurred to me, although I knew the catechism, and had read some of the Bible, that I had never read it through, and I thought if I read it regularly, that God would know it, and somehow, it would have some influence on my mother's and sister's fate. So I shut myself up in my room and never came out of it all day until I had read through the book of Genesis. Next day I read all of Exodus, next all of Leviticus, next all of Numbers. But the last two days had been rather tough on an urchin, eleven years old. So, when the next day came, I thought the half of Deuteronomy would do, and the balance on the sixth day. When I started again the seventh day I thought I would remember more if I took a little less, and I resolved to cut down to a chapter in the morning and a chapter at night. This became interesting to me, and after I had finished my self-allotted portion I used to read on when I felt so inclined, until I was tired. This habit begun at eleven years has been continued through life, with this improvement : soon after it was known that I was reading the Bible regularly, someone, perhaps my old aunt, took the Prayer Book, showed me the calendar, and pointed out to me that by following the Prayer Book lectionary one would read through in a year, excepting a few chapters, the Old Testament, the four accounts of the Gospel, the Acts of the Holy Apostles twice, and the Epistles four times. I immediately adopted the plan, and through boyhood, youth, manhood, and old age have kept it up. How many times I have thus read the Bible through, and how imperceptibly it has colored my thoughts and swayed my life ! In my childish ignorance, I thought God needed to be propitiated by my act, but for the blessed overruling of His Divine Spirit how often I have thanked God, who thus led me to take His Word as a lantern to my feet and a light to my path. How good a thing it would be if all young people would begin in early youth thus regularly to read the Bible. It would make their youth cleaner, and purer, and sweeter, yes, and happier.

My mother and sister had a safe and pleasant passage to New York, and the former returned to us in the fall.

In the spring of the year 1841, the rector of the church in Georgetown, the Rev. Robt. T. Howard, called at our home and asked me to take a stroll with him. In the course of our walk he told me that Bishop Gadsden had sent him notice of his intended visitation of the parish, and that he, the rector, wished me to give in my name for confirmation. I was only a child, just thirteen years old, and it was the first time the subject had been proposed to me. I expressed some hesitation to the rector, but he told me that as I knew the catechism, it was now my duty to be confirmed. I told him that I would give in my name if my mother approved of it. With my mother's approval, accordingly, I sent in my name, and that was the only conversation he had with me, and that was all the clerical instruction I received for preparation for this solemn step. I confess I knew nothing of the origin, or history, or obligations imposed in the rite, but I remember that after the suggestion had been made, and my mother had consented, I became very desirous to be confirmed, though I knew very little as to what it meant. Bishop Gadsden arrived, and on Saturday he took tea at our house, the rector being there also. During the evening I was brought in and introduced to the bishop as one of the candidates. He said, " Is not this child rather young ? "

He then began to catechize me. I was very much scared, but the catechism was one thing I was safe in. I could not have told who Nebuchadnezzar's grandfather was, or the names of Job's daughters, but I did know the catechism from beginning to end ; all of mother's children were drilled in that, and it had been the monthly custom of our former rector, Rev. P. T. Keith, who left us for Saint Michael's Church, Charleston, in 1839, to gather all the children round the chancel rail, and hear them say the catechism. There was no exposition of it given, but, expecting that monthly exercise in public, we all of us got the words pretty thoroughly by heart, and were made Prayer Book Churchmen thereby.

So the bishop could not trip me ; I repeated it all, and he was so well pleased, that he said, '' I have a good report of you from your rector, and you certainly know the catechism remarkably well, and you can come forward.''

So, on the 18th day of April, 1841, when I was thirteen years, two months, and eighteen days old, I was confirmed with eleven white candidates, and eight colored.* My youngest sister and myself were two of the twelve white. That service and that Sunday I shall never forget. I felt at the time that something great had been done.

When we returned to the house, I went into my room, and prayed a simple child's prayer, but I know it was very earnest. That day there began in me the desire and the purpose to study for the ministry. But after my confirmation, not one word was said to me by the rector. I did not know that I was expected, or had the right to, come forward to the Holy Communion. I just went on as before, saying my prayers, reading my Bible, going to church. I note in passing that mother always had family prayers, morning and evening; a sacred, blessed custom almost universal in those days—now, alas, almost universally neglected. As I look back to this event, I have often wondered if my experience was that of many others in the different parishes; no confirmation classes, no instruction, no following up. If so, what wonder that the church is full of members who know very little of her doctrine or history. I was confirmed in April, 1841. I never communed until Christmas Day, 1845, but of that I will speak further on.

* Miss Sarah Henning, of Georgetown, is the only white member of that class, beside myself, who is now alive.

CHAPTER III

FIRST SCHOOL EXPERIENCE

*Threatened disaster averted—Mr. Cotes's school—I leave it
shattered in health—Country leisure restores me—Good
influences—I determine to become a communicant.*

IN the spring of 1842, my mother took my second sister
to Bordentown, to place her at school at Madam
Murat's. My sister Eliza she brought home in the fall.
During this fall a great trial came to us. I was too young
to know how it came about, but it was evident that the
mismanagement which caused it could not be laid to my
mother's charge.

It came to light that the house which my father had
built, and where all his children were born, the house
which my mother supposed had been left secure to her,
was, with all the silver and furniture, obliged to be sold,
so that she was to be stripped of the last penny. There
was nothing before us but to give up the town house, and
live in the country in winter, and on the Island in the summer. My mother's support henceforth came out of the
income allowed by the court for the expenses of my sisters
and myself. It was a dreadful struggle and many an unhappy day and evening did my mother and I pass together. It was so hard to give up her home, bound to
her by so many ties. Soon the house was advertised for

sale, and we were waiting to be turned out of it. As we had a refuge on the plantation, no one had offered any help.

On the evening before the sale, we had our usual family prayers and went to bed. I could not sleep from distress.

The light had been put out, and I was lying in bed, when I heard the buzzing of a fly. I listened for some time, and it annoyed me so much that I got out of bed and lit the candle. Up on the ceiling I saw a large fly entangled in a spider's web, and the old spider at a little distance off, looking on, ready at the right moment to make his fatal attack. The poor fly, by his desperate efforts to get out, was only making things worse. My sympathy was excited ; so getting on a chair and taking a stick, I managed to break the web and get the fly out. It shook itself vigorously, and flew off, while the spider beat a retreat and got beyond my reach. I went back to bed and began to think. If I was sorry for the fly, and let it out of its danger, would not God be sorry for the widow, and her fatherless children, who were all trying to be Christians, and would He not send somebody to let us out of the trap that a worse than spider had put us in ? I fell asleep.

Next day I went to the place of auction, and heard our house put up for sale—I, a poor boy of fourteen years, with a weeping widowed mother at home.

I heard someone say one thousand dollars—and the crier sang out, " One thousand dollars, one thousand dollars, one thousand dollars ! Is no more offered for this valuable property ? Once, twice, three times,—gone ! "

The auctioneer asked who the purchaser was ? A. W. Dozier, my father's old law partner, then came forward, and said he was the purchaser. The big tears rolled down my cheeks. Then the furniture and the silver were put up. Oh, the agony of that hour ! Someone bid ten dollars. I nearly fainted as it was all knocked down by this auctioneer. As I turned to leave the place Mr. Dozier came up to me and taking me by the arm, said, "I have bought the house and furniture in your name. Come and sign a paper at my office."

I was only a child, but the incident of the spider and the fly recurred to my mind, and I told him of it.

"God had not forgotten you," he replied ; "but I had to keep quiet, lest if it had got out that I was going to buy the property in, someone might have run it up. But nobody made a bid. I wish I had bid one hundred dollars ; I could have got it at that, for everyone felt so much for your mother. Reading the agony on your face, no one would have bid a dollar against you."

He advanced the money, and I, a boy of fourteen, gave him my personal bond for one thousand dollars, insured and assigned. I paid the interest and insurance out of my income ; the one thousand dollars in full a few days after coming of age.

I was now getting to be too old a boy to be kept at a small village school, and the question arose, where was I to go ? One of my sisters was at Morristown at school, but mother could not bring herself to send me so far away, as I was not strong.

In those days, Mr. Cotes, an Englishman, had the most promising school in that region of the country. He took a limited number of boarders. It was an expensive school, and resorted to only by the sons of people of property and position, so that it was necessary to enter a boy's name for a vacancy a year or two ahead. Mr. Cotes, happening to come up to Georgetown to visit Mr. William Bull Pringle, at his plantation, some six miles out of town, I was sent to him on my horse to have him enter my name. The old man had but one eye, and he struck me with terror the first time I saw him. I never did get over the terror and dislike with which the man inspired me. My name, however, was entered by him for the next year, and I rode off wishing most sincerely that he had said he had no place for me. In those days the school term was for the whole year, saving the holiday in December and April. The poor children had to endure the drudgery of studying all through the summer months.

In May, 1842, I went down to Charleston, and was enrolled as a pupil with Mr. Cotes.

I never can forget a lesson I received the second day at dinner. I had helped myself as usual, when Mr. Cotes, at the head of the table, asked me if I was going to eat all that was on my plate? Never having come in contact with such manners, I flushed up and felt indignant, and answered, I did not know whether I would or not. "Well," he said, "I will pass it over to-day, but henceforth help yourself to as much as you wish, but whatever you put on your plate you must eat." He entered into no explanations, and I was too angry to eat any more. The old man had a rough way, but reflection soon told me he was right. Whatever was left on the plates was wasted; servants would not eat it, and he kept no dogs. There were some fourteen or fifteen boys at table; if each of us left a good sized piece of butter on our plates, the aggregate of wasted butter would almost suffice for the next meal; and so of everything else. Multiply each day's waste by the ten months, and it was clear our carelessness would be the cause of a dead loss. I have never forgotten that lesson, especially when, in after years, I had to provide for three hundred boys. Mr. Cotes's first rebuke has been very efficacious in saving my pocket.

The next lesson I learned was from seeing in an outbuilding walls covered with all manner of vile scribblings. Brought up with the greatest care by my mother, with my sisters as my principal companions, I was innocent of that form of evil. This writing and those drawings were new to me, and with the perversity of human nature I looked at things I ought not to have seen, and read, although a great deal of what I read I did not understand ; but the effect was revolting to my moral sense. That lesson has served through thirty years to make me take care, as the head of a great boys' school, that no writing be permitted on any of the walls of the institution, a precaution quite as conducive to the morals of the boys of to-day as the lesson from wastefulness was to economical management.

I had not been long at Mr. Cotes's school before I was attacked with nervous depression. When I went down to breakfast a great lump would rise in my throat, and I could not swallow a mouthful, even of coffee, and I would go to school weak and scared and miserable. I stood out the summer of 1842, and the winter of 1842–43, until September, 1843, when I was taken down with nervous fever, that soon became typhoid, and I was desperately ill.

My old doctor, Dr. Wm. T. Wragg, watched me devotedly, but told my mother that it had been brought on by my unhappiness at school, and when I recovered later, in October, he said, that to keep me longer at my books would be death to me. That I must go home and hunt, and fish, and ride, and not study for months.

Of course I was withdrawn at once from school, and taken to Georgetown. The country house was furnished, and I owned a riding horse. A fine gun, powder, shot, and a fishing outfit were purchased, and with a trusted man-servant in charge of me, I was sent alone into the country to carry out the doctor's directions. Nearly all negro women are good cooks, so orders were given that one of them should be brought from the fields to do my cooking. A supply of light reading was sent with me, and I was turned loose. As my sister was engaged to be married, it was not convenient for the whole family to join me in that country life which my mother always detested.

During the fever that nearly cost me my life, I had grown rapidly, and was now nearly six feet tall, as thin as a lathe. This overgrown lad of fifteen and a half was thus thrown on his own resources. It was the most injudicious thing I ever knew my mother to do in her rearing of me, yet she trusted me fully, and was unsuspicious of harm.

During that winter it became necessary, in some business arrangements, that I should read my grandfather's will, and there I learned that these two plantations and two thirds of the slaves would be mine at the age of twenty-one. As I roamed at large over these fields, several hundred acres of rice-land, and several thousand acres of pine-land, I came to the long village row of houses, occupied by the slaves. All of this I regarded as prospectively mine. To a boy the acres seemed endless, and the slaves numberless, and the negro village a little town. A rice-pounding mill, barns, cattle, hogs, horses, mules, farm utensils, filled my imagination, and I remember how, as the impression grew of what was mine, the desire and purpose to study for the ministry became gradually weaker, until at last it died away. I was enjoying the foretaste of a free Southern planter's life, and it had its own attractions. But I was alone, with no companions, perfectly unrestrained, a man in stature, a boy in age and experience, with fast-returning vigor and strength, conditions around me offering many temptations to sin, and memory recalls some three or four occurrences that I know have been blotted out of God's book of remembrance, but which, though he has repented of them, one never forgets.

The latter part of April, when it was no longer safe to

remain on a rice plantation, saw me returned to town quite restored to health. But from September to May my books had been utterly neglected. I had read a good deal, but chiefly light literature—all of Scott's novels and manyrothers, a little history, and a good part of Shakespeare's plays ; but I had pursued no serious study. My Bible reading was never intermitted one day, but for that what might I not have done, or what might I not have been ? I remember that the question of the renewal of my studies seemed to be an open one, but I told my mother that I would not consent to give up my schooling ; I had the means, I said ; I was still young—it was then the spring of 1844, and I had reached my sixteenth year on the 31st of the previous January. I had still five years before my majority, and what was I to do with those five years ? To school I would go, but where ? Nothing could have induced me to return to Mr. Cotes's, and Doctor Wragg urged that I be sent to the interior, as best for my health. Mount Zion Academy, or College, as it was called at Winnsborough, under Mr. G. W. Hutson, was selected ; so I packed up, and started on the steamer *Anson*, a small river steamer that plied between Georgetown and Charleston.

On the boat I met Mr. Thos. Pinckney Alston, who gave me a letter of introduction to his son Charles, then a student in the South Carolina College. Mr. Alston's son William had been a classmate of mine at Mr. Cotes's school. It was Friday, the 2d of June, 1844, that I got on board the train in Charleston, at seven o'clock in the morning, and it took all day, till near six in the afternoon, to make the one hundred and thirty-six miles to Columbia. That was the rapid transit of those days, fifty-three years ago. On Saturday I went up to the South Carolina College, and presented to Mr. Charles Alston my letter of introduction from his father. He was courteously kind and showed me everything about the college, and finally took me to his room. There he went through his private store of books, and one set he pointed to as specially his choice set. He was a devout, earnest Churchman, and I remember Kirke White's poems, *The Imitation*, by Thomas à Kempis, Taylor's *Holy Living and Dying*, Sutton's *How to Live and How to Die*, and other books of that stamp, and I left him very much impressed.

He invited me to take a seat in his pew at Trinity Church, Columbia, of which Doctor Shand was then the venerable rector. It was on Trinity Sunday, June 4, 1844, that I sat with Christopher Gadsden, Charles Alston, and three others in the pew. There was a celebration of the Holy Communion, and all these young collegians remained, and I came out.

As I walked back to the hotel, for the first time in my life, I asked myself the question, Why was not I a communicant? It had never been put to me before. I thought to myself, " I have been confirmed; why do those young men stay in, and I come out ? " But I found no answer. As I was leaving the pew, Mr. Alston whispered to me, " Come up and spend the evening at my room." I went to dinner at the hotel, and spent the afternoon walking about Columbia, as I had never been in the place before. After tea, I lit a cigar (an over-indulgent mother had permitted me that winter to acquire the habit of smoking) and strolled up to the college.

I expected to spend a social evening, smoking, and perhaps taking a glass of beer. As I approached Mr. Alston's room, I heard the low monotonous sound of someone reading. I knocked and was invited in. As the door opened I saw the room was full of young men all sitting quietly round. I was simply motioned to a chair, and the reader went on. There were fourteen young men in the room, and they had just begun the evening service.

All the forms of the Church were observed : we stood,
and sat, and knelt, sang, and responded, and after the
hymn came the sermon. I do not recall one syllable of
it, nor whose it was. I do not think I heard a word of it
at the time. But the spirit of God was doing His work
through the example of those young men. It all came
over me with a convincing power. There I was in the
South Carolina College, a place, to say the least of it, not
particularly odorous of sanctity at that time. Here were
fourteen young men assembled in the midst of a somewhat
godless surrounding, separating themselves from all that
was worldly, and hearing a sermon, not ashamed of the
Gospel of Christ. I contrasted their life with mine. I
suppose that my life had been as free from vice as any
other young man in five thousand, but it had not been a
life that led up to the life that these young men were
leading. My thoughts were intense ; my emotions deep.
The service ended, I was introduced to those I did not
know. I shook hands all around, went up to Mr. Alston,
and simply said, '' Thank you,'' declined to stay, and
started for the hotel.

On reaching my chamber I locked my door, and there
on my knees poured out my soul to God, thanking Him
for that day, and all its blessed influences. I claimed the
cleansing blood of my dear Saviour, and asked to be received at the Supper of the Lord. The peace sought was
given me, and I went to bed, happier than I had ever been
in my life. Of course, so marked an event in one's life
clings to the memory, and the slightest detail is vivid
still. In looking back, I have often thought that in my
neglect of the Holy Communion I had been more sinned
against than sinning. The spiritual life of the Church,
or of its clergy, did not seem in those days to be felt by
the people, at least I had never seen or felt it ; and in all
these years, from April, 1841 to June, 1844, I had never

even been told that the blessed Sacrament was meant for me, as a means, and help, to keep the solemn vow I had made at my confirmation. Yet I had needed help, for in those three years I had done some few things that my conscience then, and there, sorely condemned me for. But the Saviour had me in His tender care all the time.

CHAPTER IV

A WISE SCHOOLMASTER

I go to Mount Zion College—Happy and profitable days under a wise schoolmaster—Turkey stealing—My success as an actor—I forswear gambling—My opinion and practice with regard to lotteries and raffles—Boyish pranks—The power of confidence.

THE only railroad in existence in the State of South Carolina, in 1844, was the South Carolina Railroad, for a long while the longest road in the world. It started from Charleston, and at Branchville, sixty-four miles thence, it forked, one branch going to Augusta, Georgia, the other to Columbia, South Carolina, and at each of these places it stopped. The town of Winnsborough, where Mount Zion College was situated, is twenty-five miles north of Columbia, and the only means of transportation, was by a four-horse stage which ran three times a week, and it took eight hours to accomplish the journey, for the road was rough and hilly.

On Monday the 5th of June, 1844, I mounted to the seat beside the driver, and started off at seven o'clock in the morning, a light-hearted boy. The events of the day before had been a reality to me, and I felt that I had turned my back on the past, and was in many things entering on a new life. I never had wallowed in the gutter, nor had I experienced those excruciating agonies in the conviction of sin that we sometimes read about. The pangs of conscience with me had been sharp and short. In my inmost soul I had always loved God, even from a little child, and His ineffable love, shining all through His Word, as I read it systematically for five years, had pierced my inmost being. When I felt contrition, I threw myself at the Saviour's feet, and knew that He had taken me to a loving Father who, for His sake, had freely, fully, and finally forgiven me all that was wrong in my past. At that early age, I had learned what God's Word said, that Jesus had borne my sins in His own body on the tree, and I believed it as a fact; so that with a merry heart I started on my journey to my new school, among total strangers; for I did not know a person either in the town or the school. We arrived about three in the afternoon, and the stage drove straight up to the college.

There I found over one hundred boys, who, of course, all gathered in a crowd to see what sort of a chap was this low-country planter's son.

At that period there was a distinction· and difference between up-country and low-country people very generally recognized. This is not so much the case now, since the means of intercommunication have improved and the intercourse of the two sections has become general and frequent. I was rather handsomely dressed, for my tailor was Charles D. Carr, the leader in that line in Charleston. I have no doubt that the boys looked upon me as a dude or swell, neither of which words, by the bye, had then been coined. I know I looked upon them as a pretty rough set of fellows, blunt and bluff, but no doubt honest. But here and there I noticed boys of a gentler type, some of whom soon became my intimate friends. I was led up to Mr. Hutson's study, a little flustered. But the first glance at Mr. Hutson put me at my ease. A more complete contrast to Mr. Cotes cannot be conceived.

Mr. Hutson was a large man, with a most benign countenance, and the sweetest smile I had at that time seen on the face of a man. He rose to greet me, and as he advanced I perceived that he was slightly lame, one leg being somewhat shorter than the other. He had a cigar in his mouth, held between his lips right at the end of the cigar, and in the middle of his mouth. I found out afterwards that out of school he always had that cigar in the same position. I often wondered how he managed to secure it and keep its balance. His words of greeting were gentle and reassuring, and I loved the man at once, and did to the end, and even now revere his memory. He ordered me to be taken to my room, and there I found assigned as my chum a relative of Mr. Hutson named John Harrington. At first we did not take to each other, and were soon at sword's points. But, somehow or other, we learned to value each other's qualities, our enmity passed away, and we became bosom friends, so that one was seldom seen without the other.

The room—well, it was the exact opposite to the tidy one I had left at home, and it took me some time to break myself into it. The first night found me, soon after I had gone to bed, candle in hand, on a hunt. It did not take very long to find the game, for the bed was lively, with more dwellers in it than the legitimate occupants. There was an extensive cremation that night, and many nights, as the candle was run along the seams and under the ticking. Carbolic soap, kerosene oil, hot water, and fire, all were used, until we got that room more exclusively to ourselves. I found that the boys brought their water, and cut their own wood, for we had no water-works nor steam-heaters. And here the training I had received at home came in. I had owned a body servant, whose sole duty was to wait upon my orders, and of course there had been no need for me to do anything toward waiting upon myself. But mother had often said that no one knew what he might be compelled to do before he died, and so she sometimes made me put my room in order, light my fire, bring the water, and clean my own boots. It was not often done, but enough to insure that I knew how to do it. So when I saw these boys so engaged, I thought I would make myself disliked if I hired a servant, which I had the money to do ; I therefore set to work, and did as the rest of the boys did, much to their surprise. As I found out afterwards, when they heard I had come from the rice section of the State they expected to see a soft, green, self-indulgent noodle, and to have much fun out of him. But I undeceived them at the start as to my capacity to run abreast with them.

The first serious jar came when I was counted in to go off at night to steal turkeys for a secret supper. I drew the line very emphatically there, and expressed my astonishment that boys calling themselves gentlemen could engage in such mean rascality. They did not see it thus. It was not theft they said, only a boyish lark, full of fun. I took the ground that I could see no difference between the crowd that would indulge in such a lark and the darkies who robbed the chicken roost; indeed the former were much worse, for they knew, or ought to have known, better. There was a long discussion. I succeeded in drawing a few over to my side, and they never again joined that crowd. In fact, the stand I took greatly lessened the frequency of the abomination. But it marked a departure. There were other evil practices in which I was invited to take a hand, but in vain. At last all knowledge of these pranks was kept from me. It did not make me popular, but it did secure me respect.

The boys at Mount Zion were allowed to go to the

church which they preferred, and of course I went to the
Episcopal church, the first Sunday after my arrival.   I
had intended to introduce myself to the rector, and inform
him that I had been confirmed, and desired to go to the
Holy Communion.   The first service threw me into myself.   The Prayer Book is often badly handled, and it does
seem strange that educated men should so often seem to
be incapable of appreciating the power and the beauty of
the liturgy.   And the Bible,—how often those chapters
are murdered!   I could no more have opened my heart
to the clergyman than I could have done so to an oak log.
Perhaps it was my fault, but I was only a boy making my
way among strangers.   I just shut myself within myself,
and kept on trying to nourish my religious life as best I
could, with surroundings not altogether elevating.   For a
time I went conscientiously to the Episcopal church,
morning and afternoon, alone, for there was no other
church boy there; but it was an irksome task, relinquished
at last when another interest arose, of which more anon.

I was very fond of declamation, and after a while in-
fused a taste for it into some of my fellow-students.   From
one point to another we went on until we formed a Thes-
pian Corps.   Mr. Hutson took a very great interest in it.
He had the stage in the large school house fitted up with
shifting scenes, and encouraged us with his presence, and
aided us with his criticisms and approval.   Artemus
Goodwyn and myself always took the female parts of the
plays, and Mr. Hutson was so well satisfied with one
private exercise, that he consented that we should invite
the public.   A theatrical exhibition was a novelty in those
days in that community, and I am sure very many in
Winnsborough had never witnessed a play.   So our show
was crowded.   *Jeremy Diddler*, and *Box and Cox*, and a
number of laughable performances were given, and received with vociferous applause.   We made such an im-

pression that some of the gentlemen of the town, Hugh
Aiken and his brother James, some lawyers, and others,
formed an association in the town and invited us to join.
Mr. Hutson selected a certain number of us and gave his
consent. Goodwyn and myself were among the number.
The association fitted up more elaborately a large upper
room over Mr. Aiken's store; and there we gave several
exhibitions. We became quite aspiring, and selected *The
Lady of Lyons* for presentation. We gave a great deal of
time to it, and Mr. Hugh Aiken (afterwards colonel in the
Confederate army, and killed in a night skirmish ten days
after the burning of Columbia), played Claude Melnotte to
my Pauline. I was most elaborately got up, with a wig
of long hair, and a dress made by some ladies of our
acquaintance. It was before the days of hoop-skirts, but
the ladies wore their skirts very full. I had on seventeen,
and often since have wondered how I walked.

Before the play, by request, I recited *The Maniac* in
costume. The effect was very startling, for as the curtain
went down a piercing shriek came from the audience.
One of the ladies had been thrown into hysterics. Had
she seen the fun that was going on behind the curtain she
would not have given way in that manner. While quiet
was being restored in the immense audience, for the town
and country round crowded in to see the play, the actors
were getting themselves ready. The curtain rose and
dead silence prevailed. Mr. Hutson sat in a conspicuous
place, and soon the anxiety wore off his benign face, and
his perfect satisfaction as to how the play was going gave
us great encouragement. At times the applause actually
stopped the play; and during the scene where Pauline
recognizes Claude and rushes into his arms, the audience
went wild. It all comes back to me with great distinct-
ness. After the play they made us raise the curtain again
and again. We bowed and bowed and smiled, while the

audience seemed not to have enough of it, until in sheer
desperation we quitted the stage, leaving the curtain up,
and declined to appear again.   I have no doubt our heads
were quite turned at the time, and indeed it must have
been a great success, for, in the years that have since
passed, I have met people who have told me how well
they remembered that play, and my Pauline.   Only the
day before yesterday, November 2, 1896, a venerable and
distinguished old gentleman spoke of his having been
there, and he said he had never forgotten the occasion.
It was our final triumph.   Some of us found that it was
taking too much time, and the excitement and the applause were unsettling us, so we thought it best to stop.
Goodwyn and I retired, and that soon broke up the association.

We had as Greek teacher an Irish gentleman not of the
old school.   I remember almost with shame how we would
torment the poor man.   He had no hold on us, and we
did not respect him, and when that is the case, boys can
be—what can't they be ?   Sometimes we would work him
into such a rage that he threatened to cane us.   I think
if he had he would probably have had a fight on his
hands, although we richly deserved a caning.   He went
gravely to Mr. Hutson one day and demanded the right
to thrash us, saying, in England boys older than we were
thrashed.   Mr. Hutson told him if he thought he could
do it to go ahead, but he cautioned him that these American boys were not English boys, and it would be well for
him to insure his life before he attempted the castigation.
He never tried it.   Mr. Hutson heard of some of our
pranks and took measures to stop them by administering
punishment in his own way.   But he did not keep that
teacher long, and his successor was a different man, and
never had any trouble with the same boys.

It requires much wisdom and more grace to be a

teacher, but all the faults of a schoolhouse are not found behind the desks. It is a pity that many who are unfit take up the noble profession, and it is a greater pity that so many children have to suffer from their deficiencies.

At Mount Zion College we had what was for those days a good laboratory and a full supply of apparatus. Chemistry and physics were Mr. Hutson's forte and hobby, and I devoted much time in his department. I preferred these to all other branches, and often have wondered how it was I did not follow them up, for if I had then any talent at all it ran in that line. Some of us would follow Mr. Hutson into the laboratory after school hours, and the old gentleman, as we thought him, but he was not old, would give himself and his time to us. I think he was partial to such boys ; he certainly was very kind to them, and we all loved him, and some of us would leave play and everything to get the lessons he set us. If we found them too long we would perfect ourselves as far as we could and then tell him we were not prepared on the rest. Sometimes he would say, '' I did not expect so much ; I only gave you that to try you.'' He had our affection, and I think that it was more to please him than to get information that a few of us were quite studious.

Mr. Hutson allowed the boys to play cards provided we did it openly and without gambling ; consequently there was very little gambling in the school.

One incident I still recall. I was playing whist one Saturday out in the yard, under a large oak tree. The boys had heard me say I never had played, and I never would play, cards for anything beyond amusement, and this day they put up a trick on me, and after we got into the game, I discovered we were playing for a blackberry-pie. I went on and played the game out and lost, and the blackberry-pie was bought from the old woman who was loitering around to beguile the dimes from the boys

by her digestion-ruiners. The pie was cut into four and
my portion handed to me. I declined, saying it was the
first and it would be the last act of gambling in my life;
and it has been so. I have always had an instinctive
horror of the vice. I never bought or held a lottery
ticket, and have studiously avoided even a chance at the
raffles which I think disgrace church fairs. Fairs, raffles,
grab-bags, post-offices, dances for raising church funds, I
have always held as abominations, and travesties on religion and charity.*

I remained at Winnsborough from June 5, 1844, until
October 4, 1845. During that time I never took part in
any of the mischief in which many of the boys engaged
except on one occasion. From some cause or other, my
chum and I agreed to go out one Friday night and have
some fun. We turned our coats wrong side out, mashed
in our hats, and went after this imaginary fun. Four
main roads crossing each other at right angles formed the
approaches into the town from the surrounding country.
Cotton fields surrounded the town and came down to its
limits. A high fence enclosed them, and we two boys
pulled down this fence and turned it across the road, and
joined the two side fences, completely blocking it. We

---

* Only once in my life have I taken a chance at a raffle. Accidentally I found one day that a parishioner, driven to great straits
as the result of the civil war, had given her silver forks and spoons
to be raffled. They were very massive and handsome, and often in
her husband's lifetime (he was an intimate friend), I had used
that silver at their table. I knew what it had cost her to make
that sacrifice. Twelve chances being still open at $2.00 a chance,
I subscribed for all of them. I requested the man in charge to
cast the dice for me, and if either of my chances won to send the
raffled articles back to the lady with all the money, and to say
they were returned by the winner on condition that they should
never be raffled again. A man who had only one chance won, so
my good intentions were frustrated.

piled the rails one on the other in the Virginia worm-fence style, and put the " rider " on. It was most laborious work, but we went from one road to the other until we had all four blocked. We then entered the town, and finding a light wagon in a yard, we drew it to the front door of a large girls' school, and by great effort got the hind wheels up against the door. We then went off quite innocently and waited till morning for the explosion.

No one was in our secret and not the slightest suspicion rested on us, and next day we strolled down-town expecting to hear ourselves well abused, and to listen to various threats against the perpetrators of the outrage ; but we waited all day in vain. Not a word or comment. We found out that some countrymen coming in with cotton, had discovered the obstruction, and supposing it to be the work of some mischievous boys, pulled the fences down and passed through the town without saying a word about it. Even the owners of the fields that we had exposed, by taking down the fences, made no disturbance, and so we had all our trouble for nothing. It was a silly thing, but it was our first and last escapade.

I must relate another incident of these days. One Friday night, two friends from town came up to get my chum and myself to go to their office and play whist. They were grown-up men, lawyers by profession. From early youth I had always sought my friends among those who were older than myself, and these two gentlemen soon after my coming to Winnsborough had taken me under their wing. When they came for us that evening I went up into Mr. Hutson's study to get permission. He had retired, so I wrote a note and put it on his desk telling him whom we had gone with, where we could be found, what we would be doing, and adding that we would return at eleven o'clock. Going down stairs, the four of us walked with as much noise as we could make

so as to attract attention, went down-town, and came in
punctually at eleven o'clock, to find the door locked.   We
went to the other door of the landing which was always
open, and that, too, was locked.   We were sure the boys
had done it, so we tried one window after another, and all
were fastened down.   We then realized that it was not
the work of the boys, and that old J., as we fondly called
Mr. Hutson, had done it.   We were nonplussed.

We sat on the steps and were not complimentary to
Mr. Hutson.   My note was on his table, we had done
nothing secretly, and we thought our treatment very
mean.   Neither of us used profane language.   (I never
used an oath intentionally but once ; I was then a small
boy ; the evil word slipped out, and I was so ashamed of
it, that I left the playground and I went and told my
mother.   The ungentlemanliness of profanity was sufficient without the sin of it to give me an abhorrence of it.
And I can say, with no mental reservation, in all these my
sixty-nine years, that was the only time I ever intentionally cursed.)   But we did not say pretty things about Mr.
Hutson.

After a time I remembered that some quarter of a mile
off in the woods I had seen a long ladder, and I suggested
to Harrington that we should get it and put it up to the
second story to John Robinson's room window and thus
show Mr. Hutson whether he could bar us out or not.
So we went and got it.   It was a heavy tug, but at last
we got back and put it up to the window, and I, being the
lightest, went up and waked Robinson.   I scared him out
of his wits, but got the sash raised at last.   Meanwhile I
had noticed a white object far back in the dark, and
thought it was Robinson's shirt.   I told Robinson old J.
had locked us out but we meant to show him we could
get in.   Now Mr. Hutson had a singularly musical voice,
and from that white spot came that voice.

" Yes, Mr. Porter," he said, " and if you will go to the proper entrance you will be admitted."

As I have said, he was a large man, and he wore his vests low and exposed a broad shirt-bosom, and it was this I had seen, little dreaming it was Mr. Hutson himself.

I slid down the ladder, alarming Harrington. " What is the matter ? " he said ; " are you hurt ? " " No," I replied, " worse than hurt ; old J. is at the top of the ladder ; he has heard every word we have said, and we shall be sent home to-morrow."

He had indeed been listening, and was just about to open the door when he heard my proposition to get the ladder. He was the soul of humor, and he could not resist the joke of letting us go to all that trouble ; he had waited for us, had seen us come with the ladder, and followed us to Robinson's room.

When we got to the door it was open, and all that Mr. Hutson said was : " Young gentlemen, if I had known who it was that had gone out I would not have locked the door."

We went to our room, but not to bed. We did not lie down that night. There was so much confidence implied in his remark, and to think that we seemed to have betrayed it ! We could not make out why my note had not informed him. We were two miserable youths.

The next morning at half-past six we went up and said our lesson in Ancient Geography ; Mr. Hutson was as kind as ever, perhaps a little more so. Sunday passed, and Monday, and still no word of reproof. Tuesday morning, we came out of the classroom, following old J. as he mounted the stairs. As spokesman, I asked a word with him. He stopped, and said " Certainly."

" We wish to go home, sir," I said.

" For what ? " he asked.

"We have apparently trespassed on your confidence, though I had written you a note, and neither of us wish to stay when confidence is gone."

"Who says you have lost my confidence?"

"Why, you said, sir, had you known who had gone out, you would not have locked the door; intimating you did not think we would ever go out without permission."

"Well," he said, "I repeat it. I did not get your note until the morning. I had gone to bed with a headache. I had got wind of a contemplated raid on a watermelon-patch, and I thought the boys engaged in it had taken advantage of my indisposition and had gone out. The noise you made woke me up, and thinking the crowd had escaped, I took that method of locking the doors and fastening the windows to catch them, but if I had known it was only you two, I should have felt sure that it was all right. To show you how far you have lost my confidence, Mr. Harrington and yourself may go out any night and every night, and stay out as long as you like, and you need not ask any further permission." And with that he left us.

Mr. Hutson knew that neither of us would avail ourselves of this comprehensive permit, and he was safe in offering it. In fact from that day till the day I left, neither of us ever left those grounds until we were sure Mr. Hutson knew all about it and had given his consent. But the dear old man paid us off. He knew that both of us visited a number of young ladies, and he went round and told each of them the whole story, with some embellishments, and whenever we went out those girls would give it to us, with their additions and comments, until we had to threaten that we would cease visiting them. This won a respite, for our friends did not desire our visits discontinued.

Many years after I had left school I went to visit Mr.

Hutson in Winnsborough, and we talked over old times. He had not forgotten the occurrence, and he chuckled over it, and pictured the ladder-scene to perfection. Of that lesson hundreds of boys have derived the benefit. I felt the power of confidence, and have cultivated it during the thirty years in which I myself have been at the head of a great institution for boys. I always trust a boy ; I take his word and allow no one to question it. When he proves himself unworthy of confidence, then I send him off. But there are comparatively few boys who will not respond to confidence. Boys are sometimes surprised at the confidence I put in them. Evidently they have not been reared that way at home, which is a sad pity for the boy, and for the home.

CHAPTER V

FIRST LOVE AND ITS CONSEQUENCES

How I made good use of my time—First love—The course never runs smooth—I enter upon a business career—Work without pay—My first communion—I rebuke ribaldry—I renew my suit and am rebuffed—A snake in the grass— I show myself a member of the Church militant—The perils of conviviality—The horrors of a slave sale.

I WAS now in my seventeenth year, and in more than one sense had made good use of the months I had been at Mount Zion College. This will be seen from the sequel, which it is necessary to refer to in order to explain the sequel of my life.

There were fourteen beautiful girls in Winnsborough, any one of whom was calculated to make a sensation in any society, and to make a susceptible young fellow's heart beat quicker at the sight of her. For some little time I flitted around, but gradually was drawn to one particular house, that of Miss B., a universal belle, who had all the older men at her feet. She was a lovely woman, and very kind to me. I looked up to her as an older sister; but she had a younger sister just my age. At that time I thought this latter the handsomest woman in the world. I have seen many women since those days, but none have ever effaced the impress of that face. Her figure and her carriage were grace and dignity itself. Her manners were charming, her mind bright, and her disposition equal to her external appearance. Is it any wonder that I was soon deeply in love ? I thought of her by day and dreamed of her by night. She was indeed a boy's ideal. Some persons laugh at a boy's love—puppy love they call it. But I know one boy that loved as really, and deeply, and holily as man ever loved. All my spare evenings were spent with her; we walked together, and. read together, went to church together. Her mother was a Methodist, but I did not care much about the Methodists; did not enjoy the preaching ; service there was little, or none. I did, however, care about Miss B., and it was a pleasure to be in the same building, and to have her sitting in the opposite pew or bench, and to walk home with her after the exercises were over. And so things went on. I thought then, and think still, that I had a good deal to satisfy me, that my attentions were understood and were not unpleasant to her or to any member of the family. In the month of September, 1845, the 24th, I could restrain myself no longer, and on one of those occasions that present themselves under such circumstances, I gave utterance to language, to feelings, which for months had been declared in actions. It was met evasively and disappointingly ; I was not rejected, but I was not accepted. I was left miserable. I had given my whole heart so entirely that I wanted one in return. I left the house that night and a veil was over all nature ; nothing looked or seemed to be as it had been before. A few days after, my good Samaritan, Miss B., went to walk with me, and told me I was a silly boy ; it was all right, but that we were too young to enter into an engagement. Neither of us had seen any thing of the world, and it might be a delusion, and it would be unjust to both of us to bind ourselves by a word we might wish to break. It was consoling but not satis-

fying to an ardent boy. I was a boy in years but circumstances had matured me. I have seen many a man
at twenty-two who was much more of a boy than I was
at seventeen. This check turned the whole current of my
life. I wrote my mother that I had made up my mind
that I would not go to college. Since for a long time I
had been the only male in the family, I had assumed its
headship, and what I wished to have done was usually
agreed upon. I intended to go to rice planting after passing through college, and I now urged as an excuse that I
had noticed that few planters were business men, and as I
wished to succeed when I went to planting, I thought a
business training would be of greater advantage than a
collegiate course. This was true, but the real reason
was, I was so desperately in love that I could not stay in
the small village with the object of my attachment and
see her every day and yet not be her accepted suitor. I
was young, and I fear somewhat self-willed ; still it was a
pure, honest, earnest love that pervaded my whole being.
My mother consented to my leaving school, and very
easily procured a position for me in the counting-house
of Messrs. Robertson & Blacklock, of Charleston, the
largest rice house at that time, probably, in the world. In
after years I have often felt the need, and the want, of a
collegiate training, and sometimes have seriously regretted
that I was turned aside from college ; still the ways of
Providence are not ours. If I had not received that three
years' business training, I never could have carried on
the work assigned to me in after years by the Providence
of God, and which has required much business knowledge
and acquaintance with finance to carry out.

On the 3d of October, 1845, I accordingly bade farewell
to school, to Winnsborough, and to Miss B. But I left
one whom I thought I could trust to look after my interests, and to keep me informed if anyone else was going

to see her too often for my happiness ; determining to return to Winnsborough, if that was the case, and to press
my suit. I arrived in Charleston on the 5th, and on the
8th of October presented myself to the members of the
firm. Mr. Robertson was quite dignified, and somewhat
stern. His first remark was : " Well, sir, what sort of a
clerk are you going to be ; will you attend to business, or
spend your time in King Street (the shopping street)
walking with the girls ? "

Mr. Blacklock did not give me time to answer, but
quickly said, " I do not think that is a fair question, nor
a cheerful greeting to our young friend. The proof of the
pudding is in the eating. And I think it would be well
to allow him the opportunity to decide what kind of a
clerk he will be. He comes to us with such commenda-
tions that I expect entire satisfaction in taking him ; I
should like to have him with me in my department."

My heart went out to Mr. Blacklock at once, and I
never had cause to take it back. I took no notice of Mr.
Robertson's remark, but said to Mr. Blacklock, " You
shall have no reason to be disappointed in me, sir."

I was to be paid no salary, and I never received a penny
from the firm. They knew I did not need anything for
my support, but I have often thought they made a great
mistake. It was a very rich house, and as after events
proved, I did not disappoint them, and I think it would
have added some pleasure and zest to my work if I had
received a due compensation ; but never so much as a
theatre ticket was given me in three years.

This was the first time that I had returned to the low-
country since I left it in June, 1844, and I had nothing to
draw me to the Holy Communion in Winnsborough, but
as soon as I arrived I wrote to Rev. Mr. Howard, rector
in Georgetown, informing him of my intention to make
my first communion on Christmas Day, 1845. There was,

in fact, nothing in my life to prevent my coming forward. My disappointment in love had in no wise caused me to forget my duty to my Saviour, though I loved with the intensity of an ardent nature. No woman living could force me to forget my obligations to myself and to my God, and I did not make a fool of myself. So on the 25th of December, 1845, I received the emblems of the broken body and outpoured blood of Him who had died for me. I am now nearly sixty-nine years old, and in all these years I have never but once left the church and turned my back upon this evidence of transcendent love.

My mother, my two sisters, and self, received together at my first communion. On my return to Charleston, in January, 1846, I offered myself to the rector of St. Michael's Church, as a Sunday-school teacher, and continued to be one for four years. I am often amused in these latter days to hear young men excuse themselves for lying in bed on Sunday morning too late for church by saying that they work so hard. I know I used to be on the wharf at seven o'clock every morning, and stay at the counting-house every night till ten, and sometimes eleven, o'clock at work, but I never found myself too tired to be at my class in Sunday-school at half-past nine in the forenoon.

Here let me illustrate the changes in church matters. I was the youngest and only young male communicant in that old parish. I heard afterwards that I was known by the old ladies as the young disciple. The next in age to me was Mr. W. C. Courtney, who was just ten years my senior. It is not so now, thank God. Then the clergy wore black gowns to preach in, with long white bands around their necks. Men did not kneel in church ; it was very funny to see them come in and put their faces into their beaver hats, for a second or two, to say a preparatory prayer, I suppose. The offerings were taken up in the hats of the wardens and vestry, standing by each door with a white pocket-handkerchief thrown over the hat. When a corpse was taken up the aisle, all the pall-bearers made a table of the coffin and put their hats on it. The *Te Deum* and the *Gloria in Excelsis* were always read. The first time the *Te Deum* was sung at Saint Michael's Church, I remember the commotion was so great that one might have thought the whole of St. Michael's Church, steeple and all, had gone bodily into the Church of Rome. The *Gloria Patri* was never used till the last psalm for the day ; then it was read. It was very bad manners to join in the hymn, and to respond to the service was vulgar. One wonders how the Episcopal Church ever survived such misuse of its liturgy and neglect of its privileges. The Holy Communion was ad-ministered (to have spoken of a celebration would have been heresy) on the first Sunday of the month, and the whole congregation left, save a small remnant of dear old ladies, and some decrepit men. Occasionally a curiosity like Mr. Courtney and myself stayed back, the congrega-tion departing with the major benediction. It is all changed now, as everybody knows, but, oh, what a fight it has been !

I soon found out what my work was to be in the counting-house. Mr. Blacklock was king of the rice market ; until he came and fixed the price no one thought of offering to buy or to sell. Before he came down to the office my duty was to go to all the wharves at which rice vessels lay, and have two barrels of each brand of rice taken from the vessel and headed up ready for the king. As he arrived at the office, I gathered up my bundle of old shot-bags with strings in them, and sallied down to the wharf, with my coopers all ready. As soon as Mr. Blacklock put in an appearance, out went the heads of the barrels ; I then filled my sample-bags, left

him, went to the office, spread them out on newspapers,
marked the brand on the margin of the paper, and
waited for orders.   Any lot designated as sold was
rolled out of the vessel, weighed and delivered, after I
had taken the weights of the barrels in my book.   I then
returned to the counting-house to make out and deliver
the bills for distribution before nine o'clock in the morning, which was done by another clerk.   My firm did an
immense business, and often I have gone home so tired
that I would fall asleep in my chair before a cup of tea
could be got for me.   And this went on from October to
the middle of April, for three years.

In summer we had very little to do.   Mr. Blacklock
was very kind to me, and kept me with him all the time.

A part of my duty for the first year was to go to the
post-office, after getting my sample barrels ready, and to
get the mail from the firm's private box.   Quite a number
of youths of my own sphere of life would gather there,
also waiting for their employers' mail.   Sometimes the
conversation was not edifying, and on one occasion a certain youth began to tell an exceptionally disgusting story.
I stopped him, calling him by name, and said, " One of
two things—you know that I am a communicant of the
Church, and you take this method of telling me that I am
a hypocrite, and I must be if your language is enjoyable
to me ; or, not wishing to insult me, you take this method
of driving me out of the company."

" Dear fellow," he replied, " neither.   It is so seldom
that one of your age is a communicant that I did not
know it, and I apologize, and will never repeat this," and
he never did.   All the other boys said they liked to see a
man show his colors, and promised that I should not be
offended in this way again.   If at any time I came up to
them and anything improper was going on, at once
someone would say, " Come, fellows, let 's change this

conversation. Porter does not like it.'' I mention these incidents, which are true, hoping, if ever this story of a life gets into print and is read, they may have some influence for good.

I had been receiving very favorable reports from my supposed friend in Winnsborough, when one day I heard, in the month of February, that Miss B. had come to Charleston to go to school to Madame Du Pree, the fashionable girls' school of the day. I am afraid that I got the samples somewhat mixed that day. I found out that young gentlemen were permitted to call on the young ladies at that school on Saturday, provided they went in the morning. So the first Saturday I asked for leave for a short while, got myself up in the best style, and called. In due time Miss B. came in, beautiful as a sunbeam, but she met me like an iceberg. She was the lady—she could not possibly be anything else—but oh, how cold! She froze me up. I tried to be agreeable, but thoughts and feelings were paralyzed. I did not make a long visit, and as I went down those steps, the thought of how we had parted and the fact of how we had met put me in a rage. I knew I had done nothing to merit this ; I was her equal, socially and financially. I had offered the pure heart of a pure life, and she had disappointed me. My idol had shattered itself. I vowed that no woman should ever have the second chance to treat me thus, and that cost me what it might I would never see her as a girl again; and I never did. I even avoided the place where she was, and not until 1869, twenty-three years afterwards, when the Protestant Episcopal Diocesan Convention met in Abbeville, she wrote and asked me to be her guest. I accepted, and took the opportunity to ask the meaning of that morning at Madam Du Pree's. She asked why I had never given her the opportunity to explain ? I told her, wounded pride. She had married, and I had mar-

ried, and both were true in heart and life to husband and
wife, but I told her that she had made me almost a woman-
hater; that for three years, till she married, there had
been a lingering hope that the block would be removed,
but I would not seek to do it, and after she was married
it was too late. But now, if she could, I asked her to re-
move a painful remembrance which had been with me all
these years—the remembrance of a bitter disappointment
in the character of the woman I loved. She asked me if I
remembered a person whom I thought a friend. Certainly
I did. Well, she said, he began after I left to visit at
her house constantly, and he had the impudence to fall in
love with her and to address her, and he took the opportunity to traduce me in every way ; made statements of
things which he said I had said. I said to her, "And
did you believe him ? Did you believe that I was capable
of such things ? " She said, " I was only a girl," and
she asked, " Have you not known what wounded pride is ?
I did not stop to do you justice, but resented it. I came
fresh from all these statements to Charleston ; you called.
I was full of indignation and I forgot myself and showed it;
but long, long since I have known how you were traduced
and the motive of it and have wished for this opportunity,
for your course towards me showed how deeply I had
wounded you." I thanked her, for it took away that long-
kept sorrow. And so it appeared by falsehood the destiny
of two lives, perhaps, was changed. My dear wife knew
all about this. I have always had the likeness of that girl
of seventeen hanging in my study, and many persons have
taken it for the likeness of my wife, for they were singularly alike. But when she would say, " Why, that is my
husband's first sweetheart," and surprise would be expressed that she would permit it to remain there, she
would say, " I never met her, but I love that girl, for if she
had married my husband I could not have done so, and I

am under great obligations to her.'' I suppose that everybody has had some romance in life. As a married man
myself, and she a married woman, there has never been
one thought or feeling that I believe would meet the dis-
approval of heaven; but the memory of that holy love of
youth has been with me all my days, and will be to the
end.

I had a fair supply of pocket-money, consequently had
a sufficient number of so-called friends to share it with me.
There are always a certain number of youths whose home-
training is different from what mine had been, and their
moral natures not pitched on a high plane, and there are
innumerable pitfalls in the way of youth. I did not find
my pathway exempt from them, and the influence of
companions was not always beneficial. I remember on
one occasion I found myself very dangerously near to the
point of yielding to persuasion to evil, but the grace of
God was stronger than the influence of the devil, and I
resolutely said no, and left the party. I went home, and
into my room, and locked the door, and took my Bible
and opened it at a chapter in the Gospel according to
St. Matthew, and knelt down, crossed my hands on the
Bible, and took a solemn vow, that I would never gamble
for the value of a pin, would never take a drink in a
saloon or bar-room. I had never tasted anything
stronger than wine, and I would never go to any place
that I could not ask my mother to go with me, nor ever
be in the company of anyone I should be ashamed for her
to know about. And I solemnly asked my Heavenly
Father to record the vow, and if I broke it that He would
punish me at once. I was only eighteen years old, but
how often have I thanked God for that vow ! I never but
once had any trial afterwards to break it, for I felt an impassable barrier had been placed between me and the
common temptations of youth. That prayer, that God

would punish me at once, was a great help. As I look
back just fifty years, I know that the vow of my youth
was the best thing I ever did, for by the grace of God I
kept it solemnly, save on one occasion, and in the training
of the thousands of boys who have been under my care it
has been a useful lesson that some have profited by.

About the only amusement that I did really enjoy very
much in Charleston was the theatre. I liked to dance
occasionally, for I saw no harm in it then and see none
now. I like to see young people dance; but the theatre
was almost a passion with me, and whenever I could be
spared from the office at night, I would go if the play was
good and the actors of the first order, such as the elder
Booth, Charles and Mrs. Kean, Forrest, and especially
Burton, the comedian, who started the audience in a roar
of laughter as soon as he appeared, and kept them at it
as long as he was on the stage. I admired also Mr. Crisp,
the father of the late Speaker of the House of Representatives, and Mrs. Mowatt, and others whom I have forgotten. I never missed a chance.

On one occasion, McCready, the great English trage-
dian, was in Charleston, and I went every night. He
was playing *Macbeth*, and between two of the acts I went
out for a few moments. On my return, as I pushed open
the green baize door of the foyer, I encountered an old
schoolmate, William Mazyck, and he accosted me with a
surprised expression, " Why ! are you here ? " " Yes,"
I said, " I am here, and why not ? " " Oh, nothing, but
somehow I did not think you ever came to the theatre."
I passed on and took my seat. But the pleasure of the
performance was for a time spoiled. " You here ? You
here ? " kept ringing in my ears, and I began to think
whether I was doing anything wrong. I looked around,
and I saw a number of very good people at the play, and
I argued, " Why cannot I be here as well as they ? " As

the play progressed I forgot the incident and soon was lost in the performance. It certainly was a great treat. After I returned home, I took my Bible to read as usual, and as I closed it I was conscious that I had been so absorbed by McCready's acting that I had paid no attention to the lesson, so I read it over again, and suddenly "You here?" rang in my ears.

I began to think whether Mazyck thought that I, as a Sunday-school teacher and a communicant, was out of place in a theatre. Perhaps he was himself troubled, and I was a stumbling-block. In myself I felt no scruples— the play was an education—but perhaps he might have thought otherwise. And at last I got down on my knees, and there it occurred to me that I had very little to give up for Christ, and if my pleasure brought any reproach on Him, I would make the sacrifice, and would never go to the theatre again while I was in the counting-house; and I never did, though I was there three years after this night. But the sacrifice involved a very great struggle.

I so disciplined myself that I never read a word about the theatre, what actors were in the city, or what play was on the stage. Often, if I had to go anywhere in the neighborhood of the theatre in Meeting Street, I would go down Queen to King, and up to the market, and return in the same way. I was afraid to trust myself, lest if I passed the theatre and found by the handbills some good thing was there, I would not be able to resist. It did my character good, gave me strength of will; but I feel sure it was a sad mistake, and that my profession did not demand it of me.

I have mentioned that I have never turned my back on the Lord's Supper but once in fifty-one years. I was perfectly conscious that at Charleston I was living a different life from ordinary youths, and I have no doubt was indulging a spirit of self-satisfaction, if not of self-righteousness.

One Friday evening, however, after leaving the counting-house, I was overtaken in a fault that I felt was inconsistent with being a communicant of the Church. Some might have attached little importance to it, but I did, and it troubled me very much ; so that on Sunday when the morning, service was over, I came out, instead of remaining to communicate. I was very fond of the Rev. Mr. Young, who was the rector, and of Mr. Keith, the assistant at Saint Michael's, and I ought to have gone to either of them on Saturday and have told them my fault. I am quite sure either of them would have said to me, '' You were wrong, but you have done nothing heinous ; you are truly sorry for it ; come to the Holy Communion confessing your sins and have the assurance of your Father's forgiveness, which we, as priests in His Church, with the authority of our Communion, declare to you in His name.''

I was nineteen years old, and did not know then the proper course ; but I went home, and in my room I knelt down and asked forgiveness, and that by God's grace I would never again place myself in such a position as to make it questionable in my mind whether it was right to go to the Holy Communion.

Now Bishop Gadsden had asked the rectors in Charleston to arrange it so that a celebration would be held in one church in the city every Sunday. The second I knew was at Grace Church, so after teaching my class at St. Michael's I went there. I remained with the communicants, and waited, trying to know whether I was doing right to go to the chancel-rail, and earnestly praying. I waited until the last four or five communicants went up, hesitating, until I felt I must go. Little did the Rev. Doctor Spear, who was the celebrant, know what was going on in that youth's heart and mind, or with what calm and peace he turned away after receiving those emblems of a Saviour's love. I thanked God, and vowed as I returned to the seat, that I would watch myself more carefully, and lean less on myself and more on God's grace; and at sixty-nine years old I am able to say I have never since felt I had no place at the Lord's table, and have never again left or refused to partake of His body and His blood. I am trying to make a faithful record of my life, its evil and its good. This sketch may some time or other be read by one whose conscience troubles him, and I trust that he may be induced to feel that it is only following the devil, who, if he once gets the advantage of us, or through our own carnal weakness we do wrong, if he induces us to stay away from the communion once, he will persuade us twice, and so on, till he has us in his power. No, to err is very human, but go and tell it to some faithful priest of God and get his counsel and his prayers, and if he is a true man, he will tell you to come and cast your burden on the Lord, and to receive the assurance of His pardon at His feast. I think, with no human counsels, the course I pursued was evidence that I was led by the Spirit of God.

Sometime after this I was returning from paying a visit to my old grandaunt (the old lady who was born on the 12th of May, 1780), when, at the corner of Hasell and Meeting Streets, I met a half-dozen of my young companions. They wished to know where I had been. I told them.

" Tell that to the marines," they said ; " a young fellow like you spending your evenings with an old lady."

" Well," I replied, " I do not care whether you believe it or not, it is true."

" And where are you going now ? "

" Home," I said ; " where all of you had better go."

" No," they said, " we are going to a certain street and you have to go with us."

" I will not do it," I answered.

A couple of stout young fellows seized me, one on each arm, and said, " Go you shall."

There were too many to resist without a row, and every one of us was a member of some well-known family, so I yielded, apparently, and went along.

They thought they had made an easy conquest, so letting me go, we walked along, and I threw them off their guard. We got as far as Saint Mary's Roman Catholic Church, when, seeing my opportunity, I made a rush and, being a very good runner, I distanced them, and ran into the Charleston Hotel.

There was then a large glass rotunda in the middle of the hollow square. The boys came in close behind me. When in there I turned on them and said, " Now desist, or I will expose you. I would sooner die than go where you said you were going."

I was in a rage, for one of the weaknesses of my nature is a quick, high temper that I have had to battle with all my life, and it was well up that night. I remember saying, " Try that again and we become strangers to each other, and though I never carry any weapon except a penknife, I will put it into the first one who attempts it."

They saw I was in earnest and they apologized at once, saying they did not know I was in such dead earnest ; they only meant to have some fun, and thought that I would be like the rest of them. The effect of it was, we all went out into the street together, and everyone of us went to his own home.

The law required every one sixteen years old to turn out in the militia companies, or to join a fire company. I chose the latter, and joined the Phœnix Fire Company. It was composed of young men of the best families of the city. We were called the White Kid Company, but dudes or not, we generally took the prize as being first at fires, where we stayed the longest. The company was a social organization, and they had a supper or a punch treat once a month. I went now and then at first, until I discovered that a dear young friend of mine who was a member generally got under the influence of the punch. I then determined to go to all of them. In the meanwhile, having great influence over my friend, I extracted a promise from him that he would only drink as much as I did; and he kept it. I would help myself to one glass of punch, and make it last through the evening, and he did the same. For some time it was pretty hard on him, but he was a true man and kept his promise, and years afterwards when we had both gone to rice-planting, he said he owed his being a sober man to my influence. I had saved him at those monthly suppers of the fire company.

I was once called upon to perform the hardest task which up to that time had fallen to my lot. One of the many evils of the institution of slavery, was the separation of slave families that would arise at the death of an owner, when the estate had to be divided, or the debts of the estate forced a sale. Mr. Richard O. Anderson, the same gentleman who some sixteen years before had bought my mother's slaves, died, and his negroes were all sold to go somewhere in Georgia.

They were brought to Charleston and had to be reshipped, and I was directed by Mr. Robertson to go and attend to it. Of course I had been too young to know any of them when my father owned them ; but some of the older ones, and many of their descendants, were in that lot of slaves. These appealed to me as my father's son not to let them go. Their entreaties, that I would take them back to the old plantation which they knew was still in the family, and not to allow the separation of some of the families, affected me profoundly. As the prospective heir of an estate, with a fixed income, but only a minor, I was powerless. I did all I could to console them, and made it as easy as possible ; saw them all aboard, and the vessel sailed for the South. I went up to the counting-house, and into Mr. Robertson's private office, the tears streaming down my cheeks, and I said, " Mr. Robertson, I have done as I was told to do, but I wish to say it is the first and it is the last of such a job. If I am again required to do such a business as that, I beg to retire from the office I hold."

Mr. Blacklock quickly said, " I see what it has cost you, and you never again shall be required to repeat it." And I was not.

CHAPTER VI

MY LIFE AS A SOUTHERN PLANTER

A question of Georgian civilization—I engage in a dispute where bloodshed is just averted—I retire from business— The life of a Southern planter—Advantages of a business training—Look not upon the wine—A negro hypocrite—The slaves' view of marital responsibility.

IN the month of July, 1846, my mother's health failed ; so I took a three months' leave from the counting-house and went with her to Clarksville, Georgia, in the immediate neighborhood of the Tallulah and Toccoa Falls, to which we made many trips. There was a pleasant party of old friends taking the same trip—Mr. and Mrs. Francis Porcher, Mrs. Cuthbert, Edward L. Parker, Henry Blanding, and ourselves. All of the party save myself are now dead.

One day while staying at Clarksville our party visited Madison Springs. I was seated with a party of young men on the piazza of the local hotel after dinner, and information was there received that Judge Daniel, of Georgia, had made a brutal and murderous attack with a knife on Alexander H. Stephens, afterwards Vice-President of the Confederate States. Of course, this fracas was the subject of general comment, and I was the only South Carolinian in the crowd.

I rather imprudently said to all these Georgians (most of whom were all about my own age—a little over twenty—fortunately a few older men being present), " I am astonished at this display of barbarism ; if a Circuit Judge and so distinguished a man as Alexander H. Stephens can be engaged in a bloody fight, what could be expected of other men ; this, I think, is a reflection on the civilization of Georgia ! "

Coming from a citizen of another State, my words set fire to the crowd, and I found I had a fight on hand.

I had nothing but a penknife, for I have always had a contempt for the habit of carrying concealed weapons, but the men angrily began to close in on me. I pushed my chair up against the wall of the house, satisfied, however, that my time had come.

Just as one of the young men, however, was about to attack me, one of the older men came forward, and getting himself between us, put out his hand and said, " Mr. Porter, I thank you for the implied compliment to Georgia. You gave her civilization credit for the impossibility of such an occurrence. You are right, sir, it is a reflection on our civilization ; it is an outrage." He lined himself up alongside of me. This was the turning point. The men ceased talking. One after another joined me with the gentlemen who had come to my rescue and soon the majority was on my side.

I then apologized to all of them for my thoughtlessness, while I did not retract the honest sentiment, and the whole party applauded me that I had not showed the white feather. We soon became very good friends. It was a very striking illustration of how a mob can be quelled by the courageous firmness of one man. If that gentleman had not left the crowd, and come over to me and said what he did, I would most probably have been murdered in the next ten minutes.

It also illustrates how careful a man should be in the use of his tongue.

At the close of the month of August, mother and I took our seats in the stage, and left Clarksville for Greenville, South Carolina. There were no railroads, then, in all that section of country. The last of September we again took the stage, a two days' travel to Columbia, South Carolina. This was the summer of 1848. I then returned to Charleston and resumed my place in the Robertson & Blacklock counting-house on the 1st of October. About the middle of December I went to the private office of my employers and told them I would be twenty-one in six weeks, and that I should then enter on my planter's life, and tendered to them my resignation as clerk in their employ, with many thanks for all the kindness received from them.

Mr. Blacklock said, " We have been expecting this, but we do not wish you to carry out your intentions."

He added, " The planter's life will never suit you ; you are a born business man. I have kept you constantly with me, for you are the only clerk I ever had who took so much interest in the business, or who gave me so little trouble."

I thanked him for his good opinion, but there was nothing else for me to do.

" No," he said, " go and make all your arrangements, and as soon as you are of age, sell your plantations and negroes, put your money into this firm and we will make you junior partner."

It was a great surprise, and, of course, I was much flattered, but I declined the offer, saying I intended buying from my sisters all their slaves, and reunite the estate on the plantation where my grandfather had lived and was buried.

He tried much persuasion, and told me I was making

the mistake of my life, for I would never make a planter of myself. I was firm, however. He then said, " Of course, you are familiar with our books. You know a great quantity of wine and brandy (whiskey was not then a common drink) is sent into your neighborhood. Take my advice and never take anything to drink before dinner, nor after dinner," and then he added, that he was the sole survivor of all the young men who had gone into business with him, and whose habit it was to go to the French coffee-house, the fashionable saloon of that day in Charleston, South Carolina, to take a drink at eleven o'clock, which he never did. They were all dead, and most of them from the effects of strong drink.

I thanked him, but told him that I scarcely knew the taste of brandy or wine.

" Well," he said, " remember what I tell you." And I did.

Mr. Robertson, in the meanwhile, had written a check and put it in an envelope. "Mr. Porter," he said, " if you will not stay with us, we wish you to take this and buy a watch, and wear it as a memento of your being with us."

I had been there a little over three years, and this was the first present I had received. I already had a handsome watch, so I bought a horse with the gift of money. I shook hands with the gentlemen and retired from their employ.

Had I not spent those three years in business I am sure I never could have done the work which in after years, in the providence of God, has been committed to my hands. I have often thought what a difference it would most probably have made in my after life, if I had accepted the offer, and become a partner in that house.

This was in 1848. In 1860, South Carolina seceded from the Union, the Civil War began, all of my associates

of my own age went into the army, most of them as officers. Most probably I should have been with them and
shared the fate of so many of them. It is scarcely prob-
able that I would have been alive to write this story of a
varied life, for though in the army from the beginning to
the end, I was there as chaplain, and non-combatant,
thereby running no risk of being killed.

In the week before Christmas, 1848, there was a very
distinguished actor in Charleston. I had not been to the
theatre for two and a half years, but I think it was
McCready, the English actor, who had arrived in the city,
and I was paying a visit to a very lovely girl who afterwards married my friend, Joshua Ward, and as we talked
about the actor, I asked her to go with me and see him the
following evening. It was an extraordinarily cold night
for our latitude, and I dressed in evening dress, with a
light overcoat, and took a frightful cold. A day or two
after, I went up to Georgetown to pass the last Christmas
at our town house, before taking possession of my property
on the 31st of January, 1849. My cold increased, and
soon developed into a severe attack of pneumonia, and on
the 21st of January, just ten days from my majority, I lay
at the point of death, "so near and yet so far." For
several days my life hung in the balance, but by the 31st,
my twenty-first birthday, I was slightly better. I had
now reached the day when I could secure ample provision
for my mother, and at once made my will, giving her my
estate in the event of my death, thus rendering her again
independent. But my life was providentially spared, and
I rallied soon after I came of age. I sold the town house,
paid Mr. Dozier the one thousand dollars he had loaned
me when I was a boy of fourteen, and moved to the residence on the plantation. There was a great deal to do.
It had been so long an estate under the management of
overseers, after my brother's death in 1841, that buildings,

and river banks, and fences, needed much repair, ditches
had to be cleared and new ones cut.

I soon found my business training was of great use.
The entire negro settlement was at once rebuilt, brick
chimneys put where clay ones had been used ; a children's
house, where they were daily cared for, was built. I contracted a large debt in buying my sisters' slaves, who had
been hired out, as my sisters had no rice land, and the joy
of those people was very great when they came back to
their old home, and it was soon apparent to all my people
that a master, and not an agent, was in charge.

I at once organized a large Sunday-school for all the
children, to which many of their parents came. Mother
kept house for me, and assisted me in the Sunday-school.
Georgetown is eight miles from the place, and we rode
to church in the morning, came back to dinner, and gave
the afternoons and evenings to the instruction of my
slaves.

Now I had a man named George, who was a Methodist
class-leader, who did the preaching, and I had learned
from boyhood to look up to him with great respect.
Those Sundays that we could not go to church, I gathered
the whole of my slaves together, and used parts of the service, read the Bible, gave them some lay preaching, and
sang a great many of the hymns, with which they were
familiar, letting George '' line them out,'' as they called
it, and let them sing their own tunes. When the full
volume of sound would rise, it was inspiring, and often
exciting, for negroes in their own melodies, the old plantation songs, have musical voices.

Not long after I had gone into the country, I received
an invitation to go over to Waccamaw to a great hunting
party which was gotten up to welcome me into the circle
of planters. Of course I went.

We took our first drive, and started three or four deer,

but got none. The rallying horn was blown, and the hunters gathered about eleven o'clock by a clear stream of water, and at once out came the flasks of brandy, and my health with a toast was to be drunk.

Mr. Blacklock's parting warning came to my mind, so I took a cup, and stooped down and filled it with water, and said I was ready for the drink. Oh, that would not do, they all said,—it was expected of me to join them. I turned to my host, who was Joshua Ward, who knew me well, and I said, " Josh, I do not wish even to seem to be rude, but I was warned against this by our common friend, Mr. Blacklock, and without interfering with your custom, you must let me join you in this cup of water."

That ended it. It was known I would not drink before dinner, and though always asked, was never pressed. I attribute to Mr. Blacklock's few wise words the fact that I passed through my planter's life and all through the Civil War, and I am sure I have never taken half a dozen glasses of any kind of stimulant before dinner, in my life, and never made it a daily habit to take any. When I was fifty-five years old my old physician, Doctor Wragg, who attended me at fifteen with typhoid fever at Mr. Cotes's school, urged that my peculiarly anxious life was such a strain on my nervous system, that I must take a glass of whiskey-and-water every day at dinner, and that is my habit whenever I am at home. Never a drop before nor after dinner, but only one wineglass measured out at dinner. I hope that if this story is ever read that no one will think I am a fanatic. I approve of a good cigar, and a good glass of wine, or if necessary a good glass of whiskey, if it is desirable for the health. These things are to be used in moderation and received with thanksgiving.

After the manner of Southern country gentlemen, we entertained a great deal, and were seldom without friends staying with us. Some young ladies visited my mother, with one of whom I saw that mother was quite anxious that I should fall in love. I liked to please my mother, but love-making is one thing that no one can do for another. Love that induces a true man to seek a wife, or a true woman to accept a man as her husband, is not manufactured. Match-making is a poor business, and I am not so made that anyone could do that for me. The woman that was to be my wife, and the mother of my children, had to be one who could establish herself in my respect, admiration, and affection, without anyone's aid. The memory of my first love had become hallowed. The lady had married, and I thought of it only as a sweet, pleasant dream of the long, long ago. But I knew that something like it would have to come again, when next I thought of marriage. I did not know how rich a blessing God was keeping in store for me.

There was a great variety in my life and always much to do, and I believe I realized the solemn responsibility of holding my fellow creatures as slaves. I did all I could to house my people well, to feed them plentifully, to clothe them warmly, and to provide for their religious instruction, while their daily tasks of labor were such as they could easily fulfil. I worked harder in the counting-house, and have since worked harder than any slave I ever owned.

One day I received quite a shock in my barnyard. I had no steam thrasher, though I was preparing for one, and the rice was thrashed out by flail and bob. Every afternoon the hands took their last floor of straw off in a bundle on their heads, as they went to their homes. On the day I speak of, my overseer came to me, and said, "Mr. Porter, you think a great deal of George, the Methodist class leader."

"Yes," I said; "a great deal. He is a good man."

" No," the overseer replied, " he is a grand rascal."

" Be careful," I said; " I will require you to prove it."

" Oh, that can easily be done. The rice," he said, " is well headed, but it is not turning out as much as it should, and as I suspected something was wrong, I hid myself in the cow-pen, where the hands threw their bundle of straw, and waited an hour or two after dark, when I saw a long line of the hands enter the cow-pen, and George was in the lead. They went to each bundle of straw, opened each, and took out of every one of them a parcel holding from a peck to a half-bushel of rough rice. This they took down to the swamp and pounded it. I followed them in the dark and watched the whole process, until they returned with the clean rice to their homes."

Now, to every family a certain amount of rice land was allotted which they could plant with white seed, not gold seed, so that they could have as much rice of their own as they needed ; and not being allowed to have the gold seed, which was the crop rice, they could not cheat us. Besides, there was a garden to each house ; each could raise as many hogs and chickens as they wished, and each thrifty family had a cow and a calf. Of course, some took care of themselves, while others, like white people, were thriftless.

" Well," I said to the overseer, " are you sure George was among them ? "

" Oh, yes, he was the leader of the gang."

" Call George to me."

He came.

" George," I said, " the overseer has made a grave charge against you, that I can scarcely believe, although he is so sure. I wish to know what you have to say."

I then repeated the overseer's story.

George listened very attentively, and finding the facts so circumstantial, and no way to avoid them, he said, " Yes, Mossa, it is all true."

" What," I said, " you, a preacher of righteousness on this plantation, and yet you were found heading a gang of thieves. No wonder the crop was falling short, as eighty odd bundles, abstracted every evening, would soon make a hole in the pile. Did I ever refuse to give you anything you asked for, George ? "

" No, Mossa."

" Do I not give you enough to eat ? "

" Yes, Mossa, plenty."

" Then, sir, what does it mean ? "

" Oh, Mossa, you know it is only nigger—but, Mossa, I no tief (steal) de rice."

" Not steal the rice," I said ; " and yet you tell me that you took it from this barnyard, with others, hid it in a bundle of straw, got it in the dark, and pounded it in the woods."

" Yes, Mossa, all dat is so, but I no tief de rice—Mossa, enty nigger belong to Mossa ? "

" I believe you do," I said.

" Enty rice belong to Mossa ? "

" Yes, it does."

" Well, sir, if rice belong to Mossa, and nigger belong to Mossa, and nigger eat de rice, enty Mossa still ? "

The logic was irresistible, but the excuse so ludicrous, I found it hard to restrain my risibles and to appear very angry.

" Well, sir," I said, " is that the kind of doctrine you teach your hearers, my slaves ? Then I break you right here as a preacher, and if you preach again, I will show you that the rice and nigger do belong to Mossa, and will have nigger given a good thrashing."

Investigation showed that I had long been deceived in the man, and I am sorry to say the same character largely prevailed in all that class. The Methodist class leaders used their position of influence, to the gratification and indulgence in much immorality and corruption. I could tell a number of stories in illustration, and any old Southern planter who may read this could add more. It is supposed it was a common thing to separate colored husbands and wives. My experience was, that it was difficult to keep them together. Conjugal fidelity was rather uncommon. I had a man named Peter ; he was very tall, and was called long Peter ; he was married to a very respectable woman, and they had a large family of children. One day long Peter came to me, and said he wished to take another wife.

" Well," I said, " Peter, the trouble is, you cannot do it. A man in this country can only have one wife."

" Oh, yes, Mossa, but I want to leave this one, and get a young gal. She is too old for me."

" You rascal," I said, " and what does your wife say to this ? "

" Oh, she does not wish me to leave her."

" And you shall not," I said.

So calling both together, I told her all that had passed.

" I am not going to punish you," I added, " but I mean to make Peter live with you."

I then directed the overseer to fix up comfortable quarters in the barn and every night to see that the man and wife had food, water, and a bed, and to put them in the barn, and lock them up together.

This lasted about a fortnight, when Peter said, " Dat will do, Mossa. I see you is 'termined, and I will live with Elsey—let us out."

I did so, and the fellow did live with his family as long as I owned them, but as to his fidelity, I cannot vouch.

CHAPTER VII

END OF MY PLANTATION LIFE

The institution of slavery—Its missionary results—An inherited responsibility—The good side of the African— Emancipation—I begin to feel that I had missed my vocation—I determine to enter the ministry—My friends encourage me—A time of study—The episcopal examination —The end of plantation life for me—A painful ordeal.

THIS seems to me a good place to record my views as to the institution of slavery. I could not help it that I was a slave-holder. I was born to it, and inherited it. It had come to my ancestors from the English, and afterwards from the cupidity of residents in the Eastern States. I do not believe there is anywhere on record, that the slave trade was carried on by Southern people. I do not say this by way of reproach ; as I have said before, those who brought and those who bought them lived up to the light of their day, and God, who oversees the wickedness of man, made it the greatest missionary work ever done by man. Not five hundred thousand naked African savages were brought over to America before the trade was stopped, and had they remained in Africa, if they had not been eaten by the king of Dahomey, their descendants would be naked African savages still. Whereas the descendants of those five hundred thousand number eight millions at the present day, of whom two thirds are professing Christians. It is all bosh when the negroes of the South are classed among the heathen. Their religion may not be of a high and cultured type, their morals may be below our standard, but considering the advantages, influences, and restraints of each race, the morals of the blacks are not one whit lower than the morals of the whites, relatively speaking. And among these people I have met with some noble traits. I have known some true Christians. I have sat at the feet of an old black Mamma, and have taught her the words of the Apostle's Creed, and learned from her receptive faith, how to believe it myself. I love the African race, and think they are the most wonderful people (taking all their history) of the present day, and yet, I believe they are an inferior type of men, and the mass of them will be hewers of wood and drawers of water till the end of time—at the least, to the end of many generations. Do for them as we will, a black man will never be a white one. I think I was born opposed to slavery. I do not remember the time when I did not hate it. Yet what could I do to abolish it? When I came of age, and inherited those that had been left me, when I bought my sisters' slaves, and brought them all back to the old plantation, what could I do but keep them? I could not free them, if I had wished to, and I was not such a philanthropist as to be willing to make myself a pauper by emancipating; the law forbade that. If I had so desired, I could not have taken them to many of the Western or Northern States, for the law prohibited that, but if I could have taken them to some free State, how would they have been supported? To have transported a large number of men, women, and children without a dollar into a strange land, would have been worse than barbarism. Much has been written on the subject, and much can be written. In sections of the

South, it was truly a patriarchal system.   In some families an institution almost sacred.   But when one generalizes, he fails to describe things as they are.   In some sections, and in some families, the institution was anything but patriarchal.   There were many things in it possibly that were lovely, and there were many things hateful.   The dependence of these people on their masters and mistresses, their love and care for our children, their tender faithfulness to us in sickness, what old Southern slave-holder can forget all this ?   Where, but on a Southern plantation, could a family go to bed, night after night, year in and year out, surrounded by hundreds of African slaves, your own, and those of your immediate neighbors, with the sideboard and the drawers unlocked, all loaded with old family silver, and all the doors and windows of the house left open, and never a fork or a spoon to be taken ?   What could have been, what is there in the records of history more sublime than the fact when in the four years of civil war, when the South was invaded by army after army, not only of Americans but of hordes of foreigners, and our slaves were sent from the coast country into the interior, with our wives and children, while all able and respectable white men were in the army, these slaves not only protected these women and children, but regularly worked for them, while they knew their slavery was at the real bottom of the strife ?   Yet in all those bloody, awful years from '61 to '65, through all the South there is no record of a single murder committed by a negro on a white person, or a single outrage or indignity offered to any woman.   I say it is a proof of the manly nobility of the negro, for which the Anglo-Saxon race should be grateful, as it redounds to the credit of the masters of the South, as evidencing the feelings with which their treatment in general had inspired the slaves.   It was a joyous sight in olden times to see in nearly all our plantation families, all the house servants come in to morning and evening family prayer, and to go to their church meetings and hear them sing. When the war broke out, there were within five as many negro communicants in the Episcopal Church in South Carolina as there were white, and the Methodists and Baptists counted them by the thousands.

It would extend this subject too long to tell all I know and feel about it, yet I thank God the negroes are free. I think their emancipation was cruel in the way it was done—cruel to them and cruel to us. More unwise still was the haste with which the ballot was put in their hands ; but it is done, and I do not know a Southern man who would restore slavery if he could.

Sometime in the winter of 1850, I was asked to deliver an address to the Odd Fellows, for I had joined the order, and accordingly I wrote and delivered the address, which resulted in a request that I would deliver the 4th of July oration. Up to the war, the 4th of July was a great day with us, and someone always read the Declaration of Independence, and an oration was given. I did my part, and this led the constituency about the Sampit section, to desire me to run for the Legislature. I took it up, and gave some dinners to the masses, and made some speeches, but it was not to my taste and I declined to enter into politics, or rather to accept any office.

I made a very good crop of rice in 1850, and also in 1851, and do not recall anything of very great importance, except that I found that I was growing very tired of the plantation life. The novelty had worn off. The necessary routine of managing, controlling, punishing, etc., of the slaves soon became very irksome. I tried to be, and I know I was, a conscientious, careful, Christian master, and I know my people were as well cared for, and had as many comforts and privileges as any laboring people in the world. They were a light-hearted, happy gang ; still they had to be governed, and made to obey, and I was very tired of it.

I remember I was riding one day through the woods, going from my lower to my upper plantation, about three miles, to see how the hands were getting on with their work. I was alone, and thoughtful, when suddenly stopping my horse, I turned his head towards the woods, and when I was hidden from the possible sight of any passer-by, I sat on the horse, and offered an earnest prayer that God would lead me to a life more useful, and more satisfying to my nature, than the control and discipline of negroes. I had then no thought of seeking the ministry. That had all passed away from my mind, if not from my heart. I was not conscious of a wish for it, or a thought about it, but I have looked back since, and that ride through the woods, that prayer on horseback, has seemed to me the beginning of the end of my planter's life.

This was sometime in the month of February; planting began in March, and I was very busy. Sometime in the month of April, 1851, my aunt, Mrs. Mary Ford, came to pay us a visit. We had returned from church, and after finishing our usual service with the plantation hands, we took dinner, and sat around the fire, for it happened to be cold weather. The conversation turned upon the incidents of my father's life. My aunt was devoted to him, and mother and she had a great deal to tell me of his words and ways. I had often heard many of the incidents before, and was well acquainted with his characteristics, but this night all that was said sank into my mind with increased power, and took possession of me. What a blessing to children to have parents they can revere !

It was after eleven o'clock at night before we retired. I went to my chamber, read my Bible, said my prayers, and undressed. I had stooped down to take off my socks, when there passed over me an overwhelming sense of misery. I raised myself up, and looking steadily into the fire, I said aloud, "I am very unhappy. Well," I continued, "and why am I so unhappy?" I had everything that a reasonable man could wish; my fortune in these days would be considered as poverty, but in those days I was as well off as the most of my neighbors. There were a few young men with more property, but many with not so much. My life record, from the time of my youth, could stand the blaze of the fiercest light turned on it. I had nothing to hide, nothing to be ashamed of. My social position was of course assured. I knew I was esteemed among men. I was in the vestry of the church, was a delegate at twenty-one to the Diocesan Convention from my parish, my health was tolerably good, though not robust. I had a well-furnished house, a good library, was a steady reader. Had my servants, horses, guns, and dogs; could come and go as I pleased, and yet, after surveying the situation and conditions, I said, "Still, I am very unhappy, and why is it so?"

I was seated on a chair in front of the fire, and had drawn my right foot up on to the chair with my finger in the top of my sock, half pulled off, and there I sat, and pondered.

Gradually the thought entered my mind that I was unhappy, because I was not fulfilling my destiny. "And what is that?" It soon took definite form in the thought that I had purposed, when a boy of fourteen, to study for the ministry, and I had given it up and had driven it from me.

"Pshaw," I said, "it is too late, that cannot now be!" and I drew off my sock, and with impatience threw it across the room.

I put the light out, and jumped into bed, and tried to drown thought in sleep; but it was of no avail. Sleep had fled. My broken purpose seemed to stand like a phantom before me, and I could not drive it away. I then began to reason with myself. I had left school, had gone to business, had left it for the planter's life, had been at it a little over two years.

Was I not volatile, unstable, restless, would I not create this impression upon all that knew me ? Then I answered myself, " What has brought this broken purpose back to me ? Why does it stay there ? Is it the Spirit of God calling me back ? If it is the Spirit, what matters what anyone thinks of me ? "

Then I thought, " It is impossible. I have given up systematic study for nearly six years, have almost forgotten my Latin and Greek, have read a great deal, but have not studied."

Then I answered myself, " I had a good grounding, I did not have a dull mind, I had a strong will, and if I determined to study, what was to hinder me from studying and learning what any other man could learn ? " And again I asked myself, " Is this the Spirit of God calling me ? if so, shall I hesitate to accept the call, because of the labor of study ? "

Thus objections melted away, for I was fond of books, and study with an object would soon become a pleasure.

Then came the financial question. What of my debt to my sisters ? My business training soon arranged how that could be settled. Then last came the question of the disposition of my property. I knew I could not be a rice planter and a clergyman in active life at the same time, and to sell my hereditary estates, my plantations and negroes that had been in my family so long ! No, I could not do it, and I turned over in bed dismissing the subject. But it was no use. I tumbled and tossed all night, battling with myself, and with this conviction, that the reason I was unhappy was, that I was not fulfilling my destiny, until at last I gave way and made a full surrender of myself.

Jumping out of bed, I knelt down at the bedside, and said, "Lord, if Thou dost wish me, here am I. I give myself to the ministry of Thy Word. Thou must lead me and make the way by which it can be done. I give myself to Thee, my God, through Jesus Christ, Thy Son."

Just then a large clock in another room struck four. I immediately crossed the hall to my mother's room and told her of my resolve. Wakened out of sleep to receive such information, she at once began going over the difficulties which I had already solved. I listened, and then told her I had gone over all of them, but that I believed that I was called of God, and I dared not, nor did I wish to refuse the call. She prayed that God would guide and bless me, and then I went back to bed and to sleep.

My aunt, when she heard of it at the breakfast table next morning, said she was not surprised, and no one would be surprised, for it seemed the most natural thing, and if I did not make a good minister, she did not know what young man could.

This was encouraging as the first echo from the outside world.

After attending to the affairs of the plantation, I rode down to Georgetown and called on the rector, Rev. Robt. T. Howard. He greeted me warmly, and said he had been expecting to hear this for some time, and then gave directions what I was to do. He and I both wrote that morning to Bishop Gadsden, who in time replied, informing me that as soon as I felt equal to standing an examination in Latin and Greek, and other studies required by Canon, he would appoint examiners. Soon after leaving Mr. Howard, I met Mr. Benj. H. Wilson in the street. He was not a religious man, but had always been friendly with me. I told him what was going on. He took my hand and gave me a friendly grasp, saying, " I am quite prepared for this. Your friends have all said you would sooner or later enter the ministry, and I am glad it has come so soon.''

Here my first difficulty was completely answered. If my friends had gathered from my life any such impression, it had not been from any intimation I had given, for I had not one thought of it myself. I had put it away from me when I was fifteen, and I was now twenty-three years old.

I of course immediately began an earnest and systematic course of study. And when I felt that I could pass an examination, I informed the bishop, who appointed Rev. M. H. Lance and Rev. Robt. T. Howard to be my examiners.

They were not very rigid, and I was recommended by them to the Standing Committee with the bishop's approval, and was received as a candidate for priest's orders. The next point was the financial, and proper arrangements were made respecting my debt to my sisters. Then came the last, the disposition of my property. The crop was all planted, and the final disposition was not to take place till after harvest. In the meanwhile I called all my slaves up and told them how I felt called of God to go and preach the Gospel, that when I was ordained, I could not tell where I would be sent, and that I certainly would leave the plantation. I told them that they had now two years under a master, against twenty years under overseers ; they knew the difference. If they preferred it, that I would continue to own them, but they would not have my protecting eye. If they would take my advice, they would let me select for them a master ; that I would promise them to choose some gentleman whom I believed to be a Christian, and if I could not find an owner to suit my views, I would not sell them.

Their first impulse was to refuse to be sold, and with the emotional nature of negroes, they set up a wail and howling which was very distressing. I anticipated this, but it quite upset me. I told them that I would give them a week or a fortnight to decide. I took the most intelligent of them aside, and gave them my views in full, and advised them to counsel the people to choose a master. In the given time they were all called together again, and it was a pathetic scene. Master and slaves were in tears, they made protestations of love and desire to die in my hands ; still they felt that I had advised them of their good, and they would trust me to select a good master for them. My heart was very full when the decision was made, but negotiations were entered into with different parties for the land, which was finally sold to Mr. Lance to be delivered January 1, 1852, while I undertook the more difficult part of finding an owner for the slaves. I sent a certified list of all of them with the doctor's certificate as to their physical condition to Mr. Philip Porcher of Charleston, the most respectable broker who attended to such matters, asking for the valuation of them, and in due time received his appraisement. I settled on Dr. Allard H. Flagg, of Waccamaw, as the best man I knew, and deducted sixteen thousand five hundred dollars from their appraised value, in order that they might all be sold to one man with no separation. This was effected in October, 1851, and the slaves were to be delivered early in December, after the crop was disposed of. The summer passed and the time came.

Mother had gone to live in Charleston. I disposed of the household furniture that we did not need, and made ready for removing the slaves. I chartered a steamer to come to the wharf at the barnyard, and the pilgrimage began. God knows what it cost me ; my distress was greater far than those people felt. I closed up my house, and went to the negro settlement, and moved the procession. All their household goods, their pigs and chickens, their cows and calves were all put in motion, all marched down to the steamer, I following on horseback. I saw them all on board; then drawing them all up in line, I shook hands with every one from the youngest to the oldest, and left the boat, which soon steamed away. I was left the only living creature on the plantation.

Though my father had been buried in Georgetown in the churchyard, my grandfather, an aunt, and uncle had according to an old custom been buried in a ground set aside on the plantation, near his old residence. In the summer I had a deep ditch dug all around and a high bank thrown up.

When the steamer headed down the river, I mounted my horse, and looking neither to the right, where my grandfather was buried, nor to the left, where my residence had been, I rode as straight as I could go to the road which led to Georgetown, and turned my back on my old ancestral home. It is now forty-six years since that day, and I have never had the nerve or resolution to visit it again. The intense anguish of that occasion cannot be understood by anyone who has not passed through the same experience.

And so closed forever the chapter of my Southern planter's life.

CHAPTER VIII

A PLANTATION RECTOR

I begin my theological studies—The Rev. Alex. Glennie—
The plantation rector—I become a lay reader—I success-
fully pass a canonical examination—In the meantime I
meet my fate on the trip to Georgetown—Love and mar-
riage—My missionary zeal is severely tested—My wedding
trip.

I TURNED my face and my attention now to the new
era of my life. Having made every arrangement
which enabled me to close my business as a rice planter,
I had to determine what was wisest and best to be done
next. My mother went to Charleston, to live with my
old aunt, old enough to have been born the day that
Charleston was surrendered to the British. I had determined to go to New York, and enter the General Theological Seminary. My family doctor, and both of my
brothers-in-law, who were doctors, most strenuously advised against this. They represented that I was not
physically strong, and would not be able to stand the
winters of the North. They convinced me that my plan
in this particular was inexpedient. With the advice of
Bishop Gadsden, therefore, I applied to the Rev. Alex.
Glennie, of All Saints, Waccamaw, asking that I might
go to him, and study under him. Mr. Glennie gladly

consented, so I went over to the parsonage of All Saints, Waccamaw, early in the month of December, 1851. Rev. A. Glennie was an Englishman, who had come over as a tutor in Mr. Francis Weston's family, had taken orders after some years, and had been elected rector of the parish. His duty was to hold service at the parish church on Sunday morning for the planters. The parish was over twenty miles long, and some of the parishioners lived on Sandy Island, and had to cross the Waccamaw River to get to church, so it was impracticable to have more than that one service. However, there were upwards of six thousand slaves in his parish, and his heart went out to them, as to sheep without a shepherd. The masters of the people gave him every encouragement, and very many of them built very comfortable chapels on their places.

He often went to some neighboring plantation, and held service at nine o'clock, returned to the parish church at eleven, dined on a cold dinner, and after officiating in the afternoon in other plantations, would get back home between eleven and twelve on Sunday night. During the week he daily visited two or three plantations, and all the children at each would be assembled at the chapel, and he would orally teach them the catechism, portions of the church service, several of the selections of the Psalms, and many hymns. Three, and sometimes four times a week he held service at night, at the last plantation he reached in the afternoon of his rounds. On these occasions the plantation hands were taken from their tasks a couple of hours before the usual time for stopping work, were sent home for supper, and got themselves tidy for service. Most of the masters, mistresses, and children attended these services. On most of the plantations, the wife and daughters of the owner of these slaves regularly taught the children, not only on Sunday, but three or four times a week, carrying on Mr. Glennie's instruction. The result was a great many more communicants among the slaves than among the owners.

It is true there were thousands of slaves, and only one hundred and fifty whites. Yet though these people could not read, they had learned the service so well, that the responses were always full and hearty. Mr. Glennie was a saintly man, guileless as a child. He was never excited, and never depressed.

I think Mr. Glennie was the first parish priest in the diocese of South Carolina who systematically ministered to the slaves as part of his parish. He was eventually elected Bishop of Africa, which appointment he wisely declined, probably under the advice of a judicious wife.

As to myself and my studies, there was nothing to do but study, and I did it faithfully. At that time the diocese of South Carolina was very Calvinistic in its theology. Fortunately, Mr. Glennie was neither Calvinistic nor very low church in his views, and therefore I had free scope to read the authors of either school. Every instinct of my nature rebelled against the Calvinistic system, and I never have been able to see how anyone could believe understandingly the church catechism and be a low churchman.

After I had been with Mr. Glennie some little while, he asked me to help him in his mission work. With my assistance, he began to hold four services on every Sunday on four plantations, and the week-day catechising was doubled.*

The question naturally arises, what was the eventual

* I still have the original entries in my note-book of services held, and catechisings, and they number twenty-three of the former and twenty-six of the latter each month for three years, summer and winter. I did it all at my own expense. I kept my own horse, paid my board, and did all that work, and never received one penny for it.

outcome of all this labor ?   Until 1862, Mr. Glennie continued his work, for after I had left in 1854, he got a
deacon to help him, and kept up what was being done
while I was there.   In 1862 the war had begun, and
everything like order was broken up.   The slaves were
removed into the interior and scattered.   The river
planters were all ruined, many of the older men had to
give up their plantations, some of the younger men had
been killed, a comparatively few of the emancipated
negroes struggled back.   The whites were unable to have
a minister for themselves, and so far as we know that
entire work perished.

How often had I seen handsome equipages, four-in-
hand, driven to that parish church, which after the war,
for many years remained closed.   There were none to
minister at its altar, and few to attend, or to support a
clergyman.   As for the poor negroes, their comfortable
homes were gone, and such as survived were mostly
wandering vagabonds.   That dreadful war !   Its consequences are seen on every side in this blighted Southland,
and are grievously felt even after thirty-two years have
passed.

In the month of June, 1852, I had covered so much
ground in my theological reading that I wrote to Bishop
Gadsden asking him to appoint a time and place for my
first examination.   He directed me to report in Charleston
immediately.   The examination was appointed by him to
be held at the house of Rev. Christian Hanckel, D.D.,
Rector of Saint Paul's Church, Charleston.

On the day fixed, a somewhat formidable array of
clergymen took their seats round the room in which I was
to undergo my ordeal.   I was fortunate enough to have
as chief examiner, the Rev. Paul Trapier, Rector of Saint
Michael's, whose equal as a catechist I never met.   He
soon learned what books I had studied, and by his wise

method of questioning, elicited replies from me which
surprised me as to my own knowledge. What at first
was a trial, and an anxiety, soon became a pleasure, and
the five or six hours passed quickly. When I was asked
to retire to the next room, to await their decision, I left
the room with the feeling that I had passed satisfactorily.
In a little while I was recalled, and informed by Doctor
Hanckel that my examination was a gratification to the
examiners. Nearly all of them were my strong personal
friends, and were deeply interested in my success.

I afterwards learned that they had put me, not only
through the canonical subjects required in the first examination, but also well into those of the second. Rev. Dr.
Hanckel, Rev. Paul Trapier, and Rev. P. T. Keith had
no Calvinistic tendencies, and were rather pleased that
the young candidate was very decidedly pronounced in
his views on that subject.

On the morning after the examination I went down to
the steamer to return to my work and studies at Mr.
Glennie's house. The steamboat was to stop at Georgetown. Little did I imagine that morning that I was on
the eve of perhaps the most important event in my life.

The day was bright, the sea was calm, a gentle breeze
cooled the atmosphere, and a few passengers took their
seat on the promenade deck under the awning. There
was one young lady seated there, whom I thought I knew.
She was dressed with exquisite taste, and wore the
daintiest white sun-bonnet, so that one saw as through a
vista, and half-hid, in the distance, her lovely Grecian
face. I recognized Miss Atkinson, and immediately approached, and took my seat beside her. When we were
children we had often played together on North Island,
had waded in the surf on the beach, and romped over the
sand-hills. Her father was a rice planter on Winyah Bay.
She had gone, while quite young, to her uncle, Mr. Stead-

man, afterwards Admiral Steadman, of the United States Navy, to be educated in Philadelphia, and from that time we had very seldom met. The trip from Charleston to Georgetown was some eight or nine hours, and we sat together and talked the whole way. She left the steamer at Georgetown, but I continued my voyage to Waccamaw. A day or two after my return to Waccamaw I went over to Georgetown, to see my sister, who was then living there. That was my pretext for the journey, but the real truth was that a certain white bonnet, lovely face, gentle, modest, retiring manner, kept mixing themselves up very much with my studies. I had accordingly told Mr. Glennie I would have to let my little darkey friends off from a catechism or two, for see my sister I must.

While I stayed at Georgetown, I found myself inclined to see much more of Miss Atkinson than of my sister. July and August passed, and September began, and decided indications were given that my feelings were becoming serious. So, on the 27th of September, 1852, I asked Miss Atkinson to take a stroll with me in the cool of the afternoon and there and then, on asking her to be my wife, I found that I had won her love and confidence. There was no reason why our engagement should be a long one, the 16th of December, therefore, the anniversary of my father's wedding-day, was fixed as the time for our marriage.

This settled, I returned to my studies and work on the Waccamaw, with periodical visits to Georgetown, but not to see my sister. The dreaded yellow fever had raged in Charleston during the summer, but late in October it was pronounced safe for strangers to enter that city, and Miss Atkinson and her young brother Charles went there—she to make preparations for the approaching event.

Ten days after they had arrived in the city, I received a letter from the mother of my fiancée, saying that both her daughter and son had been stricken down with the yellow fever. Fortunately the steamer was then in the Waccamaw River on her way to Charleston, and of course I took passage for the city, which I reached to find both patients suffering from a mild type of the disease, from which they soon recovered.

On the 16th of December, 1852, Wednesday, at 1 P.M., we were married at the church, Prince George Winyah (where both of us had been baptized and confirmed), by the Rev. Robt. T. Howard, the rector. Immediately after the ceremony, we took the steamer and went over with Mr. and Mrs. Glennie to the parsonage at Waccamaw.

My missionary zeal was soon put to a somewhat severe test, for three days after our marriage I was summoned to catechise the negro children and hold service at Mr. Joshua W. La Bruce's place on Sandy Island. I did not feel very much inclined to begin work so soon again, but Mrs. Glennie, who would never hear of Mr. Glennie breaking an engagement, insisted I ought to go. In a private consultation which my wife and myself had held, we entirely disagreed with our good hostess; but when the boat came over for me from Mr. La Bruce, I was induced at the call of duty to leave my three days' bride. It was a raw, damp December day, and I took a very bad cold, and on the 26th of December, just ten days after my marriage, was a very sick man, and remained so nearly all the winter. But I have never regretted this act of somewhat Quixotic zeal.

When the summer of 1853 came I determined to take my wife on a wedding trip, and we left for Charleston. Under a change of air and diet my health began to improve at once, and we started off for the mountains.

CHAPTER IX

BRIGHTER PROSPECTS IN MY WORK

The Episcopal fund of South Carolina — A recalcitrant Standing Committee causes me to store my carpets—I am appointed as lay reader to a struggling mission—A beggarly upper room—Meanwhile I am made a happy father—Brighter prospects for the Church of the Holy Communion — The angel of my life's work—Incident in my parochial success.

IN the month of October, 1853, Rev. T. F. Davis was consecrated Bishop of the Diocese of South Carolina, and was at the same time rector of Grace Church, Camden. Up to this date, the diocese of South Carolina had never paid its bishop one dollar's salary. What money the diocese paid had always been given to the assistant of the church of which the bishop was rector. Some forty years before the episcopate of Bishop Davis, General Huger had begun an Episcopal fund whose accumulations had passed through many vicissitudes. At last, by the efforts of Mr. J. F. Blacklock, enough had been raised to pay the bishop four thousand dollars a year and release him from the onerous duties of a parochial cure.* Bishop Davis did not know at the time of his consecration what

* I wrote a full history of this fund, and published it in *The Diocese*, our Church paper, in 1895.

the condition of the fund was. He expected to continue as rector, and wrote to me at Waccamaw early in December to come to him in Camden with a view to becoming his assistant. To Camden accordingly I went. He presented me to the vestry, and at his request, I was elected to be his assistant, the appointment to take effect as soon as I was ordained. " And that," the bishop said, " would be in January." I could not canonically be ordained until May, 1854, as I was to be under the bishop's immediate supervision; he thought there would be no difficulty in ordaining me some months in advance of that date. So certain were we that the Standing Committee would make no objection, that I measured all the floors of the parsonage, and on my return to Charleston, bought all the carpets.

The application for permission to ordain me in January was sent to the Committee, but an application from Mr. R. W. Barnwell, another candidate for orders, for a dispensation of several months, had unluckily come before the Committee at the same time. The Standing Committee felt themselves in a quandary, and refused both applications. Bishop Davis was very much hurt. It was, however, explained to him that there were reasons well known to him why it was inexpedient to further Mr. Barnwell's views, and they could not grant one dispensation while refusing the other.

The bishop took the ground that the cases were not parallel ; that while it was unwise to place so young a man as Barnwell in sole charge of a large city parish, such as Saint Peter's Church, Charleston, to which he had been elected, I was much his senior, and was to be with, and under, the bishop of my diocese. The bishop then informed the Standing Committee that it was the first, and it would be the last request he would ever make of them, and it was. He never again made a similar application to them. I can testify that so long as I was a member of the Standing Committee, and up to the bishop's death, there never came a communication from him to that Committee. From my own personal standpoint, I can trace the hand of Providence in this incident. Had the Standing Committee granted that dispensation, I should have been ordained deacon in January, 1854, would have gone to Camden, and possibly have remained there. The whole current of my life would have been changed. Yes, and the destiny of many thousands would have been changed. This is a bold assertion, but if any reader follows on as this biography is unfolded, he will see that the assertion is not too strong, nor too bold.

I had the carpets stored away, wrote to the vestry of Grace Church, Camden, declining their call, and returned to Waccamaw.

Just before Christmas I received a letter from Rev. E. A. Wagner, saying he had resigned his position as rector of the Church of the Holy Communion, Charleston, and had named me to the vestry. I replied that I would not be ordained until May, and could not consider his suggestion. However, within a week I received an invitation from the vestry of the church to take charge as lay reader until my ordination, when they would elect me their minister. Accompanying the vestry's invitation, was a letter for me from Bishop Davis, saying that the work at Charleston was an important one, that he wished no break in its continuity, that as the people could pay me very little salary, and I had a private income sufficient to support myself while building the church, and gathering a congregation, he earnestly desired me to take the work for which he had no clergyman whom he could recommend. Regarding the bishop's desire as nothing less than a command, I took my wife to her mother to Georgetown, on the 2d of January, 1854, and going myself to Charleston, sought out the chairman of the vestry, Doctor Phillips, whom I questioned about the parish of the Holy Communion. He let me know that there was no parish in reality and no church.

The so-called parish of the Holy Communion, as I learned, had originated in the following way: Bishop Bowen lived in the upper wards of the city, and desiring a chapel of ease, had, before he died, held a few services in his own house in Ashley Street. To take up this work, Bishop Gadsden had called a meeting on November 7, 1848, and organized a parish with wardens and vestry. One clergyman after another had been trying their hands at building it up, and in six years they had gotten so far as to buy a lot, for which they had paid three thousand dollars, and to lay the foundations of a small cruciform gothic edifice of forty-five pew capacity. Things were now at a standstill. After telling me this, Doctor Phillips took me to see the building in which the little congregation were worshipping. It stood on the grounds of the United States Arsenal. Major Hagner, the commandant at the arsenal, was an Episcopalian, and had loaned an unoccupied storeroom to the congregation. We climbed up a rough pair of stairs, mostly a ladder, and found ourselves in this desolate room, a place about seventy-five by thirty-five feet. It was neither ceiled nor plastered, there were no sashes in the windows, no carpet, and no stove. A little rail divided off the sanctuary at one end, a curtain hung over the place for a melodeon, and on one side was a small font. Bare benches filled the rest of the forlorn-looking place.

I asked Doctor Phillips if this was the result of six years? The warden answered very hopefully. He was quite sanguine, and did not seem to think the work offered me was unpromising to a young man. I took care not to let him know my opinion about it. I promised to

look over the neighborhood, and advertise service for the
following Sunday.

The four following days I went over the ground, and
found that from Boundary Street, as Calhoun was then
called, to the limits of the Neck, as it was termed, from
King Street to the Ashley River, there was no place of
worship of any description, except Saint Paul's Church,
and the congregation there was principally a congregation
of planters' families, who came to the city in summer. At
the same time there was evidently a good mission field, so
I determined to give it a trial.

Sunday came, a raw, drizzly, gloomy day. I went up
to the arsenal and climbed up the stairs. I found the
room was nearly empty. The congregation in fact consisted of Doctor Phillips, one or two other adults, and a
child, Jane Waring. I waited some ten minutes beyond
the hour advertised for service, and by that time just
eight persons were on the benches. After service, I went
to my old aunt's, where my mother was, feeling very blue.
And indeed all the ladies protested against my taking the
position, one of my aunts being very emphatic, and saying I would be a fool to waste my young life on a broken-
down enterprise that had not the faintest prospect of
success. That Sunday afternoon, however, it cleared off,
and to my surprise I found some twenty-two persons in
my new mission chapel. The congregation of the morning had acted as missionaries, giving glowing accounts of
the new lay reader, and these curious people had doubtless
come to see what sort of a young man he was. I was introduced to my flock, only one of them, a relative named
H. Laurens Toomer, a member of the vestry, being known
to me. After the service was over I took a decisive step.
Calling Doctor Phillips apart, I said to him, " I left my
wife at Georgetown in ill health. I am starting to-morrow
for that city, but will be back on Friday. I can under-

take the work in this place on the following conditions. If I see all these windows on my return filled with sashes, a good stove set up, a carpet up the middle of this room, and a door shutting off the draught from the stairs, I will put a notice in Saturday's paper, announcing this improvement and advertising divine service. If these improvements are not made, I shall put a notice in the paper to the effect that I will officiate here no longer ; for I could not ask people to come to a place where they would catch pneumonia.''

I almost took the old Doctor's breath away.

'' Why,'' he said, '' we have been here six years and we have not had any of these things.''

'' Yes,'' I replied, '' and after six years where are you now ? Now, if you are in earnest about this mission, I will be in earnest, too. I will do all I can to make it a success, but you will have to show me that you mean business. Among the members of your vestry there is quite means enough to furnish all I ask. Do as I suggest, and we will go ahead ; I will accept your invitation. Refuse to do it, and I need not come back again.''

'' Very well,'' he said, '' I think I can guarantee you all that you demand.''

I left for Georgetown on Monday, the 9th, and on arriving at the wharf, I noticed that I was the subject of observation, and as soon as I got ashore, several parties came up and congratulated me upon being the father of a fine boy. The mother, they said, was doing well. On reaching the house, I found that at the very hour that I was holding in the upper room of the arsenal the first service of what was to become the influential parish of the Church of the Holy Communion, my first-born son had come into the world—a son to whom God, in His own Divine Will, committed a special function, namely, that of inspiring a work which has blessed thousands, and is still going on. This work, in all human probability, would not have been attempted by me if that son had not lived, and had not, by his death, awoke in me a passionate longing to help the children of others.

Amid the great rejoicing in the house that day, January 8, 1854, the little stranger was to be given to God, who had sent him to gladden our hearts. The following Friday I returned to Charleston, and going immediately to the arsenal, found workmen busy there. A stove had been set up. The sashes were nearly all in, the ceiling was going on, and a strip of carpet stood in a roll ready to be laid down. The carpenters promised to finish the work by Saturday night. I accordingly repaired to the newspaper office, and wrote an advertisement, saying that the room had been made comfortable, and inviting all who were interested in the mission to attend the next Sunday, as regular services might be expected hereafter.

On Sunday morning, the congregation had swelled to over fifty, and in the afternoon to seventy-five. Of course I was very much encouraged, for I realized that if so many came to a service conducted by a lay reader, there was certainly need for the mission. The following Sunday, the 22d, I gave notice that I would at once organize a Sunday-school for white children in the morning, and for colored children in the afternoon. I requested that all who had children to send would remain after service with such of the congregation as would help as teachers. Quite a moderate-sized class was quickly formed, and during the week I began a house-to-house visitation. I commenced at Boundary Street, visiting as many houses as I could, and gathering a good number of children's names. I notified several who had volunteered to be teachers, and we opened with a Sunday-school for the whites. It took a few weeks to let the negroes know that there would be a Sunday-school for them, but when we were well under way, we had a large gathering of negro children. The teachers of the white school all enlisted for the colored, and I had to call in more. We had started so well, that an enthusiasm was created, and the room soon filled up pretty well. I went into every hovel in all that section of the town, and found among many whites a dense ignorance, scarcely conceivable. Many nights did I spend going from one lowly habitation to another, and with a light-wood torch in one hand and a Bible in the other, read to them the Word of God, sung a hymn, and prayed, and so induced a number to come to service who had not been to church for years. My congregation was largely composed of very poor people, with here and there a family of a higher class. Among the friends of some of my vestry was a Presbyterian and his wife, Mr. and Mrs. B. He heard a good deal said about the rapid strides the mission was making, and living in the neighborhood, he once dropped in to service with his wife. They came once and again ; he became interested in the work, and his wife being a great musician, and he having a fine voice, they offered to take charge of the music for me. A melodeon was purchased, and a choir formed. They attached themselves to the parish, and being not much older than myself, we became fast friends.

CHAPTER X

A HARD APPRENTICESHIP

I take permanent abode with my family in Charleston—Am ordained deacon and preach my first sermon—I begin to think of building a church—My appeal for help offends some conservatives—The liberality of others—The "amende honorable"—Yellow fever, and my experience of it.

WE had our son baptized John Toomer on the 24th of February, 1854, and being satisfied that the work I was engaged in would be made successful, I brought my family down to Charleston, and purchased a house in Rutledge Street. On the 16th of May of the same year I was ordained deacon by Bishop Davis. The Rev. T. P. Keith, who had baptized me in Georgetown, was my presenter.

I preached my first sermon as an ordained minister on Sunday the 20th of May, and my text was from the Acts of the Apostles, eighth chapter, fifth verse : " Then Philip went down to the city of Samaria, and preached Christ unto them." I still have the original manuscript. The sermon was preached in the upper room at the arsenal. I have never found any other theme than that which Philip took in all these forty years, and I trust my dear Lord will tell me I preached Him faithfully. The building was very full, for of course I had many relatives and friends who came to hear the new young minister. I was in my twenty-sixth year. I was dreadfully scared at first, but as I warmed up, I know I forgot myself, and remembered that I was there to preach Christ, not myself, and at the close of the service was much encouraged by the warm greetings I had from many of my hearers. The comment that lasted longest in my memory was an expression of sympathy, " He promises well, but how sad it is that so delicate-looking a man should have gone into the ministry ! His life will be so short," and now I know of but two persons except myself who were at that service and still survive. So little do we know of the future !

* Soon after this I asked the vestry to call a meeting, to review what they had done, and find out what they proposed to do, for I had no idea of staying permanently in the upper room at the arsenal. Some eight hundred dollars had been collected by me in Georgetown ; this I held in reserve until I discovered the vestry's views. I soon found out that they had already purchased for $3000 a lot on Ashley Street, corner of Cannon, and had laid the foundation of a small cruciform building, which was to have narrow lancet windows, and to contain forty-five pews. I thought the situation unfortunate, and so it proved, and will prove until the city is built up far beyond its present limits with substantial buildings. On seeing the plan, I told them it seemed to me to be that of a pretty village chapel, set in a surrounding of trees, but very much out of place at the corner of a city thoroughfare ; that in this warm

* The entire salary paid by the congregation to the lay reader and minister for the year had been $236. The Society for the Advancement of Christianity, seeing our progress, voted to the vestry for salary $250. I had gone to them without the offer of a dollar, and though I could live without their salary, as soon as we began to get a congregation I told the vestry that it would be a better parish if it learned at once to help itself. The total offering for the first year was $423.70.

climate the congregation would be steamed, and besides, I did not propose to devote my young days to the building of a church that would always be a mission. I wanted a church which in time would be self-supporting, and declined to serve, if that plan was carried out. The vestry were as much taken aback as when I requested that the upper room should be made comfortable, but my business training now came into use. I was firm, and would yield to no arguments. The result was that the plan was abandoned, and Messrs. Jones & Lee employed to furnish another. I was not in the vestry, and Messrs. Jones & Lee's design was adopted without consulting me. When I saw it, I told them that it was that of a respectable-looking omnibus stable, but did not look much like a church. However, I would build it, provided, when the congregation could afford it, a church that was a church should be built. I then brought out my Georgetown subscription, and told them we must begin at once. This was on the 2d of July, 1854.

On reviewing my work to date, I found that I had collected from the 8th of January to the 2d of July, three thousand six hundred and sixty-seven dollars; that the congregation now numbered seventy-nine whites, and thirty-seven blacks; that there were thirty-one white children and thirty-five black in the two Sunday-schools; that the church had twenty-one communicants.*

After visiting from house to house to get aid, I asked the Rev. Mr. Keith, Rector of Saint Michael's, to let me

---

* I remember the first day I went into Broad Street to ask for aid to build a church, a gentleman whom I approached met me by saying:

"The Church of the Holy Communion? Why that is a chimera floating in the brains of a few up-town people which will never be realized!"

"Well," I said, "chimera or not, I have ten thousand dollars preach in behalf of the church. He consented, and I preached, he announcing there would be no offering. My text was Titus, third chapter, part of first verse, "Be ready to every good work." I began by saying:

"A beggar again. Methinks I hear this thought running through the minds of my hearers. But I wish to say that I am no beggar. I am a minister of the Church of which you are members. I believe what you believe, and I am charitable enough to suppose that we are actuated by similar motives. My duty is to show that the work I present is a good work. Then your duty is to see how ready you are according to your ability to help it."

I then told of the work, its needs, what we had done, its prospects, and then very practically showed how each pew could help.

Concluding, I said that the rector had announced that there would be no offering, and I did not wish one; I needed more than the small change usually put into the alms basin, and requested any who were interested to send their subscriptions to Messrs. R. & B. Mr. R. was one of the vestry, Mr. B. was a vestryman of Saint Paul's. Next day I went to the office of Messrs. R. & B. somewhat fearful, for when I got back to the vestryroom, Mr. Keith did not say one word about the sermon, and under Saint Michael's porch a large gathering were evidently discussing the sermon. I touched my hat, and passed on, no one saying a word. As I entered Mr. R.'s office, the old gentleman threw up his spectacles on his head,

of my own, and if it becomes necessary I will put this sum into it, and we will see if this chimera cannot be made a reality."

He looked at me steadily and asked:

"Are you in earnest? and do you mean that?"

"I certainly do," I said.

"Oh, well," he replied, "if that is the way you are going at it, come to my office and take my subscription."

So I gathered the first money.

and said, " The very man I wish to see. Now I look upon you as a son, and I wish you to go home and burn that sermon.''

Then he gave me such a talking to that only his preface made me stand it.

" You will not get a dollar," he said. " I will not give you one myself."

When I got a chance to get a word in myself, I said, " Mr. R., was my sermon scriptural ? "

" Oh, yes, entirely so."

" Was it clear ? did I make out my case ? "

" Yes," he said, with animation ; " I did not think that you could write such a sermon."

" Was it courteous ? " I asked ; " for if it was not, I should like to apologize."

" It was," he said, " perfectly so."

" Well, then," I said, " it was scriptural, it was clear, and it was courteous ; why, then, should I burn it ? "

" Oh, but to think of a young man standing up, and talking to Saint Michael's people, old Saint Michael's, in that plain, practical way, telling them what they ought to do, and then how to do it. Why, who ever heard of such a thing ? If that is the way you are going to preach, you will ruin yourself. You will not get a cent. Go home and burn that sermon, burn it, so that you can never preach it again."

" Well," I said, " I thought I had been ordained for that very purpose, to tell people what they ought to do, and how they could do it. I will not burn it, and bid you good morning."

I was terribly sore. I strolled up Broad Street, and at the door of the Bank of Charleston, I met the president, a noble layman.

" Good morning, my young friend," he exclaimed, " I am glad to see you. I congratulate you on that sermon yesterday ; you have made a profound impression ; you will build the church. The sermon has been on every-one's lips, and only in praise."

"Why, Mr. I. K. Sass," I said, "You take my breath away. I have just come from Mr. R."—and I repeated the conversation.

" Pshaw," he answered, " our friend knows more about selling rice than he does about sermons. Come in, and I will show you whether you will get a dollar."

He drew his check for one hundred and bade me God-speed. I felt better.

The next friend I met was Mr. Charles D. Carr, who had been my tailor since I was a boy. He called me into his store, and came up rubbing his hands and slapping them together, saying, " I was never more delighted in church in my life. It was good to see a young man get up in old Saint Michael's Church, and preach a sermon like that. You did shake up the bones ! Why, you made them all look up and wonder.

" Come in," he said, " and let me give you my check. Here is one hundred dollars, and I will duplicate it when-ever you need it.

" Now," he continued, " I wish you to go and see Mr. Jas. L. Petigru ; he was delighted. Did you see that crowd under Saint Michael's porch when you passed ? They had gathered around Mr. Petigru, who was speak-ing in the highest commendation. You must go and see him."

I left him, and as I reached the corner of Saint Michael's Church, Mr. Petigru himself turned out of Meeting, into Broad Street.

As we met, he said, " I believe I am speaking to the Rev. Mr. Porter ; I wish to congratulate you on your effort yes-terday ; that is the best sermon of the kind I have ever heard, and if I could have gotten to the foot of the pulpit without making us both too conspicuous, I would have congratulated you before all the congregation. Why, sir, you came with a definite object, you stated it forcibly, and then proved to us it was our duty to help it, and how the least person in the church could do his or her part.''

Mr. Petigru stood at the forefront of the bar, and was a power in this community, and he overpowered and confused me. '' Your church is built, sir,'' he continued, '' and if you always preach like that I prophesy a successful ministry.''

Taking from his pocket a check, he handed it to me. It was a large donation from Mr. Petigru, for he was not a man of much means. It may well be supposed that I went home in good spirits, to gladden my young wife, who had passed an anxious morning.

It was about six weeks after I had been to the counting-house of Messrs. R. & B., that I thought I would go there again.

Mr. R. met me very cordially, saying I had not been there for a long while.

I made some excuse. '' You were not a good prophet,'' I added ; '' I did not burn that sermon, and I have eight thousand dollars to my credit on it. Mr. Petigru was very complimentary.'' I knew that Mr. Petigru was Mr. R.'s ideal, and had much influence over him. '' Indeed,'' he replied. '' Well, before you go, I wish to add my mite to the sum,'' and drew his check for five hundred dollars.

The summer of 1854 came on, and with it the dreaded yellow fever. We were short-handed ministerially, some of the rectors being away, and I had a great deal to do.

I was overworked, and caught the dreaded pestilence three days after ground had been broken to lay the foundations of the new Church of the Holy Communion. My old physician, Dr. W. T. Wragg, who had attended me in typhoid fever when a boy, was soon at my bedside, and told me mine was a mild case. "Well," I said, "I thought one born near the swamps of Carolina stood in no danger."

On Friday he thought me so much better that he directed stimulants. I fancied champagne. My wife gave me a wineglassful, and I felt so much worse, that I thought I had not taken enough, and she gave me another wineglass. As I swallowed it, it seemed like a ball of fire at the pit of my stomach. I at once became desperately sick. The Doctor was sent for, and was dismayed at the change. He tried many remedies and finally he said, "I have tried stimulants and alkali, let us try acids." A lemon could not be found in the city, but oranges were got. My tongue was like a piece of hard dry leather. I could not extend it beyond my lips. My wife squeezed a plug of orange, and wherever the juice fell it released my tongue. I motioned for more. It was given me, and the relief was instantaneous, so that I fell asleep.

As soon as I was able to move, the vestry insisted on my going into the country to recruit.

CHAPTER XI

HARD WORK AND FOREIGN TRAVEL

*I am ordained priest—A second son is born to me—The
Church of the Holy Communion finished and consecrated
—The growth of the work—My wife's health begins to
fail—Our voyage to Europe—I found a successful Industrial School—Its history and work—I become an army
contractor—A laughable incident.*

THE building of my new church went on during the
winter. The convention of the diocese was held in
the following May in Camden, and I was there ordained
to the priesthood, in Grace Church, on the 13th of May.
A second son, Theodore Atkinson, was born to me on
July 25th ; he was baptized in the arsenal.* On the 26th
of October my church was finished and consecrated by
Bishop Davis, Rev. Paul Trapier preaching the sermon.
There were fourteen priests beside the bishop present, and
all save the Rev. Dr. C. C. Pinckney and myself are dead.

Thus in one year, nine months, and eighteen days from
the day I held my first service, in the upper room of the
arsenal, a church had been built, and we had moved in
with sixty-six white adults as members, sixty-eight children, forty-three white communicants and five colored.

* He has been in the ministry since 1879, and for the past twelve
years has been my assistant.

A total change took place in the personnel of the congregation as the months went on as a higher class of people came in, and most of the very poor dropped out. I did all I could to keep them, but it seems impossible to keep that class in a congregation of well-to-do people.

The indications of growth in our work continued, and were seen in the increase of offerings. The third year they amounted to $1,833.80. The fourth year the rector's salary went up from $300 to $975, and the offerings of the parish amounted to $4,337 in 1857.*

In the summer of 1857, our young son Theodore was desperately ill, and his devoted mother seldom had him out of her arms. That illness of the child cost us much in after years. He had scarcely recovered when I was summoned to Fernandina, Florida, where my sister, the wife of Dr. I. F. Lessesne, resided. She had lost her eldest child, a most interesting girl. On my return to Charleston we were caught in a cyclone, and had to anchor in one of the creeks which flow through the marshes between Fernandina and Savannah. I was a week in getting back to Charleston. Mr. George A. Trenholm met me in his carriage at daylight at the station, and on the way home told me that Mrs. Porter was lying at the point of death. She had been taken ill three days before, and they could

---

* I find in the parish register an entry made by myself, that I built a house on Gadsden Green, on a lot given me in trust by Mr. Theo. D. Wagner, and rented the double house to two poor families at $2.00 per month. This is a beginning of what I meant to be a series of homes for the poor at moderate rents, long before Mr. Peabody's munificent gift for the same object in London. The war came on three years afterwards, and no rent was ever collected. I paid the taxes for twenty-one years, when by consent of Mr. Wagner, and by authority of the court, I vacated the trust in 1879, and sold the lot and house for a trifle. After the war it was impossible to carry out my plans. This was one of the many good things destroyed by that awful war.

not communicate with me, for they did not know what had become of the steamer in which I had sailed. For weeks my wife hovered between life and death, but in the winter rallied somewhat, though she never quite recovered her health.

In the spring of 1858, Mrs. Porter continuing very feeble, Doctor Wragg desired us to go abroad, and the vestry, of which Mr. George Trenholm and Mr. Theo. D. Wagner, were members, insisted that we should go. The Doctor ordered a sea voyage; and so we sailed on the 9th of June in a fine barque, the *Mary Washington*, and reached Liverpool in twenty-one days. My salary had gone up to one thousand dollars, and I was quite able to take the trip, but Mr. Wagner sent before me a check for fifteen hundred dollars, saying he wished me to have a perfectly easy time. Mr. Wm. L. Trenholm, son of Mr. G. A. Trenholm, afterwards Comptroller of the Currency, U. S. Government, and now president of the Security Company, New York, was living at Aigburth, near Liverpool, and most hospitably entertained us for some time. We travelled through England, Scotland, France and Switzerland, and returned, sailing on the 18th of October, in the steamship *Persia*, for New York. With Mr. Wagner's gift, the fifth year of our parish life, the offerings amounted to $5,700. As I look back it seems to me my Broad Street friend's chimera had substantially materialized.

While my congregation had totally changed, and instead of the Church of the Holy Communion being a church for the poor, a great deal of wealth had gathered into it, I continued to keep in touch with the poor, and in my visits, I found one class for whom no provision had been made. I doubt if any city ever existed where every conceivable provision was better, or more thoroughly made, for the relief of poverty in general than here in the City of Charleston. There was a Fuel Society, so that the poor could get all the wood they needed, Garment Society, Hat and Shoe Society, a Benevolent Society, which looked after the homeless and sick, and all these works were the united efforts of the non-Roman bodies, chiefly, however, Episcopalians and Presbyterians ; for the wealth of the community were in these bodies. But I found there was no provision for poor women who wanted work, but were very unfitted to do good sewing, though they were willing to work if they had it. So I told my people if they would let me have their plain sewing, I would have it done for them. It was an expensive experiment for me.

My scheme was largely responded to, and bundles of cloth were sent to me, but when the work came back if it did (!!) it was so shockingly done, I had to buy other material, and quietly have it made up by good seamstresses, without telling my secret. I said, if it did come back ! I several times found a drunken husband had resented the intrusion into his domestic circle, and had thrown the goods in the fire.

I was quite desperate. I saw there was a need, but how to meet it. An English woman came to me one day asking employment and a home. I found out that she was a good seamstress, and I employed her. I gave her a room in the Sunday-school building and fed her from my table. I told her I did not know exactly what I wanted her for, but I would find out.

A day or two after, I met a pretty little poor girl in the street, and asked her if she could sew. She could n't, but wished she knew how. I took her by the hand and led her to the English woman, and said to her, " This is what I want you to do ; take this child, and teach her everything you know about a needle." The child stayed two or three hours, and went home happy. The next day she brought a little friend. In two weeks the teacher had a larger class than she could manage.

I explained matters to my people. Volunteers came forward, and so I established the first industrial school for girls in this State, and as far as I know in the South. Very soon, some of the mothers came with the children, and so my object was reached, namely, that of educating these people for themselves. We soon had so many operatives, and they made so much progress, that we found it difficult to get a sufficiency of private work to keep them going. So I went to Hayne Street, and made a contract for hundreds of pieces of plain underwear. Gradually we grew more ambitious, and took contracts for common pantaloons and coats. Then we introduced a sewing-machine, and had a woman taught ; this example was contagious, and we at last acquired thirty-two sewing-machines. We had men employed to do the pressing and cutting. The institution became entirely self-supporting ; here my business training was very valuable, for we kept a regular set of books. Ten cents was stopped from the cost of making each garment, and every cent of the rest given to the workers. This ten cents bought the machines, paid the men, and met the expense of fuel and light. Each day before work a few collects, and a hymn, and the Creed were used to make up a service of song and praise. I proposed to the workers that they would save time, if their dinners were provided in the factory which could be done for ten cents each. They all agreed, so we had a kitchen opened and a table spread for them. The women numbered fifty-nine. The children's industrial school went on, the ladies of the congregation coming to my aid in sufficient numbers to carry on the cooking arrangements, and the work of the school.* One day in the

* Christmas, 1861, these operatives presented me with a silver goblet and waiter, inscribed, " From Grateful Hearts to the Founder of the First Industrial School in the City." I have it now ; a grateful servant took them with the rest of my silver when we were

spring of 1859, Mr. Wm. Matheson, who was at the head of the largest ready-made clothing store in the city, came to see this much-talked about establishment. He stood at the door for some moments, and looked at the busy scene, then said :

" Mr. Porter, are you a tailor ? "

" No," I said, " nor the son of a tailor."

" Where, then, did all this come from, how have you done it ? "

" Oh," I said, " like Topsy, it just grew,—grew from one little girl."

" Will you turn this factory over to me ? " he asked.

" Yes, it has grown too large for me, it takes too much of my time ; I will gladly do it on one condition, namely, that you pay these hands just what I do. Do you see that group of three women in that corner ? One at the corner, one at the sewing-machine, and two fixing work ? Do you see how well they look, how well they are dressed, and how contented ? When I found them they were starving, they had sold everything but one bed, and were about to be turned into the street for house-rent. Now their wardrobe is supplied, their house is comfortably furnished, and I have six months' rent deposited for them in the savings-bank. If you take this institution on my terms, I will give you the house-room free."

" But I can't," he said, " I have to make a living."

" Yes," I said, " and to make graves for these poor people while you are making your living out of them. I

raided on in Anderson, S. C., in 1865, by soldiers from North Carolina, and hid the silver in the woods, and when they demanded it of me, I could truthfully say I did not know where my silver was, for the servant, without saying a word, when she heard the Federal soldiers were coming, gathered everything up and disappeared and did not return until they had gone. This little token is a pleasant memory of the past.

will be frank with you. I did not expect to meet such success in this industry, but I soon saw the possibilities in it, and I hoped to force you and others to give more than starvation wages, for I shall carry this on until I have hundreds in it. My congregation have given what I asked to start it, dining-room and all ; now it carries itself, with a little surplus, and you see how the operatives are faring.''

'' Well,'' he said, '' it is a revelation, and though you may hurt me, I say God bless you, and your effort for the poor.''

I must finish here the history of this school. When the war broke out, Colonel Hampton sent to me for uniforms for the Hampton Legion, and to illustrate the preparation the South had to make for that gigantic war, I may mention that I went to every factory in Virginia and North Carolina in vain search for a suffucent quantity of cloth of the same color to uniform one thousand men. I came to Charleston, and from Messrs. Wm. Ravenel & Co. purchased ten different kinds of cloth for the ten companies, and took them to my industrial school, and there the uniforms were cut and made. I had fifty-nine women in the building, and three hundred and fifty outside working at their superintendence ; for our troops, just after the first battle of Manassas or Bull Run, were in a deplorable condition. Major Hatch, Quartermaster of the State of South Carolina, heard of this, and in the name of the State took possession of our school which was the only organized establishment of the kind in the State or in the South. After I had finished the uniforms of the Hampton Legion, I took them to Virginia, and left Major Hatch in charge, and most of the work done for the South Carolina troops was done there. Later on, when the shells made the lower portion of the city uninhabitable, the Confederate Government took possession of the lower story, and the Confederate Post Office was kept there until Charleston fell into the hands of the Federal Government. When I returned to Charleston in 1865, I went with my sexton to look at the wreck. The colored sexton told me the Freedmen's Bureau people had carted off all the sewing machines, and nothing was left. Thus another great and beneficent work perished, the result of that dreadful war. I have never been able since to revive the work, but many persons who had come in there to help, had learned the work, and after the war supported themselves in consequence.

I must enliven this sad page with one laughable thing. When we were at the height of our uniform work, a dear young girl, bright and pretty as a rosebud, came to me in great distress, holding up an unfinished pair of pants, saying, " Do, Mr. Porter, tell me what is the matter ? I can't get these things to fit."

I took them and said, " Well, my dear, if you will rip them apart, and put both of the fronts together and the backs together, you may get it right. You have a front part and a back part now stitched together, and I don't think this is natural."

It brought a merry laugh, but she had learned something.

CHAPTER XII

SECESSION THUNDER-CLOUDS

Good works of Mr. Wagner and Mr. Trenholm—I experience the power of faithful prayer—Secession in the air—I witness the signing of the ordinance of secession, but do not sign it—The ratification mass-meeting—The firing of Fort Moultrie—Capture by secessionists of United States arsenal in Charleston.

I HAVE mentioned among my helpers Mr. Theodore D. Wagner, and Mr. and Mrs. George A. Trenholm. Mr. Wagner and his family had come to me from St. Michael's in 1856, Mr. Trenholm and his family in 1857, from St. Peter's Church. A more generous, large-hearted man than Mr. Wagner scarcely ever lived. Few are alive now who knew of his benevolence, but in his day no case of suffering that he ever heard of went unrelieved. I only had to tell him what was needed to be done, and he did it, for he loved to do it. Hundreds were the recipients of his kindness ; doubtless he was often imposed on, but that did not chill him. Absolutely unselfish, he seemed to disdain hoarding, and spent as freely as he made. He belonged to the great mercantile firm of John Fraser & Co., of which Mr. Geo. A. Trenholm was the head.

In business Mr. Trenholm was a king. He was the absolute master of local banking, and the cotton trade.

He had his ships, and his word in Broad Street and on East Bay was law ; but it is of the man I would write. He was tall and handsome, and graceful in his manners. I said, when speaking of Mr. J. W. Hutson, that he had the sweetest smile of any man I ever saw, save one ; that one was Mr. Trenholm. His alms were not so well known as Mr. Wagner's, but I, his pastor, saw what he would not let the world see, and many families that the community knew not of, were made comfortable, and lived in ease by his generosity. He had the clearest mind I ever met with ; there was scarcely a subject you could propose that he would not throw light upon. He was the least resentful man I ever knew ; of those who did him much harm, he never said a harsh word ; of his family circle he was the very light. Great as he was in business, he seemed to leave all at the gate when he came home, and was as tender to his dear wife (who was a perfect Christian woman) as if he were a young lover, and to his children, climbing on his shoulders, and hanging round his neck, he was devoted. It was a pleasant home to which to go. He succeeded Mr. C. C. Memminger as Secretary of the Treasury of the Confederate States. He, with Mr. Wagner, inaugurated the blockade-running. They brought immense stores, and guns, and ammunition into the Confederacy. It is a sad commentary on life that the generation of to-day, even in this community, have little knowledge of the greatest man who ever lived in it.

Knowing the difficulties of collecting money to build churches, Mr. John Bryan and I had organized a Church Building Association in 1857. The officers were the Bishop, as President *ex officio*, Dr. C. Hanckel, Vice-President, Rev. A. T. Porter, Secretary, and John Bryan, Treasurer ; the Rev. Messrs. P. Trapier, C. Wallace, A. W. Marshall, D.D., G. H. Elliott, C. C. Pinckney, Messrs. J. K. Saas, I. F. Blacklock, C. Edmonston, E. L. Kerrison, C. B. Heyward, F. Elford, G. A. Trenholm, Trustees. We assisted twelve churches to the amount of $4475. The society lived six years, and the civil war crushed the life out of this institution also. But for the war it would now be a power in the church.

In the early part of the summer of 1860, my wife took the two children to spend the summer with our two friends, Mr. and Mrs. Joshua Ward, at their beautiful home on the French Broad, in Transylvania County, North Carolina. I remained at my work in the city. In September I was suddenly summoned to go to the mountains, as our oldest boy was desperately ill with typhoid fever. When I arrived, the doctor gave me very little hope, but said if he could induce perspiration he would see some chances for the child's life. I have always been a firm believer in the power of faithful prayer ; God may not grant what we ask for, but He never forgets one true prayer, and the faith that makes it.

I accordingly left the sick room and went up the side of the mountain alone, and prayed, that if it were possible, this cup might pass from us. The child was then nearly five years old, and had grown to be the handsomest child I had ever seen, perfect in figure, and spiritual in expression, with a bright, intelligent mind that seemed to run only on spiritual things. I recollected on that mountain's side, how, when he was three years old, I was taking him from Charleston to Georgetown in a steamer. The ocean was like a mirror, and he was leaning over the railing, looking out at it.

He said, " Papa, how smooth the sea is, do you know what makes it so smooth ? "

Seeing him lost in thought, I asked him what made it so smooth.

" Why, papa, don't you know ? God has stooped down and rubbed His hand over it."

" Out of the mouth of babes and sucklings hast Thou perfected praise." Those words have often given me courage in a life that has been full of the rough, and the smooth. Such was the child's mind even to the end. After my earnest wrestling in prayer, I returned, and went and looked at him. There was no change, and I went out seven times, and said the same words, with the addition, " Nevertheless, Thy will be done."

When I returned to the room the seventh time, I noticed on the boy's lips a chain of perspiration drops.

Then I knelt at his bedside and thanked God, for I knew that the crisis was past. He began to mend, and in a couple of weeks was up and about again.* The rest of the summer passed pleasantly ; there was little communication with the outside world and we were in profound ignorance of what was going on. Early in October we crossed the mountains to Greenville, and came down on the railroad to Columbia. When we reached there we found the State of South Carolina was wild with excitement. The presidential election was coming on, and everyone said that if Mr. Lincoln was elected the State would secede. Dear old Doctor Shand, with whom we stayed, had caught the infection, and seemed ready to buckle on his sword. I remember the conversation round the fireside. His young son, then a boy, since a distinguished lawyer, Mr. Robert W. Shand, and I took the opposite side, and said secession was a second nullification madness. My father, I had always heard, was opposed to the idea, and was a Union man, though he died before that nullification folly came to a head. And I had im-

* Dr. Arthur Flagg, who attended him, said his recovery was a miracle. That same Dr. Flagg, with his family and servants, were all swept into the sea in their house in the fearful cyclone and tidal wave of 1893, which swept the coast of South Carolina. All of the party were drowned save two—some nineteen persons.

bibed his views, and, as I said, to me it seems madness. I remember Mr. Shand's son, a boy, saying, "Father, secession will not be a peaceable measure ; it will mean war, and war will mean the emancipation of our slaves."

The old gentleman could not stand still ; he said it was all nonsense, and got so excited that we became amused, and teased the dear old saint, for saint he was, by depicting the horrors that would come.* We left at once for Charleston, and found the fever of excitement was raging. In November the Legislature met, and after a stormy debate, called a convention to secede from the Union, Lincoln having been elected. A laughable story of Mr. J. L. Petigru is worthy of record. He was walking up Main Street in Columbia, and was met by some countryman who asked, "Mister, can you tell me where is the lunatic asylum ? "

"Yes, my man," he said, "it is off down that street, they call that the asylum, but it is a mistake. Yonder," pointing to the State House, where the Legislature was in session, "is the asylum, and it is full of lunatics."

Mr. Petigru was to the end a pronounced Union man, and such was the veneration in which he was held, that he said what he pleased, and he said many sharp, bitter things in those five years' of war, but no one took offense, nor molested him. Day by day the excitement increased, and when the Legislature called the Convention we had all become crazed. I was in my thirty-third year, and

---

* We little dreamed what we said in fun was more than realized in that very town of Columbia, and in that very house, for it was burned down by Federal troops five years after. And Dr. Shand was struck by a soldier, and a trunk that he and a servant were carrying from the burning house was violently taken from him. It contained all the Church Sacramental silver, and has never been recovered.

became as enthusiastic as the rest. I look back now and wonder how it all could have been as it was.*

The Convention assembled at St. Andrew's Hall, Broad Street, afterwards burned down. The room was cleared, but my wife's brother, Samuel T. Atkinson, was a member of it, and I sat quietly by him and was not turned out. I think I was the only person not a member who was present.

Chancellor B. F. Dunkin, Mr. Robt. W. Barnwell, and others made conservative speeches, but the fiery eloquence of the secessionists prevailed, and the vote was ordered by the roll call. The ordinance of secession was read, and a stillness that could be felt prevailed. The members were called alphabetically, and my brother-in-law's name was first called—" Samuel T. Atkinson."

In a subdued, but firm voice, he said, " Yea."

Yea after yea, was answered until every name was called, and the vote was unanimous.

Then each went up and signed the paper, and the deed was done, which cost millions and millions of money, tens of thousands of lives, destruction of cities and villages, plantations and farms, the emancipation of five millions of African slaves, the entire upheaval of society, the impoverishment of a nation ; and let loose a demoralization which has left its impress on the whole land, North and South. It was a deed which made the North rich and the South poor, and has made Southern life one great struggle from that day to this.

---

* Many years afterwards I was in Mr. C. C. Memminger's office, and I said to him :

" Mr. Memminger, I am now as old as you were when this city and State went wild ; why did not you older men take all of us young enthusiasts and hold us down ? "

"Oh!" he replied, "it was a whirlwind, and all we could do was to try to guide it."

Someone, from a window of the Convention hall, gave a sign to the dense mass of men who packed Broad Street outside that the ordinance had passed, and then a mighty shout arose. It rose higher and higher until it was as the roar of the tempest. It spread from end to end of the city, for all were of one mind. No man living could have stood that excitement. If there were any like Mr. Petigru, they hid themselves; for he alone would have dared to be silent that day. This was Thursday the 20th of December, 1860. Bonfires were lit that night in every street ; processions were formed and went to the houses of different public men, and forced them to come out and make a speech.

A crowd came to my house, and yelled, and called out, but I would not go out. I did not know what to say, until my friend Wagner somehow got into my house, and insisted on my going out to the upper piazza and saying something. I did not say much, but it was in somewhat of a discordant strain. I urged that we required to stop shouting, and do something, for the event of the day meant serious business. Mr. Wagner often afterward talked to me of that speech, for the crowd did not go away pleased; but experience showed my young head was more level than the head of some of my seniors.

On Friday morning, Judge A. G. Magrath, the United States Circuit Judge, in the presence of the bar, rose from his seat, and in a most dramatic manner, took off his gown, and laid it on the chair, saying, '' The office of United States Judge is vacant.''

The act started the enthusiasm of the day before ; everybody took to shouting. As the wave or sound died down, the news flew from mouth to mouth that James Conner, United States District Attorney, had resigned. Men hugged each other in the streets, and every one ran hither and thither to hear what next. Would old Mr. Alfred Huger, who had been postmaster, it seemed, forever, resign? No, he would not lose his head as the rest of us had, he would wait and see. Nearly everyone who held a United States office hastened to follow the example of Mr. Conner.

A ratification mass-meeting was called for Friday night, and was held at the South Carolina Mechanical Institute Hall, next south of the Circular Church.* The large building was packed, and the throng in the street was immense. It was all one way in Charleston.

Judge Magrath was the first speaker. He stood on the left of the stage facing the audience, and began (I give his very words) :

"Fellow citizens : The time for deliberation has passed." He paused, and started across the stage to the right, walking in slow measured steps. Everyone who remembers Judge Magrath's walk, will recall him as he passed a large handkerchief through his hands, from one diagonal corner to the other. He said not a word more, and the audience waited until, in an impassioned voice and gesture, he added:

" The time for action has come."

At that moment there went up a universal yell, presage of what has gone into history as " the rebel yell." It died out, and rose, and died, and rose for several minutes before the Judge could proceed. And I, fool as I was, yelled with the rest of them, and threw up my hat, and no doubt thought we could whip creation. It was very dramatic in the Judge, a fine piece of acting, but alas, the prologue of what a tragedy !

Some other hand must portray the military scenes of that week. The flame of enthusiasm extended from the seaboard to the mountains, and all South Carolina was ablaze. Matters somewhat settled down until the following Friday, December 27th. Christmas had come in between, but we all forgot Christmas and its joy. Early

* Burnt on December 11, 1861.

Friday morning a dense smoke was seen issuing from Fort Moultrie on Sullivan's Island, and the impression got abroad that it had accidentally taken fire. Major Macbeth at once chartered a steamer, and ordered, contrary to city ordinance, two fire-engine companies (the Etna and the Vigilant, or the Phœnix and one other company, I forget which) to go and assist Major Anderson in extinguishing the flames. I saw the engines on the steamer. While she was getting up steam, a client of Captain Edward McCrady, Jr., came from the island in a small boat, and gave the information that the guns had been spiked, that the interior of the fort had been fired and rendered useless, and that Major Anderson and the garrison had shut themselves up in Fort Sumter. The situation began to be realized.

I do not think that anyone can portray the scenes of that day. There was no more shouting, but men and women were hurrying to and fro, with an excitement words cannot express at all. The wildest rumors were started, everyone supposed that Fort Sumter was full of shells, and that Major Anderson had trained his guns on the city, and we should soon be bombarded.

News flew through the State, and through the whole South, that fighting was going on in the streets and blood was flowing like water, and company after company from the State, and from Georgia, volunteered to come to our aid. Of course, there was not truth in any of the reports and aid was declined, but the United States arsenal was occupied, and the Washington Light Infantry, Captain Pinckney's company, and Captain McCrady's (I do not remember any other) were ordered to capture Castle Pinckney. I have a ludicrous account of the capture of the arsenal written by one of the " picked twenty " that is too good not to be put in permanent shape and will be found in the appendix.*

* Appendix A.

CHAPTER XIII

WAR IN EARNEST

My chaplaincy in the Washington Light Infantry—The delusion of secessionists as to peace—Fort Sumter is fired on —The surrender of Major Anderson—Some difficulties of recruiting—Some young Confederate heroes—Bull Run.

THE Washington Light Infantry was organized in 1808 and was the oldest volunteer company in the State. I had been elected their chaplain in 1858, succeeding Mr. Gilman, a Unitarian minister, who had succeeded the Roman Catholic Bishop England, and he succeeded Rev. R. Dewer Simons. I am therefore the fourth chaplain, and have held the office for thirty-eight years. On Saturday, 28th, I received a note from Captain Simonton, afterwards Colonel, and now United States District Judge, asking me to come to Castle Pinckney, and hold service for the boys. I did so and preached a sermon, choosing my text from Second Timothy, ii., 3, " As a good soldier of Jesus Christ." Thus I had the honor of preaching the first sermon to the troops in the civil war. The Church of the Holy Communion I had, of course, closed on the occasion.

When we were rowing back after the service, Pinckney Lowndes said, " Look here, Chaplain, you have scared us out of our wits ; you tell us there will be fighting, and fighting means killing and wounding. So we are all ready to resign right away and go home."

Of course he was joking as to the latter part, but the first was true. I did not believe that this question could be settled peaceably.

The Friday night after Major Anderson had gone to Sumter, I went down to walk on the Battery, for I was oppressed and depressed. Events had followed so quickly one on the other, that the reality of the situation began at last to appear. On the Battery, I met Colonel James Chestnut, ex-Member of Congress. I remarked to him, "These are troublous times, Colonel ; we are at the beginning of a terrible war."

" Not at all," he said, " there will be no war, it will be all arranged. I will drink all the blood shed in the war."

So little did some of our leaders realize the awful import of what we were doing.*

Some time later in the winter of 1861, the Washington Light Infantry with the Rifle Regiment were sent to Sullivan's Island to guard the north end, for the fleet was at anchor outside the bar. Why they did not land a force and take Sullivan's Island, and from there march to Mt. Pleasant, and Charleston in the rear, I have never heard explained. A strong force could have captured the island at any time for months after Fort Sumter fell. I went down with the company, coming off and on to the

---

* Twenty-four years afterward, Sunday falling on February 22d, the anniversary of the Washington Light Infantry, I, as usual, preached to them at the Church of the Holy Communion, and I used the same manuscript, writing a short introduction, without altering one sentence in the sermon. I could have preached it at the foot of the Bunker Hill Monument in 1860, for it was as applicable there as here. I note this to show the spirit that animated some of us in those trying days. There were only six or eight of the old command left and present ; many of my last hearers had not been born when the sermon was first preached.

city ; holding service in the morning at the Church of the Holy Communion, and at night at the camp.

One evening the officers were sitting round the table playing whist, when a sergeant, who was in command of the pickets, came rushing in as pale as a ghost. '' Captain ! Captain ! '' he exclaimed, '' the boat is full of creeks.''

He was so excited (or scared) that he had put creeks in the boat, instead of boats in the creek. The Company was turned out and we all went to do or to die. But as it was a false alarm, we neither did nor died, but came back to quarters and went to bed. Some old bills of Klinck & Wickenberg, who were the grocers of most of us, show how sadly far off we were from the real state of the case. Champagne, madeira, and sherry, paté de foie gras, and French green peas, sardines and Spanish olives, Spanish cigars, with other luxuries, formed then the staple of our stores of soldiers' fare. The time came when a sweet potato would have been an acceptable luxury, if we could have had enough of them.

The fateful day of April 11, 1861, came. At four o'clock in the morning, I heard the boom of a cannon. I happened to be awake, and ran in and woke up Captain Simonton, saying, '' The first gun has been fired ; Fort Sumter has been attacked.''

We were all soon upon the beach.

Shot after shot was following from Fort Moultrie and battery Gregg on Morris Island. But Sumter looked grim and was silent. Not until full daylight did Major Anderson open fire, but when he did, he gave it all round. We could see the shot strike the beach and ricochet along the sand. Many of us ran after them; some of us went into the tower of the Moultrie House. I suppose the crowd of us was seen, and our position being the most elevated point on the Island, must have been taken for a post of observation, for soon shot after shot struck the building. At last one shot crashed into the tower in the story below us. It was getting too much of a good thing, and we scrambled out of that place without " looking upon the order of our going."

On the second day, Moultrie set fire to Sumter, and every gun we had at Fort Johnson, Battery Gregg, and the other batteries on Sullivan's Island opened simultaneously on the devoted Sumter. It was enveloped in smoke and bombarded by fifty guns, and out of the smoke came a flash. Anderson had answered back.

I witnessed then a scene that I doubt was ever equalled. The gallantry of the defense struck the chivalry of the attackers, and without a command every soldier mounted the parapet of every battery of the Confederates and gave three cheers for Major Anderson. Soon after the white flag went up, firing ceased, and Major Anderson had surrendered.

The most remarkable thing about that fight was, that not a man received a scratch on either side, and no blood was shed until the next day, when Major Anderson was permitted by General Beauregard to salute the United States flag before it was hauled down. On that occasion, a gun exploded and killed two or three Federal soldiers. So ended the first chapter of that story written in blood, in sorrow, and ruin.

Soon after the fall of Sumter, the Washington Light Infantry was ordered back to Charleston, and I continued at the church. Colonel Gregg's regiment was sent to Virginia, and a call was made for the companies and regiments to volunteer. A meeting of the Washington Light Infantry was called, and after much debate, it was resolved that the time had not come to leave the State.

This was a great mortification to not a few of us.

The next day I was walking through Washington

Square, when I heard my name called. Looking around I saw J. M. Logan following me. He was a clean-faced, handsome boy with a sweet, gentle expression, almost like that of a girl.

" What do you think of the action last night of the Washington Light Infantry ? " he asked.

" I am distressed," I replied, " such action by the oldest organization will have an injurious effect."

" No man can now afford to look back," Logan said, " and I am glad of it. Will you help some of us to get up a company of volunteers ? "

" Who are the ' some of you ' ? "

" Theodore Klinck, Wm. A. Dotterer, and myself wish to get up a company, but we need an older man to lead."

" Very well," I said, " ask Klinck and Dotterer to come to my house to-night, and bring the roll of the company."

They came. We divided the roll into four lists; each took the men over whom he had the most influence, and agreed to see them the next day, and to report at my house the next night. The next night we had a roll of about thirty. We then proceeded to advertise a call of all the Washington Light Infantry who had agreed to form a company to go to Virginia, to meet in my Industrial School rooms the following night. This was the first public notice of our movement, when the thirty came, and a large number of others, so that we enrolled about sixty. These elected W. H. Peroneau, Captain ; Klinck, 1st Lieutenant ; Dotterer, 2d Lieutenant, and T. M. Logan, 3d Lieutenant.

We met next night in the same place, to hear who had accepted. We learned that Peroneau had declined, but a number of names was added to the roll. E. L. Parker was then elected Captain, but he declined. Mr. Benj. Johnson was then elected. As he was known to but few of the company, and lived some sixteen miles from Mt. Pleasant, in Christ Church parish, I was asked to go to him and offer him the command. Next day, accordingly, I went over to Mt. Pleasant, hired a buggy and horse, and drove to his plantation. I arrived there towards the dusk of the evening, and was warmly and hospitably received. He had no idea of my mission. It was a happy Christian home I found at the plantation. I have often recalled my feeling of pain when I arrived as a harbinger of evil to them.

We passed as happy an evening as was possible to me, with the knowledge of my object in my mind. At last the servants all came into family prayers, and after the family had retired, I informed my host of my mission, telling him that he had been elected Captain of the Washington Light Infantry Volunteers for Virginia, and asked him to accept it.

He was much startled and said, " It has come sooner than I expected, but I cannot answer until the morning."

Next morning after prayers, and breakfast, we strolled out. I had noticed, as we left the house, deep traces of the night's anxiety on the face of Johnson's lovely wife, but I saw in her eye that she would not stand between her husband and his duty to his country. So when Mr. Johnson accepted the election I was not surprised.

I hastened back to Charleston. Logan was waiting on the market wharf, and when I gave him the signal agreed on, he did not wait to meet me, but rushed off to the bulletin board, and put up a notice of the acceptance of the commission by Mr. Johnson. He then called a meeting at the Military Hall in Wentworth Street. I met the volunteers and related to them all about my visit, and announced Mr. Johnson's acceptance, adding that he would be in Charleston the next evening to take command.

The evening came, the hall was crowded. Mr. Johnson was in the building, the committee, Klinck, Dotterer, and Logan, were with him. The meeting, after some delay, was called to order with myself as chairman. The newly elected Captain then rose to his feet and said, "Gentlemen, I hold myself bound to you, by the promise I made to Doctor Porter, but here is a telegram from Colonel Wade Hampton, offering me the place of Lieutenant-Colonel in the Legion he is raising to go to Virginia. What am I to do?"

We immediately released him from his engagement to us and begged him to accept Colonel Hampton's offer, and he left the building. Gallant man, he was killed at the first battle of Manassas, as Lieutenant-Colonel of the Hampton Legion.

The task now before us was greater than ever. We had to meet the men and tell them of our disappointment. Three men had been elected Captain, and all had declined. I resumed the chair and Logan made the announcement. It fell upon the men like snow upon flowers. Murmuring and discontent appeared. Klinck and Dotterer spoke, but a motion was offered and seconded to disband. I then left the chair, and taking the floor, made a speech.

I gave the meeting a detailed account of every movement in forming a company from the beginning, and gave our pledge, that if mover and seconder of the motion to disband would withhold that resolution, and give us one more day, we would find the right man by the next night, or would oppose them no longer, but agree to disband.

To this they assented, and Logan and I went off in hope, although absolutely nonplussed. We could not think of a man.

Next day about eleven o'clock we met at the corner of Church and Broad Streets, where the Charleston Library now is, and neither of us had found the man. While we were talking, James Conner came out of Paul and Brown's grocery store, and walked up Broad Street, towards St. Michael's Church. Instinctively I slapped Logan on his back saying, " What fools we are ! Why, there is the very man whom of all men in this community we want. He is far ahead of all the others we thought of."

" Go after him ! " said Logan.

I crossed over, and before we reached St. Michael's I had offered him the unanimous vote of the company as Captain. We stopped under St. Michael's porch, he hesitated, said he must take time to think.

" No time, Mr. Conner," I said ; " Now ! we must have an answer now ! we must go to that meeting with our man, or they will disband to-night."

" Well," he said, " on your assurance that the election is unanimous, I will accept."

I ran back to Logan, and if there were two happy men in the city, we were those men.

We put up a notice of the meeting for that night, urging every man to be present, as the business was vital. We kept the secret from all but Klinck and Dotterer, and when we met, the hall was crowded. We four were jubilant. Logan nominated James Conner.

" Will he accept ? " came from all quarters.

" He will, if the election is unanimous."

I put the vote *viva voce*, and the yea was a yell, for he was a distinguished lawyer, and immensely popular. How we had never thought of him before was a wonder to us. When I put the negative—" There are none here," was the answer ; " we are all aye."

Conner was waiting in the building, and Klinck, Dotterer, and Logan at once waited on him and escorted him in, and he was greeted with a tremendous cheer. As soon as I could be heard, I said, " Men, here is the Captain we pledged to you last night." Turning to Captain Conner,

I proceeded, '' I resign the chair to you, sir, and turn over the command.'' *

The company offered themselves to Colonel Hampton, and was made Company A of his Legion. How they demeaned themselves, is recorded on a monument erected in Washington Square, within fifty feet of the spot on which Logan and I held our first conversation. The long roll of killed shows how they fought. I delivered the oration when the monument was finished.

The Hampton Legion went to Virginia, and Captain Conner had promised me whenever a battle was imminent to telegraph me, '' Come at once,'' and I would understand. I soon after received the telegram from him, and left as soon as I could, but reached Manassas Junction four days after the first battle of Manassas.

---

* James Conner rose to be General; he lost a leg in Virginia. After the war he was foremost in council, and his influence and cool bravery saved this city from awful carnage at the time of the riot in 1876; but for him many lives would have been lost, and thousands of negroes would have been massacred, and the consequences no one can foresee. Klinck and Dotterer were both killed. Logan won his spurs, and was the youngest General in the Confederate service when the war ended.

9

CHAPTER XIV

MY WAR EXPERIENCES

The plague of measles in the Confederate camp—I go to the front — The work of an army chaplain — A grateful " Yank"—Red tape and ragged uniforms—" Confederate mismanagement"—The Christian General—Search for a dead soldier—Pipes and Piety.

THE people of the South blamed Johnson and Beauregard for not pressing on to Washington, but one week after that battle our demoralized army was one great measles camp. It is no exaggeration to say, you could perceive the measles in the air. Ten thousand troops from Washington could have wiped us out.

I went at once about my work looking up the wounded and sick and had my hands full. I had two canteens, one of whiskey, and one of water, which I filled, and often a Federal prisoner drank one, or the other, and then a Confederate, or *vice versa*. I remember going into a shanty where a number of men were wounded. I went up to a Confederate soldier, and he said, " Chaplain, go first to that man over there ; he is worse off than I am."

I went, and found a soldier wounded in the knee, and suffering very much. I got a pitcher of water and poured it over his leg, until I had deadened the pain. Then I asked his name and regiment, and where he came from.

He was from Rochester, N. Y. Assuring him my question did not spring from idle curiosity, I offered, as I was
close to headquarters, to write to his mother and sisters,
and tell them he was not seriously wounded, and would
be taken care of; my letter would go, I added, by the
first flag of truce. He became very much affected, and
the big tears rolled down his cheeks.

" Mister, did you say you came from South Carolina ? "

" Yes," I said.

" And you treat a Yankee so ? "

" Yes ; we are not barbarians. You are a wounded
prisoner, and have no business to be here, but you will be
well treated."

" I did not expect it, I did not expect it, and from a
South Carolinian, too. If I ever get well, I will fight you
no more."

I sent the letter ; I have forgotten the name of the
sender and the address ; I do not know whether the letter
was received, or what became of the man. My duties
called me elsewhere.

The Legion was some miles from Warrenton Junction,
and I found my way to it. The sick, and there were
many, were in a sorry plight ; so I got Colonel Hampton
to let me have an old store, and permission to go to
Charlottesville, Virginia, to the Women's Relief Association storehouse, where was Rev. Robt. W. Barnwell, the
same man who applied for a dispensation of time, and with
me was refused by the Standing Committee in 1854, and
I procured a large amount of stores, took them by rail,
and soon fitted up a large hospital, which added much to
the comfort of the men. The soldiers were in rags, and
Colonel Hampton sent me on an expedition to get uniforms for his men. When I reached Charleston I told
some of our influential citizens the condition of all our
troops. A meeting was held at the Bank of Charleston,

and a delegation consisting of Judge Magrath, Wm. D. Porter, Henry Gourdin, Wm. Bull Pringle, and myself were sent to Columbia to see Governor Pickens and to tell him of the soldiers' needs, and to offer any assistance that the banks in Charleston could give. Governor Pickens listened impatiently, drew out a drawer, and read with much emphasis from a document he had in it, a list of the articles he had at his disposal, not enough to supply half a dozen regiments a month and added, he was much obliged to us, but the State did not need the aid of the banks. Judge Magrath looked at me, dropped one eye and winked, quietly holding up his hands, and we broke up the audience. The committee returned to Charleston with gloomy forbodings.

I returned to Virginia with the uniforms, and after some time got a furlough to go back to South Carolina. While in camp I shared the bed of Captain Conner, and took my meals with Colonel Hampton. A slapjack with sorghum was a luxurious dessert in those days.

The day I started for Richmond a long train of sick and wounded soldiers was to be sent off, and I was to be put in charge of them. When we reached Warrenton Junction we were sided off on the Y., and I never pass the spot that I do not think of that awful day I had with some eight hundred men, all needing medicines, food, and water. A number of them died in those cars. We had to send a long way for water, and did manage to gather a little coarse food and there we were kept until late in the afternoon. Having some cigars, I went into the baggage car and offering the conductor a cigar I begged him to let me sit there awhile, for I was worn out with the day's labor. I just happened to look at my watch, and said, "With luck we will be in Richmond in forty-five minutes," when an awful crash came.

The train stopped, the car was filled with steam, and I

was flung to the end of the car, with two or three boxes piled on me. I was not, however, hurt, so as soon as we could, we got out. We found we had run round a sharp curve, and had struck a freight train stalled there laden with wheat. Our train had gone through three of the freight cars, splitting them open, and our engine was bottom up, some fifteen feet below the embankment, the engineer with his ribs broken. Somehow nothing else had left the track. Instead of reaching Richmond in forty-five minutes, we were twenty-five hours, with a train of wounded and sick soldiers. This is a typical instance of Confederate mismanagement. The want of organization and administration, I verily believe, was what neutralized the magnificent fighting, the splendid endurance, of our soldiers. Had other departments done as well as the troops in the field, there is no telling what might have been the issue of the war.

I made several trips backwards and forwards to Virginia, but as I was only the chaplain of the Washington Light Infantry Volunteers, two companies that were in the legion, and there was a chaplain for the rest, I accepted the appointment as chaplain of the 25th South Carolina Regiment, Colonel Simonton, as the old Washington Light Infantry was a part of it, and went over to James Island with my new command.

Before leaving the Hampton Legion, I record that I had purchased a small silver Communion set, and used it in divine service under the trees in the open field. Colonel Hampton and many officers and soldiers were accustomed to receive the Holy Communion there. Colonel Benj. Allston, of a Texas regiment, now Rev. Mr. Allston, brought to me Colonel Pender of the 8th North Carolina Regiment, and after full instruction I baptized him, surrounded by all his regiment. He was afterwards made a General and was killed retreating from Pennsylvania.

Such was the character of my army ministrations. On James Island, as chaplain of the 25th Regiment, Colonel Simonton in command, I had a service of prayer and praise with a short sermon every night ; for owing to the inspection and dress parade and other military duties I could not get the men before midday. Having no house to worship in and few trees, the intense heat of the sun made Sunday morning service impossible. Eventually, however, Gen. R. E. Lee had ordered inspection and dress parade so arranged, that time could be given all the chaplains to have a morning service in all his regiments. I knew General Lee, so I wrote to him and asked him to extend the order to the whole army, expressing my profound respect and esteem for him, and winding up my letter by telling him what a source of strength and comfort it was to many of us to think that in this time of our country's sore distress that he, in whose hands, humanly speaking, our destiny rested, was himself leaning on the Divine Arm for strength and the Divine Wisdom for direction.

Of course I knew General Lee, but scarcely expected that he would remember a young chaplain who had in no way distinguished himself, and consequently I did not look for a reply. But in due time I received an autograph letter from the General, in which he gave me full directions how to accomplish my aim, and expressing his pleasure that the chaplains appreciated his order. He added his appreciation of my expressions about him, and only wished they were deserved, but he added, " It is true that I am daily seeking guidance from our Heavenly Father, and do lean only on His arm for protection."

The letter was a foolscap sheet, written from top to bottom. It was dated the day before the beginning of that series of engagements which culminated in the utter rout of Pope, and the second battle of Manassas. With his mind full of the plans for that campaign, that he should turn aside, and write to an obscure chaplain five hundred miles away, was perfectly characteristic of that glorious man, that great soldier, that greater Christian gentleman, whose fame will grow more brilliant as the years go on, until the children's children of South and North grow to be proud of the great American, who has shed lustre on his country.*

At the second battle of Manassas, Charles Steadman Atkinson, a younger brother of my wife, named after an uncle, his mother's brother, a rear-admiral in the United States Navy, was killed. I took a furlough, and went to Virginia to look for his body. I had taken him when he was quite young to live with us. I had sent him to school, and he went from my house to the army.

All we knew was that he had been buried on the field near a farmhouse not far from a cowshed, and that he had been shot in the forehead. I went to Warrenton, which was full of wounded men from Manassas and Sharpsburg, and received great kindness from the rector, Rev. Dr. Barten. Having purchased a coffin, I went on the search. It was a gruesome hunt.

After a while I spied the ruins of a farmhouse, where a cowshed was still standing, and near it was three graves. One of these I believed to be my boy's, but which? I do not know why, but I determined to try the middle grave. The man I had with me, and had brought the coffin on his cart, dug away about eighteen inches of earth, and we came to some rough boards ; these we removed, and there was a soldier wrapped in a blanket. Those who had buried him had put side boards up, so that the thin cover of earth had not reached the body. I turned back the blanket from the face, and found it was the body I was

* I lost that letter with other valuable papers at the burning of Columbia. I would give a great deal could I recover it.

looking for. A bullet-hole was in his forehead. I recognized my boy at once, for dissolution had not disfigured him. I took one long look at him, covered the face, and the man and I lifted the body, placed it in the coffin, and started back for Warrenton. We had scarcely started, when, looking at some distant hills, I saw a long line of blue-coats emerge from the horizon.

We were in a comparatively open plain. I was dressed in Confederate uniform, and I saw that we were perceived. I therefore directed the carter to keep the road, while I struck off for a ravine and twisted around under cover until I was satisfied I was out of range. As I did not wish to be captured, and go to a Northern prison, I did some good dodging.

I reached Warrenton in safety, and after a while the wagon came with the corpse. Dr. Barten read the service for me, and we laid the boy, for he was only a boy, as, alas, so many other Confederates were, in the churchyard, where he awaits the summons to arise. I placed a stone over his grave.*

Having finished this mournful duty, I hurried to the hospital, where there were two thousand six hundred wounded men lying.

On my way to Richmond, I had supplied myself with a

---

* The burial of my boy in Warrenton recalls a fact that few know. After the war was well on, and there was danger that Charleston might fall, Mr. Robert Gourdin, who was a devoted disciple of John Calhoun, went at night with a trusted few and removed his body from its tomb in St. Philip's churchyard and buried it in another part of the grounds. It was feared that if the city fell animosity might induce the violation of the grave of the great Carolinian. After the war it was exhumed and replaced, and the State, through the exertions of Hon. W. A. Courtenay, erected the monument over him in his resting-place in St. Philip's churchyard. John Gregg, the then colored sexton, is the only one, I think, now living who was present.

quantity of smoking tobacco, a stock of Powhatan pipes, and some reed stems. Carrying as much of these commodities as I could handle, I entered a large ward. As I came in some of the men looked up, and I said, '' Boys, I have brought you some tobacco ; all who want some raise your hands.''

There was a general hand-showing, and I went round and gave out all I had. Much disappointment was shown by those who had not been served, until I went back to the parsonage and brought another supply. Eventually everyone who wanted a pipe had one. When they got to smoking, they looked happy. Soon after this someone called out loud, '' Now, Chaplain, give us some prayers,'' which of course I did.

Three or four days after a runner came in, saying the Federals were upon us. I therefore bade the boys good-bye. Putting on my knapsack, I took to the road, and walked over to Culpepper Court House, and so returned to James Island.

CHAPTER XV

THE BLOODY "CUL-DE-SAC"

Tent worship—The Federals in the bloody "cul-de-sac"—I am under fire—Scenes of slaughter—A strange incident—Church plans at Charleston—A financial blunder, for which I am scarcely accountable—What might have been had I followed my business instincts.

IT was my habit to gather every Sunday night in my tent a number of the young men who had fine voices. Colonel Simonton allowed me to keep my light burning as long as I wished.

On Sunday night, June 15th, there were about a dozen of them, and after singing many hymns, they concluded with "Bow down thine ear, O Lord," from Moses in Egypt.

"And now," I said, "let us all kneel, and join in the Lord's Prayer," which we did, and I rose, and pronounced the benediction after the prayer. We then shook hands and bade good-night.

At 4 A.M. the long roll beat, the whole camp was astir, and in a twinkling the troops were on the double-quick to Secessionville, for an attack was being made on the battery.

There is a narrow tongue of sand projecting from the village of Secessionville with a bold creek on one side and a wide impassable marsh on the other. At the narrow point which adjoined a wide cotton field a strong battery had been built by Colonel L. M. Hatch, whose death is in to-day's paper, January 12, 1897. (I read as I drop my pen for a second.) There was a dense fog and the attack was well planned. The Federal troops advanced, over-came the pickets, Capt. Thos. Simons in command, and before those at the battery were aware of it, pickets and Federals together rushed in on them. A desperate hand-to-hand fight ensued. The enemy were knocked on the head with empty bottles, for there were plenty of them, shot with pistols, clubbed with butts of rifles, and driven off, so that the guns got them in range and played havoc with their ranks.

By this time reinforcements had poured into the battery, the Louisiana Tigers and many others. Our regiment was marched to the flank, so that the marsh lay between us and the battery. As the fog lifted, the second assault was made by the Federals. It was a brave assault, but scarcely to be called war. The cannon poured shot into their shelterless ranks, the parapet was lined with men with rifles who knew how to shoot, and we were on their flank, concealed by a thick wood, dealing death. It was an awful slaughter ; for when once the Confederates had awakened to the situation, the attacking party found themselves in a sort of *cul-de-sac.*

As our regiment had over a mile to run, in taking up its position, Doctor Ravenel, the surgeon, and I took our horses and followed, riding down into an open cotton field. The enemy, fired upon from the woods by our men, re-turned volley after volley, and some of the balls began to whiz past our ears.

" Look here, Doctor," I said, " this is no place for you. You are wanted to help wounded men ; take my horse and go back to the field hospital, for I don't wish my animal to be killed, and I will go on and see if there is anything for me to do."

I walked down towards the edge of the woods, and took my stand in the open cotton field. I could see nothing, but the bullets were uncomfortably close, and too many to be pleasant. Colonel Hagood (Afterwards General,* and then Governor of South Carolina) rode out of the thicket and asked what I was doing there ?

" Waiting," I said, " to see what I can do."

" I order you, sir, to leave," he said.

" Well," I replied, " you are not my Colonel, and I will not obey you."

We both laughed, though the situation was pretty serious.

" Well," he answered, " go, then, and sit behind that stump, or you will certainly be killed for no object."

" I will obey that order."

He went back into the thicket, and I went for the stump. It was the stump of a large pine tree. A moment after two bullets struck the stump. Jumping up, under the impression that I was in the exact range, I went out again into the open field. I would have lain down between the cotton hills, but unfortunately they ran the wrong way. Had they been crosswise they would have been a protection ; for it is remarkable how slight an obstruction is a protection in battle. They ran lengthwise, however, and I had scarcely reached the ground when a whole volley scattered round and over me, flinging the dirt upon me. I do not know why I escaped death. I must have been shielded by a merciful Providence, who still had some work for me to do. With a bound I stood upright and said to myself, " This is a mean way to die ; if I am to be shot, I will fall like a man." But soon my attention was drawn in another direction, for young Christopher Trumbo came running out of the woods, and holding up his hand, exclaimed : " Oh, Mr. Porter, see what the Yankees have done to me ; they have shot off my thumb."

*General Hagood died Jan. 5, 1898.

" Thank God," I said, " they have not shot off your head. Go to the rear ; you will find Doctor Ravenel waiting for you."

A few seconds afterwards three men came out, two supporting their comrade between them. He was spitting blood and the others were carrying his gun. I found that a bullet had struck him, but his belt or buckle had turned it, and he was suffering merely from concussion.

" Go back, men," I said, " you are needed there. Give me this man ; I will take him to the rear."

They went back very reluctantly, and I did not blame them. I took the man, and we had not gone far, before a shower of bullets enveloped us. Fortunately, a quarter drain was at hand, and we got into it. As the fusillade stopped, we started again, and reaching the rear, I turned the wounded man over to the Doctor and returned.

When I got near the edge of the woods, a dead man was brought out ; it was Fleetwood Laneau. I helped with his body, took him out of range, and went back to meet the body of R. W. Greer ; did the same for him, and returned to meet Thos. N. Chapman's body; repeated for him what we had done for the others, and went back to meet them bringing I. H. Tavener, shot through the body. These were four of the twelve who had been singing in my tent at twelve o'clock the night before, and the sun had just risen. Such is war !

We had to take poor Tavener farther than we had carried the others, and by the time I got back to the field, the battle was over. Four as gallant assaults as have ever been made had been made by the Federals. They fought with determined desperation, but the more men they brought the more we killed, for it was a narrow place, in which they were compelled to keep advancing, so that we mowed them down like wheat. We buried over a thousand of their dead, in the immediate front of the battery.

While I was on James Island a circumstance occurred for which I vouch, while I share in the wonder it may excite in the mind of the reader. I wished to have a celebration of the Holy Communion, but had left my Communion set in Virginia.* I tried to buy proper vessels in Charleston, but could not. I did not feel authorized to take the sacred vessels belonging to the Church of the Holy Communion, and the only things I could get were fluted tumblers. These I used in the Communion Office. After the service I washed them, and put them in the basket, saying I would see they were never used for anything else. I wiped the second tumbler, and put my hand into the covered basket to put the tumbler in ; it slipped out of my hand and fell on the other tumbler, and broke both into the smallest fragments. There was not a piece left large enough to put a teaspoonful of water or wine in. There was not a distance of two inches between the tumblers when the one fell on the other; all of us around were amazed and awed. I upset the basket, and gathered the fragments and buried them. Some may think a plain, practical man, as this narrative shows I have been, has no superstition in his make-up. But I do not deem it superstition, when I say those glasses had been used for the most solemn rite in which man can engage ; they had contained consecrated wine, the symbol of the Redeemer's shed blood. Most likely sometimes they might have been used for drinking whiskey out of them, and it was not meant that they should be profaned by such use again. I never again had the opportunity to administer the Holy Communion to the soldiers ; we were kept moving about and were so constantly on the alert, that there was no chance for me to do so.

Some Sundays, however, I used to run up to Charleston

* This set General Logan has recently presented to the relic collection in Richmond.

and hold service at the Church of the Holy Communion. It was at one such service, held in January, 1863, that I stepped forward in the chancel, just before the sermon, and told the congregation I felt that the war must soon end, and I wished to build a church that would be a church, to cost not less than two hundred thousand dollars—two hundred thousand dollars as a thank-offering to Almighty God for the restoration of peace. I proposed that we would raise the walls of this present church, make a two-story building of it, and give it as a home to widows and orphans of the Confederacy who might be in need. Mr. Geo. A. Trenholm, who was then the Secretary of the Treasury of the Confederate States, happened to be in church. He, the next day, wrote me a letter expressing approval of my views, and enclosed a check for fifty thousand dollars, telling me to invest it as I pleased, to collect all I could from the congregation, and go on with my plans. He added that whatever deficiency there was, he would supply the same. His wife would give the organ, he said, his children the stained-glass windows. He told me that if I would select a lot, Mrs. Trenholm would pay for it. I bought the lot in Rutledge Avenue, nearly in front of what is now Radcliffe Street, and where Mr. George Wagner has his brick house, and Mr. Trenholm gave me his check for $6500 for the purchase, in the name of Mrs. Trenholm. With this beginning and his assurance, I was very happy. Before depositing Mr. Trenholm's check I unfortunately showed it to a certain banker, and told him my plans. This banker was a noble layman, but he made me make an awful blunder.

" What are you going to do with this $50,000 ? " he asked.

" I am going right down to the wharf to buy cotton with it. There are now fifteen blockade runners in port. I will put three bales on each steamer, and if three

steamers out of five get through I will sell the cotton on
the other side, deposit half the proceeds there in England,
sell exchange for the other half, and keep at it until I
have the whole fifty thousand in gold on the other side.''

'' You shall do nothing of the kind,'' he said.

'' And why not ? Here is Mr. Trenholm's authority
to do as I please with it.''

'' If you act so, it will show the church has no confidence in the cause, and the money will do more harm
than good.''

I did not see it in this way, and my business instincts
told me I was right, and I answered, '' Confidence or not,
this is trust money of the Church. As to my own money,
you know, sir, I have sold all my bank stock, railroad
stock, private bonds, and have bought from you Confederate eight per cent. bonds. That was my own, and I
have shown my confidence, and put everything in Confederate securities save one house in Ashley Street, and if
there was any market for real estate, that would go too,
but I have no right to risk this trust fund, and I will not
do it.''

'' I will go and see Mr. Trenholm,'' he replied, '' and
he will stop your cotton speculations.''

I wish now that I had let him go. I might have had
time to set three or four agents to work, to buy the cotton
before Mr. Trenholm could find me. Even if I had gone
myself to Mr. Trenholm I might have out-talked my
friend the banker, for I am sure Mr. Trenholm would
have been on my side.

Foolishly I gave in, and bought Confederate eight per
cent. bonds, which after the war I sold for $350, just
enough to purchase carpets for the chancel and aisles of
the old church. The war ran on sixteen months longer,
and blockade runners went regularly during that time.
If I had carried out my original plan with regard to that

fifty thousand dollars, I could have sent hundreds of bales of cotton to England, and at the price of cotton here and there, I could have had a million dollars for the church after the war; could have rehabilitated this desolated diocese, and not have been struggling as I am now to keep alive that very parish of the Holy Communion, and the still more important work of which an account will come later.   Here was a banker's judgment against a poor parson's, the class that has to do the hardest financiering of any among men, but who, as most laymen think, know nothing about finance.

10

CHAPTER XVI

SOME OF THE HORRORS OF WAR

*The shelling of Charleston—I am in the thick of it—A work
of mercy—"Mamma, I saw him die!"—Yellow fever—
The death of my first born—"O Lord, save Thy people,
and bless Thine heritage"—Grief and patience.*

THE Federals had been shelling Charleston from Morris
Island for two years. It was a senseless waste. It
cost the United States a great deal and did little harm to
the city; many shells fell short of the city, many struck
in the burnt district, or exploded in the streets, and
the damage was inconsiderable. St. Michael's and St.
Philip's steeples were the targets   St. Philip's was struck
and injured a good deal, St. Michael's twice. The last
shell fired struck the chancel and revealed a large window that had been bricked up. There is now a handsome stained-glass window put in by the Frost family,
in memoriam. This senseless bombardment in no wise
furthered the object of the war. It killed some eighty
inoffensive old people, men and women, but did not hit a
soldier, for there were none in the city to hit. They were
all on the fortifications.

The Federal admiral has been blamed for not steaming
in and taking the city. He knew better than his critics.

'The harbor was magnificently fortified, the channel was filled with torpedoes, and on every spot in it one hundred guns of the largest calibre could be concentrated. No vessel afloat could have been above water a quarter of an hour. By the zeal of the blockade runners, and the indomitable will of the people, as soon as Sumter fell, fortifications had been planned and constructed, so that the place was impregnable. Thus Charleston was never captured, although it was evacuated when General Sherman marched through South Carolina to Columbia.

During these terrible days Rev. Mr. Howe, Rev. G. M. Green, and myself were then the only Church clergymen in the city, and very few others of any denomination. We divided up the hospitals and each of us visited them daily besides performing our parish duties. The Rev. Mr. Dehon, son of the great Bishop Dehon, had died of disease taken in attending the hospitals. But our calamities were augmented by the fact that in August yellow fever was brought into the city by a sick sailor on one of the blockade runners. Smallpox was also prevalent. I heard Doctor Ozier, the then most prominent local physician, say that there was a case in every third inhabited house in Charleston. Of course we clergymen had a great deal to do. We were forced to open our doors to the shelterless. Dr. Wragg, from Broad Street, when burnt out, I had invited to my house, which had twelve rooms in it. Mr. Allston Pringle, from lower end of King Street, A. O. Andrews, from Hazel Street, both shelled out, took refuge at my home, and were there until the war ended.

One incident of these days affects me in the remembrance. When General Sherman was marching through Georgia, the Federal prisoners at Anderson were removed to Florence in this State. A temporary track had been laid through Spring Street across the Ashley River bridge, and leading to the South Carolina Railroad and Northeastern Railroad stations. The box-cars, for that was the only kind we had, often stopped at our corner, for my house is corner of Rutledge and Spring Streets. Many of the poor men were down with scurvy.

I accordingly laid down a store of onions, and as each train stopped, I sent out my two little boys Toomer and Theodore, with loaves of bread, and bags of onions and fresh water to the prisoners. On Wednesday, October 20, 1864, these two children had gone as usual with their stores to help the poor fellows, when I suddenly saw them running back weeping bitterly. The eldest, Toomer, nearly eleven years old, threw himself on his mother's knee, and said: " Oh, mamma, mamma, I saw him die. I know he is our enemy, but I saw him die in a box-car. Maybe he is some boy's papa, and suppose my dear papa was a prisoner, and was to die in a box-car, what should we do ? "

The child sobbed bitterly, and it was a long while before we could comfort him. Such was the child, as handsome a boy as was to be found anywhere, and apparently in high health. But even then I felt a sort of foreboding, and on Friday I called to see a youth who was very ill with yellow fever. He had been an orphan under the care of an aunt, and I told this woman not to distress herself, as I had seen so many cases of fever, that I was justified in assuring her that, judging from his symptoms, he would not die, and he did not. " But," I said to her, " I am passing under the shadow of a great cloud. I do not know what it is, but I feel I am about to be greatly afflicted."

She tried in vain to cheer me.

On the following Saturday I was writing a sermon on the text, St. John, iv., 49, " And the nobleman said, ' Sir, come down, ere my child die.' " When writing, my boy came to me and said: " Do, papa, come and help me raise my kite, I cannot do it by myself."

I was inclined to put him off, but I had been in the habit always to grant my children's requests, if I could, so I went, and raised his kite for him. How glad I have been since then that I did it ! At supper time (a frugal meal, for we had not had butter for months, and our only sugar was sorghum molasses, with only a substitute for tea and coffee) I noticed that my child did not eat his supper. I said to him: " You do not seem to fancy the molasses ; perhaps your mother can spare you some milk."

He took the milk, but still did not eat his supper. I noticed it, and he said: " I do not feel very well, and if you will excuse me, papa, I will go to the fire."

I told him to go, and my wife, happening to look at me, observed there was a look of distress on my face.

" Oh, my dear," she said, " you are too anxious."

" You do not remember, wife, that there is a pestilence raging."

The shadow of a great gloom settled on me. I pushed off from the table, and said, " We will have family prayers, and then you can go to bed, my son."

When we rose from our knees, the dear boy still knelt, and was asleep. I went to him and took him up.

" Oh, papa ! " he said, " I am so sorry I went to sleep at prayers, but I am so tired."

I said, " Put your arms around papa, and give him one good hug." He did—it was the last. I took him on my back, and carried him upstairs, and in seventy-four hours I brought his lifeless body down again. Doctor Wragg was in the house and had done all that could be done, but the boy died of yellow fever. In twenty-four hours, my other two children, and my sister's little orphan girl, my adopted daughter, were all down with it. Their cases were mild. Toomer's was violent from the beginning. His pathetic pleas for ice wrung our hearts, for the fortune

of the Vanderbilts could not have bought a pound in
the city of Charleston. We had no ice machines then,
and we could get nothing from the North. The last day
Toomer repeated the collect he had studied for Sunday,
the Gloria in Excelsis, the Creed, the Gloria Patri,
verses of the Psalter, hymn after hymn. But his nerves
seemed to have received a shock. The condition we were
all in seemed to prey on his mind. The crash of shells
falling in the city, and bursting every few minutes, the
alarm of fire every now and then, the poor food we were
eating, the prisoners passing our door—all seemed to weigh
him down. At last he clasped his hands, and turning up
his beautiful eyes, he said, " O Lord, save Thy people,
and bless Thine heritage." Then, putting his two hands
in his mother's (she was standing on the left side of the
bed, and I on the right), he said, " Mamma, it is so hard,
it is so hard," then turning to me, he put his hands in
mine, and said, " Papa, let me go, let me go." I, consenting, said, " Go, my darling, if Jesus calls you."

I sank on my knees, and before I could raise my head,
he had gone,—gone to be with our dear Lord, gone to his
life-work in His presence. Is it any wonder that whenever I have since heard those words in the Te Deum, " O
Lord, save Thy people and bless Thine heritage," my son's
dear voice has sounded in my ears, and this scene risen
vividly before my mind ?

A remarkable incident connected with the church happened while he was dying. In September, 1864, Mr. T.
D. Wagner had said, that as there was still some debt on
the church and on the Sunday-school, and it was no
time to have debts, he wished to know the full amount
still due. I accordingly told it to him, namely, $3,360 on
the church, and $5,145.95 on the school-house, for the in-
terest was unpaid for three years, and had increased the
original amount due. Mr. Wagner gave me his check for

the sum, and thus we satisfied the mortgage on the church and school-house.

It was while I was standing at the bedside of the dying boy, a package was handed me from the post office. I threw it unopened into a drawer and some days afterwards opened and found these satisfied papers. This my son, therefore, was born the hour that I was holding the first service at the arsenal, 8th of January, 1854, and the papers freeing the finished church from debt, were handed me whilst he was dying.

Little Toomer was buried the 26th of October, at Magnolia cemetery, by his brother and sister, for we could not get to Georgetown on account of the blockade.*

On the 27th of October, I was called upon to bury a lad named Knox, at St. Paul's Church, who had also died of yellow fever. I was about to refuse, but my dear wife said, " Husband, God requires of you to set an example; go and do your duty."

So I went, and as I met the corpse at the door,—it was in the same kind of coffin, one even of the same size,—I seemed to be burying my child again. I reeled, and almost fell, but gathering myself together, I read the service through, and from that time just kept on with my duties; preached the next Sunday, although with a heart as nearly broken as a man's ever is; and I believe if I had not gone right to work, and kept at it, I should have become crazy. I did not grieve less because I did what duty required, but it gave me strength to bear. There is a large lot attached to my house, and I laid it out in a handsome flower-garden, bought some plants and worked hard, when not engaged in ministerial offices, just to drown thought, and tire myself, so that I could sleep. The other children all recovered.

* I removed their bodies to that place, and to my family burying-ground in January, 1870, but the anguish was too much for me, and brought on a hemorrhage while the removal was being made.

CHAPTER XVII

Non-combatants driven from Charleston—My lost sermons—
Adventures of some port wine—Burning of Columbia—
Drunkenness and robbery enter with General Sherman—A
panic-stricken people.

MATTERS were getting worse ; it was determined to hold Charleston to the last extremity, to fight street by street, if attacked, and orders were issued to re-move all non-combatants from the city; especially women and children.

I therefore started with my family to Anderson, but before we reached Alston, twenty-five miles from Colum-bia, the train was halted. An immense freshet, we were told, was coming down the river, and had carried away some trestles in the railway-bridge, so that we were com-pelled to return to Columbia. When we arrived there, old Doctor Reynolds and his wife opened their hospitable doors to us, and leaving my family with them, I returned to Charleston. Sadness greeted me. General Hardee, who was in command (an attendant, by the by, of the services of the Church of the Holy Communion), sent for me, and told me that General Sherman * had left Savan-

* When General Sherman was marching through South Caro-lina, the Federals burned many buildings in Camden, among them

nah, and was moving on Columbia. This would force the evacuation of the city. He added, " Unless you are prepared to take the oath of allegiance to the United States government, you had better leave.''

As I had been too pronounced a man to be left undisturbed, I told him that I would take that oath when the flag of the Confederacy was furled, but not till then. Charging me to secrecy, he ordered me to leave ; so, on Sunday, 10th February, I bade the congregation farewell, telling them that I was going to leave the city for some time, and the church would be closed until my return. On Tuesday, I left by the Northeastern Road for Florence, to go thence to Columbia, for the bridge on the Congaree had been washed away. I took with me the sacramental vessels of the church, in a large black box, and we reached Columbia on Wednesday night. I had placed a box containing books and clothing, sermons and valuable papers, in charge of a friend, Mr. Wm. Allston Pringle ; but in the confusion, he lost the box. I never saw the box or books again, until four years afterwards. The Sisters of Mercy sent me a half-dozen of the books, which had been rescued by a kind-hearted Roman Catholic priest, where, or how, I have never learned. The sermons, clothing, and valuable papers, I never heard of again.

I wonder if any of General Sherman's men read the

the Protestant Episcopal Theological Seminary. Bishop Davis wished to revive the same, and I asked Mr. Welsman to donate for that purpose a building in Spartanburg, which had been built for a church school for girls, but had been vacated through the failure of the enterprise. Mr. Welsman generously consented. The seminary lasted a few years, but the diocese was too poor to sustain it, and it was closed. The trustees sold it, and Converse College, a school for girls, is flourishing there. The interest is donated to the Theological Seminary at Sewanee, University of the South. If I had not asked Mr. Welsman for that building, Sewanee would not be getting that $500 a year.

sermons ! They were some of my best, and I would like
very much to get hold of some of them myself.

Wednesday, General Sherman's army had now reached
the Congaree River, and fighting had begun below the
city.   Three days after my departure from Charleston, a
portion of this army was distinctly visible on the heights
outlined against the sky.

Shells were suddenly thrown into the city of Columbia
without warning, and as I was one day walking in the
street, I saw a shell strike the corner of the house just in
front of me, next to the house where my family was staying.   In the front piazza a group of terrified women were
standing.   There is still a gash in the west end of the
State House made by one of those shells.

General consternation prevailed in that city, which was
filled with women and children, refugees from the coast.
The shelling did not continue for any length of time, for,
to the credit of General Sherman be it said, as soon as he
learned that an over-zealous officer was shelling Columbia
without orders he immediately stopped it.   Such was the
report at the time.   The Confederate General Wheeler,
with his cavalry, then in Columbia, was in full force, and
one of his captains meeting me, asked if I could tell him
where he could procure a pair of stockings.   I went immediately to the store of the Ladies' Relief Association,
where Mr. Edwin L. Kerrison was in charge, who told me
that he would give me a box of socks, on condition that I
helped him move some of the wine and liquor which was
there.   He feared the soldiers would break in and the
consequences might be serious.   Seeing a number, I think
one hundred and forty-four cases of port wine, marked
Ladies' Relief Association, which had arrived after running the blockade, I agreed to Mr. Kerrison's proposition.
This wine would be of service to the sick.   I then went in
search of the Captain, and giving him the box of socks,

asked him for a squad to protect me in carrying this wine through the streets, which he did; and with the help of Doctor Reynolds's waiting man and a truck, I safely disposed of one truck load of wine.

I then went about the city endeavoring to reassure such ladies as were without a male protector. During all these hours a constant firing was kept up above and below the city ; in the midst of which, at night, we retired to bed, but not to sleep—an anxious, careworn people.

The city of Shushan was perplexed. I shall record what came under my own observation, which was noted at the time ; I trust nothing that is written in this book will stir up an angry feeling in a single heart. My life is a striking illustration of God's Providence, and nothing is further from my wish or intent than to engender strife.

The events of which this part of my narrative treats have passed into history. My effort ever since General Johnson surrendered has been to make peace between the people of the North and the South ; and by the blessing of God on my humble efforts, I have been the means of bringing many on both sides to a better understanding.

During the shelling of the city on Thursday, the 16th February, a large quantity of cotton was brought in great haste out of many houses and yards, from both sides of Main Street, and put in the middle of the wide thoroughfare. This cotton had been stored in every conceivable place, and when the shelling began, the owners became frightened, lest the shells should set the bales on fire, and they hurriedly brought them from their hiding-places. In some of the other streets immense piles were heaped up. I remember a large pile in front of Mr. W. F. Dessaussure's house. But the cotton in Main Street was in one straight line, not more than a couple of bales high, and much of it was loose cotton. On Friday morning the 17th, between two and three A.M., there was a terrific explosion, which shook the city like an earthquake. Hastily dressing myself, I hastened into the street where I learned that an explosion had taken place at the depot of the South Carolina Railroad, where a quantity of blockade goods with much powder and fixed ammunition was stored. In the general demoralization of the hour, a number of persons had gone there, with lighted torches, to help themselves to goods, which they knew would otherwise fall into the hands of the enemy. By accident the powder was ignited, the depot was crowded, and many lives were lost.

While out inquiring about the explosion, I met Gen. Wade Hampton and staff, in front of Hunt's Hotel. The coming day was just lighting up the eastern horizon, and I said to General Hampton, " Do you propose to burn this cotton ? "

" No," he replied, " no need ; for General Sherman will not stay here. He has indeed marked his course with desolation, and this cotton he would certainly destroy as he is destroying all the railroads, but he is pushing on to General Lee's rear. The cotton, if saved, will be something for our poor people to live on after the war."

He then asked me to go to the Preston mansion, and take my family there, as it would be safer with someone in it. General Hampton also advised me to get notes from the ladies in the city asking protection, as he thought they would need it, and was sure it would be given, for the city was now evacuated. I bade him good-bye. How handsome he looked that day, as he sat on his horse, of which he seemed to be a part, for he was a superb rider ! I saw him with his staff ride out of the city, just before the sun rose, and we did not meet again until the flag of the Confederacy had been furled forever, and the mighty contest, with all its heroic deeds and unparalleled sufferings, had become a thing of the past.

My wife declined to go to the Preston mansion, so I went and urged the old servant not to betray the hiding-place of the Preston family silver. He promised, but the pressure was too much for him, and he revealed the place and all the silver was taken away. Soon after the Federal soldiers entered Columbia.

Following General Hampton's suggestion, I went over to the Presbyterian Theological Seminary, where I saw Mr. Daniel E. Huger, and many ladies, to whom I gave the General's message. Several ladies went off to write the notes ; many I had already from others.

While I was waiting for the notes, I heard for the first time in four years, floating on the morning air, the tune of " Yankee Doodle." At that time I would rather have heard the awakening notes of the Angel Gabriel's trumpet. Hastily gathering as many notes as had been written, I ran to the Main Street, and met the advancing column of the incoming enemy, soon after they entered the town. As they were marching down the street, many stragglers fell out of the ranks ; but I moved on among them unmolested, for I had taken the precaution to put on my clerical clothes. Very soon I saw with great apprehension many persons, white and colored, rushing out of stores and houses with pitchers and buckets. I heard this was done to propitiate the thirsty soldiers. It was soon evident what was in those vessels, for many of the soldiers became intoxicated, and to this cause we owed some of the horrors that followed.

As soon as the column halted and stacked arms, the weary and drunken men threw themselves on the cotton bales in the middle of the street. Thinking the officer in command would make his headquarters at the State House, which stood at the head of Main Street, I went there, and found a perfect orgie in progress. Many trophies and mementoes of a not inglorious past, especially of the War of 1812, the Florida War, and the Mexican War, battle-flags and swords, etc., were in the possession of drunken soldiers, and were being pulled to pieces and tossed about. Some of the men were wrestling and boxing. Altogether, the scene was so intensely painful and mortifying, that I quickly returned.

Going back down Main Street, I found Colonel Stone, the officer in command, and told him the city was full of unprotected women and children, and appealed to him as a man and a soldier to give me some guards for them, calling his attention to the drunken state of his men. He courteously directed me to go to the Market House, farther down the street, where I could find his Provost Marshal. He at the same time wrote on one of the notes orders for as many guards as I needed.

On my way to the Market House I saw the first bale of cotton take fire. The soldiers who were sitting and lying on the cotton had begun to light their pipes, and a spark or a lighted match must have fallen on the loose cotton, which of course took fire. I was within twenty feet of the first cotton fired that day. The flames soon spread, and the men, cursing those who had deprived them of their resting-place, quickly got away from the burning piles.

I saw General Sherman and his staff ride down Main Street, at about 9 o'clock A.M., and when he came in, the burning cotton was still smouldering. At that time he was ignorant of the cause of the fire, and naturally supposed it had been kindled by the retreating Confederates. I met him that afternoon at the house of Mr. Harris Simons. He had been intimate with the family in past years and was kind and considerate in his general bearing. He seemed to deeply deplore the terrible condition of things, but said it was his duty as a soldier to stamp out the rebellion, as he called it, hurt whom it might. He gave a special personal protection in writing to the family, but notwithstanding this they were robbed and burned out that night.

On leaving, I walked some distance with the General, and had some conversation regarding the preservation of the library of the College. He remarked that he would sooner send us a library, than destroy the one we had ; adding, that if better use had been made of it, this state of things would not exist, and that I must go and tell the ladies they were as safe as if he were a hundred miles away. I went home and told the ladies at Dr. Reynolds's house, to which several families in their alarm had fled for refuge. It was about half-past eight at night, when I told the ladies what General Sherman had said, and they only replied, " Do you believe him ? Go on the roof of the house and see for yourself."

A Captain of the Federal army had billeted himself on us, and was welcomed by us, as we thought he could protect the house. This officer went with me to the roof of the house, and we there saw that the whole of Columbia was surrounded with flames. I pointed this out to the Captain, and said I believed they were going to burn Columbia.

" No," he said ; " those are camp-fires."

I told him that I had been four years in camp, and thought I knew what a camp-fire was. Then I pointed out several residences on fire, the owners of which I knew, namely, Mr. Trenholm, General Hampton, Colonel Wallace, and a number of others. The environs of the town were ablaze. Then a fire broke out in Main Street, near Hunt's Hotel, caused by an overturned lamp in a saloon, which ignited the liquor, and as the flames spread, two or three small hand-engines were brought out which I saw Federal soldiers work on. Suddenly three fire-balloons went up, and in ten minutes eight fires broke out simultaneously across the northern street of the city, about equal distance from each other, and stretched almost entirely across the town.

At once the men who had been on the engines a moment before turned in and broke them to pieces. I saw this from the roof of the house.

" See that ? " I said to the Captain.

He gave one long look, then darted down the skylight, and we never saw him again.

A gale of wind was blowing from the north that night, and that soon caused the fire to burn freely, so that in a short time the city was wrapped in a lurid sheet of flames. Coming down from the house, I told the family that their fears had become realized.

" Columbia is being burned by the enemy."

They gathered up some trifles, prepared themselves for flight, and awaited anxiously the progress of events.

The house in which we were was of brick, surrounded by trees, but a wooden house, that of Mr. De Trevilles, was on the same block, with a brick Baptist church in the rear. It seemed to me that unless the house itself was fired we should probably be safe.

Going into the street I there beheld a scene which, while memory lasts, I can never forget. Streams of pale women, leading their terrified children, with here and there an infant in arms, went by, they knew not whither, amid the fierce flames. They hurried on, leaving behind them forever their burning homes, and all they contained. To their everlasting honor be it said, no cry escaped their lips, no tears rolled down their cheeks. Fearless and undaunted, they moved amid the surrounding horrors, silent, self-contained, enduring. In silence, the pale procession passed on. When the history of heroic women is written, let not those Carolina women be forgotten.

The streets were filled with soldiers mounted and on foot, in every stage of drunkenness. The whole of General Howard's Fifteenth Corps, we learned, had been turned loose upon us. Shouts of derision and blasphemy filled the air. Cries of "There are the aristocrats!" "Look at the chivalry!" were yelled into the ears of these defenseless women. Men seemed to have lost their manhood, and the mere beast was in the ascendant. Be it said, however, that although these poor women were in their power, there is no recorded instance of a white woman having been assaulted or outraged. So much cannot be said about the colored women, who were not so well treated. Amid all this confusion there were occasional explosions of ammunition and shells, as the fire reached their place of storage. The bursting of barrels of liquor, the falling of brick walls, the howling of the wind, for it was blowing a gale, and the swish of the flames leaping wildly from house to house made up a terrific uproar. I, myself, saw men with balls of cotton dipped in turpentine enter house after house. Some would take bottles of turpentine, throw the liquid round about, and then set it afire. It seemed as though the gates of Hell had opened upon us. It did not take long to fire the whole town.

Amid the accumulated horrors of fire, pillage, a drunken soldiery clamoring, with ribald insults, the awful night wore on until half-past eleven o'clock. Then it was that the only house in the block besides Doctor Reynolds's, being in the very next lot, was fired and the ladies of the household, fearing to be enveloped in the flames, insisted on seeking protection at General Sherman's headquarters. Our flight, therefore, was determined upon. My first thought was to take the silver service of the church out of the box to which it belonged ; this I left open on the floor and put the silver in an open box under my bed, merely throwing a cloth over it. After gathering a little clothing for the children in a blanket, and putting our infant Charles in the arms of a faithful colored nurse, my wife, Theodore, and Josephine, my adopted daughter, Doctor Reynolds, his wife and daughter, and his wife's sister left the house. There we found ourselves in the blazing streets, amid an infuriated mob of men called soldiers, and at once joined the dreary stream of refugees, whose perils and uncertain fate we were compelled to share. Through street after street we pushed our way until we had reached a house within a square of General Sherman's quarters, and as there had been no fire set to any of the houses near the officers' quarters, we determined to stop at this house. The people to whose house God's hand had thus led us, received us well. The reader will learn what remarkable consequences followed upon the chance that made us stop at that house.

Before the gate of Mr. Miot's house there were hitched two horses, belonging to two Federal officers, a captain and a lieutenant. As soon as the ladies had there found a place of safety, Doctor Reynolds went out into the street again, saying he would go back to his house, which contained all the mementoes of his life. He would go back and see the last of them. We earnestly entreated him not to go, and one of the officers to whom the horses belonged seeing this venerable, gray-haired man in the street approached us, and joined in the request that Doctor Reynolds would not venture back, as he might be insulted, or ill-used, by some of the drunken soldiers. The Doctor, however, insisted upon going, and the young officer soldier—he was about twenty-eight years old—then said, "I will go with you and protect you." The two left us about half-past eleven P.M. Meanwhile one of the ladies stood guard at the back gate, while I stood at the front gate. The hours of the night dragged on, and although soldiers came repeatedly to the house, and threatened us with many ills, they did not molest us further.

CHAPTER XVIII

LIEUTENANT McQUEEN

We arrive at a place of refuge—I confront General Sherman—At my expostulation he stops pillage and debauchery—I am robbed of my shawl—Restitution and repentance—A noble Yankee—My first fiery meeting with Lieutenant McQueen—I apologize.

IN the meantime no tidings came from Doctor Reynolds and the officer who had gone with him. Mrs. Reynolds and her daughter, as time passed, became almost frantic with anxiety as to his fate. Added to the horrors of the dreadful night, was the uncertainty as to what was to come next, or what was going on in other parts of the town. The fate of the helpless women of Columbia pressed very heavily on our hearts, and the few men who were able to exchange a word during the night, had given each other a pledge that any outrage offered to a woman, should meet with the instant death of the offending party. The certainty that such an act of vengeance might precipitate a general massacre, the dread that to burning and pillage, outrage and bloodshed were possibly to be added, served to make that night a period of inexpressible agonies. No language can convey an idea of the actual sufferings endured by our citizens, from nightfall till dawn.

But suddenly a gleam of hope appeared in our little

circle in Mr. Miot's house. About three in the morning, the officer who had gone with Doctor Reynolds returned alone. Doctor Reynolds had told him my name, and as he came up to me at the gate, he said: "Mr. Porter, Doctor Reynolds begs you to bring the ladies back, for we have saved the house, and the presence of the ladies will make it more secure."

I frankly confess, I did not believe him. I could not imagine what he had done with Doctor Reynolds, and I thought he only wished to lure the ladies into the street, that he might help the others to rob them of the few articles they had saved. I accordingly left him at the door to ascertain for myself the condition of Doctor Reynolds's house before returning to bring the ladies out. The reader may imagine my indignation when turning into the street which I thought led to my house, I saw it in flames. I was standing there half-petrified by the perfidy of the officer, when General Sherman came by. The burning city made it bright as day ; the General recognized me, and I said in reply to his remark, " This is terrible," " Yes, when you remember that women and children are your victims."

I was desperate and had lost all fear of him.

" Your Governor is responsible for this," he said.

" How so ? " I asked.

He said: " Whoever heard of evacuating a place and leaving it full of liquor ? My men are drunk, and this is the cause of all. Why did not your Governor destroy all this liquor before he left ? There was a very great quantity of whiskey in the town when we arrived."

" The drunken men have done much," I replied ; " but I have seen sober men fire house after house."

Just then an officer rode up, and saluted the General, who recognized him and said, " Captain Andrews, did I not order you that this should stop ? "

" Yes, General, but the First Division are as drunk as the first regiment that came in yesterday morning."

" Then, sir, go, and bring the Second Division and have this stopped. I hold you personally responsible for the immediate cessation of this riot."

Captain Andrews rode off. The Second Division from Stark Hill, General Woods commanding, was brought in; the drunken mob was swept by them out of the city, and in less than half an hour, not another house was burned. The discipline of that army was superb, and we all felt that fire and disorder could have been prevented or sooner arrested, for thirteen hundred houses were burned that night, and seven thousand women and children driven into the streets amidst the scenes which, as an eye-witness, I have described.

The General passed on, and I turned back to go to the ladies, relieved by the order I had just heard given. I had wrapped myself in a shawl purchased in Brussels in 1856, which I had used in Switzerland, and of late in camp on the picket-line. As I was hastening back, I was met by a drunken sergeant and two privates, and as they approached, the drunken man seized my shawl, saying, " What is a rebel doing with a shawl ? " He jerked me towards him, and drew off, and struck me a violent blow on the left temple. The attack was so sudden, and the blow so severe, that for a moment I was staggered, but gathering myself up I began to tussle for the shawl. The privates advised me to desist, as the man was drunk, and they could not answer for him ; he, moreover, was armed, and I was not. Believing that discretion was the better part of valor, I yielded, and the man wrapped the shawl around him, and walked off. The three had not gone far, when another Federal soldier who had just come across the river, and had not been in the riot, came up and said, " Stranger, I saw that man strike you, and steal your shawl ; it is an outrage.'' Dropping his gun from his shoulder, he continued: '' I am ashamed this night to own that I belong to this army ; I enlisted to fight and to preserve this Union ; I did not come to free negroes, or to burn down houses, or insult women, or strike unarmed men. Stranger, I have a mother and two sisters,'' and raising his right arm towards Heaven as he leaned upon his gun, he said, '' Oh, my God, what would I do if my mother and sisters were in such a plight as these poor women are in here to-night. Stranger, if I were a Southern man in the sight of this burned city, I would never lay down my arms, while I had an arm to raise.''

The time, the surroundings, the words, the manner, added to his words a certain thrilling eloquence. I looked at the man, all blackened with powder and smoke, with profound admiration and intense surprise.

I told the speaker for the sake of humanity, I was glad to meet one man who seemed to have a human heart in his breast. He then said, '' Stranger, if you will hold my blanket and knapsack, I will get that shawl for you.''

Suiting the action to the word, he dropped his encumbrances at my feet, and with fixed bayonet, started in pursuit of the sergeant who had my shawl. A few paces off he met a comrade whom he induced to join him, and the two men overtook the three men. The privates left the sergeant in the hands of these two men, who at the point of the bayonet, brought him double-quick back to me, and my friend said, '' Now apologize to that gentleman for striking him, and give him back his shawl.''

The sergeant made every apology, for he was quite sobered by his sudden arrest. He confessed that the devil had taken possession of him this night, but he was very sorry, and if he could be of any service, he would stay and protect me.

Thanking the true nobleman who had acted so grandly, I recorded his name in a pocket Bible, subsequently stolen from my pocket that night. By that step I lost a name I would give much to recall. It would afford me great delight to meet that man again. I think his name was White ; I have an impression that he was in an Iowa regiment.

All this consumed a great deal more time than it has taken me to tell it, and when I got back I found the officer I left there waiting at the gate, very impatient at my delay. On seeing me he cried, " Where have you been ? I have taken your wife and children home, and your wife is miserable about you."

" What," I said ; " you have taken my wife and children back to that burning house ? "

He simply said: " The house is saved ; your wife's hand was, indeed, slightly burned by a falling spark, and your little daughter fainted in getting back, but they are now safe, and Mrs. Porter is almost distracted about you."

Had I not seen the house in flames ? and yet this man coolly tells me this tale. He had taken all that was dearest to me somewhere, I knew not where, and I resolved that if there had been foul play the life of one of us was near its end, and I determined mine should not go first.

No doubt someone reading this will think, How shocking for a Christian minister ! Yes, to you it may seem so ; but to read of it, and to be one of the actors are very different things. Yes, reader, war, and all its concomitants, are sinful, devilish ; war is begotten of Satan, and born in Hell ; there is nothing good about it; but before you condemn you must be placed in the same circumstances (which Heaven forbid), and then you can understand my feelings. I said to him, " Go on, and take me where you have taken my family."

We passed through the street in which the scene I have described took place, turned down the next street, and there stood Doctor Reynolds's house, evidently unharmed. This, with a Baptist church, was the only building unburned for some ten blocks around. I saw I had done the soldier a great wrong. The revulsion of feeling was quick and violent. Extending my hand, I said: "Lieutenant, I have judged you unfairly; I ask of God and you pardon. I thought you were a villain, and now I find I am under great obligations to you."

He took my hand, and shook it warmly. "Pardon you, certainly. I knew by your countenance what you felt, and it is perfectly natural, after this night's experience. I do not wonder you have the worst opinion of every member of this army; but we are not all alike. There are some gentlemen and Christians among them yet; God help them if it were not so! Such a mob as this has been would be swallowed up by your army in a few days."

He then told me that his name was Lieut. John A. McQueen, of Company F, 15th Illinois Cavalry, of Gen. O. O. Howard's escort, and his home was Elgin, Kane County, Illinois. It was God's Providence that brought us together, for much that this biography will relate has been the result of the fact that this young man went home with Doctor Reynolds that night.

I found the ladies and children all safe in Doctor Reynolds's parlor. They gave me glowing accounts of the gentle tenderness of Lieutenant McQueen, and of the protection he had been to them. Doctor Reynolds told, how, when he returned to his house he had found it a pandemonium. It was filled with soldiers, and they had broken open drawers, and boxes, and trunks, and had scattered the contents everywhere. The box in which the church plate belonged was smashed, but the common box under the bed, in which I had put the silver, and covered it over with a towel, had escaped notice ; the boldness of the ruse had thrown the robbers off their guard, and so the silver service of the Church of the Holy Communion, Charleston, South Carolina, was preserved. When Lieutenant McQueen entered the house, he ordered every man out, and as he was an officer they obeyed. He placed a sentinel in the front and rear, and stationed soldiers on the roof. He proceeded to form a line of our servants from the well to the house, and passed buckets of water to the roof. Being a brick house, and surrounded as it was by trees it could not take fire excepting from the shingled roof, or from the inside.

The fire having swept past the block, and the house now being under guard, Lieutenant McQueen had considered it safe, and had returned to the house in which we had taken refuge, for the ladies and myself, as I have related. Several parties who had been burned out took refuge with us and the ladies being much exhausted, I opened a box of the wine I had saved, and they found it very beneficial. The next day I gave a box to Miss Reynolds to distribute among the many sick ladies in the city. One box I gave to the Rev. Dr. Shand for Sacramental purposes, and had it not been saved, the Holy Communion could not have been administered for months, for there was not another bottle of wine in Columbia. The remainder I turned over to the Rev. Mr. Jenkins and to Doctor Raoul, and distributed some to the sick soldiers in the hospital.

The week after this a certain lady came to me, and demanded the wine. I told her all of it was inaccessible, except the box of wine that Doctor Shand had, and she said that it was her wine. I said, " Madam, it was marked Ladies' Relief Association, and I did not know that you constituted that body." I told her that there were 144 cases of it, and she had better look up the 138 boxes that I had failed to save. She was very indignant, but there was nothing to be done. I did not recognize her as the Ladies' Relief Association. I had saved the wine, and had given it all away to the best objects.*

After seeing my family safe, I went out to help others. I went to the home of Mr. G. M. Coffin, an old friend of mine, and with the assistance of some negroes moved all his furniture into the large lot behind Doctor Reynolds's house. I then sat down by it to watch, and from sheer exhaustion fell asleep. The sun was high when I awoke, and every piece of furniture was gone. I have no doubt the very people who helped me to move it took it while I slept. It was during that sleep the Bible with the soldier's name who had given me back my shawl was taken from my pocket.

Saturday beamed upon us in all the beauty of a clear winter's day, but the sun shone down on a blackened, desolated city, and a broken-hearted people. On Sunday the Rev. Robert Wilson, son-in-law of Doctor Shand, preached an eloquent sermon, and a large number gathered at the table of the Lord. It was a solemn hour. What searchings of heart there must have been! For after all we had endured at the hands of the enemy, we still could go to this feast of love, where all wrath and bitterness must be left behind. We thanked God that so many could go to that feast, and sobs were heard from many of the women, and tears ran down the cheeks of the

* Years after this I received a letter from Mr. Stevens, then a clergyman of the Church, the same who commanded the *Citadel Guard*, who had fired on the *Star of the West* at the beginning of the war, asking me to tell him about some wine I had in Columbia, for this good woman was circulating astounding stories as to Dr. Shand and myself stealing some wine from her. I wrote to him the account, and he put the slander to death.

men.   Reader, you would have to be placed in like condition with us, to understand the full meaning of the first
Communion after that dreadful night.   The record of that
hour is on high, and I trust faith and love have been
accounted of God for righteousness to the little band, who,
with failing hearts, but trustful, still went to their Master's board and said, '' Thou hast stricken us, but we will
not believe Thou hast forsaken us.''

CHAPTER XIX

McQUEEN'S ESCAPE

*We bid farewell to Lieutenant McQueen—I provide him with
a letter which afterwards saves him from Southern bullets
—Hearing of his further peril I hurry to his assistance—
He is finally restored to the army of General Sherman—
Story of my adventures.*

MONDAY, 20th of February, 1865, was another day
of balmy beauty such as often occurs at midwinter
in the South. But we were spent and utterly exhausted.
The reaction of panic and sorrow had set in, nor did we
know what trials yet awaited us, for the Federal army
was still in the city, and the awfulness of our condition,
and the desolation which was all around us, began to be
realized. All hearts were sad, and despair was visible in
every face. Suddenly, about noon, there was a stir among
the soldiers, and regiment after regiment, and train after
train, passed rapidly through the streets. General Sherman had received tidings of the evacuation of Charleston,
and he started to intercept General Hardee and the Confederate forces. It was not long before the unwelcome
host was gone.

And here begins a new chapter in my experiences.

On the day General Sherman left Columbia, Lieutenant

McQueen lingered until near four o'clock, fearing some stragglers might harm us. We at last became uneasy for his safety, for his army had gone some time, and I feared that he would be shot if our scouts met him alone. At length I said to him, " There are men enough here to hold you as prisoner, but I pledge you my life to see you safely returned to your lines." I could not counsel him to accept me as a companion, as my presence with him might give him trouble hereafter. He, of course, would not entertain the thought of taking me with him, and as he was entirely in our power, the temptation to hold him for the sake of saving him from danger was very great.

In spite of these considerations, all of us, at about five P.M., with an amount of emotion that can easily be imagined, gathered around this young man to bid him good-bye. He had come among us as an enemy, and was leaving us as a brother beloved. General Hampton, with two hundred thousand men, around us, could not more effectually have protected us than he had done. As he mounted his horse, I begged him to stop a moment, and running into the house, I asked my wife, if she had not some token of remembrance she could give McQueen. She handed me the gold pencil-case from her chain. This I took to him, telling him Mrs. Porter had sent it to him. He held it in his hand for a moment and said: " Did Mrs. Porter give me this? Tell her I thank her, and will never forget her, but—" handing it back, " Tell her I never could persuade anyone that a Southern woman gave me a gold pencil-case in Columbia. I would not have a piece of jewelry from this city for any amount of money. I never could convince anyone I had not stolen it."

This suggested another thought. I begged him still to wait, and running into the house, I hastily wrote a letter to General Hampton or any other Confederate into whose hands he might fall. This I gave to McQueen, and I said: "Keep this with you ; it may be of service. Use it in any emergency which in the changes and chances of war may come."

I knew the woods would be filled with Confederate scouts, and that his life was in danger, so long as he was alone and without escort. I charged him, if he went to Camden, to show kindness to our blind Bishop Davis, and to his family, and to do his best to stop this barbarous style of warfare. He promised me that he would, and nobly did he redeem his promise. Commending him to God, I parted from him, neither of us expecting ever to meet again.

No time was now to be lost for self-defence in Columbia, for we were like a wrecked crew in a dismantled ship. General Sherman, at the request of the mayor of the city, had left us some muskets for our protection. We found, however, that not one could be fired. He also left us some cattle, such as only starving people would eat. That night we barricaded our houses, and drew out guns from places where they had been secreted, and organized the few men into a home guard. On the following day, the committee of gentlemen who had undertaken to manage affairs, persuaded all to make a joint stock of their provisions. We had all things in common, and agreed to take rations for each day. I think the most trying thing I ever did, was to go with Mr. Alfred Huger and Mr. Daniel E. Huger and others of that stamp of gentlemen, and stand for hours in the crowd of women and children, white and black, until our turn came to get a few quarts of cornmeal, and a small piece of bacon. This we did for example's sake, and it had the happiest effect, for the population of the poor were thus cared for. This was a matter of some difficulty, until we could send out beyond the belt of forty miles around us, which General Sherman had made a desolate waste, and draw provisions from these sections that had escaped the invader.

A month, to the day, passed before I could get any conveyance to take my family out of Columbia. At length, Mr. E. L. Kerrison, who by great forethought had sent his carriage and horses beyond the reach of the enemy, lent his conveyance to us and we were able to leave on the 17th of March. In all the past month we had heard rumors that Winnsborough and Camden had been partially destroyed, and that the Federal army had left the State at Cheraw. Mr. John Cheeseborough and his family were with us in our flight. We camped out the first night, and reached Newberry the next day. There we found the railroad intact, and next day went by the cars to Anderson. On the way going up at Hodges Station I met Mr. Wyatt Aiken, afterwards Congressman, who told me he had just returned from Darlington, where he had been looking for the body of his brother Hugh, then a Colonel, the same who had played Claude Melnotte to my Pauline, years before in Winnsborough. Hugh Aiken had been killed in a skirmish near Darlington, ten days after the burning of Columbia, and his brother added: " Your friend McQueen was wounded in the same fight, and would have been killed but for a letter from you, which saved his life. He drew this letter from his breast pocket, saying it was from the Rev. A. Toomer Porter, of Charleston. Fortunately it fell into the hands of a soldier, who knew you, and after reading the letter, the Confederate said, ' You must be an uncommon Yank, to have such a letter from Mr. Porter, and I will take care of you.' " *

Mr. Aiken added: " There are plenty of men who, instead of facing the enemy, stay behind. The brave heroes

---

* Our army was so outraged after the burning of Columbia, Winnsborough, and Camden, that they did not take any prisoners alive. War, diabolical war !

of the rear, think your letter a forgery, and McQueen an impostor. They have threatened to take him from the farmhouse where he was carried, and hang him, notwithstanding your letter.''

I thanked him for his information, and at once determined on my course of action. On telling my wife the circumstances, we both agreed that it was my duty to go and see what I could do for the prisoner. When we reached Anderson, I made all arrangements for the family, for Confederate money was still available, and we had a supply of that. I felt the family was secure, so the next day, strapping my historic shawl on my back, with some underwear, I took the train for Newberry, and started to look for McQueen. Where he was I had not the slightest idea, but if he was in Darlington district—though the district is as large as Rhode Island almost—I determined to find him, if above ground. If under it, I would find out who had put him there.

At Newberry I left the train, for there the road stopped, having been destroyed between that place and Columbia by the December freshet, and by the Federals. It took me two days to walk to Columbia, both days in the hardest rain I have ever been in, and that without an umbrella. At Columbia I stopped in an old mill, on the outskirts, made a fire and dried my drenched clothes. Next day I succeeded in getting a seat in a wagon, with no springs, the extemporized body being placed directly on the axles. The old, lame mule pulled six of us thirty miles to Camden, and I paid fifty dollars in Confederate money for the ride ; there was no Society for the Prevention of Cruelty to Animals down there. When I reached Camden, I began my inquiries about McQueen. Something induced me to go to the old Lord Cornwallis house, which was used for a hospital. Going first into one room, then into another, I finally opened a door without the slightest idea who was in the room. There were about a dozen Confederate sick and wounded lying on the floor ; but my eye caught that of one dressed in blue. He suddenly rose from one of the beds, and turning to me, he raised his arms and exclaimed, '' Thank God, home again.'' Seeing who it was, and that he was about to fall, I sprang over the beds, and caught Lieutenant McQueen in my arms. Laying his head on my shoulder, for a little while he sobbed, and I confess the tears were running down my cheeks at the same time. The scene created a sensation. Here was a Confederate in captain's uniform and a Federal lieutenant clasped in each other's arms, and weeping. The soldiers looked on amazed.

'' Wait, men, until I tell you this man's story, and you will weep, too.''

And they did wait, and when they heard it, McQueen became a hero at once.

I soon learned from him that he, with a squad, was out on a scouting party forty miles to the right of his army, after dark. They were attacked, and thinking they were being pursued, they retreated. The Confederates, on their part, thought they had fallen into an ambush and fled. In the skirmish two Federals were killed, and two wounded. McQueen was one of these latter. Among the Confederate casualties, Colonel Aiken was killed. The Confederates, on cautiously returning and finding McQueen, one of them had drawn his pistol to shoot, when McQueen held up my letter, and it saved his life. A litter was made for him, and he was taken to the home of Mr. Postell, who had lost his arm at Petersburg. He was a private in the company of Capt. Thomas Ford, an adopted son of mine, who had often mentioned my name in the hearing of Postell. Postell said that although he did not know me, still for his Captain's sake, he would take care of McQueen. Finding, however, that his life was in

12

danger from harboring a Federal soldier, Postell had
brought McQueen by night to Camden, only a week before I arrived there, and had placed him here under the
Confederate authorities. McQueen had been shot in the
groin about ten days after the burning of Columbia, a
month before I found him.

The delight of McQueen, when he saw me, cannot well
be described ; he said home was at once before him. He
now felt sure of safety. How he could get there he did
not know, but he felt sure he would soon be home. I
went into the town and found that he had protected the
Bishop's family, and many others, and had saved every
house that had not been burned between Columbia and
Camden. When I told the people that he was in the hospital, wounded, and a prisoner, all who had received
kindness from him, visited him, and loaded him with
attention. The blind Bishop went to him and laid his
hands on his head and blessed him. Finding that he was
sufficiently recovered to travel, and there being only a
surgeon and a quartermaster representing the Confederate
government in Camden, I obtained leave of the surgeon
to take charge of McQueen, while he held me responsible
for any damage that might occur from his giving me the
prisoner. The quartermaster gave me an old lame mule,
and Mr. De Saussure loaned me an old buggy. The young
ladies made up some biscuits, and fried some chickens ;
Mr. W. C. Courtney gave him a suit of citizen's clothes,
and Bishop Davis his linen duster. We put his uniform
in a bag under the seat, and he put on the citizen suit.
I placed my wounded friend in the buggy, and walked
alongside, driving the mule. Thus we travelled sixty-
four miles in two days to Chester. At night we lodged
with farmers. As we passed through the country lately
traversed by General Sherman's army, the people who
were poor, distressed, and stripped of their provisions,

took us in. I used to tell them about the burning of Columbia, and how one of the Federal officers had proved himself a Christian indeed ; and when they expressed a wish to meet such a man, I would introduce my companion, and then McQueen received the best they had. He remarked that he never met such a forgiving, benevolent people.

When we reached Chester, I gave the mule and buggy in charge to an acquaintance and never heard of them again. We entered the train, when I fortunately met Colonel Colquitt,* whom I had known in Charleston. I told my story, and asked and gained his protection, which was necessary, for I had nothing to show for my having this " Yank " in charge. Though of course he wore no uniform, McQueen's speech betrayed him all the while, and I therefore advised him to be silent. It was a risky business to undertake at such a time, for I was in the midst of soldiers incensed and infuriated by the march through Georgia, and the desolation of South Carolina. As I think of it, thirty-two years after, I wonder how I dared to do it, and how we escaped without one unpleasant incident. But I was aiming to reach Richmond. I knew Mr. Davis, the President, and Mr. George A. Trenholm, one of my vestry at home, was in the Confederate Cabinet as Secretary of the Treasury, and I felt certain that with his aid I could send McQueen through the lines.

Before we reached Salisbury, mingled rumors of disaster and success came floating around us, no one knew how or whence, for we had no telegraph. When we reached Greensborough, the rumors gained substance. We found we could get no farther, so with the aid of Colonel Colquitt's permit, I turned to Raleigh, thinking to see General Johnston there, and proceed on to Smithville. But the

* Afterwards Governor of Georgia and United States Senator.

battle of Bentonville had just been fought, and when I met General Hardee, at the station, he bade me stay there with McQueen, until he could see General Johnston, for Sherman was advancing, and Johnston was retreating. I was advised by Hardee on his return from Johnston to take McQueen back to Raleigh, and await General Johnston there.

We went back, and I took McQueen to the Rev. Dr. Mason's house, where, after they had learned his story, the best they had was at the disposal of my companion. I called on General Johnston the next day, at Mr. Rufus Tucker's house. He had been told by General Hardee of McQueen's noble conduct, and he at once sent his Provost Marshal to Doctor Mason's house with a permit for McQueen to pass over to General Sherman without exchange. He told me if my friend would remain quiet in the place where he was, he would be in the Federal camp, as the Confederates were in retreat. I went there, and bade McQueen good-bye. The scene of our parting I pass over ; I doubt if either of us has ever forgotten it.

CHAPTER XX

A touching story of General Johnston — The last scenes of the war—My blank despair—My wife's distress over my dejection—I read the providential working of God in history—Light through the clouds—I resolve to do my best for home and country.

I HAD now travelled over seven hundred miles, by rail, on foot, in a wagon without springs, in a buggy, amidst many dangers, to set McQueen free. I would have travelled seven thousand to show my gratitude to that gallant man.

McQueen's safety being assured, my own movements now occupied me. General Johnston asked me what I was going to do, and I frankly told him I was puzzled as to my next step. General Johnston then placed me on his staff, and gave me a horse, granting me authority to do what I could to help the soldiers. Of this great soldier I must tell the following :

Once, while waiting for dinner in the anteroom of Mr. Tucker's house, where General Johnston, General Hardee, and myself were the only three present, I told General Johnston that all South Carolina felt his removal from command at Atlanta. The General answered that my partiality had gotten the better of my judgment.

"No," I insisted, "a black pall fell over the State when you were relieved ; we all felt that General Sherman would never have reached Columbia if Johnston had not been removed from Atlanta."

The gallant soldier rose, and walking hurriedly back and forth in the small room, said: "Since you have said so much, I will tell you. I was in command of as splendid an army as general ever had. It was stronger and larger the day I reached Atlanta than it was the day I began to retreat. It took me seventy-three days to fall back seventy-four miles. I never lost a wagon or a caisson. I put almost as many of the enemy *hors de combat* as I had in my army. Men who were at home flocked to me. I had put fifteen thousand of Governor Brown's militia on the fortifications, and Atlanta was impregnable. I had 'tolled' General Sherman just to the place where I wanted him, *i. e.*, between two rivers. I had divided his forces, and would have fallen on one part, and if the God of battles had not been against me, I would have crushed that, and fallen on the other, and an organized command would not have gotten back to Chattanooga. Three brigades had marched three miles to begin the fight when the order came."

By this time the General had become so much excited, that the tears gushed from his eyes, and he strode out of the room into the piazza.

General Hardee and I had risen to our feet, as excited as the General was, and as he went out, General Hardee fairly sobbed, as he said: "Yes, and the grand old man does not tell you, but I will. He went to General Hood, and asked him to withhold the order until the battle was fought. Johnston stipulated that if it should be a victory it should be Hood's, if a defeat, he would not come from the field alive. If it would only be a check, Johnston could fall back on Atlanta, recruit and resume operations.

Hood, however, refused. The rest we know ; history will tell of the desolation and ruin that followed.''

Soon after this conversation, dinner was announced. I sat between General Johnston and General Hardee. As we were eating soup, a telegram was handed to General Johnston, and as soon as he had read it he rose from the table and called General Hardee out. In a little while General Hardee called me out, and handed me the telegram. It ran thus :

SALISBURY, N. C., April, 1865.

GEN. JOS. E. JOHNSTON :

I have not heard from General Lee for three days, but from reports from stragglers, he has met with a great disaster. Come to me.

JEFFERSON DAVIS.

General Hardee then said, '' General Johnston, you, and myself and the telegraph operator alone know the contents of that telegram.''

'' Where is General Johnston ? '' I asked.

'' Do you hear that train ? He is on it, and has gone to the President at Salisbury.''

'' What now,'' I asked, '' is the next move on the military chess-board ? ''

'' If that is true,'' General Hardee said, '' that General Lee has been defeated, the war is over ; this is only an armed mob. We have nothing but the débris of an army, except the forces with General Lee. We have but twelve thousand armed men here, and propose to surrender at Hillsborough. We intend to retreat at once, and no firing will be allowed. For any man killed now on either side will be a murdered man. You will go with me.''

He gave quick orders, and the armed mob was put in

motion. Mr. Tucker pleaded with me to take a favorite negro boy, a pair of fine mules and a wagon for my easier transportation, and I consented, drove off, and followed after the army. We camped for the night six miles from Raleigh, and I slept on the same blanket with General Hardee in a roadside schoolhouse. The next day, when we reached Chapel Hill, General Hardee told me that it was all true, General Lee had surrendered, and this army would be disbanded in three days. He warned me that a disbanding army was dangerous, and my mules might be taken from me. He advised me to leave at once, and spread news that the war was over.

Remonstrance was useless ; he was imperative ; so I left, and made for Pittsborough, where relatives of mine, the Hills family, resided. I stayed with them that night, and I never saw so much old family silver in one family in my life. There were a number of large clothes baskets filled with it. I told them that as there would be no Federal army through there, their only danger was from the emancipated negroes. But none of it was taken ; they saved it all. The next day I started towards Cheraw, in the wagon. It was an exciting ride. At every farmhouse where I stopped, to learn the way, I was told which was the straightest route, but not to go down that road, for the woods were full of deserters and bushwhackers, and it was not safe. But that was just the road I had to take, and I rode in hourly expectation of an attack. I did not have even a pocket-knife with me, but I was not troubled by any one. I followed the track of General Sherman's army when he was coming from Cheraw, and was seldom out of sight or smell of some memorial of that destructive march. I reached Cheraw in safety, and there rested, and then made for Columbia. I was going back there for those groceries which I had hidden in Doctor Reynolds's cellar, and thither I carried the news of the collapse of the Confederacy, but the news was not believed. There were no telegraph lines to Cheraw or Columbia, and no word had been heard. At Columbia I found what was of great importance to me, my barrel of sugar, bag of coffee, two boxes of candles, and roll of leather, all safe and sound. To Mrs. Reynolds I gave some coffee and sugar, and loading my wagon I went all the way back to Anderson.

I had been gone a month, and my wife had not the slightest idea where I was. There had in fact been no way of letting her know that I had found McQueen, and great was the joy when I drove into my yard. I at once called my servants together, and told them they were free, and could leave me if they so desired, but not one left. The groceries were a Godsend, as Confederate money was now useless, while sugar, coffee, leather and candles were as good as gold, and we lived by barter.

The third day after my arrival at Anderson, a rumor reached me that a party of raiders, from Asheville, North Carolina, had looted Greenville, and were on the way to Anderson. By the afternoon some young men from the outlying farms rode furiously through the town, with the news that the Yankees, as they were called, were on us, and it was not long before a squad of these raiders were galloping through the town. They had on the Federal uniforms, but the force was principally a set of deserters and bummers, and therefore the more dangerous. They had heard the Confederate Treasury had been removed from Richmond to Anderson, and they were after that. The fact was, that all the printing-presses of the Treasury had been brought to that town, and had been put into a schoolhouse, on the lot where the house was that I was living in. This was a large building that had been used as dormitories for a boarding-school, or college, as they called it, where we were living, and this large schoolhouse in the lot was where the printing-presses had been placed to print Confederate money, and eight per cent. bonds; which had been done *ad libitum*. It was nearly dark when the squad rode into my lot, and I went out and met the leader. I said to him, "The war is over; we have laid down our arms; General Lee and General Johnston have surrendered to General Grant and General Sherman, and you are liable to trouble as marauders."

The man either did not, or pretended he did not, believe me, and said he had come for the Confederate gold that was on my premises. I told him if there was any he would have to find it, for I did not know where it was. "There is plenty of paper money," I added, "and bonds here, but nothing else."

One of my faithful servants, the nurse of my baby Charles, had, without my knowledge, gathered every piece of silver in the house and disappeared. The officer dismounted, and brought five or six of his men into my house. They went to the dining-room and opened the sideboard, and every closet and drawer where the silver was kept, and finding none, asked where my silver was. I told him I did not know; when last seen by me all those places were full of silver, but where it had gone I could not tell. He called up my servants and questioned them; they all professed ignorance. I noticed that one of them named Ann was missing, and felt quite comfortable, for I felt sure she had the silver somewhere, but where, I truthfully did not know. Finding nothing downstairs, the officer led his men to the foot of the staircase, but a cousin of mine, Mrs. Christopher Mathewes, who with her children was refugeeing at my house, stood on the lower step, and said, "You do not go up those stairs unless you do it with violence." She was a strikingly handsome young woman, tall and graceful, with raven hair and brilliant flashing black eyes. She was a beautiful figure as she stood there defying these men. They paused. She said: " On the word of a lady, there is no silver, no jewelry, no money upstairs ; nothing but our wardrobes, and you shall not, if you are men, invade our chambers ; if you are beasts there is nothing to be done."

The leader was cowed, and turning to me he said, " Show me where the paper money is."

I knew it was worthless, and was glad to get them out of my house, for my wife, who was in very delicate health, had become very nervous. I led him out. As we were walking along, he threw up the lapels of my coat, and put his hand on my watch-pocket. Finding no watch there, he said, " What is a man like you doing without a watch ? "

" You do not expect a man who has been through Sherman's army to have a watch ? "

" Where did you meet Sherman ? "

" In Columbia," I said.

He only grunted, " Oh!" and said no more about my watch, which I had slipped into my shoe when they came into the yard, for I had had experience.

The schoolhouse was full of very expensive machinery, and the squad of soldiers ransacked the building, of course finding nothing but paper. They were furious with rage and disappointment. They examined the presses carefully and asked, " Are these the presses that ground out your money ? " I told them they were the same, and then the work of destruction began. They smashed every machine, leaving no two pieces together. They did not fire the building, for which we were specially thankful.

Thus was I an eye-witness on my own premises of the last remnants of the Confederate Treasury. The party left, but the rascals had gone to the stable and carried off

Mr. Tucker's two fine mules, and left two old broken-down horses in their stead.

After those robbers had gone out of the town, Ann came out of her hiding-place, and brought every piece of silver with her. She had rescued my plate of her own accord. She was a faithful servant, and died in my service some ten years afterwards, faithful to the end.

When the excitement was over, I was somewhat mentally broken down, for all this time, of which I have given account, the loss of our dear boy had been gnawing at my heart. The stirring scenes I had been in had kept it down, but now all was over, and the Confederate flag was furled, and the cause for which so many lives had been given, and so much suffering endured, was lost. I was overcome. I was, with the rest, left penniless ; my securities were worthless ; I thought I had a little real estate in Charleston, but no money; nothing but that sugar and coffee and leather to live on, and a house full of people to support. There was not a blanket in the house—all had been sent to the soldiers. There was not even a piece of flannel, for the ladies had given all to make bags to put powder in for cannon. The ladies were dressed in domestic ginghams woven by country women. The curtains were cut up for skirts. There was nothing but blank despair, and my heart failed me. I said, '' Napoleon was right ; God was on the side of the strongest battalions.'' The question of right was after all a mere question of might, and such a God could not command my love or obedience. The thought that a cause in which Robert E. Lee and Stonewall Jackson, such men, such eminent Christian men, had drawn their swords, should fail, made life worthless, and I folded my hands and wished to die.

It was thus that my religious and intellectual outlook was changed.

I had always been fond of history, and had a large collection of historical works ; so for many weeks I went early every morning up to a room by myself and read until past midnight, scarcely going to meals. My dear wife did all she could to cheer and rouse me ; for my mental depression almost broke her heart. I read a long list of English history, Michelet's *France*, Lamartine's *History of the Girondists*, Motley, Prescott, Gibbon's *Rise and Fall*, and finally Grote's *Greece*. I simply devoured the books and read with lightning speed. My edition of Grote is in twelve volumes. I finished the book after twelve o'clock one night, when I got on my knees, and thanked God for the lesson I had learned. I went down to our chamber. My wife was sleepless, and going up to her bed, I took her hand and said : " Wife, I have been a great fool ; here I have been throwing away my faith in God, my interest in life, my duty to you and our children, under a gross delusion. The records of history show that every great nation has been baptized in blood, that failure does not mean wrong in the defeated, but the results have always thrown the people forward. Had we succeeded, slavery, which we hated, would have been perpetuated with the sentiment of the world against us. It would have been a cankering sore in our body politic ; it would have been a source of continual strife between the United States and the Confederacy; this would have made a standing army in each government a necessity. This would have revolutionized the form of our respective governments, and in fifteen more years we would have been engaged in a war of extermination, for one side or the other would have to be masters of this continent. God has permitted the wrath and ignorance of men to work His will. But freed from the incubus of slavery, I believe there is a future for this dear Southland yet, and I am going to do all I can to make it. I was, and am still, true to the lost cause ; but I am not going to hug a corpse and carry it about with me ; I am too young for that ; I am just thirty-seven years old, and I have you, our two children and our adopted daughter to make a future for, and God helping me, I am going to do it.''

What a burden I rolled off that precious heart that night ! We thanked God that the evil spell was gone, and she said, '' Feeble as I am, I will do all I can to help you.''

CHAPTER XXI

HOME AGAIN

*I return home—The darkey in uniform yields to a bluff—
The iniquities of the Freedmen's Bureau—" Give us this
day our daily bread"—The prayer is answered—Confisca-
tion or robbery?—The good George Shrewsbury—I open
the Church of the Holy Communion once more—My sermon
on " Set your house in order," and how it was received.*

THE old horses had been well fed, so the next day, I
started in the wagon drawn by my sorry team, and
bound for Charleston. When I reached Abbeyville, Mr.
Edward Miles, afterwards rector of St. Luke's, where he
died, asked for a seat. I carried him five miles, but it
was too rough for him, and a returning vehicle took him
back to Abbeyville. I pushed on alone towards Edge-
field, where I had a relative, Prof. F. S. Holmes, the
person who after the war, first discovered the phosphate
rock which did so much for Charleston. When within
six miles of Mr. Holmes's house, one of the old horses
tumbled over and died. I was in a fix, but unbuckling
the harness from the dead horse, I took his place and led
the other one. It was an uncommonly tough walk.
Next day I left horse and wagon at Mr. Holmes's, and
never heard of either afterwards. I then walked over to

Aiken, where I met the Rev. J. H. Cornish, a man whose characteristic was to do everything he could for another, totally forgetful of himself. He had a small pony and an old buggy, and offered to take me over to Orangeburg, where we arrived after many difficulties.

Once at Orangeburg, I went direct to the United States official, told him who I was, that I wanted to return to Charleston, and had come to take the oath of allegiance to the United States government, which was required. I duly took the oath, not *con amore*, but with no mental reservation. The trains were run by the army of occupation, and no fares were charged refugees returning home, so I got on the car, and we dragged along at a snail's pace, for the track was in a dangerous condition, and I reached Charleston in the afternoon. I went directly to my house, corner of Rutledge and Spring Streets, and as I came in sight, I saw tall corn waving above the fence. The whole of my beautiful garden and the large lot was a cornfield. That was shock number one. Number two, came in the form of a burly black, dressed in United States uniform, with a gun on his shoulder, passing in front of my door. As I approached he stopped in front of the gate, and said, "You cannot go in dey."

"Why not?" I said; "this is my house."

"No 'taint," he answered; "b'longs to de Freedmen's Bureau."

"Does it?" I said; this was a revelation. I had never heard of that institution.

I saw that he was one of the island negroes, dressed up in a uniform; so I thought I would try him to see if he had lost the sense of obedience; so I looked at him very sternly, and in an authoritaitve voice, said, "Look, here, darkey, that is my house, and if you do not get out of the way I will make you."

I am sure I do not know what I should have done if he

had not assented. It was a case of mere bluff, but he dropped his gun from his shoulder, caught hold of his woolly head by a front curl, scraped his feet, and said, " Yes, boss, go in."

As I went in, I stood a few moments inside the gate and was pretty well stirred up to see the beautiful flower-garden I had left in February turned into a cornfield. As I went to the piazza door and pushed it open, someone, I saw, was behind it. I recognized the English woman in whose charge I had left the house (the same I had begun my industrial school with). She immediately said, " You cannot come in here ; I have positive orders not to allow you in."

This was a pleasant welcome home, but after I had brushed aside an armed darkey and got in at the gate, this woman angered me ; for I had been a good friend to her in great need.

" Madam," I said, politely, " I never strike anyone, but if you do not get out of my way I shall knock you down."

She took fright, and ran into the house, and up into the third story, and locked herself in.

There was an old colored servant in the yard, named Lydia. My grandfather had given her to my father when he was married. She had cooked for him, and for mother after his death, until I was married and went to house-keeping, but had not done any work for some years. She lived on my premises, and I supported her, and when I had left the city in February, I left her with four large hogs, a yard full of poultry, a barrel of rice, and a barrel of grist, so I knew that she could not want for food. As soon as she heard my voice, she came as fast as her old feet could carry her, and threw her arms round me and kissed me on either cheek, crying : " My child has come home ; but they rob you, my child, of all you had in the

13

house ! They broke open all the closets looking for the wine you had ; but I so glad they did not find any.''

As soon as I could disengage myself I went into the house, and it was empty. There were twelve rooms in the house, and I had left them all filled with furniture. Besides my own, Mr. Alston Pringle, Doctor Wragg, and Colonel A. G. Andrews had a quantity of theirs in the house. Old Maum Lydia could only tell me people had come with wagons and carted it all away. The English woman would not open her door, and I did not wish to break it down, but she had some furniture in the chamber she was occupying. My sexton soon came and told me the Freedmen's Bureau people had taken it. He led me to the house of one of the carpetbaggers who were in the employ of that institution which did the negroes so much harm. It defrauded them of their savings in the bank it established, and by feeding them in idleness, and putting the worst ideas in their heads, caused such an annoyance to us white people, and it became such an abomination that the United States government abolished it as soon as it discovered its mistake in creating it. I went into the house, and there I saw my furniture ; the parlor was filled with it. I looked in a chamber, and it, too, was so furnished.

'' Why,'' I said, '' madam, you have all my furniture here, and I have come for it.''

'' It is confiscated,'' she said.

Confiscated, indeed ! If the United States government had gone round and taken our furniture, it would have been a small business ; we would have to submit, but I said : '' The government knows nothing about this ; and it is pure and simple stealing.''

The woman had a pan of hot water on the stove ; she looked at me and then at the pan. I saw by her eye that it would not be long before I got the contents of the pan, so I beat a retreat, and never recovered one article. When order was restored, and this driftwood was moved out of Charleston, shiploads of the people's furniture were sent North by these vagabonds and there was no redress. I had said to my old servant, "I am very hungry, as I have no money and have had no dinner." "Oh, my honey," she said, "I will get a dinner for you." So when I got back from the furniture hunt, I found rice, and a chicken, and some eggs. I sat on a chair she brought me, and in one of her plates, with her knife and fork, by a table she furnished, I ate my first meal at home. After dinner my sexton and I went round to the church. It was a sorry sight ; carpet and cushions, and books were all gone ; even in the Sunday-school room the children's library was all gone. All the sewing-machines and furniture of the Industrial School were missing—all taken by the same set of lawless thieves. My sexton told me that most of the people, white and colored, were living on rations furnished by the government. I found a part of the city, about the Northeastern Railroad had been burned at the evacuation, which added to the portion burned on the 11th of October, 1861. The city looked very desolate. I did not wish to see any of my people at their homes, and in their present plight. After going over the church and the schoolhouse, with a heavy heart I went out, and leaned on the iron railing which then surrounded the church, and on looking down Cannon Street, I saw a country negro girl fantastically dressed in some old finery she had picked up somewhere, followed by three plantation negro men. The girl was singing at the top of her voice, and as she came near I caught the words, which were as follows :

"You may paint and you may rub,
You may wash and you may scrub,
But a nigger will be a nigger till he die—Yah ! Yah ! Yah !"

" Dat 's so,'' exclaimed the three men.

It was such unexpected testimony to a great truth that I had a hearty laugh, and it did me good. My never-failing friend, Mr. Theodore D. Wagner, took me into his house for the night.

The following morning I went early down-town to post a notice, that there would be service at the Church of the Holy Communion next day. The Rev. J. M. Green and the Rev. J. B. Seabrook were the only Episcopal ministers in the city. The Rev. W. B. W. Howe had been sent out by the Federals because he would not use the prayer for the President of the United States while the Confederacy was still in existence. He and I had been the only two at active work there. Mr. Keith, Doctor Elliott, Doctor Pinckney, Doctor Hanckel, had all left. Mr. Shanklin and Mr. Dennison had died of yellow fever. I was the first Episcopal clergyman to return.

On my way through the market, I met George Shrewsbury, a colored butcher ; he belonged to that respectable class of free colored citizens, who were so numerous in the city of Charleston before the war, and who had always commanded the respect and esteem of the white population. He had acquired some wealth ; he was a member of the Methodist Church, but like many of the colored members of that denomination, he preferred that his children should be baptized, married, and buried by an Episcopal minister. I had performed several services for him and his family, so that for many years there had been a kindly feeling between us. When he heard in February that I was going to leave the city, he came to my house, and said, that if I was afraid that my servants would leave me, although his family had never acted in a menial capacity, he would guarantee that I should be waited on by some of them, if I would only remain in the city, and as long as he had any meat at his stall in the market, I should have some. Of course, as it has been recorded, I declined his kind offer. But when we met this fourth day of June, 1865, he was delighted to see me, and expressed his gratitude that the gentlemen were coming back, for Charleston was not home without them. After his welcome, I said, " George, do you know the Lord's Prayer ? "

" Of course," he said.—" But do you know what it means ? " I told him that I feared I had never before known its meaning. [Reader, are you sure that you understand it ?] " I had for very many years," I went on, " said, ' Give us this day our daily bread,' but George, I am afraid that I relied more on my bank account than on Him who had given me that. To-day I have not a cent, and nothing with which to get my dinner, but I find in the Bible this command and promise, ' Dwell in the land, and be doing good, and verily thou shalt be fed.' And now," I said, " I intend to do all the good I can, and God knows I must be fed, or I can do no good, so I shall leave the whole matter in His hands." I left my colored friend with a cheerfulness more apparent than real, and posted my notice. I went back home with some foolscap paper which I had asked someone in town to give me, got a pen, and with some ink borrowed from a Dutchman's corner shop, wrote my sermon for the next day, the 5th of June, 1865. My text was from Isaiah, the thirty-eighth chapter, part of the first verse, " Thus saith the Lord, Set thine house in order." I finished writing my sermon, and my old cook provided a dinner for me, and I went out on the veranda, and sat on the floor smoking an old pipe.

I was thinking of my sermon, which I knew would strike a discordant note, and wondering whether it was discreet, when a ring at the street bell took me to the door. It was George Shrewsbury, who with many apologies offered me a roll of money, one hundred dollars in greenbacks. He said he had intended buying some cattle with it, but that he had had no rest since I had passed through the market. To think that a gentleman in my position had no .noney was an idea he could not take in. I declined the loan, as I had no security to offer. "My property here," I said, "is held by the Freedmen's Bureau, and they have stolen all my furniture ; you saw me sitting on the floor. I do not own a chair." He insisted, saying that if I refused the loan, he would think that I regarded the offer as a liberty on his part, and that I was offended. Of course I could not let him go away with such thoughts, so I said, "I will give you my note for it."

"I do not wish your note, sir, you know you owe it, and I know it ; when you can return it I know you will. If you never can do it, it will be all the same ; I am paid enough in knowing that I have added to your comfort."

I confess my eyes were not dry ; first, from the thought that I should be in the condition to need such aid, and next that it should come from one not in my own sphere, nor even of my own race. Money was then worth in Charleston anything the most extortionate chose to ask. I could not repay the one hundred dollars for eighteen months ; when I paid the last five dollars, I told him, "I shall owe you one hundred dollars on interest account."

"You owe no interest, sir ; I have been abundantly repaid in feeling I was the means of relieving you in a sore time of need, and whenever you wish it again it is at your disposal."

George Shrewsbury will come on the stage later on. I resumed my pipe, feeling decidedly more comfortable, and quite sure I had made no mistake in my sermon for the next day. Sunday morning came. I held service and gave out the text, "Set thy house in order." I paused, and added, "For thou shalt live, and not die,—though that is not how the sentence reads." I reviewed the text, and then urged the hearers to turn their backs on the past, and look to the future; not to waste energies on vain re-grets, but to realize that they were on a wreck and to save life they must build, out of materials at hand, a raft to bear them to the shore. They were in chaos, but out of the confusion they must lay a basis for future building. It was their duty to accept as a fact the freedom of the slaves, and to act accordingly ; the negroes had not freed themselves, and had acted well, and needed our aid ; if we would, we could keep them as friends, and not drive them over to the Northerners, whom they would look upon as their deliverers, and would become subservient to them. I added, that I should try to get into a free school-board as soon as there was one, and do all I could to educate the negroes, that they might learn that liberty was not licentiousness. I said as free men they would surely be given the ballot, and we should offer it them when they could read, write, and cipher, and owned five hundred dollars of freehold property, etc.

The church was packed. A number of United States officers were present. Governor Aiken came to the chancel before I got out of it, thanked me for my sermon, and said : " If this is the way our public men are going to speak, there is hope for the old land yet ; we shall live, and not die." Not so did all my hearers take it. It was the first time that they had the concrete facts presented to them, and they were told they had something to do— they, as well as the negroes and the Yankees. An old cousin of mine, a late wealthy rice planter, then with his family living on government rations, was especially sore. He growled at me after service, " Why, you have gone over to the enemy; you have turned abolitionist!"

" Well," I said, " Cousin Laurens, I expect I feel as much as you do ; I am with you in the common ruin, but I am not going to stay in the débris. I have taken the oath of allegiance to the United States government. I thought it wiser than to expatriate myself. I think it wisest not to look upon the government to which I have submitted as an enemy, but as a protector. We need money, we need immigrants, to fill up the gaps ; we will get neither without order, and we will get no order without peace. Turned abolitionist ! What have we to abolish ? The victorious arms of the Federal Government abolished slavery, and I, for one, thank God it is done. I would not have done it so suddenly ; it means suffering, and wholesale death to the poor blacks. If more judgment, and less passion, had been shown, the negroes could have been freed, and the South not left so destitute, and the whole country would have been the better for it. But it is done, and now, if we have any sense left, let us make the most and the best of it.'' This conversation was held in my vestry room, immediately after morning service. Poor man, he had come in quite angry with me, but as I talked, he saw the wisdom of it, and the tears rolled down his cheeks, and he said : '' No doubt, Toomer, you are right ; but it is hard, oh, so hard ! ''

CHAPTER XXII

A DESTITUTE BISHOP

I make a business venture which is highly successful—My home is again furnished—I dissipate the despair of Bishop Davis, and see that his wants are provided for—" Porter, have you Aladdin's lamp ? "

MONDAY morning I walked down Hasell Street, to a store that had been kept by the Messrs. Kerrison, and is now the dry goods store of the P. D. Kerrison Co. A Mr. John Wilson, a good-natured Irishman who had been a sutler in the United States army, then had the building as a grocery store. I walked boldly up to him, and said : " You are Mr. Wilson, I am the Rev. A. Toomer Porter, rector of the Church of the Holy Communion."

" Yes, I have heard of you."

" Well," I said, " as I do not think you have heard anything very bad, I have come to ask you to give me a credit for five hundred dollars. I have nothing on earth to offer as security but my face and my character."

He smiled and said, " What I have heard of you makes me glad to know you have come back to this disordered city. But why do you want so much credit ? You may get what you need for your family, but why five hundred dollars at once ? "

" George Shrewsbury," I said, " has loaned me a hundred dollars. Of this I wish to keep five dollars so as on a pinch to get a loaf of bread with. Ninety-five dollars I need to pay freight to Anderson. I will have to wagon from Orangeburg to Newberry. If you will let me have the groceries, I will go round, and try to get five hundred dollars more credit in dry goods. Not a store has been opened in Anderson, and if I can get there first, I can pay you something on account in thirty days."

I now felt the good of my business training at Robertson and Blacklock's Rice House.

" You shall have the credit. I wish you luck ; you look as if you mean business."

" I do mean business, my friend. I have a family to support, and my wife is in delicate health, and she will soon have nothing whereby to get food for the children. Yes, I mean business, and George Shrewsbury has enabled me to get at it."

I went round and got credit for five hundred dollars in dry goods from different parties, telling each why I asked it, and none refused. I then wrote to Christopher Mathewes, a cousin, who was at my house with his family in Anderson, to meet me on Thursday at Orangeburg, and to have two wagons to go to Newberry. On Thursday I got a permit for transportation, and met Mathewes with the wagon at Orangeburg. We loaded up that evening, and camped a few miles out of town, he sleeping in one wagon and I in the other, each with a pistol, for it was the first lot of groceries that had gone through a disordered country, and the risk was great. We reached Newberry on the third day, and though it was Sunday, I felt that God knew it all, and as we could only get a flat open dirt car for our goods, we rigged up some boards on the sides and ends, and put our goods on the car and started. We danced a fisher's hornpipe on that car, keeping things from going overboard, but we succeeded. I had gotten the keys of a store which Mr. Wagner owned, and loaned me, he being much amused at my undertaking, but commending my enterprise. When we reached Anderson, our cargo was a great surprise, and a crowd gathered at once. I told them that as we would open the next day, they might bring their money, gold and silver and greenbacks, and get anything they wished. We hauled our goods to the store, and Mathewes and I shut ourselves in and worked nearly all night getting the goods opened and arranged. I very much fear, if the truth has to be told, that the advanced price was a very heavy percentage. When we finished, we took some large pieces of brown paper, and in large letters printed on it what we had.

We went to bed full of expectation and excitement. Next morning betimes we were at the store, but not before some customers were waiting, for the news had spread far and wide. The doors had not been opened ten minutes before the store was crowded, and it was all we could do to supply the wants of our customers. They brought nothing but silver and gold, for things they had not seen for four years were before them in quantities, and each seemed afraid lest what they wanted would be gone before they could get their share. Stockings were emptied of their hoardings, and our till received it. By the evening, we had taken eight hundred dollars, and I am almost ashamed to say, a good part of the one thousand dollar stock still on hand. I sent Mathewes to look for a good man next day to help as clerk. In the evening I got my wife to sew the coin in a belt. "Now," I said, "Mathewes, you must carry on the store. I will go back to Charleston, establish my credit there by quick payments, get one thousand dollars' worth of groceries, and come back to you. I can now manage by myself the transportation."

Early next morning I took the train to Newberry, and made my way back to Orangeburg, engaged four wagons to wait on me, and in less than a week I walked into Mr. Wilson's store, and said : " I have eight hundred dollars in hand. I want enough out of it to pay transportation, and will pay you three hundred dollars on account of the five hundred dollars, and three hundred dollars to the dry-goods people. Now I want one thousand dollars credit on groceries."

" Five thousand dollars, if you want it," Mr. Wilson said ; " for this beats all I know. How have you done it ? "

I made out my list, and told him to send the goods to the station that day, then went round and paid the three hundred dollars to the dry-goods people, who offered me all the credit I wanted, but I needed none, for I found it was the grocery line that had the profit in it, as food was much more needed by the people.

The following days we still had a crowd at our store, and in three days I had money enough to pay the debt in Charleston. By this time I had waked up some of the men, and I heard of several who were going to Charleston for goods ; but we had skimmed the cream. It was the only store in Anderson where our kind of goods could be had. When I had money enough to pay the debt, to have some for transportation, and a little for my own needs, I said to Mathewes : " I shall now leave you in charge, for I must go home and resume my legitimate business. I must gather up my flock, rebuild the parish, and go on preaching the Gospel."

It was now the first of July, and I left next morning after having paid all my debts in less than fifteen days, gained unlimited credit, and supported my family. In November, I returned to Anderson for my family, took from the store money to pay our passage down, with such trifling furniture as we had, and a little to supply our pressing necessities, presented the contents of the store to Mathewes to support his family on, which he did for nearly a year. At the Broad River I put my few articles of furniture with my library and servants in a flat, and had them floated to Columbia. There I procured a carriage and took the family to Columbia, thence to Orangeburg, and so back to Charleston. There I borrowed two chairs from the corner shop, the children sat on the trunks, friends lent us a bed or two, and a few days later, the Spanish Consul having a sale of furniture, I bought for a song, furniture for the dining-room, our bedroom, and the children's room, as well as a sofa. The odds and ends I subsequently brought from Columbia, and that was all we had for some years.

And here we were at home, in November, 1865, and I was then nearly thirty-eight years of age, with a wife totally broken in health, two children, a boy of ten years old and one of three, with an adopted daughter, and not a dollar of income, still the owner of two houses, the one I was living in, and the other in Ashley Street, next to the Sunday-school house ; this latter unoccupied. Of course there was no salary from the church. The Sunday offerings barely paid the sexton and organist, leaving little for the rector.

When I returned to Charleston in July, I found a letter from McQueen, who said that if I was in any trouble about my property, I must write to General Howard, as the latter requested. I did write, and Howard immediately directed General Saxton to release my property, and return it to me, which was done; so when my wife came back, at least the house was ours. I was not idle, and very soon regathered such of the fragments of the congregation as remained, while a few new families came in to us.

The journal of the convention of February, 1866, shows that I had, in that summer of 1865, from the 5th of June (exclusive of my shop-keeping) baptized thirty-two whites, and eleven colored ; nine had been confirmed in my parish ; there were nineteen marriages and forty-one burials. Our congregation numbered one hundred communicants and sixty Sunday-school children. Our communion alms amounted to one hundred and eighty-one dollars. Since the cessation of hostilities our communicants were about one hundred, but as the congregation was just collecting, after our total break-up, the number cannot be definite. One very pleasant feature was the steady attendance of my former colored congregation, and their quiet, respectful demeanor.

In 1866, I invited Bishop Davis and daughter to stay at our house, which they did ; my wife's ingenuity accommodating them, without their knowing our straits. One night, before going to bed, the dear old Bishop said to me, " Porter, I am the dying bishop of a dead diocese."

" Oh no, not so bad as that."

" Yes," he said, and he ran over the churches that had been destroyed, the communities and parishes that had been wiped out of existence. The Theological Seminary was burned, the library scattered, fifty thousand dollars endowment gone, Bishops' Fund gone, Aged and Infirm Clergy Society gone, Widows and Orphans of Clergy Society gone, Advancement Society gone. " I myself, besides, have received no salary for 1865, I have nothing left at home, and look at me, my coat has been turned."

His pants were threadbare, and his hat—what a hat it was !—and no overcoat. It was a pitiable tale. I had overlooked the Bishop's wants, for I did not know he had received no salary. But anticipating that he would be depressed, I had seen Mr. Evan Edwards about the Advancement Society, and Mr. John Hanckel about the

Bishops' Fund, and all the treasurers of the other socie-
ties, so I said: "To begin with, the Bishops' Fund has
some $58,000 saved ; Society for the Advancement of
Christianity, $34,000 ; Aged Clergy Fund, $35,000 ;
Widows and Orphans, $57,000 ; the Theological Scholar-
ships, $7000, all saved."

The Bishop was half reclining in an armchair. He
raised himself on his elbow, and turned his sightless eyes
towards me, saying, "Porter, how do you know that such
good news is true ?"

"I am reading you the report furnished by the different
treasurers."

He leaned back in his chair and said, "Thank God, it
is not as bad as I thought."

I said, "Bishop, our own cares have so absorbed us,
we have forgotten your needs, but I promise you in as few
hours as it can be done, you shall have the best suit of
clothes in Charleston, and your family shall be provided
for."

He asked me, "How are you going to do it ?"

"Leave that to me," I said.

Getting up, he said, "Porter, you are the first live man
I have met with."

"Oh," I said, "Bishop, I am too young to give up
yet."

"Well," he said, "I have heard enough for one time
and I will go to bed."

Next morning he told me he had slept soundly all
night, the first night's sleep for months.

"And now," I said, "Bishop, I wish you to lie down
here till I come for you." And off I started for Broad
Street. I soon arranged for the Bishop's relief, by appealing to several church people. And the next day I took
his hand, and put in it a roll of bills.

"What is this ?" he asked.

I said, " It is $650, and you will have your suit of clothes day after to-morrow." Then I told him what I had done. " This money is for yourself and family, you are not to give it away." But I believe he did give it nearly all to some of his poverty-stricken clergy.

He said: " Porter, have you an Aladdin's Lamp ? "

" No," I replied, " but you have some noble, warm-hearted laymen in the Church, and they only had to be told of your need, and this is the result."

CHAPTER XXIII

Bishop Davis at the Diocesan Convention of 1866—Churches and parochial schools for the colored people—Good resolutions are no use without practical performance—I take steps toward the carrying out of certain good resolutions passed by the convention—The Bishop sends me North to collect funds for the Theological Seminary and colored school—I am kindly received in New York by Dr. Twing, and in Brooklyn by Dr. Littlejohn—Munificence of Mr. A. A. Low.

THE war was over and now a new chapter in my life opened. I will detail it from the beginning.

Bishop Davis in his address to the Episcopal Convention of February, 1866, in Grace Church, the first held after the war, said : " Let me say, too, that I have received the strongest memorials of kindness, and to testify my recognition of these in the spirit of Christian affection and fellowship. The Freedmen's Aid Commission, in the Department of Domestic Missions, in the Church of the United States, is now in active operation. Through it I have received communications from our Northern brethren in the spirit of Christian kindness, and sympathy, offering to us aid and coöperation in the instruction, both literary and religious, of the freedmen of this State."

The education of the freedmen, and their instruction in the Christian doctrine of the Church was discussed at this convention, and resolutions were passed advocating the work.*

The Board of Missions to the colored people elected were Revs. C. C. Pinckney, C. P. Gadsden, A. T. Porter ; Geo A. Trenholm, E. L. Kerrison, and Thos. W. Porcher.

Immediately after the adjournment of the convention, Mr. Trenholm and myself conferred on the subject. The resolutions sounded well, but were worthless without action. We therefore set out to look for a building, to establish a colored school. Mr. Trenholm thought it would do harm to select any inferior or obscure building, and we settled on the Marine Hospital belonging to the United States Government as just suitable. The place had been condemned and was not in use. How to get possession of it was the question. The Bishop had his Diocesan Theological Seminary very much in his heart, and had said much about it in his address ; he wished to revive it, so one night after the convention had adjourned, he said, " Porter, this diocese, unaided, cannot restore the Seminary, or open a school for colored children, and some one must go North to raise money. I am blind, and I cannot go, and you are the man, and I am going to send you."

I refused at once. " Why," I said, " Bishop, I do not know a single person at the North, and I do not know how to go about it."

" Nevertheless," he said, " go you must, as soon as the spring sets in."

He was positive, and I yielded. The Bishop went home, and I was left to prepare for my mission.

On the 4th of April, 1866, I sailed in the steamer for New York. I had left green peas in my garden at home,

* See Appendix B.

but when we arrived late on Saturday night, and had put up at the New York Hotel, April 6th, I found myself in the midst of a snowstorm. I knew nothing of New York, and on inquiring for a church to go to, was advised to go round to University Place, where there was a service held by some Episcopal congregation temporarily. It was a dreary day, and a dreary service, and very poor preaching. I forget what congregation it was, and who was the preacher. I had not been in New York since I was a boy of thirteen, when Canal Street was high uptown. On Monday, New York turned out, and as I stood in the hotel door, I was bewildered with the throngs of people going up and down. I stood a long while, not knowing what to do at first, nor where to go. I thought I was a fool, on a fool's errand. How could I ever get a hearing from these people? I had my credentials, and my churchly instincts told me I should first present them to the Bishop of New York, Doctor Horatio Potter. The Bishop received me courteously, heard my story, gave his sanction to my efforts, and gave me a letter to Rev. Dr. Benj. T. Haight, of Trinity Parish. The Doctor was cordial, but I went back to the hotel no further advanced than when I left in the morning.

And so each day passed. I was miserable, and felt that I was unfit for the mission committed to me. I was nearly returning home. Up to Friday morning I had made no acquaintance, and of course no advance. It occurred to me that I would go to the Bible House, where the Protestant Episcopal Board of Missions had their rooms. I went there, and the first person I met was the Rev. A. T. Twing, the General Secretary, a large, stout man, with a bright, cheerful face. I had to introduce myself, tell my mission, and show my credentials.

I was listened to very cordially, and words of encouragement were spoken, but no line of action was indicated, until I said I was an entire stranger, knew no one, that there was a small coal of love in my own heart, and I hoped that I might find some other heart where there was a like coal, and perhaps the Holy Spirit might fan the two into one bright, burning flame.

Doctor Twing opened his strong arms, and throwing them around me said, " You blessed rebel, yes, there are plenty of coals up here in many hearts, and the Holy Spirit will flame them into love ! " and he gave me a squeeze that nearly took my breath away. He said, " I will put you on the track, and if on one line we do not succeed, we will try another until we do." He wrote a warm letter to the Rev. A. N. Littlejohn, D.D., then rector of Holy Trinity, Brooklyn.

" Take this right away, and if nothing comes of it, return here."

I left immediately, feeling that I was at length started. I went over to Brooklyn, and was relieved to find the Doctor at home. I sent in my card, with Doctor Twing's letter, and was shown into the drawing-room. The Doctor soon entered, stately and reserved, but courteous. I stated the object of my visit and the Doctor drew me out. I was the first Southern clergyman he had met since the war, and he asked me many questions. As our conversation proceeded, his reserve melted away, and he became kind, sympathetic, and tender. I felt the tears running down my cheeks, and said, " Doctor, you have succeeded in doing what Federal bullets never did ; pardon my weakness," and I brushed aside the tears. Very abruptly the Doctor got up and left me in the drawing-room alone, without saying a word. I felt the awkwardness of my position, and was about to beat a retreat, when the Doctor returned with a bottle of old port wine, and two glasses, and filling them said, " We will drink a glass of welcome to you and wish you success. Now, where are you stop-

ping ? Go and get your luggage, and come and make
this house your headquarters.''

I had found a coal, and it was a live one. I soon had
my trunk at the parsonage. We went into his study, and
he gave orders that he was not to be interrupted except
for some urgent call. Neither of us took off our slippers
until we went to dinner that evening. He told me that I
must preach the next day. Before the sermon on the following day, the rector stepped forward to introduce me.
Never was a brother presented more favorably or lovingly.
He told his people of the hours we had spent together, and
never had he more cheerfully given his pulpit to anyone.
I was quite overcome by it, but in a moment or two, there
was a new state of feeling, for numbers of the congregation
in each of the aisles and in the gallery rose to leave the
church. Quick as a flash, and in a stentorian voice, the
rector directed the sexton to lock the doors, and then I
never did hear such a rebuke as he uttered. Every soul
sat down at once, and with this preparation, I ascended
the pulpit.

I knew that I was agitated; I felt that I was pale; but
after an earnest prayer, I gathered myself together, and
in a steady voice, that I knew penetrated to the farthest
point, I announced my text, '' I am Joseph, your brother,''
paused, and gave the whole text, and then the book,
chapter, and verses. The effect was instantaneous. I
could see at a glance that I had riveted the attention of
every person in that congregation. All speakers feel when
they have the ear of their audience. I felt it, and it re-
assured me. Everyone knows that a manuscript read is
very different from a manuscript preached with emphasis
and emotion, and as I went on, it suddenly struck me,
'' This may be taken for more than I mean,''—when,
leaving the manuscript, I said : '' My brethren, I hope you
will not misunderstand me. I would not have you, under

a false impression, give me a dollar for the Theological Seminary, or for the colored school we wish to open. My sympathies were all with my people. I did all I knew how to do that became a minister of the Gospel of peace to help them, but when, in God's providence, we laid down our arms, we did so in good faith, and all wise men among us are making not only the most, but the best of our condition." I then resumed my manuscript, and did not alter a word.

The service closed, and the offering was made ; I had never seen so much money put on the plates before. When we went into the vestry-room, Doctor Littlejohn did not say a word, but he came up to me, and folded me in his arms, and I have never forgotten it. We had not taken off our vestments before the vestry-room was literally packed with the members of the congregation, men and women. I was greeted with, " Your text, sir, your text, and your sermon was worthy of it.". I had to go into the aisles to greet the people. I think I shook hands with two thirds of them. It was a long time before we could get into the rectory; then Doctor Littlejohn expressed his gratification. The people followed us there. I confess it was a very happy day to me. The offering, with what was sent in, was about one thousand dollars.

A day or two afterwards, I received a note from Mr. A. A. Low, who said he had heard of the sermon, and enclosing his check for five hundred dollars. He stated that the rector of Grace Church would call on me with the request that I would repeat the sermon at that church on the following Sunday ; which I did with full appreciation, and great success. If this is ever read by any Southerners, please remember that this was in April, 1866, and that the sermon preached had been submitted to Mr. George A. Trenholm, late Secretary of the Confederate Treasury, and had received his commendation and approval. It was preached as it was written, and contained no sentence that compromised me or the South, and yet it was received by my Northern brethren in the manner I have described.

On Wednesday I was invited to a reception given to me by Mr. A. A. Low.

There was a large assemblage, and among them there was a certain guest, who, no doubt perceiving his questions were annoying, still plied them vigorously, until becoming a little provoked, I said, " Well, sir, we Southerners are better Union men than you are."

" How can that be ? " he asked.

" We, sir, need population, and money ; we can get neither until we have quiet, protection, and peace. We can now get these only from the government of the Union, and therefore that government is a necessity to us."

" Oh," he said, " if you are such good Union men, how do you like the Freedmen's Bureau ? "

Well, at that time that subject was like a red rag to a mad bull, and I found my temper, which I am sorry to say has always been quick, was somewhat getting the better of me. I had used all the tact and skill I possessed to avoid unpleasantness, but the true inwardness of the man was now revealed. I said, " Sir, if you had your study in your place of worship, and found out that your vestry, or deacons, or whatever your lay officials are called, had bored gimlet-holes in the ceiling, and hid themselves above you to spy on you while in your study, and you were to find it out, how would you like it ? "

" I would not submit to it," he said.

" Well," I said, " that is just what we think of the Freedmen's Bureau, and we will not submit to it."

With this, Mr. Low came quite hurriedly, led by his youngest son, then a boy, now the distinguished Seth Low, LL.D., President of Columbia University, New York. He had heard the conversation, had realized its

import, and went for his father, whom he brought up to
where my unkind interlocutor was standing, with a group
around us.

"I am very sorry, Mr. Porter," said Mr. Low, "to
hear of the annoyance to which you have been subjected.
I invited you to have a pleasant evening ; please take my
arm and come with me, but let me say to Mr. —— that
he in no wise represents my views."

"Thank you, Mr. Low, for this deliverance," I said,
taking his arm, and turning away with him. I was immediately surrounded by a number of persons, who seemed
to vie with each other to efface the impression which they
saw had been made. While thus engaged, I saw a tall,
military-looking man pushing his way towards me.
Someone proposed to introduce me, but he came forward
and extended his hand saying : "I have no need of an introduction, Mr. Porter. I am Captain Worden, who
fought the *Monitor* against the *Merrimac* in Hampton
Roads. Confound that fellow! I have heard what has
passed, and am glad to see the man has left. I heard you,
sir, on Sunday at Holy Trinity. When you announced
your text, I thought it was the happiest selection I had
ever heard. You won your audience as you uttered it.
And as you went on, my interest, and the interest of the
congregation became intense; and when you stopped, and
left your manuscript, and with the honest frankness of a
gentleman, told this people fearlessly what you had done,
I felt as if I could walk up to the pulpit and grasp your
hand, for you were pale and excited, and as you raised
your hand one could almost see through it. You had the
marks of the mighty struggle in every line of your face,
and when you resumed your discourse, I drank in every
word, and when it came to the offering, I opened my
pocketbook and gave you its entire contents, and gladly
would wish to be able to give you a hundred times more.

There are two classes of Southerners for whom I have a profound contempt—that class who stayed North during the war, made money, enjoyed themselves, and expended their energies in abusing the North, and praising the South ; for them I have a contempt that they did not go to the help of the men they praised. And the other class are those who come up here now, and say they had no sympathy with the South and they did nothing to help in the struggle. Contemptible blackguards ! To have lived among a nation of heroes, fighting the greatest fight in history, against such tremendous odds, enduring, suffering, with a heroism which was magnificent, and then to say that they did not sympathize, and did not help. Such fellows would be dangerous in your kitchen, for they would steal your spoons. I wish it were in my power to go South, and rebuild every house that was destroyed; yes, and oh, if I could bring back to life all who were killed on either side, and if I had the power I would blot out from the pages of history the record that the war had ever been fought! ''

I have quoted Captain Worden accurately. I felt I could embrace him, and, had I been a Frenchman, would have kissed him on either cheek.

To continue my account of Mr. A. A. Low. Later in the fall I said to him : '' I own a house in Charleston in a prominent part of the city, on a lot one hundred and seventeen by two hundred feet. On it is a large building used by the servants ; for before the war all of us in any position had around us a swarm of people as old family servants, each in the other's way, causing a constant drain on our incomes, but no one thought of doing without them. Now this is changed. I have no use for such a building, and if I had the means I would cut the building in half, divide the lot, and make two additional buildings.'' I then told Mr. Low that I wanted five thousand dollars, and as the property was unencumbered, I offered to mortgage it to him. Mr. Low made me the loan and I built the two small houses. Mr. Low went to Europe, and I found I needed fifteen hundred dollars more, for I had to add to my house some servants' quarters ; his son, Mr. A. A. Low, Jr., loaned that to me. I pledged all the rents and paid off the loan to three thousand two hundred dollars, when one day I received a generous letter from Mr. Low with my bond returned cancelled and the mortgage satisfied. This was indeed a generous gift.

Many years after, I received a letter from Mr. Low, saying that I possessed qualities which made him desirous that I should move to Brooklyn, and if I would come, he would let me select the style of architecture and would build a church for me, and I could name my own salary, and he would guarantee the same to me for my lifetime. I was then receiving a salary of eight hundred dollars from the Church of the Holy Communion. I thanked Mr. Low, but told him he had greatly overestimated me, and declined his offer. He then wrote, if I would come he would endow my school. This was a great temptation. My dear wife was then a great sufferer ; she had been paralyzed some time before, and was in bed. I took the letter to her and said, " Now, wife, what must I do ? "

The gentleness and tenderness of that dear wife never shone out more brightly than that day ; her clearness of vision and cool calmness of judgment never left her.

" My dear," she said, " do you believe that God gave you the work you have in hand ? "

" I do," I said.

" Has He blessed it and made it successful ? "

" To a marvellous extent," I answered.

" Has He in any way withdrawn His presence ? "

" No," I said, " but is not this His will, that the work can now go on with an endowment ? "

"It may be," she said, "but is it not true that you possess the power of acquiring a remarkable influence over boys, that you have their confidence as very few men are able to win? Are there not some things in life more valuable than money?" and she ceased.

"Which means," I said, "you think I had better stay where I am, and fight the great fight of faith where God has put me."

"I do," she said.

I went down to my study, wrote to Mr. Low, thanking him, but telling him why I must decline. He wrote me oh, how kind a letter! and said, whenever the people of Charleston were tired of me the offer was at my acceptance. From time to time Mr. Low would send me a personal check for my private use, and was a generous annual contributor to my work to the last year of his life. I have his likeness framed, and keep it as one of my treasures. His sons, Mr. A. A. Low, Dr. Seth Low, and his stepson, Mr. W. G. Low, have continued to be my generous friends up to the present time.

CHAPTER XXIV

MY SCHOOL

I plead the cause of South Carolina before the General Board of Missions, New York—" The most eloquent appeal ever presented to the Board "—I am very successful —I open in Charleston a school for colored children—President Johnson assists me and I obtain the Marine Hospital for my school.

BISHOP DAVIS had authorized me not only to plead for the support of the Theological Seminary and the colored school, but to appear before the General Board of Missions of the Episcopal Church, and to lay before them the condition of his diocese. Rev. Dr. Littlejohn arranged for me to meet the Board the Friday after Mr. Low's reception, and I appeared at the given time. I remember as present Rev. Dr. A. H. Vinton, Rev. Dr. Montgomery, I think, Rev. Dr. B. T. Haight, Rev. Dr. Littlejohn, Mr. John David Wolfe, Mr. Stuart Brown. There were others whose names have escaped my memory. They received me courteously and asked me to state my case. I began to tell of the desolate condition of the Church, when it rose up in my mind that South Carolina had been, up to the war, the third contributing diocese to missions, and that now prostrate, she was asking by my lips that she should be aided. I became very much agitated and said: " Gentlemen, the vision of the past has risen before me; the present overwhelms me; I cannot proceed," and my head fell forward, and the tears rolled down my cheeks.

Doctor Montgomery rose hastily, and came forward, and said, " You need say no more," and he took my hand and pressed it warmly.

Each member of the Board did the same. There was not a dry eye in that room. It was in 1866.

I bowed out of the room, and soon after Doctor Littlejohn came out, and told me they had voted six thousand dollars a year to this Diocese of South Carolina, and they paid that amount for several years. Doctor Littlejohn told me that my appeal was the most eloquent ever presented to the Board. " Oh!" I said, " Doctor Littlejohn, I could not speak, my voice failed me ; my heart was so full."

" Yes," he answered, " and you filled the hearts of all the Board ; you had no need for speech."

Soon after this I was invited to go to Boston to address the Convention of the Protestant Episcopal Church. Bishop Eastburn was then Bishop. At a given time it was moved that the Convention suspend business, and that I be invited to address the Convention. The Bishop hesitated, but the resolution was pressed with so much earnestness, that it passed unanimously, and I ascended the pulpit to address the Convention of Massachusetts upon the relation of the Church in South Carolina to the colored people. When the invitation was given I had prepared a written address, which I duly delivered. On its completion I received an ovation, and I heard from all sides declarations that it was refreshing to hear the Southern side, from the frank mind of an earnest Southern man. I made then a host of friends who stood by me for many years afterwards. On my return to New York, I called to see the Rev. Dr. Thos. House Taylor, rector of Grace Church.

He had not seen me since I was an infant, but he recalled the kindness he had received from my grandfather and from my father. His own father had died and had been buried from my father's house. He remembered he had been my sponsor. He was about to sail for Europe and begged me to take his pulpit for two Sundays, which I did.

After finishing my engagement at Grace Church, I thought the time had come for me to give up my efforts for the Theological Seminary, for I found it did not greatly interest the people. The total result of my mission was sixty-six thousand dollars for missions in the diocese, Theological Seminary and colored school. This was not all collected at once. The six thousand dollars a year was continued for missions, I think, for six years ; the rest was for the Seminary and the school. I then went down to Washington, and called on General O. O. Howard, who was very glad to see me. He was at the head of the Freedmen's Bureau. I showed to him the resolutions of our Diocesan Convention, and told him of Mr. Trenholm's and my selection of the Marine Hospital, and that as it had been condemned, and we wished to get the government to sell it, that I had nearly five thousand dollars towards its purchase. He took me to the White House to see President Johnson, introduced me, and told the President my object. The President listened very attentively, and turning to General Howard, said : '' This is the pleasantest thing I have heard from the South. I told you so. Let these gentlemen alone ; they will do the right thing. Yes sir ; get a bill through Congress authorizing the sale of the Marine Hospital and I will sign it.'' Then taking up his check-book he filled out a check for a thousand dollars and said, '' That is my subscription towards its purchase.''

General Howard undertook to frame the bill, and had it

passed. The President signed it, and the building was ordered sold. I telegraphed Mr. John Hanckel to buy it for me. No one supposed it would sell for more than our first bid of one thousand dollars, but Mr. Yates, the Seamen's Chaplain, who was very much disconcerted at the sale of the Marine Hospital, bid on it and ran it up to nine thousand eight hundred dollars. Hanckel's mettle was up, however, and he was determined to have it. It was knocked down to him for me. He telegraphed me the amount ; I was staggered. However, I went to General Howard, and told him the situation, and somehow between the Freedman's Bureau and the Treasury, they arranged it so that a deed of gift was made in trust to me, Mr. George A. Trenholm, and Mr. Bennett, a colored man. The only condition they added was that there should be no restriction to anyone in using the advantages of the institution on account of color, race, or previous condition, the Board to be self-perpetuating. The money I had collected at the school was to go for repairs and furniture.

I then returned to New York, and again Doctor Littlejohn used his influence, and brought me before the Board of what was called the Protestant Episcopal Commission to the Colored People of the South. This time I was successful in rousing some enthusiasm, for it was a new work, and I went into the subject inspired by my success in getting the building. I remember how I was plied with questions, and how I answered them all with the most direct frankness. Rev. Dr. A. H. Vinton was most particular in his interrogatories. The result was the Board was determined we should have six thousand dollars a year for the colored school, provided that, as principal, a white man from the North should have charge. To this I assented. The building was repaired, the furniture was procured and the school was opened with a roll of eighteen hundred colored children. I selected fifteen Charleston ladies, and gave them five hundred dollars apiece salary and kept the school going for four years, when the facilities for the education of the colored children in Charleston exceeded those of the white, under the city common school system, and as the interest flagged in the North, the appropriation fell off, and I turned the children over to the city's care. Thus, at the suggestion of the Bishop, by virtue of the resolutions passed in the Diocesan Convention, the first large school for colored children opened solely by the white people in the South, was here in the city of Charleston. When the school was closed, I turned the building over to St. Mark's congregation and we established a library, and a general meeting-place for instruction and amusement, which was kept up while I was rector of that church, but fell through and remained idle until 1895, when a Mr. Jenkins, a colored Baptist preacher, through the intervention of several of my white friends, obtained from me, the sole surviving trustee, a temporary lease for a colored orphanage, until such time as I hoped the city would take the matter in hand, when I could make such disposition to them as the trust allows. I have printed in the appendix an article which appeared in the *Messenger*, on October 19, 1896, the paper of the colored people, printed at the Colored Orphanage.*

While I was at the North I had studied the papers very carefully, and, as the result, I wrote to Mr. George A. Trenholm, saying I was sure the next move would be to give the ballot to the negro, and I begged him to get a dozen leading men together, and create a public sentiment on the subject. It would be well, I said, if the negroes, when they could read, write, and cipher, and owned five hundred dollars in real estate, should have the suffrage given them by the South. This arrangement would be an incentive to education, to thrift, and to economy. If,

* See Appendix C.

on the other hand, they received the suffrage from the North, as well as their freedom, it would involve troubles innumerable. If we moved first, it would forestall hasty, ill-considered action on the part of the North. Mr. Trenholm wrote me he agreed with every word, but begged me to be very careful how I expressed my views.*

* During my visit at the North, and in the course of all the work I have related, some caustic critic wrote a very severe article in the Charleston paper, attacking me for all the work I was doing at the North. The paper was sent to me, and being of course very indignant, I wrote a reply and sent it to Mr. Trenholm, whose cooler judgment withheld it, and he with others replied to my vituperator and quite silenced him. I never found out the name of my critic. The record I have made is strictly accurate, and the reader can judge how far I was deserving of attack. On my return South I paid the Bishop $5500 for the Theological Seminary, which was kept open as long as the fund lasted, and was then closed. I collected for purchase and repairs of Marine Hospital as a colored school, $6300, and obtained a grant of $6000 a year for four years for running expenses, and $6000 a year for six years for Missions in the Diocese of South Carolina. It does not strike me, looking back, that my mission to the North was an unsuccessful one.

15

CHAPTER XXV

A KIND PRESIDENT

How I obtained Mr. Trenholm's Pardon

PRESIDENT ANDREW JOHNSON, having required certain persons to ask for a pardon before they could be restored to citizenship, and their property recovered, none of the Cabinet officers of the Confederate States had then complied with his conditions and been pardoned. One night, therefore, during the winter of 1866, being at Mr. Trenholm's house, I said to him, that if he would ask for a pardon, I was sure I could get it for him.

He had been Secretary of the Confederate States. Mr. Trenholm flatly refused to ask for a pardon.

"I have done nothing of which I am ashamed," he said, "and have committed no offence for which to ask Mr. Johnson's pardon. I will not do it."

"Well," I said, "will you write me a letter telling me your views, as to what the duty of the Southern people is, what you think will be, and what ought to be, the course of the United States government?"

"That," he said, "I will do with great pleasure; but I do not know of what avail it will be."

He wrote the letter, and it was a masterly production, as was everything from his pen. Gen. Daniel Sickles

was then in command of Charleston. He was not popular
with our citizens, but I had a purpose, so I called on him
with this letter of Mr. Trenholm's, and told him I wished
him to recommend his pardon, which was essential to the
welfare of the city and State. Men like Mr. Trenholm
should be able to resume business.

General Sickles read the letter carefully, commented on
its strength and elegant diction, and said he would return
it to me the next day. But that afternoon he sent an
orderly on horseback with a note to me, and the letter
most enthusiastically endorsed. I went to Mr. Trenholm's house that night, and told him that I was going to
the North the next day, to get his pardon. I did not tell
him of General Sickles's endorsement.

When I reached New York, I went to Doctor Littlejohn, and asked him to sign the petition for Trenholm's
pardon, and to get Mr. A. A. Low and three or four other
Republican gentlemen of influence to sign it. Doctor
Littlejohn kept the paper two or three days, and returned
it to me signed, with his name, and that of Mr. Low, Mr.
Pierrepont Edwards, Mr. Cyrus Curtis, and one or two
others. I happened to see in the morning's paper that
Gen. O. O. Howard was to dine that day at five o'clock
with Mr. Chittenden in Brooklyn. I went over, and sent
my card to the General, and he came down at once, leaving
the dinner-table to meet me. I apologized for the intrusion, but asked his endorsement of this paper.

" I am always glad to oblige you," he said, and after
reading the paper added his name to it. Thus fortified, I
took the evening train for Washington.

Next morning I went to the White House, and in the
lobby I met Mr. J. B. Campbell, a prominent lawyer from
Charleston.

" What are you doing here ? " he asked. " Come for a
pardon ? "

" No," I said; " I am too insignificant a personage to need one.   I have come to get Mr. Trenholm's pardon."

" Go home," he said.   " Your attempt is a waste of time ; I have been here three weeks and can't get it," and we separated.

The President was not approached then through a private secretary, but a porter at the door let in the callers. I saw this, and approached the man, but it was no use. I sat by him, however, and set about to ingratiate myself with him, but he would not take my card in.   At dark I went to the hotel to eat my dinner.   I had not tasted a thing all day.   General Howard was in Brooklyn, and I knew no one of influence in Washington.   Next day I found out that the porter was fond of a cigar, so I gave him one after another of some fine cigars I had, and by this bribery and corruption secured his promise to take in my card.   He at last opened the door, and I walked in, but there were a dozen persons in waiting, and one by one they went up to the President.   The President was very gruff to some.   Suddenly Secretary Stanton came in, and he and the President went off into an adjoining room. I thought, it is all up with me to-day ; all the other visitors seemed to think so, too, for everyone left, and I was left alone.   I sat on the sofa and waited.   There was loud and stormy talking in the room where the Secretary and President were, and presently the Secretary passed through the room with flushed face.   The President followed, and seeing me, he asked, in the roughest manner, " What do you want ? "

" A pardon, Mr. President."

" For whom ? "

" For Mr. George A. Trenholm, late Secretary of the Treasury of the Confederate States."

" Ah," he said, " and what are you doing with such a paper ? "

" Mr. Trenholm, sir," I answered, " has been as a father to me, and I am his pastor."

" Then, sir, you are the proper person to be here ; but there is a set of sharpers who are making money out of this pardon business. I have just recalled eighteen from South Carolina, which I find were costing money to the pardoned. I mean them to get it without paying for it."

As he was talking, he was looking over the paper I had handed him, and his eye rested on General Howard's name. Looking at me, he said, " How did you get General Howard's name on this paper ? "

Knowing that a man who has given his check for one thousand dollars does not often forget it, I said: " Mr. President, you see so many persons you have forgotten me. But General Howard introduced me to you ; you signed the bill for the sale of the Marine Hospital, and you gave me your check for one thousand dollars towards its furniture."

His manner changed in an instant. He extended his hand, and said, " Call in the morning early." Turning to the porter, he added, " Admit this gentleman alone, and the first one in the morning."

I gave the man at the door a tip, and went away quite delighted.

I was at the President's door at eight A.M. the third day. At nine I was admitted. The President met me very cordially, saying : " I must apologize to you for my brusqueness last night. I had not had a glass of water all day, I was tired out, and had just held an unpleasant interview. I have read the paper and have signed the pardon, and it has given me the greatest pleasure to do so." He then called his son Robert, and told him to go with me, and to show me the offices in rotation, to which I was to go with the paper, which the President wished attended to at once. Notwithstanding the President's directions to his son, it was nearly five in the evening before I got the last signature and seal on the pardon, and I walked back to Willard's Hotel triumphant.* I told Mr. Trenholm before leaving I would not communicate with him until the pardon was procured, and if it was, I would telegraph, " All right." As I was going up to the telegraph office in the hotel, I again met Mr. Campbell. " You still here ? " he said.

" Yes, but I am going home to-night."

" I told you it was a waste of time ; you can't get it."

" No," I said ; " I cannot get again what I have already obtained."

" What do you mean ? " he said.

" I mean that I have Mr. Trenholm's pardon, and if you do not believe me, suppose you look at it," and I handed him the document. He took it and read it, folded it up and returned it to me, and said, " How did you get that ? "

I replied : " That, sir, is my business, not yours. Certainly by no aid from you."

I accordingly telegraphed Mr. Trenholm, and left for home in the eleven o'clock train. I need scarcely say with what grateful welcome I was greeted by that household next day.

I do not think it is apparent in this record of the years '65, '66, or '67, that I was carrying the burden of a great sorrow. The death of our son had thrown a shadow over life's pathway; the sunlight did not seem so bright, nor the flowers so fair. Very few were the days or nights, that sometime I did not give way, but never before anyone excepting my wife, who felt as keenly as I did, but was braver and stronger than I was. Many a night had

* Mr. Trenholm's letter with those endorsements is in the archives of the government.

she heard a sob from the depths of my heart, and she would gently rebuke me.

" Husband, is that right ? Are you not afraid that you are murmuring, and that leads to rebellion ? "

" No, wife, I bow, but my heart seems broken, and I cannot help it. The world shall not see my grief, and I try to keep it from you, but you read me so thoroughly that I can hide nothing from you." I believe that God's loving providence had given me all the work of these two years, and added to me grace and strength in mercy and love, so that I was taken out of myself.

It was only in my quiet hours that the realization of our loss oppressed me, and on the 25th of October, 1867, about two o'clock in the afternoon, I started out on my usual pilgrimage to his grave. It was a fine, bracing, autumnal day, and too early for frost ; everything was green, and all nature was beautiful. Magnolia Cemetery is two miles from Charleston, and as I walked thither, I had not the faintest conception that I was approaching the crisis of my life. When I arrived at my destination, as there was no other person in the cemetery but myself, I knelt on the grave, and prayed for absolute submission, resignation, and comfort. As I was thus kneeling on the mound, my head buried in my hands, I wept bitterly; how long I cannot tell. Suddenly I heard a voice saying to me, in distinct, articulate tones, " Stop grieving for the dead, and do something for the living."

I say, articulate ; for, though there was no audible sound, yet I heard as distinctly as if someone had spoken, the words quoted—so distinctly, that I raised my head to see who had intruded upon the privacy of my grief. No one was visible, the sun was shining bright, the sky was cloudless, the birds were singing in the trees. The impression was so strong that I had been spoken to, that I said aloud, " What can I do for the the living ? " Again

I heard the same voice saying, "Your child is enjoying what you are only hoping for; but see his young companions who are mostly poor orphans without churches or schools. Take them and educate them."

"Educate other people's children," I said to myself, "when I scarcely know how I am to educate my own?"

I had fifty cents in my pocket, and was uncertain where the next was to come from, but I became conscious of an influence upon me such as I had felt once before, when I passed that night which determined me to give myself to God, and to serve in the ministry. I was four hours at that grave alone with God, for I have not the shadow of a doubt that the spiritual world had enfolded me, and as I talked aloud I seemed to be answered, and heard my child's dying words, "O Lord, save Thy people, and bless Thine heritage."

The warm reception I had lately received at the North, suggested the thought that if they had so readily helped the colored school, would they not also help to educate the white children?

I knelt upon my child's grave, and used these words, "Heavenly Father, if this is from Thee, give me wisdom, give me zeal, give me continuity of purpose, and open the hearts of people to me, and I will do it ; but if it is only a fleeting enthusiasm, let it pass away as a morning cloud, for Jesus' sake."

Reader, I have never shed a tear for that child from that day to this. There never has been a day since that he has not been in my thoughts, but the glorious work that he has done on earth by his prayers in Paradise has made me look upon him not as gone but as waiting for me. The sun went down as I rose from my knees, and I could not walk fast enough to get home, but ran a great part of the way.

As soon as I reached the house, I lit a five-cent tallow

dip, in a ten-cent tin candlestick, and took it into my un-furnished front room down-stairs. I then called my wife. We went together into this large empty room, darkness made visible by this one candle on the mantlepiece, and I put my arm around her waist, and told her what had oc-curred at the grave of our child. I told her that I had never thought of such a work till that hour, that I had no training to keep a school, and no money to begin it with, but if she were willing to give up the rent of the house in Ashley Street, that six hundred dollars a year would be a start. It did not take her a moment to decide. Throwing her arms round my neck, and looking up into my face, she said : " If God has given you a work to do, go and do it. Certainly, give up the rent of the house. I never expected, as your wife, to have to do this, but if you will go in debt, and furnish the chambers that the Freedmen's Bureau people stripped, we will take boarders to feed us."

" But you cannot do it," I said. " You are too feeble ; it is as much as I can do to keep you alive now."

" Am I not your wife ? " she answered. " You will re-quire strength to do your part, and cannot God give me strength to do mine ? " We both sank on our knees, consecrated ourselves to our work, and asked God's bless-ing. There was more light than the candle's in that room ; it was illumined by the Spirit of God. He saw the sacrifice she made ; it was all the living we had, and he accepted it ; and to my wife, not to me, the Church and the State are indebted for all the glorious work that has been done these thirty years.

I sent a circular, addressed it to each clergyman in the State, and, where there was no clergyman, to the lead-ing layman, asking them to give me a list, first of orphans, of widows' sons, of motherless boys, or of boys whose parents were alive, but unable to send them to school. I then notified my tenants that at the end of the month I would need the house in Ashley Street, which I had hitherto rented at fifty dollars a month.   I next went round and begged odds and ends of furniture, crockery, clothing, and table-linen, until I had sufficient to begin on.   I told Mrs. John Bryan, the widow of my old friend, I would need a matron; and for a home and her food, but no salary, she agreed to take charge.   I then looked around for a principal for the school, and selected Mr. John Gadsden, who had a school of a few boys in Summerville.   I told him I could not guarantee a salary, but would pay him as soon as I could.   When he accepted I went to grocer, baker, and butcher, and told them I had paid eight thousand dollars for my house before the war, and I could probably sell it for three thousand, now that my wife had renounced her dower, and if I found I was running in debt, I would sell the house and pay them.   Somehow everyone I approached seemed to catch the spirit that was in me, and to feel they must help a thing which was begun in so remarkable a manner.

There was a Federal officer at the citadel, who heard of my intention and he sent me word that there were one hundred iron bedsteads at the citadel, which had been condemned, but were not too bad to be used.   If I wanted them, he would present them to me.   Of course I was grateful.   I used those bedsteads for twenty-five years, and passed them over to the colored orphanage at the Marine Hospital last year.

In the meanwhile, responses to my circulars literally poured in upon me.   One letter was particularly touching. It was from a widow, in Walterborough, South Carolina, who said that Sunday as it was, she was compelled to write.   She had just returned from church, where she heard the circular read by the rector.   Up to that moment, the cloud that overshadowed her had been impenetrable ; it seemed as if God had forgotten her. She appeared, at least, forsaken; but that circular had opened the cloud, and let in upon her a ray of light, which had come from the Throne of God into her darkened heart. She had a fine boy, fifteen years old, whom his father before he died had taken through Cæsar, but now his education had been stopped, and there had been no earthly hope for him. But now my circular had changed all this, and she was going to send him whether I would take him or not.

CHAPTER XXVI

EDUCATIONAL NEEDS OF THE SOUTH

The ravages of the war in Southern States affected the cause of education—This was especially the case among the upper classes—My work was to remedy this condition of things— I open a day school for 425 boys and 125 girls—My boarding school accepts 33 boys—I advise my boarders how they should behave—A good remedy for coarseness and obscenity —Mr. Wilkins Glenn of Baltimore assists me.

I DID not feel that my mission was to rescue *gamins*, who were no poorer than before the war, but the entire wealth of the State had been swept away, and all schools existing in 1861. The mere youth, the seed corn, as Mrs. Jefferson Davis called them, had been taken into the army, and for four years had not been at school. In fact, no schools had been opened, and if they had been no one had money to pay for schooling. The wresting of our slaves from us, involved the depreciation of our land ; railroads had been destroyed, banks had failed, factories we had none ; insurance companies had all failed. There was, therefore, no source of income, and the most calamitous result was the inability to educate our children. I aimed to save for the Church and the country at large the representative families of the State. I realized that the youths from the army, now grown to be men, were most of them descended from a long ancestry, and that their class was in danger of degeneracy, through illiteracy or, perhaps, obliteration. I admit that there is no such thing as an aristocracy in a republic, but there are grades of society, and unhappy is that land which has no educated, cultured class. If everything is on a low, dead level, then ignorance and deterioration are inevitable, and, as my circular said, I was prepared to give the preference to my own church people, although quite ready to consider applications from any Christian denomination. After careful selection from among the older boys who had sent in applications, I agreed to take thirty-three, as soon as I was ready, and among them the widow's son, Josiah B. Perry.*

I began at once making arrangements for the opening of the Home for the country boys, and this took more time than it takes to tell about it, for I had to accommodate the thirty-three boys whom I had consented to take. In the course of these preparations it occurred to me that I might utilize the schoolhouse in full, and add a day-school which would only involve additional teachers. I probably could procure some who were idle, trusting me to pay when I could. At that time no large common school for whites had been opened—the common-school buildings having been appropriated by the Freedmen's Bureau, and several large schools were in operation for the colored children. I therefore consulted Mr. Trenholm, and he urged me to open the school, which I accordingly did. Teachers were engaged on my terms, and

---

* He was fitted for college, and obtained in time a scholarship at Trinity, Hartford, where he graduated creditably. Subsequently he studied law, but after a year or two of practice took Holy Orders, and is now the successful rector of St. Andrew's Church, Washington, D. C.

at the Church of the Holy Communion, on the 9th day of December, 1867, after a full service, and addresses by Bishop Davis and myself, the day-school was formally opened, with four hundred and twenty-five boys, and one hundred and twenty-five girls. I charged fifty cents a month for tuition, but such was the poverty of the people, that from the day-school and the thirty-three boys in the Home, I received in ten months just three hundred and sixty-eight dollars. I moreover gave out eight hundred dollars' worth of books, for which I received no more than one hundred dollars in return. Scribner & Co. supplied me, and generously made the school a present of the four hundred dollars balance which the school owed on this amount. On the 21st of March, 1868, the first boy came to the Home, the orphan son of highly respectable parents, a child who gave sad evidence of the degenerating effects of poverty. I wondered whether his was the condition to which all our country boys had fallen. I had been called of God none too soon.

Within a week the thirty-three boys were all in the Home, where they stayed until August. When the first five boys arrived, I took them into my study and said to them : " Now, boys, you have come here to be my sons. Your circumstances are such that you will be my guests. There is no money to be made out of you. You are here to study, and to take advantage of this great opportunity. Your spiritual mother, the Church, has opened her arms to shelter you, and to lead you on the way of life." I charged these boys never to allow anything improper or indecent in the school. I told them I expected them to attend to this.

" The boy," I added, " who writes or draws anything improper on the walls needs cleansing, and although you cannot make him clean within, you can externally. Take every such boy, therefore, to the pump, and wash him well. When I hear you have done this, I will dismiss him from the school." *

The school was opened in December, but up to the middle of March in the following year I had received little or no money. My expenses were running on, and no salaries or bills had been paid. Things looked desperate, but neither my faith nor my courage failed me. The firm conviction that God had given me this work sustained me, and how much I bore from doubting, discouraging friends whose want of sympathy produced want of confidence in my success, only God knows. How many earnest prayers went up to heaven, how many sleepless nights and waking hours of anxiety were passed, only He can count ! After the boys had all come to the Home, and everything was organized, I felt that God required of me to make personal exertions to carry out His will, by providing material means for this important work. Not knowing whither I should go, I started North, my objective point being Baltimore, where I knew there was great interest felt in the South. Although I knew none of the clergy, I called on Rev. Dr. Milo Mahom, rector of St. Paul's Church, and he invited me to stay with him. I had with him the same experience I had with Doctor Littlejohn in 1866. We talked till the early hours of the morning. What a glorious man he was ! He had a

---

 * Some years after this Mr. William Cullen Bryant, while visiting the city, called on me. He addressed the boys, and I afterwards told him how successful I had been, for in seven years I had never had to discharge a boy for obscenity. Turning to the boys I asked if they had ever ducked any one? I was somewhat taken aback by the general laugh and their emphatic, Yes ! They had, it seemed, ducked three, who had begged so hard not to be betrayed to me, as they would then have to leave, and had promised so earnestly never to offend so again, that I had not been informed of the duckings. There was a general laugh at my expense, but after such a record I was willing to endure the laugh.

splendid mind, and a heart surcharged with sympathy. He wept that night like a child as he read the pathetic appeals contained in the letters which had responded to my circular.

" Now," he said, " go into my pulpit to-morrow morning, and tell the story just as you have told it to me."

I did so. I will never forget that Sunday. It was soon after the war, and all hearts there were tender towards our people, and South Carolina in particular. The Spirit gave me utterance on that occasion ; men were not ashamed to wipe their eyes and many women sobbed. It had not been announced that there was to be a collection, but eight hundred dollars were found in the plate, and checks came next day, and it went at once to Charleston, where it caused unspeakable joy. Mr. Wilkins Glenn, a member of the congregation, then owned and was editor of the *Baltimore Gazette*, and after an interview with me, devoted several columns, day after day, in the *Gazette*, to me and my cause, and proposed to form an association to assist in carrying on the work. I stayed five weeks in Baltimore, preaching at Emanuel Church and St. Luke's, and obtained one thousand dollars from these churches, besides what was given at St. Paul's. Day after day I went through the snow from house to house—we had five snowstorms during my stay—but I returned to Charleston with sufficient to relieve my most pressing necessities.

I had scarcely reached home when I received a telegram from Mr. Glenn requesting me to return to Baltimore, which I did. Mr. Glenn had been to New York and had interested Hon. Clarkson N. Potter, Mr. Charles O'Connor, Mr. William B. Apppleton, Mr. J. S. Thayer, Mr. William B. Duncan and others, who had agreed to assist in placing me on a firm basis. Mr. Glenn called a meeting of influential gentlemen in Baltimore, who organized a society with Mr. Samuel G. Wyman as its President, and this society pledged me six hundred dollars a month, for three years. I started back for Charleston, but was stopped in Washington by Rev. Dr. Pinkney, afterwards Bishop of Maryland. He took me to his warm heart and asked me to tell my story to his people. His people, he told to show their love to him, by listening to what I had to say, responding to the extent of their ability. This they did generously, and I thus obtained money enough to pay up every debt, and to carry me to the end of the year.

The pledge of the society organized by Mr. Glenn was fulfilled, and I ended the first year out of debt, having had over five hundred children in the day-school and thirty-three living in the Home. These latter I had for the most part clothed as well as fed and educated.

There is a record of thirty years still of this biography, in which there is much to tell of the wonderful providence of God, His Presence, and Hand in the life of this institution. It will be seen how He has used one means after another to make me realize that His hand has guided, His voice has counselled. Was it a fanatical dream at the grave of my child or was it the ca'l of God? I went to that grave without one thought of a school, surrounded as I was by desolate poverty. To build up a great charitable institution then and there seemed as preposterous as to project a great cathedral in the Desert of Sahara, without one co-operator, and with no materials. Yet the record of this one year begins a series of events, as the story will unfold, of which I wish to take a reasonable view. I believe in the miracles recorded in Holy Scripture; I believe that God is the same Being now, and that if each man would ponder His paths we all would find miraculous interpositions in our behalf. But God works by human means. Through a series of years and events He had been training me for the mission of my life. When the time had come, and all the conditions were

16

favorable, He gave me my commission, and led me into the positions favorable to the necessities of the work, and then required me to use all the ability with which He had endowed me. He required me to work as though it all depended on me, while He made that work successful, or thwarted it, as in His wisdom He had seen best. If my experience can strengthen one failing heart, and encourage it in energy, patience, waiting, endurance, and faith, this narrative will not be written in vain. If I can make any heart realize that our Father is not far off, but nigh, that His hand is stretched out still, and His ear open to our prayers, if I have comforted some soul, and helped someone to cling closer to God, I shall have magnified the grace of God, and this will be my exceeding great reward.

CHAPTER XXVII

"THE LORD'S BOX"

*My method of appealing to the honor of boys—An incident
testifying to its success —" The Lord's box " —Jewels
among the lowly—My public work outside of the school—
My " Romish " tendencies—A very practical rebuke.*

THE association in Baltimore, through Mr. Glenn,
continued to send to me, each month, the six hundred dollars promised, but it was not near enough to meet
expenses, and I therefore went on in November, 1868, to
New York. The introductions given me by General
Howard, and the friends I had made in 1866, assisted me
very much. While in New York I saw the advertisement
of the sale of a building in the rear of the Church of the
Holy Communion, Charleston. As only a fence divided
the yard from my house, which held but thirty-three, and
as the terms on which the house was to be had were one
third cash, and the balance in three years, I prayerfully
considered the purchase of it, and telegraphed to a friend
to buy the house, if it did not exceed five thousand dollars.
I did not have a cent when I received a telegram to the
effect that the house had been purchased in my name for
five thousand one hundred and fifty dollars, and I must
pay seventeen hundred dollars as soon as the papers were
made out. I went round at once to see my dear friend,

243

Mr. John David Wolfe, and told him all my plans. He was a man whose ear was ever open to every story of work for the glory of God and the good of men. He scattered of his abundance through the land, and though dead, he yet liveth in the institutions he fostered and founded. After patiently hearing my story, he said, " You are as bad as the bishops,—a regular stand-and-deliver man."

Then, turning to his desk, he wrote a check for one thousand dollars, and said, " If you are good for anything, you can soon raise the other seven hundred dollars. Go and see Stuart Brown and Mr. Aspinwall, and if they do not help you, come back to me."

The seven hundred dollars was collected that day, and the amount was remitted to Charleston, and by the time the rest was due, it was all paid by the generosity of my Northern friends. Mr. Wolfe continued to be my generous friend, and gave one thousand dollars every year, until he died, and after his death his daughter, Miss Catherine L. Wolfe, continued her father's subscription until she died. How I have missed them !

I was spending an evening at Mr. Wolfe's, and an old lady was there, Mrs. Spencer. I did not know at the time she was his sister. Mr. Wolfe told her all about me, from his first acquaintance, when he found me at the meeting of the Board of Missions in 1866, and he enlarged on my present work. Mrs. Spencer asked me if this was something that was to be, or if it was now in existence. Of course I told her it was now in being. She then left the room, and when she was going away from the house, she handed me an envelope. In it was a check for five hundred dollars, which she renewed yearly until she died.

When I began the school, I placed my boys on their honor, and told them that there would be no espionage, and in thirty years, having had over three thousand under

my charge, I have seldom known my confidence abused.
The following incident is illustrative of the tone of the institution:

Two of my oldest boys had been given tickets to go to
the theatre, and the principal permitted them to go and
waited for their return. When they came in they were
under the influence of liquor. This was on Friday night,
and on Monday Mr. Gadsden told me of it. I said he
must leave the matter to me to manage, and during the
day I stayed about the premises, treating those young
men as if I were not cognizant of their misdemeanor. On
Tuesday morning after service, these two boys came to
me in the vestry-room, and under great embarrassment
stated the case. The night was very cold, they said, and
they had gone into a saloon, and each had taken one
drink, and being unaccustomed to the use of ardent
spirits, they had been overcome. They said they did not
feel at their age (one was nineteen and the other twenty)
they had done so great a wrong in taking a drink. The
wrong was going to a bar-room at all ; it was a breach of
confidence. This was their error, and they feared they had
lost my respect, and they were willing, they said, to submit to any punishment I was prepared to inflict. They
implored me not to expel them. I asked them if this con-
fession was of their own volition. They replied, "Entirely." I asked if the offence would be repeated by them.
" Never," they answered, " while we continue under your
charge."

Then I said, " Young men, your offence is as fully forgiven as it is freely confessed ; I will never refer to it
to you again."

They pressed my hand ; the big tears rolled down their
cheeks ; their hearts were too full for words ; everything
was gained, and until they finished at the school those
young men were patterns. I think that is the way our

Father forgives sinners. In after years one of these young men came to see me, and, referring to this circumstance, said it was the turning-point of his life. Had I thrashed them, he said, they would have submitted, but probably would have despised me, but when I forgave them they loved me, and would on no account have again displeased me.

Two other incidents are worthy of note, and may be of use. I had preached one Sunday at Emanuel Church, Baltimore, and on the Thursday after my sermon, the rector, the Rev. Dr. Randolph, now Bishop of Southern Virginia, brought me six hundred and five dollars, saying, '' My brother, you will be thankful for these six hundred dollars, but here is a check for one hundred dollars which might have been one thousand dollars without inconvenience to the giver.'' Then he ran over the different amounts from various parties, and when he came to the five dollar bill, he said, '' This is the most precious of all ; it is the gift of a white washerwoman.'' He had remonstrated with her saying, she could not afford to give this much, but she replied, '' It is the Lord's, not mine.''

She had then told her pastor, '' As the gentleman preached, she became interested, and said, ' I will give him all that is in the Lord's box.' ''

It seems she had a box, which she called '' the Lord's box,'' in which she deposited a certain percentage of her gross daily earnings. As I went on, she added to her mental offering the receipts of the next three days ; she made three dollars, she found two dollars in '' the Lord's box,'' so added the two sums ; she brought the five dollars as her gift to the Orphans' Home. I asked to be permitted to call on this woman, but the rector said she would be hurt if she thought I had heard this story. Some six years after this, I had preached at St. Peter's, Eaton Square, London, of which Canon Wilkinson was the vicar.

Next day I was to dine at Brighton, and at the door I met a gentleman who was also to be a guest. He introduced himself, and said, " I heard your story last Sunday, and gave you all that was in " the Lord's box " and here is five pounds."

I asked him what he meant by " the Lord's box," and he gave me an account of his rule of life. It was the same as that of the Baltimore washerwoman. He was a dentist, and put a percentage of his gross receipts in " the Lord's box," and always had something to give. If every churchman did the same, how abundant would the treasure be at the Church's command.

Another incident in a different sphere of life. I once preached in Grace Church, Newark, New Jersey, of which the Rev. Dr. Hodges was rector. The next morning the friend with whom I was staying came into the rector's study, where I was, and, taking both my hands in his, said : " I thank you for coming here ; you have helped to form the character of my child. It is my custom when my daughters are seventeen to give them a watch, and at eighteen add a chain and such trinkets as they wish. My daughter reached eighteen last week, and I had told her to go to Tiffany and get whatever she wished. Last night she was much moved by your sermon, and begged me to give to you the amount her chain and trinkets would cost ; but I refused. I feared it was a sudden impulse and that she might regret it. I told her to sleep on it, and see how she felt next day." She had done so, but she had just come to him and said, " Do, Father, give Mr. Porter the full amount, and make it a great deal more."

He cautioned her that he would not give her the usual gift that year, if she thus gave it to me. She persisted, and her father did give me the amount and much more.

To anticipate. In 1874, I preached in the same church. The congregation was large, and after service I received

words of appreciation and sympathy from very many, but
that did not go far towards feeding a hundred hungry
boys, and paying for educating five hundred. The rector
gave me fifty dollars, his wife gave me a marriage fee
of ten, a Presbyterian lady sent me fifty, and a Southern
woman from Georgia, who happened to be present, sent
me twenty. Nothing else came from that large congregation in the way of substantial help ; but next day, when
I was leaving, a colored servant girl, who had come from
Augusta, Georgia, with her former owners, followed me
to the door, and slipped into my hand an envelope. " I
do not look for aid from you," I said. She replied : " May
I not do a little for your cause ? I love those Southern
people ; they were good and kind to me."

Of course I did not rebuff her, but took the envelope,
which contained a five dollar bill, rolled round a slip of
paper, on which was written by herself :

" We give Thee but Thine own,
    What e'er the gift may be ;
All that we have is Thine alone,
    A trust, O Lord, from Thee.

" May we Thy bounties thus,
    As stewards true receive ;
And gladly as Thou blessest us,
    To Thee our first fruits give."

Of all that congregation, only that humble servant was
found to show her faith by her works. I believe that act
has been written in a more important book than this.
Christ's jewels are often among the lowly ; let us not
despise a brother or sister of low degree.

In the year 1869, I was elected a member of the Standing
Committee of the Diocese of South Carolina, and have
been reëlected every year since (this is now 1897), with the
exception of three years, 1886 to 1889, during the intense

excitement in the diocese on the subject of the colored question, the position I had taken rendering me unpopular with the laity.

I was elected in 1870 as a deputy to the General Convention, and have been elected to every succeeding convention save the one held in Chicago ; I was still under the ban, but by 1889, the second solemn thought of the laity reversed it all, and since, some of those who were most opposed to me have become my warm friends.

I was elected in 1868 a trustee of the University of the South, and continued to be until 1886, when I declined a reëlection. I recall these facts only to show that the school which took up so much time did not withdraw me from the duties of the Church. I could write a long account of the condition and struggles of the early history of the University of the South ; what a very inefficient grammar school it was, and how, by the untiring efforts of Bishop Quintard, it was brought into new life.

The University of the South looms up now, in ever greater and grander proportions, the product of as much self-sacrifice, zeal, energy, and perseverance, as was ever spent on any human work.

My report to our Convention of 1869, says : " There are eighteen or twenty pupils there. Commander Maury declined the Vice-Chancellorship. General Gorgas was elected Vice-Chancellor. It is the day of small things with the Board, the grand designs of its projectors having faded into the distant future ; the heavy shadow which has fallen on all things pertaining to the South has not left this out in the sunlight of prosperity ; but a great idea never dies. This generation may only see the germ ; coming ages we trust will enjoy the blessings of the great thoughts, and high hopes, and zealous labors, of these masters in Israel, Bishops Polk and Elliott, and Otey and Cobb." Thus I wrote in 1869. There are bishops in the

Church who have graduated there since ; so that my prophecy has already been fulfilled. By referring to my parish register, I find that this busy year with the school was not an idle one in my parish. There were one hundred and thirty-seven communicants, thirty-eight baptisms, twenty confirmed, and that the parish contributed $6661 to church purposes. My salary, which had been a trifle in '67, was $1200 in '69. One Sunday in November I said to the congregation, that the hope I had of building a new church had perished, but that I greatly desired to improve the present church, and make room to bring my boys from the gallery on to the floor of the church. The next morning, before I had left my chamber, an architect and builder was sent to me by Mr. Theodore Wagner to find out what I wished to have done. Mr. Wagner promised that if my alterations were within bounds they should be made. Accordingly, we had the rear wall taken down, a recess made sixteen by thirty-five, to be used for the present as a chancel, and an organ chamber built for a new organ. The cost was three thousand eight hundred dollars, and Mr. Wagner paid for it. The vestry then sold the lot in Rutledge Avenue, that Mr. Trenholm had given for a new church, for the sum of three thousand dollars, and with this they took down the galleries and altered the roof of the church, adding twenty-five pews. Mr. John Hanckel presented a handsome stained-glass window. A marble altar and font were also presented with other chancel furniture. The vestry sold the old organ for six hundred dollars, and bought a new one for three thousand two hundred dollars, for which they borrowed the money. I think, considering this was four years after our terrible war, that it indicated much life and activity in the parish. About this time I discontinued the black gown to preach in. I had the pews arranged for the people to kneel toward the altar, and

not turn round towards the front door, as they had been
doing. I induced them to rise at the offertory, and introduced a change of colors in the hangings.

Captain Ramsey, of the United States army, who was
in command of the arsenal, I had induced the congregation to elect as a vestryman. He lost an only child, and
asked that he might place a memorial marble cross on the
super-altar, which I put there quietly. It was the first,
as were all these developments, in this diocese. One of
my parishioners, who was really a Congregationalist, from
which denomination he had come to the Church, was at
service one day, and found fault with all that we were
doing as Romish.

"Well," I said, "point out the marks." He mentioned the organ put by the chancel, the pews fixed so
that people must kneel forward, the marble altar, etc.
Finally he said, "Your dress shows your tendency." (I
had on a clerical coat and collar.)

"Well," I said, "how much are you giving for all
these changes?"

"Not a dollar; it is wasteful to be beautifying and
enlarging the church, when people are needing blankets
and food and clothes and shoes."

"Oh," I said, "I can accommodate you;" and taking
out of my pocket several lists, I said : "I always carry
these with me, for I am looking after all these things.
Here is a blanket list, and a garment list, and a shoe list
—all for the poor, and there are enough of them. On
which, or on how many of these lists will you subscribe?"
He would not subscribe to any. "Well," I said, "do
not find fault with those who are making these improvements, and have their names for small amounts on every
one of these lists. And now, about my clothes. That is
a personal matter; you are at liberty to wear any style
you please, and I claim the same privilege for myself, and

will not permit you or anyone else to regulate the cut of them.'' Poor man, if he is alive now, he would find in every church in Charleston everything done that was then being done in the Church of the Holy Communion in 1869.

CHAPTER XXVIII

THE WORK OF MY LIFE IS RECOGNIZED AND HELPED.

*I enlarge the home—New and old friends still help me—I
find a friend of my childhood in Governor Ligon—" Cast
thy bread upon the waters " — A reminiscence of my
mother's New Haven days—Mr. Charles O'Connor recognizes the statesmanlike character of my work—The class
of the refined and educated was to be saved to the South
through my efforts—Hence the support of outsiders.*

I SOON found that the home I had purchased was not
large enough, so I built an addition to it, which in
time was all paid for. I had agreed to take boys to fill it
to overflowing, which number, added to those who were
to live in the house my wife and I had given up, had
trebled my responsibilities. Relying on the pledge of the
society in Baltimore, I felt I had a nucleus to which I
might add the amounts which each boy could pay ; for
from the second year I had always required that each
should pay what he could, if it was only a barrel of
potatoes. The last week in September, 1869, I received
a letter from Mr. Glenn, of Baltimore, saying that circumstances would prevent him further aiding me. This
was a staggering blow; only my wife knew of this calamity. The school I opened as usual, but with a trembling,
anxious heart. Yet I believed I was doing the work that

God had given me, and He had been gracious to me. His resources had not failed, and He did not let my faith fail me. I left for Baltimore as soon as practicable, and some of the members of the association assured me that whatever others did, they would continue their assistance. I then went to New York; and I wish to place on record my gratitude for the uniform kindness, consideration, and affection even, with which I have been treated for thirty years by my Northern friends. Men and women of every political association, of different religious affiliations, and of different grades of society, have been kind and generous to me. I have never had manifested to me any bitterness towards the South. When it is remembered that I came from South Carolina, from Charleston, the hot-bed of secession, and frankly asked for aid for the sons of those who had been foremost in the strife, from those with whom they had fought, and that I was received with a warm welcome, and that through their generosity I have been sustained all these years, it is, indeed, to me marvellous. It evidences the power of the grace of God. I think my work is a testimony and a tribute to the goodness there is in human nature.*

From Baltimore I went, as I have said, to New York, where Mr. Wolfe, Mr. Low, Mr. Spencer, Mr. Aspinwall, Mrs. A. M. Minturn, Mr. Stuart Brown, Mr. J. W. Chanler, and others helped me. Mr. Wm. P. Clyde gave me groceries enough to carry me seven months. By the month of February I had run down to almost nothing, and things were looking very blue, when one day I received a telegram from Mr. Glenn telling me that it was important that I should come to Baltimore. I went, and if I here say that I believe that it was God's providence, I hope there will be none to regard me as a fanatic; but if this book is read, and it helps to make only one person believe

* See Appendix E.

in the precious truth of God's loving, special providence over His children, it will not have been written in vain.

Mr. Glenn told me that Mr. Caleb Dorsey had died, and had willed thirty thousand dollars to be distributed to those in need in the South ; that Governor Ligon had been left executor for the distribution of this sum, and that when I had been in Baltimore two years before, he had been struck by my Christian name, Anthony Toomer, which he had seen in Mr. Glenn's paper repeatedly, and had wondered who I could be. At that time he was not able to assist and therefore made no inquiries, but as soon as this fund was at his disposal, he asked Mr. Glenn to telegraph for me. I rode out to the Governor's residence with Mr. Glenn's introduction, and the Governor asked how I came by the name of Anthony Toomer I told him I was named after my great-grandfather and my grandfather ; the former an officer in the Revolutionary war. My mother's name was Toomer.

" Were you ever in New Haven ? " he asked ; " if so, when ? "

" In 1832 and 1833."

" How many brothers and sisters did you have, and what were their names ? "

I told him. He said, " Then I am right. You were that curly-headed little boy I used to ride on my horse. When I was in Yale College, your mother, who was a strikingly handsome woman, of most engaging and fascinating manners, and with a generous heart, was very kind to me, and it gives me great pleasure that I am able to show my appreciation of kindness, shown long ago, by now aiding your mother's son in his noble work." He drew a check for three thousand dollars, and handed it to me, saying, "You can use it for your own or your mother's needs, or in any manner you see fit." Of course it was given, every dollar of it, to the school. My mother was very glad that her bread cast upon the waters had come back to do so much good in later days.

Being in New York later in the season, I requested Hon. Clarkson N. Potter to introduce me to Mr. Charles O'Connor, who for three years had regularly subscribed to my work without meeting me face to face. Mr. O'Connor was a Roman Catholic, and I feared that he might not understand that I was an Episcopalian, and of course the boys were under that influence ; though there is no effort at proselytism made among Roman Catholics, Presbyterians, Methodists, Baptists, and Lutherans, who are taken care of as well as our own church boys. I brought this fact to Mr. O'Connor's notice, as I did not wish him, or anyone else, to give me one dollar under a false impression. Mr. O'Connor's reply was thorougly characteristic. " I know, sir, that you are an Episcopal clergyman, and if you are the man I take you to be, I have no doubt your boys will lean very much to that Church ; indeed, if you made them all good Episcopalians, I think you could make them some things a great deal worse." Mr. Potter and myself assented with a good laugh. " But," added Mr. O'Connor, " to be frank with you, it is not the religious aspect of your work which attracted me. Your aim has been to save a representative class of our fellow-citizens, which is relatively small everywhere, and we of the North cannot afford to lose that class in the South, any more than you at the South can lose that class at the North. I have regarded your action as that of a statesman, and a most beneficial political movement. For that reason I have helped and do now, (and he handed me a substantial check) and wish I could do more." He helped me until he died. How I wish, now, the broad-minded, substantial men, of whom there are still many, could see it likewise, for the work is just as essential now as **then, only it is so hard to carry it on.**

I was reading Franklin's autobiography recently, when I met the statement that the great revivalist preacher, Whitefield, who gathered money to build an orphanage in Savannah, Georgia, was accused by some miserable slanderer of appropriating the same to his own use, and Benjamin Franklin, of his knowledge of the man, vouches for his honesty. That was long ago, but human nature is the same in all ages, and an equally vile slander was sprung upon me. At the time, my wife and I were giving every dollar of our certain income to sustain the work ; were taking boarders to get money to live ; when many days I gave away the last dollar I had, without knowing where the next was to come from ; yet there was some poor soul so mean as to accuse me of making money out of my work. Of course such things are brought to your attention by well-meaning friends, and I traced it pretty surely to its source. It did me no harm where I was known, but it was spread from the same source in Baltimore, and did, not me,—for I was not living on the plane where such motives dwell,—but the work harm, and deprived me of the opportunity to assist many who needed help. It is very sad that men should live who are eager to impute wrong motives to good deeds. There is comparatively, so little self-sacrifice in the world that it is difficult for a great many to believe that there is not some ulterior purpose in an action, however benevolent it may be. But the good Lord has compassion on us all, and I am only sorry for such narrow-minded and limited souls. I have heard the same of others as of myself through the years, but dismiss the subject with free forgiveness to every traducer.

During the fall of 1869, I engaged from the State Normal School of Albany, New York, Mr. George W. Chaloner, who proved in time a very superior mathematical teacher. He was not in good health when he came to

us, but the Southern climate built him up and he lived
for fifteen years in my employ, when he died.   I brought
him from the North for two reasons.   Our young men at
home, owing to the war, had not received that systematic
education which alone qualifies one for an important position.   It is a great pity, indeed it is a great robbery, for
incompetent persons to attempt to teach.   They rob a
child of that which can never be given back, time and
opportunity.   Secondly, I wished to prove to my generous
Northern friends that in 1869 a Northern teacher could
come to the South, could teach, and be kindly treated by
the children of the best people of the land.   I never once
heard it urged against him, from first to last, that he had
come from the North.   He was a good teacher and I was
satisfied, so that ended it.   But Mr. Chaloner's coming
here is a fine illustration of how little some Northern
people understood or knew the South ; quite as little as
some Southern people understood or knew the North.   I
had the following statement from Mr. Chaloner himself.
Remember this was in 1869.   When he determined to
accept my offer there was a family meeting held, and by
every argument and persuasion he was besought to decline.   He would be murdered as surely as he came ; but
his health was poor, and he thought he would risk it
among the savages.   If he would go, they told him that
he must go armed ; so his trunk was loaded with a rifle
a pair of pistols, a dirk and a large knife, as well as
with plenty of ammunition, and he was urged to sell
his life as dear as possible.   When the parting came, it
was as with one going to sentence of death.   When he
arrived and was greeted and put to work, it did not gradually, but suddenly, burst upon him what a fool he had
been.   When he knew us as we are, he concealed his warlike arsenal, and never told me of it for some years, when
the ludicrousness of the whole thing convulsed him with

laughter. It was ludicrous, but it was sad. They were not the only people who thought this of us. Much of the legislation which has caused so much sorrow and loss to the people, sprang from this suspicion in the multitude, which designing politicians for years played upon to keep us apart. It has been wicked—it is wicked. There are thousands of good and noble people at the North and at the South, and it is lamentable how ignorant they have been of each other.*

* See Appendix F.

CHAPTER XXIX

CALUMNY AND REBUFF MEET ME

A calumny stops the flow of beneficence in Baltimore—The vicissitudes of my financial life—Reflections on God's providential care—I am roughly rebuffed by a friend of Dr. Muhlenberg—I give him a sharp lecture—He proves his repentance by a small gift.

IN October, 1870, we began the fourth year of our Home. I went to Baltimore in November, but found the doors unaccountably shut. I did not then know the calumny of which I had been made the victim, and to which I have before referred. Mr. and Mrs. S. G. Wyman, indeed, continued their aid, but I found it necessary to go on to New York ; but even there I found the task of collecting money was not easy. I was told it was a bad time to ask for help, but then, when has a poor beggar ever found it a good time ? How often one hears, what is undoubtedly true, that there are so many calls. And it seems to me we ought to be glad there are. We may not be able to give to all, but is it not an evidence that Christ's Spirit is working in the hearts and lives of so many, who, feeling the life of Christ in themselves, are trying to spread His Kingdom, trying to enlighten ignorance, to relieve suffering, to make the world brighter because they live in it ? What better use can be made of superfluous means than in helping those who have the capacity of using means for God's glory, and the opportunity, which, perhaps, the giver has not ?   Suppose there were not these calls, that no benevolent work was going on, that everything that is evil and deteriorating were left to work in human life, what would become of the world ?   If men acted on the belief that these things are in the masses, and it is best to leave them to themselves, how long would life and wealth be safe ?   On the low plane of self-preservation, we should thank God for the many calls, and respond favorably to as many as we have the ability to assist.

I remember one day during my visit to New York going with Mr. A. A. Low to Staten Island, to some celebration at the Sailor's Snug Harbor.   The meeting had gone on very well, and speeches had been made.   I had taken an obscure seat in the rear when Mr. Low began to speak, but I saw in the first few sentences that I was going to be called out.   I tried to hide but it was no use.   Mr. Low called me to the platform and I had to make a speech.   It was there I met Mr. W. H. Aspinwall, who greeted me warmly after the speech, and before we left handed me a check of a considerable amount for my work ; and he continued until his death to be an annual contributor.   Then his pious wife, a sister of the great J. Lloyd Breck, continued to be my generous friend until she died.   So much came of that invitation of my dear friend Mr. Low.

But I was sometimes terribly disheartened.   One day the Rev. Dr. Morgan, rector of St. Thomas's volunteered to give me a letter of introduction to one of his wealthy parishioners, who had just moved into a new house, newly furnished.   He appreciated the compliment of his rector in singling him out, and began to make excuses for not helping me, by telling me how much he had recently given,— thirty thousand to this object, five thousand to another, and four to another, and so on.   He estimated his recent

gifts at about forty thousand dollars. I deprecated his
giving his reasons for refusing me help. I was quite
ready, I said, to believe them good, and congratulated
him and his beneficiaries, and only regretted I was not
so fortunate as to be one of them. His conscience seemed
to be awakened, and he began to tell the conditions on
which each sum was to be given. They were such in each
case, I perceived, that his bank account had not been de-
pleted, nor was it in much danger. I learned on good
authority afterwards, that he did give five thousand of the
forty. My reflections as I left him were on the self-decep-
tion of the human heart ; how prone we are to cheat ourselves into believing we have done what we know we
ought to do.

During this visit to New York another great forward
movement was made ; it came about apparently very
naturally. I was dining with my friend Mr. Howard
Potter, brother of my early and long generous friend,
Hon. Clarkson N. Potter, who helped me until he died.
It so happened that the Rev. E. N. Potter, D.D., then
President of Union College, came in to dine. He had
happened in 1868 to sit behind me in the outskirts of the
General Convention, in New York, and he heard my comments on a speech which some idiot was making. Everything had been peaceable and lovely. It was the first
General Convention since the war, when all the South was
again represented, and all the Northern brethren had been
cordial and considerate. Then this young man, in spread-
eagle style, was just rubbing the fur of us all the wrong
way. Everybody was nervous ; there was apparent
agitation, and I was talking to Bishop Davis's daughter,
wishing that I could get hold of the man by the nape of
his neck, and throw him out of the window. Doctor Potter
seemed so much pleased with my remarks that he introduced himself. When Doctor Potter went home to his

charge in Bethlehem, he sent me, unsolicited, five hundred dollars, and a valuable box of clothing for my boys from his parish. So we were not strangers when we met two years afterwards at dinner at his brother's. He asked me if I had any boys ready for college. I said I had five, but I had no hope of sending them, as the provision at Trinity had failed me. He told me to send them to him, and that they should be no expense to me, save for their clothing. I afterwards learned that he proposed to provide for them at his own expense. One of those boys has been head master at the Porter Military Academy for several years. It will readily appear what an impetus this again gave to me and to my institution, and when it is stated that there has not been a year since that we have not had from five to ten boys, at one time twenty-six, either at Union College, Schenectady, or at Hobart College, Geneva, through the instrumentality of Doctor Potter, it will be seen what an invaluable benefactor Doctor Potter has been to the Church and to the State. Miss Catherine L. Wolfe, daughter of Mr. John David Wolfe, once told me she had given fifty thousand dollars to Union College to be invested, and the interest of that fund was to be used for the benefit of my boys. And while Doctor Potter was there it was so appropriated.

During the summer of 1870, I enlarged the schoolhouse by adding four rooms twenty by twenty, well ventilated and built of brick. I had no money at the time, but the rooms were a necessity, and I trusted in the goodness of God to assist me in paying for them. The cost was three thousand dollars. It took some time, but the debt has long since been paid. Should I record all the ways by which God has led me, this biography would be extended to undue limits, but I give two incidents only, by way of illustration.

I owed a bill of two hundred and forty-nine dollars and

fifty cents for kitchen utensils and other necessary articles. This had troubled me much, for I knew the parties had but little capital, and they had been very considerate in not pressing me. Indeed, this has been singularly true of all to whom I have owed money. Being in daily expectation of a demand on me, and not having been able to save the amount, I had made it a subject of earnest prayer. I was writing a sermon one Saturday afternoon, when the thought came suddenly in my mind, that the bill ought to be paid, and that perhaps there were letters in the Post Office containing money for me. There was no letter delivery then and no street cars ; of course I had no conveyance, so I walked a mile and a half to the Post Office, and found quite a number of letters for me. The first I opened was from the Rev. James Saul, of whom I had never heard. He stated that one of my circulars had been sent to him by a friend in New York a year before, that it had lain on his desk long enough, and now he enclosed a check for one hundred dollars for my work, if still in existence. The second was from the Rev. Dr. Pinckney of Washington, D. C. He wrote that he had one hundred and fifty dollars over what he needed for some certain object for which he had asked an offering, and he knew no work he would rather help than mine. This was just the amount I needed with fifty cents over. The bill was paid in a few minutes, and I gave thanks to God, and was cheered and encouraged by this manifestation of His care. To neither of these parties had I written ; indeed, one of them I had never heard of.

Oftentimes my work has been compared to that of Mr. Müller in Bristol, England. The difference is, his is far more extensive, and it rose up surrounded by the wealth of England. Mine rose in a desert, and has depended for help from those who had no special interest. He says he has never asked for aid save from God ; but he has annually written the story of his work, and scattered it by thousands of copies, and that is as much asking as by word of mouth. I have, however, literally laid this work before God, by day and by night, pleading that as I had not sought it, but He had given it to me, He would give me wisdom to do His will; and then I have worked as if it all depended on me, believing God required this of me. Often all my work is vain. If ever I have reason to expect results, and meet failure instead, God does not forsake me. Often when in direst necessity, in some way with which I have had nothing to do, help has come tiding me over the difficulty. Would it have come, if I had supinely sat down without exerting myself? If there were no self-sacrifice, no self-denial, no mortification of the spirit, could I prove that I was willing to do even if I suffered? I do not believe anything short of the most powerful convictions of duty, and the strengthening grace of the Holy Ghost, ever enables a man to undertake such a work. Sometimes I met with things hard to be endured. Cases like the following, I trust, are rare.

The Rev. Dr. Muhlenberg of blessed memory became very much attached to me, and one day while sitting with him in St. Luke's Hospital, he said : " I am going to give you a letter to an old man who can give you ten thousand dollars and he would n't miss it a moment ; I do not know whether he will give you anything, but give him a chance." For he certainly thought his letter would bring some aid. I called at the house Doctor Muhlenberg suggested. I told the servant, who wished to refuse me admittance, that I had a letter which I wished to deliver in person. I was ushered into a cheerless anteroom, and kept waiting for nearly half an hour before the master appeared. As he came in, in the most ungracious manner, he said, " Well, sir ? I have received your card. What is it ? What do you wish ? "

"To deliver you a letter from Doctor Muhlenberg."

He stood in the doorway and did not ask me to be seated, but took the letter most ungraciously. It was a large letter-size sheet, written on four sides. He glanced at a sentence or two, turned over the page, and then to the signature.

"Yes," he said; "this is Doctor Muhlenberg's hand-writing, and this is his signature, but—" crumpling it in his hand, he pushed it back into the envelope, and thrust it at me, saying: "there are so many impostors going about I cannot attend to it."

Utterly unprepared for so gross an insult, and feeling that I had done nothing to call it forth, I was naturally indignant, and my temper rose at once. I flushed, and grew pale, but I put my hands behind my back, and said, "That letter is addressed to you, not to me." I trembled with suppressed rage, but fortunately I had read the Book of Nehemiah that morning at my morning devotions, and Nehemiah flashed through my brain; how, before he answered the king's question, why he was of that sad countenance, he sent up a silent prayer for wisdom. I stood, accordingly, and looked at the man, did the same, and when at length I had full control of myself, I said: " I know, sir, in this great city of New York, there are a great number of unworthy persons who are going about. But for my own protection as well as yours, I presented that letter, which entitled me to politeness at least. Your insult is more to Doctor Muhlenberg than to me. Now, sir, if my personal appearance and my manners do not indicate the gentleman I belie my ancestry. But I have a message to you. I am a clergyman of the Church of which you are a member; my social position is as good as yours. I have been the rector of a prominent church for eighteen years, a member of the General Convention, and of the Standing Committee of my diocese, trustee of

the University of the South, and of the General Theological Seminary and Board of Missions. I should have been
elected Bishop of Africa by the House of Bishops, but for
the intervention of my Bishop, who said he would advise
me not to accept ; so that my position is established. It
is an apostolic injunction, ' Be courteous.' You may be
that, if you cannot be generous. Perhaps the next appeal
to you may be by some young man, as well introduced as
I am now, who, if he is met by you, as you have met me,
may go from your presence abashed and humiliated, and
may say, ' If this is the way I am to be treated, I will give
up the work.' And at your door will be laid at the great
day, some great work for Christ and His Church destroyed.
To save you from this, I must give you the Master's mind
on this subject. If, sir, you could call on Doctor Dyer,
who has visited me, you will find out whether I am an
impostor or not."

" Do you know Doctor Dyer ? " he asked.

" That is my privilege, and I count him my friend."

" I did not call you an impostor."

" No, sir ; you dared not ; but you classed me with
impostors."

" You Southerners are so high-toned and impulsive,"
he said.

" A gentleman, sir, whether from the North or South,
East or West, is always high-strung, and knows when he
is insulted."

I had been very bold before this old man, but so keenly
had I felt the indignity, that I was glad to seek an obscure
street to hide the traces of feeling which I knew must be
visible. I went back to the hotel, and shut myself up
until next morning, asking that God's grace would con-
quer the natural man, and give me strength to rise above
such unworthy conduct, if I had to meet any more of it.

A week after I met Doctor Muhlenberg, and he said,

" I heard about that visit ; you gave the best sermon that old man has ever heard. I have one hundred dollars for you from him."

I thanked him, but begged him to return it to the old man, as I declined to receive it.

" You must take it," the Doctor said.

" Some things cost too much, Doctor, and this is one of them."

The Doctor said, " You do not know what it cost that old man to give one hundred dollars, and you must take it."

" Well," I said, " it cannot go to my school ; that is God's work, and those who help it must do it for Christ's sake. I will take the one hundred dollars, and give it to twenty poor women."

" I do not care what you do with it, so you take it.

I am glad to say this is an exceptional case, and it is here recorded, not in malice, but to encourage some fellow-laborer to continue his work even in the face of insult or contumely. The good Lord sees it all and will recompense. Mr. W. P. Clyde renewed his gift of groceries, and I closed the year with a debt of sixteen hundred dollars, one thousand of it on the enlargement of the school-house, which had cost three thousand dollars. My son, Theodore Atkinson Porter, having finished at my school when only fifteen years old, I was unwilling to send him to college so young, and he was unwilling to remain in the school where he had graduated, so I sent him to London, Canada, to Dean Helmuth, but after six months I brought him back to New York,* and kept him at the

---

* He graduated in 1875, went with me to Europe, entered Berkley Divinity School, and was ordained Deacon by Bishop Williams, in 1879 ; remained in Connecticut at Pine Meadow for a year ; came home, and was ordained priest and made rector of the church in Sumter. Fourteen years ago I brought him to be my assistant

Anthon Memorial, until he was old enough to go to Trinity, Hartford. Mr. Clyde volunteered to bear his expenses through college.

at the Church of the Holy Communion and the Academy, and here he has been trained, I trust, to take up my mantle when God shall call me to lay it down. He married Kate Fuller in 1879, a devoted wife, and to me a blessed daughter; she died in 1893, leaving five children. He was married again in 1895 to Louise Salmon, by whom he has one son.

CHAPTER XXX

SCHOOL AND CHURCH FLOURISH

The good health of the school—I escape being made Bishop of Africa—I find the needs of the work met by many providential interpositions — The Church of the Holy Communion is at length enlarged and beautified—I introduce a surpliced choir—Not an innovation, but merely a revival of a past practice in Charleston.

IN 1871, the full school opened for the fifth year, but not until November, because of yellow fever. At the close of the last term we lost our first boy by death. This was William Cornish, son of the Rev. J. H. Cornish, of Aiken. His death was the result of carelessness in bathing, and eating unripe fruit. He was a communicant.*

* During thirty years there have been but five deaths in this institution (and not one of them in any way connected with ordinary disease). One from a congestive chill, one from organic affection of the heart, one from Bright's disease, one the effect of an accident which befell the pupil before he came to me, and one a case of country fever, developed three days after the boy's entrance. We have had but one case of typhoid fever, one of scarlet, a few of pneumonia, but no deaths. Taking the number that have been here I believe it is without parallel in the history of any school. It shows this is a healthy place ; it is evidence of medical skill and care ; but above all it manifests the watchful providence of God, who has spared me this trouble. I have known the time

I discovered accidentally this year that it was necessary for me to give closer attention to the personal purity and habits of the boys, and I consulted Bishop Howe as to my proper course. He told me if I had the wisdom and the tact for this side of the work, I would indeed be a benefactor and he would stand by me. I have carefully and prayerfully given close attention to each individual boy from that day to this, with very remarkable success, and I have piles of letters received from many who have been my pupils, thanking me for the care and counsel I had given them, and expressing gratitude that they had been physically, as well as mentally and spiritually, saved, by my fearless and faithful dealing with them. I am confident from wide experience, that boys often go wrong simply from the neglect of fathers and friends.

During the summer of 1871, I had been compelled to give my note to two parties, one for ninety-eight dollars, and one for one hundred and ninety-nine, for the school, and I did not know how I was to meet them. While attending a man with yellow fever, I was taken sick at his bedside with a sympathetic fever. Having once had the yellow fever myself, I was not very liable to a second attack.

The General Convention was then sitting in Baltimore, and it was the first time I was privileged to go as a deputy. The Rev. W. B. W. Howe was to be consecrated Assistant Bishop of South Carolina, so I left my sick-bed and went to Baltimore, not being able to provide for my notes, but having told the parties I would use every effort to meet them. When I reached Baltimore I found the attention

when there was scarlet fever of a virulent type, and diphtheria in every one of the four streets which surround this square, and not a single case here, while we have often had measles and mumps, and less dangerous and fatal diseases. I ascribe to God's goodness, not our merits, this wonderful exemption.

of the Church was taken up with the General Board of
Missions, Domestic and Foreign, the Missionary Bishops,
the Indians, the Chinese, and the Africans, and that was
no place for me to present the needs of the white people
of the South. I therefore kept my needs to myself, making
them known only to God, and as there was a Celebration
every morning, at seven A.M., at St. Paul's, I was glad to go
to it, to bring the burden to Him who there draws so nigh
to us. One morning as I was leaving St. Paul's, Miss
Mary Glenn met me at the door, and handed me an envelope, saying, that her sister had requested her to give
it to me ; it contained a hundred-dollar bill. My note for
ninety-eight dollars was due at two o'clock that day, in
Charleston ; so I telegraphed Mr. Hanckel to pay it
and draw on me. Two days afterwards, as I was seated in
the pew of the South Carolina Delegation, I had in my
mind that twelve o'clock had passed, and my note for one
hundred and ninety-nine dollars was due at two o'clock.
I was nervous, but felt the conviction that a kind Providence would bring it all right. A little after twelve o'clock
one of the ushers told me a lady wished to speak with me.
A woman again ! Blessed woman ! What headway
would religion or charity make without her ? It was to
a woman, at the well in Samaria, our Lord first revealed
His Divinity, a woman was first at the grave, the first to
whom He revealed Himself after the Resurrection. As
woman ministered to Him when and where tenderness
were needed, so has she ministered to His Church ever
since.

In the vestibule Mrs. S. G. Wyman met me and handed
me an envelope. She said Mr. Wyman had given her one
thousand dollars to give to such work as she desired to
aid, and she had divided it among five objects, of which
my work was one. The envelope contained a check for
two hundred dollars. I at once telegraphed to pay the

note ; and thus my credit was saved. I had not said one word to Miss Glenn, nor to Mrs. Wyman, nor indeed to any human being, but I had at the daily Celebration asked help, even as the Syro-Phœnician woman asked it on the coasts of Tyre and Sidon, and God sent His help to me. In each case the relief was exactly according to the need. If I recorded every such incident in these thirty years, this work would be voluminous. In the early days these things occurred again and again; when the work had been well established, and was widely known, God has seemed to require that I should present it to the notice of the benevolent ; but when I have been in extremity, He has always opened the way for me to go on. I believe in the special providence of God, as firmly as I do in the Atonement ; without belief in both, life to me would not be worth living.

During one of the evening sessions of the General Convention, the Rev. H. C. Potter, then Secretary of the House of Bishops, now the distinguished Bishop of New York, came in with a message from the Bishops. As he was going out he stopped at our pew and whispered in my ear, " Hail, Bishop of Africa ! " I should not have been more startled if he had fired a pistol at my ear.

" What do you mean ? " I asked.

" You are about being elected Bishop of Africa by the Bishops."

I did not sleep a wink that night. I felt the Bishops were making a mistake, for I knew I had neither the learning, the ability, nor the strength for such an office, and I earnestly prayed that it might not be done. Bishop Davis was stone blind, and every day I went for him, and took him home from the House of Bishops.

One evening he said to me : " Porter, I do not know whether you will thank me, but I prevented you last night from being elected Bishop of Africa. I told the

18

Bishops I would use all my influence to prevent your accepting, or allowing your name to go to the Lower House ; that you had a wife in extreme ill-health, and two young boys ; that you yourself were not strong ; but the chief point of all,—you were doing a work for the Church even more important than you could do in Africa.''

I told him I was grateful to him for relieving me from the situation ; for I most certainly should have declined an office for which I knew myself to be unfit. That was as near as I ever came to the Episcopate.

The great fire of Chicago occurred during the sitting of this 1871 Convention, and made it more difficult for me to collect money in New York ; but I had to have aid, or stop. My best friends told me that it was useless to try, but to try I was compelled, and I worked day and night, footsore and heart-weary, but not forsaken. After some weeks I gathered enough to make me comparatively easy until the spring. I then returned North, and for the first time stopped in Philadelphia, made some few friends, and collected one thousand dollars ; then went to New York, collected a little, and went on to Boston. This was my first visit since 1866, and my first appeal for the school. I was kindly welcomed in Boston, and from that city has come a large part of the help that has sustained me all these years.

From the time that I consented to build the Church of the Holy Communion, in 1854, I always determined, when the time came, I would try to build a church which would be more appropriate than the one we then built. I have written the account of how I was defeated when, through the gift of Mr. George Trenholm, I had had the opportunity. The first movement towards my project was when Mr. Wagner built the addition which was used for a chancel, but this was only one step.

I found the picture of the roof of Trinity Hall, Cambridge, England, had it drawn by a draftsman, framed, and hung up in the vestry-room. One of the vestry seeing it there asked what it was. I told him it was a rafter of the roof we would one day put on this church. He told me he was afraid he would never see it up. I told him I could wait ; and there it hung on the wall for nearly two years. I took occasion at each vestry meeting to bring the matter up. One night at a vestry meeting, Mr. Trenholm said : '' Gentlemen, we are none of us growing younger, and the rector has this matter of improving the church much at heart. I propose that we take steps to carry out his wishes, if he will explain them to us.''

I at once told them that I wished to take out the back wall of the chancel, and build a recess chancel ; that I would assume the cost of that if they would do the rest, namely, build two transepts, and put that roof on the church, and give me the present chancel for my choir. I told them the cost would be about seventeen thousand dollars, and proposed a scheme of subscriptions running over five years.

The vestry resolved to adopt my scheme, and we began operations next day. The present church is the result. At Easter many pledges, amounting in all to fifteen thousand dollars, payable in five years, were placed on the altar. They ranged from fifty dollars to one thousand dollars each. It was a bold venture, for the incomes of my people had then been greatly reduced, but as everyone agreed to do something, we borrowed from the bank and worked it off, using these pledges as collaterals. I gave my individual note, and Mr. Trenholm endorsed it. I also insured my life for five thousand dollars and assigned it to the vestry, so as to secure them from my pledge for the chancel in case I died before it was paid for. In the course of time the alterations were all paid for, costing seventeen thousand eight hundred dollars. It was a long, hard struggle. In the fall of 1871 I went to New York and had a very difficult time, but people were kind, even when they gave nothing. I collected a little and went home, and struggled along I scarcely know how. I again went North in the spring intending to go to Boston ; but the great fire there broke out the day I reached New York, and of course I did not go, but turning westward, I visited Pittsburgh and Cincinnati. In the former place I met Mr. J. H. Shoenberger, who was very generous to me, and often afterwards helped me. I also visited Cincinnati, and Mr. Larz Anderson and Mr. George Shoenberger gave me each five hundred dollars, with subscriptions from others. I afterwards went to Louisville, Kentucky, but was not compensated for the effort. When I look back, I realize more and more how this work has been sustained of God. I do not believe any man living could, unaided by Providence, have sustained it. During the year Mr. William Cullen Bryant, the poet-editor, visited us, and in the *Evening Post*, of New York, he gave a glowing account of the school, and as long as he lived, whenever I went to New York, he always gave me the benefit of a cordial editorial, which helped me much. Mr. J. C. Hoadley, of Boston, also visited us and gave me substantial aid.

On the 31st of March, 1872, Easter Sunday, at the visitation of Bishop Howe, and with his consent, I introduced the surpliced choir. I had for several years been utilizing the boys as choristers, but I had not then adopted a uniform, and it was not a pleasant sight to see them in their motley dress ; so I consulted Mr. Trenholm as to the wisdom and expediency of this departure.

I never will forget Mr. Trenholm's advice to me.

" I have wondered," he said, " why you did not long ago put those boys in cassocks and cottas. Now you get patterns and I will give you the materials, and if you go among the ladies and get them interested by making the garments, after they are made, they will wish to see them used; and when the women of the parish are all in favor of it you will have no trouble.''

I followed his advice, and when the vestments were ready, the ladies scarcely wished me to wait until Easter. The news of the innovation was noised abroad, and the church was crowded to excess that Easter; for we had a full choral service. Two families left the church, but ten came in their place. Two vestrymen withdrew their sons from the choir, but in six months asked that they be allowed to return. Save that, I did not have the least trouble in my parish. All liked it. Outsiders made a great stir, and it was amusing to hear how much the brethren of the denominations had to say about it; but the people continued to come, and now, twenty-five years from then, I never have an extra service that the church is not packed ; and there are very few found who do not enjoy the service. Several newspaper attacks were made upon me which I did not notice, but I was preparing a sermon, reviewing seventy years of the Society for the Advancement of Christianity, and I had to read up a great many old records, among them the proceedings of the vestry of St. Michael's. There I found an entry of a charge, so many shillings paid for washing the surplices of the choir-boys, some sixty or seventy years before. I immediately published the item. This refreshed the memory of old Colonel Fergurson and Doctor Prioleau, who remembered they had been surpliced choir-boys at St. Philip's, long, long ago. This ended the controversy. It had been done before in Charleston; it was really no innovation, and Doctor Porter was not, therefore, going to Rome. In the late spring of 1872, I was in desperate straits ; I really did not know what to do. I went to Philadelphia, and was the

guest of the Rev. E. A. Hoffman, D.D., then rector of St.
Mark's, now the Very Reverend Dean of the General
Theological Seminary, New York, who has written his
name in flames of perpetual light by his princely generosity to that great Church Seminary, and by his munificent
gifts to St. Luke's Hospital. Doctor Hoffman asked me
on Saturday to preach for him on Sunday, but I had
already accepted an invitation from Rev. Mr. Harris,
rector of the Church at Chestnut Hill. Doctor Hoffman
reminded me that I would address a much larger congregation at St. Mark's, but I felt it my duty to fulfil my previous engagement. I accordingly went to Chestnut Hill,
and on Sunday it rained in torrents. There were very
few persons in church, so I preached, but did not mention
my work. At that service two ladies in very deep mourn-
ing asked the sexton who I was, and afterwards came to
the vestry-room desiring to speak to me. One was for-
merly from Charleston, the other was Mrs. Birkhead,
from Baltimore. The latter told me that she had become
greatly interested in my work through Mrs. Heminway,
of Boston, who had established a school in Wilmington,
North Carolina, and through Mr. William Cullen Bryant.
She asked me to come over to her friend's house. Then
she said she must have been led to church to meet me, for
she never went out in such weather. Strange to say, she
had come from Philadelphia to spend that Sunday only,
and we probably would never have met had she not come
out in the storm. She had seen her only child drowned
on Long Island, and the origin of my work had touched
her heart with sympathy, and she desired to help me.
She assisted me much by giving me several letters of introduction to very prominent people, among them Mrs.
John Jacob Astor and Miss Gilston of New York, now
Mrs. Mary Winthrop. These letters, given in 1872, have
been the means in these twenty-five years of my collecting

about fifteen thousand dollars ; so that was not a profit-
less Sunday. Was it a chance meeting, or was it Providence ? These letters and their immediate result enabled
me to go on. Without them I should have been obliged
to disband the school. One of these letters took me to
Albany, where, at an old ancestral manor house, I was
most hospitably entertained, and generously helped. I
went from there to see Mr. Nat. Thayer, of Boston, with
a letter, and he gave me five hundred dollars. As the
immediate result of these letters I returned with three
thousand five hundred dollars, the gifts of people I had
never met before.

CHAPTER XXXI

UNEXPECTED HELP IN TROUBLE

Our school feels the panic of 1873—" Master, carest Thou not that we perish?"—An unfeeling bank president who finds in me his match—My congregation sympathize and assist—Seven drays full of groceries unexpectedly drive into my yard—An unjust appropriation to the Roman Catholic orphanage becomes the occasion of assistance for me.

EVERY preparation was made for our October opening, 1873, the sixth year of the Institute. Jay Cook & Co. had failed in September, and I had sufficient business capacity to know that it was the beginning of a terrible panic. All who remember the panic know that it swept through the country like a tornado. It struck us on Friday, 26th of September. It so happened that about that time I was writing a sermon on the text " Master, carest Thou not that we perish."

The sermon lay on my desk half finished, when I received a note from the president of the bank, reminding me that my note for five thousand dollars, due that day, must be paid in full. This note was endorsed by Mr. George A. Trenholm, and was given for the enlargement and improvement of the church. It was given and taken

as accommodation paper, to be renewed indefinitely, paying each time as I could. I called on Mr. Trenholm, who
was unable to help me. Everyone who remembers that
panic of 1873, knows that the richest man could not draw
any amount from any bank, North or South. I went to
the president and told him that so far from receiving payment in full, he would have to renew it in full ; he had
known what the money was loaned for, and the terms on
which it had been borrowed. He, however, remained in-
exorable. I told him so far as I was concerned he might
protest it and do his worst, but he was striking at my
endorser, and to save the credit of this latter, I would
sacrifice anything I had. Finding I could not move him,
I lost my temper and said: " Well, sir, go ahead, crack
your whip, and do what you please."

I then walked out of his office giving the door a sharp
bang behind me. I had not gone far, when a clerk came
after me, saying the president wished to see me. I went
back, and he said, " You must not get vexed."

I then told him that he was not dealing with a specu-
lator, and that he had been quite willing to take my paper.
He had known it was good, but now, in that extraordinary state of the financial world, instead of every man
standing by his neighbor and helping him to breast the
storm, people were for grinding down and crushing out
others, as if by such policy in the long run they would
help themselves. " As you measure," I added, " it will
be meted to you again."

" Well," he said, " I thought you could make some
arrangement ; but if you cannot, I will give you until
Monday."

I really did not see how I could do more on Monday
than on Saturday, but it was all I could get out of him, so
I went to Mr. Trenholm and got another note endorsed,
payable on Monday.

On my way from the bank I met the butcher George Shrewsbury, to whom I owed five hundred dollars on account of the last year's beef for the Home. After expressing his regrets, he told me that unless I paid off that five hundred dollars, he could no longer supply me with meat for my boys. Here was another shock ; what was I to do ? On Wednesday, October 1st, ninety-six boys were expected from the country, eight teachers had been engaged, and one was on his way from the North. Here I had a great institution on my hands, with neither money, provisions, nor credit, and the country trembling on the verge of ruin.

When I reached home I received my mail, and in it was a letter from my son Theodore, at Trinity College, whom I had just fitted out for the winter with a fine overcoat and everything necessary. The letter said, while at recitation, a sneak-thief had gone in his room and made a clean sweep. All this came on the 27th of September.

I could not finish my sermon; the text had become a direct, personal question, and my poor weak heart of unbelief was very like to that of the affrighted apostles in the storm ; the wind blew, and the waves ran high and filled the ship and I was about to sink. O what a calamity ! First, to those who had learned to look to this institution as the only but sure hope for the education of their children; and to me what a sorrow to see a work crumbling to pieces which had cost so much labor, for which so much had been endured, on which so much love and faith had been bestowed. I was supremely wretched. Could I have been mistaken after all, and was not this a God-given work ? I cannot describe the agony of that evening. My dear wife was at Clifton Springs, New York, under the care of Doctor Foster, for she was a confirmed invalid, and I did all I could to relieve her sufferings. I did not have her strong faith and clear mind to counsel me.

My aged mother I would not perplex with my difficulties, so we passed the evening together, and after she had gone to bed I went round at ten o'clock and locked myself in the church, and in the solemn and silent darkness, alone with God, I poured out my soul in prayer. I asked that help might come to me if it was my Father's will. I knew that man's extremity was God's opportunity; therefore I implored Him not to forsake me now in this time of need. Again and again I threw myself on the floor and prayed. I paced the middle aisle from door to chancel and had no comfort. At length at two o'clock in the morning I went up into the chancel, prostrated myself in front of the altar, and said; " Oh, my Father, if this work, which I thought and hoped was Thine, must now be ended, Thy will, not mine be done."

I rose, feeling the first sensation of calm resignation I had known in this midnight struggle with God. I went home and finished my sermon before morning and preached as I believe I never did before and never have since. My congregation were not aware of the night's experience, but I have never moved a congregation as I did that day. After the sermon I came out of the pulpit, and getting near the congregation, I told them about the note I had to meet the next day, and begged each to do what he could. Some of them offered the last dollar they had. Two or three watches, several diamond rings and breast pins, even a wedding ring were in the plates, and three hundred and twenty-eight dollars, part of it being pledged to be sent to me when the donors went home. I told the vestry to take out all that jewelry; that the sacrifice should not be made; the president of that bank should not have it. I returned each piece to the owners, and asked the trustees of the school (for it had been incorporated by the legislature the year I bought the house in the rear of the church, and, when paid for, I had deeded to them) to meet me after service. They did so, and agreed to go as a committee of the whole, to baker, butcher, and grocer, and ask for three months' credit, and if at the end of that time there was no apparent way of carrying the work on, we would wind up, and gradually pay the debt. We then knelt and asked God's blessing, and adjourned to meet the next day at eleven o'clock, and go together on our mission. Troubled as each of them was, not knowing what a day would bring forth, they were willing to leave their business and go and further this.

On Monday morning I went round to the schoolhouse, and was standing in the quadrangle looking at the two houses, wondering whether this great work had come to an end, whether these halls would no longer ring with the merry voices of my boys, whether there was to be no opening in the cloud, no hope for them, whether I had labored only for this, had prayed, battled—only for this. I cannot present in words the lonely wretchedness I was in that day; my heart was full to overflowing; tears I could not restrain flowed down my cheeks. I sorrowed for myself, for my boys, for their parents and friends. How many hearts which had suffered so much would that blow reach? It was just nine o'clock, and I was about to leave the place, when I heard a noise at the gate, which was thrown open and a dray was driven into the yard; then another, and another, until seven were drawn up in line, every one of them heavily laden with boxes and barrels. Astonished, I walked up to the drays, and there on every box and barrel was my name in full, with " Orphans' Home, Charleston, South Carolina," added. Perfectly awestruck, I looked at the drays, while I seemed to hear a voice from heaven: " O thou of little faith, wherefore didst thou doubt?"

I asked one of the draymen where these goods had come

from and where was the bill ? His answer was : " From the steamship *Georgia*, which arrived last night. There is no bill, no freight, no drayage ; I was told to deliver them to you."

I seemed to hear a voice saying, " Now stop your work if you dare ! "

I locked up the groceries, fully six months' supplies, and then went into the church, and kneeling at the altar, I asked forgiveness for my want of faith, while I thanked God for His goodness. I then went home, gathered up all my silver—spoons, forks, sugar-dish, milk-pot, and every piece of silver I owned—and getting someone to take the load, I started to go to the bank. On the way I stopped at George Shrewsbury's, told him of the groceries, and he said: " Mr. Porter, this is the Lord's work, and as long as I have a pound of meat in my stall you shall have it. Pay me when you can."

I paid him in time ; indeed, I paid him several thousands of dollars before he died, for he was my butcher for seven years. I went to the baker, who was willing to wait. Then I went to Mr. Trenholm, got a note deducting the three hundred and twenty-eight dollars, and left the time open. Then I went to the banker who held my note, and offered the renewal note and my silver. He said he did not want that ; he wanted currency, and if the three hundred and twenty-eight dollars was all I could do, he would renew it for ten days. I then saw the trustees, communicated the joyful news, and excused them from going round as the crisis was past. I had no money, but I had evidence that God was watching over our needs. Before the ten days were over, I went to W. C. Courtney, President of the Bank of Charleston, and told him how I had been treated, and he went with me to the President of the South Carolina Loan and Trust Company. The two agreed to divide the note; and when the day came, I drew the amount in bills and took them to my own banker, asking for my note.

"Where did you get that money?" he asked.

I told him it was none of his business; it was good money, and if that was the amount due, to take it, and give me my note. Things had then eased up somewhat, and people were getting over their scare, and he said, "I do not wish for it; I will renew your note for just as long a time as you wish."

I thanked him, but declined keeping it in his bank; but the intense nervous excitement of this transaction was eventually the cause to me of a long and serious illness.

I called the trustees of the school together, and told them to whom I believed I was indebted for the groceries, and we passed resolutions which we engrossed and framed and sent to the donor. We received no reply; but in June, 1874, being in New York, I went to his office and told him I knew we were indebted to him for the supplies of groceries, and before he replied, I wished to tell him that under God he had saved the institution. Had those supplies not come, credit no doubt would have been refused; I should have been obliged to stop the boys from coming from the country, and have advertised in the papers the next day that the school would not be opened. Probably I might have re-commenced it at some future day, but even a temporary cessation would have shaken the confidence of everyone in the permanent success of this work to so great an extent that I could scarcely have regained my former position.

My friend was moved by my statement, and said: "Well, you have cornered me. I must tell you that during the height of the panic, I remembered that your school opened about that time, and no doubt you would be in trouble, so I ordered the grocers who supplied my ships to send you the groceries you received." That man, God bless him!

is Mr. Wm. P. Clyde, the tried, firm friend of all these years. This was in June, and he turned to his confidential clerk, to send me at once supplies for two more months. May the blessing of God be with him and his in time and in eternity!

Be it remembered all this happened during the year of the great panic, and though I had the groceries, I had no money. During the six years past the expenses had exceeded my receipts, and each year there was an accumulating debt. There was money indeed due me from pledges of persons whose sons had been here, which if I could have collected would have paid my indebtedness; but in consequence of the successive failure of crops, the high taxes, the wretched government—for this was during the so-called reconstruction period—the people in the country had been growing poorer and poorer, and it was out of their power to pay. The Roman Catholics had for a number of years been drawing from the city treasury six thousand dollars a year to support their orphanage. I knew that this was contrary to the Constitution of the United States, and of the State of South Carolina, and I was spending a certain evening with Bishop Howe, and told him that our people were just sleeping over this imposition, but after awhile would make another move, and get hold of some of the common school fund, and I believed I was in a position to open the eyes of the community as no one else was.

" I have a larger work than they are supporting," I said to the Bishop, " and suppose I send in a petition to the City Council for the same appropriation ? I have no doubt it will be refused, but at least it will raise the question."

" Neither of you," he answered, " have any right to such an appropriation, but what is sauce for the goose is sauce for the gander. Go ahead with my approval, and let us see what will come of it."

I therefore got Mr. Henry Buist, a lawyer and a warm friend, to draw up my petition. It was a very astute paper, and proved a bombshell in the Council. It so happened that C. C. Bowen (who had married the daughter of Mr. James L. Pettigru, who was a member of my congregation) was a member of Council, and he saw at a glance that the appropriation for the Roman Catholics could not be continued unless my application were granted. Political influence was too strong to allow of discontinuing the six thousand to them, so he moved and carried through, the appropriation of three thousand to my school. I thought it was a mistake when I read the account in the paper, but it was true. The two hundred and fifty dollars a month paid my butcher's bill and was a great help, and was continued for three years, when Mr. Edward McCrady and Mr. Meminger got Mr. Johnson of Baltimore, who owned some city stock, to allow them to use his name to institute a suit to stop these appropriations.* I told both of those lawyers, " Stop both, and I

---

* In this connection I will anticipate a few years. I was elected one of the school commissioners, in charge of the city common schools, and in course of time, after the suit was forgotten, there came an application from the Roman Catholic Bishop and clergy for the support of their parochial school, they to elect their own teachers, and to have the sole management, but to draw their pay from the common school fund. Everything had been arranged, and they had secured a majority of the Board, when Mr. O'Driscol offered a resolution consenting to this petition. Mr. C. C. Meminger, in the chair, before putting the resolution, presented a written protest, which he read. It was an unanswerable paper.

"If I am the only man to sign this," he said, " I will do so that it may go on record." I immediately asked him to pass the paper to me. I affixed my signature to it. Then I made a speech and told the Board if they passed the resolution I would secure the best legal talent in the city, and would take out an injunction against the Board, preventing the payment of the appropriation. I would placard this city, and call a mass-meeting of the Protestant comam satisfied,'' but they made their fight against me, and of course won it. The Roman Catholics have had their six thousand dollars, however, ever since, and have it still.

munity, who were strong enough, if once aroused, to nip this thing in the bud. It was a stormy meeting, but the resolution was never presented; it just died.

CHAPTER XXXII

God's special providence is apparent in the way my work was supported—The incidents of this chapter will appeal to the most downcast or disheartened.

PANIC year as it was, this seventh year, opening October, 1873, closing in August, 1874, I raised in South Carolina nine thousand dollars besides the three thousand from the City Council, which shows how we tried to help ourselves ; for be it remembered the first year I gathered only three hundred at home. Generous friends at the North had given me six thousand dollars. But after all this anxiety and labor, after writing hundreds of letters, and often sitting at my desk till two or three in the morning, my overtaxed nervous system gave way. I had never received one dollar remuneration for all that has been recorded in these seven years. We had a Christmas tree and a dinner for the poor children of the Sunday and Industrial School on the 26th of December, 1873, and after it was all over I broke down. Then began a long and severe illness ; but as soon as I could be moved I was sent to Florida, where I remained two weeks, and returned home only to have a second attack, more severe than the first. I then went to Aiken, and after a while returned to Charleston, and resumed my work. I was very feeble all winter, and of course the burden was heavier to be borne; but the parish and the school went on, carried by the unseen hand of God. The last of May I went to New York, and my family physician wrote to the Bishop and the vestry that, in his opinion, if I did not have complete rest my life would be the forfeit. Accordingly, at their earnest solicitation I spent the summer at the North, making friends, and seeking aid wherever I could find it. I have grateful memories of that summer in New York, Boston, New Haven, Newport, Lenox, and Stockbridge, where friend after friend was raised up for me, through whose kindness I paid off all my indebtedness. It is not taken from mere memory, but from the record which I made at the time, that in 1874 I met everywhere an earnest desire for the restoration of fraternal feeling between the North and South. I wish it were possible for every man and woman of the South to share the experience I have had at the North. I have heard the views of those who differ from us, and have given my own with perfect frankness, never concealing my war record, or feeling that my Northern friends expected me to make an apology for the course I pursued during hostilities ; and I believe I have been the means of informing many as to the real condition of the South, and have in a number of cases induced a kindly feeling.

During the summer I preached at St. Thomas's Church, New Haven, and after service, a lady sent into the vestry-room to ask me to come to the hotel to see her. It was Mrs. Ogle Taylor, of Washington, D. C. She was on her way to New Britain, but being fatigued, stopped at New Haven for the night, and had gone to Trinity Church, which she was compelled to leave on account of some fresh paint about the church. Seeing St. Thomas's Church, she had gone over there, and was glad she had done so, as she had heard my appeal. After giving me one thousand dollars, she invited me to visit her at Washington, and promised the aid of friends whenever I was ready to do the same work for the girls of the South as I was doing for the boys. As Mrs. Taylor will appear prominently again in this record, I hope my readers will remember her name. Now, was it chance only that she came to that church that day ? I believe it was Providence. During the same year, Rev. Mr. Learoyd, of Taunton, gave me a letter to the Rev. Justin Field, of Lenox, Massachusetts, who most kindly received me, and kindness upon kindness was extended to me. I was the guest of Mrs. Ellison, whose hospitality can never be forgotten. She gave me a letter to her brother, Mr. Robert M. Mason, and to his daughters. Mr. Mason has long entered into rest, but the generosity of his daughters has never failed me in all these years. Without them, as far as I can see, this work would have come to an end long years ago. I wish to place on record as a monument to them, living in this book after I have passed to my rest, that their munificent generosity for the past fifteen years has been the nucleus round which I have gathered the means to carry on the work, and but for them it would have been impossible to continue it.

The Rev. Mr. White, then rector of Trinity Church, Newport, also kindly invited me to preach. Although I was a stranger, he did not introduce me, but bade me tell my story. As the congregation did not know who I was, I felt the awkwardness of the situation, and in as straightforward and delicate a manner as I could, I introduced myself.

Mr. Daniel Leroy leaned over to his wife, and said, " I never heard of him before, but he is a gentleman." This he told me afterwards. Mr. Leroy was a brother-in-law of the Hon. Daniel Webster, and his dear wife the sister of the

Hon. Hamilton Fish, then United States Secretary of State. Mr. and Mrs. Leroy invited me to be their guest. I was liberally assisted in Newport, and the friendship, begun then, lasted until the death of both of my friends. Again and again they entertained me in Newport. At several of the General Conventions held in New York I was always their guest. It would be impossible to tell all the acts of personal kindness I received from them, and how generous they were to this school, nor did it cease then. Mrs. Edward King, their daughter, and Mrs. King's sons and daughters, have been, and are now, among my dearest friends. Somehow, I have been with them in many times of joy, and oftener in scenes of sorrow ; so that I feel that I am one of the family.*

---

* I put on record the names of those who were my principal helpers in those days: Mr. A. A. Low, Mr. and Mrs. J. Jacob Astor, Mr. Wm. P. Clyde, Mr. W. H. Vanderbilt, Mr. Isaac Henderson, Mr. Fred Hubbard, Mr. W. H. Aspinwall, Mr. Adam Norrie, Mr. John David Wolfe, Mr. Stuart Brown, Mr. Charles O'Connor, Mr. J. Pierpont Morgan, Mr. A. H. Bend, Mr. A. M. Benson, Mr. Charles E. Bill, Mr. Charles D. Dickey, Mr. James C. Fargo, Mr. Jos. E. Sheffield, Mr. J. M. Dunbar, Mr. Percy K. Pyne, Mr. Augustus Schermerhorn, Mrs. Robert C. Winthrop, Mr. W. E. Dodge, Jr., Mr. Henry E. Pellew, Mr. John Welsh, Mr. Wm. Welsh, Mr. Geo. W. Childs, Mr. Edward T. Buckley, Mr. Larz Anderson, Mr. John H. Shoenberger, Mrs. A. M. Minturn, Mr. George K. Shoenberger, Mrs. Caroline W. Suydam, Mr. James M. Brown, Mrs. E. L. Spencer, Miss Gilston, Miss C. L. Wolfe, Mr. Saml. D. Babcock, Mr. Ed. S. Jaffray, Mrs. Ogle Taylor, Mrs. Mary Heminway, Mrs. W. H. Aspinwall, Mr. Edw. King, Mr. E. R. Mudge, Mr. Clarkson N. Potter, Mr. Alex. Brown, Mr. Howard Potter, Rev. Arthur Lawrence, Mr. A. A. Lawrence, Mr. Daniel Leroy, Mr. George M. Connarro, Mr. J. C. Sowdan, Mr. J. Carey, Jr., Mr. W. R. Robeson, Mr. R. Mason, Mr. Junius S. Morgan, Colonel Auchmuty, Mrs. Auchmuty, Miss Ellen F. Mason, Miss Ida M. Mason, Mr. C. J. Joy, Mrs. Edw. King, Mr. B. T. Reed, Mr. Jos. S. Fay, Mr. Jas. M. Beebe, Mr. H. C. Kiddar, Mrs. N. E.

I have bought and paid for a house which cost ten
thousand dollars, have added four rooms to the schoolhouse at a cost of over three thousand dollars, have paid
all current expenses for the seven years. I would like to
know if the reader thinks it was a delusion at the grave
of my child, when I began this, or was I given a work to
do by our Heavenly Father ? To God be all the praise!
He has honored me by using me as His agent, but He has
given me the friends and provided the means. Though
I have never had an income, I have only depended on what
I could collect from day to day.

I was still at the North when the school opened for its
eighth year. Mr. John Gadsden was still the principal,
and managed for a while ; but the yellow fever broke out,
and the Home boys returned into the country until after
a frost. I still had the three thousand dollars from the
City Council, and a few of the boys paid from one dollar
to twenty per month. I must have had a hard struggle,
for I see in my diary of February 27, 1875, the following
entry : " Received a letter from Mr. ——, of New York,
very cold and unsympathetic. O, Lord God, the silver
and the gold are Thine; Thou knowest how anxious my
heart is ; Thou knowest how I depend on Thee ; Thou
knowest all our needs ; Thou knowest what we are doing ;
Give us each day our daily bread; O Lord God, make my
work Thine ; make me Thine, and may many deacons,
priests and bishops be raised out of this work for Christ's
sake." That entry tells the story of these thirty years ;

Bayliss, Mr. Albert Fearing, Dr. George C. Shattuck, Mr. Wm.
Niblo, Mr. Wm. Amory, Mr. Wm. Endicott, Mr. Jno. Hogg, Mr.
Robt. L. Kennedy, Mr. J. C. Hoadley, Dr. J. J. Crane, Mrs. C. R.
Goddard, Mrs. Russell, Mrs. Annie Ives, Mr. Wm. Goddard, Mr.
and Mrs. S. G. Wyman, Mr. Fred S. Winston, Mr. H. F. Spauld-
ing. These are my principal helpers, from soon after my beginning,
and all of them continued annually to assist me during their life.

for there has scarcely been a week when it did not describe the situation. And none but God knows what a strain on the nerves, what a drain on the vital energies it has been, and how the sunshine of personal life has all gone out in the struggle. But for the sustaining grace of God, and the cheerful encouragement of my dear wife, while she was with me, I would have given up long since. I find in that diary I was particularly low-spirited on the 30th of March. I had published the first chapters of a little work on the school, and it had fallen unappreciated from the press. When, on the 4th of April, the widow of an esteemed clergyman called on me, she said she had just read my pamphlet, and supposed she was behind many others in bringing her offering. It was fifty dollars, a very large contribution for her limited means. On the 5th of April, I received a letter from Mr. Seth Low, saying he had just read my pamphlet, and if I would send him one of my two-hundred-dollar endowment bonds he would gladly sign it. These two cases came as a reproof to me; they seemed to say, " O thou of little faith, wherefore didst thou doubt ? " *

* This is a good place to remember an incident. I had continued my book, of which three or four editions have been published, brought down to 1880, and there is a great deal from 1875 to 1880. Some years after 1880, I was seated in my study, when a lady called. She asked me if I was the Rev. Dr. Porter. I told her, "Yes." She said she had come all the way from St. Louis, Mo., to look into my eyes and to take my hand, and to thank me for what I had done for her. I was much surprised, as she was a total stranger to me. She said, "I have come to see your wonderful work. I had lost my belief in God, for I had lost my faith in the efficacy of prayer, and if there is no efficacy in prayer there can be no loving, merciful God and Father. For if there is a Father in Heaven, He must hear and answer prayer. By what the world calls chance, but what I call Providence, your book was put into my hands. I read it over three times, and then knelt down and

My good friend George Shrewsbury, of whom I have
made frequent mention, died on the 8th of March. He
was the donor of five hundred dollars to the Academy.
He was a member of the City Council, though a colored
man, and he represented the conservative element in that
board.   I acted as one of his pall-bearers, and assisted in
bearing his body to the grave ; a thing it required some
nerve to do in this community, but my friends all commended me for doing it.   I was still during that year very
much pressed for money.   I owed a bill for three hundred
and twenty-four dollars which had to be paid on the 17th.
On the 8th of March I received a letter from Miss Catherine Wolfe, enclosing a check for two hundred dollars.   I
had made no appeal to her, but she wrote saying that she
thought it might help a little.   She had previously given
me, in the fall, one thousand dollars.   I received from
different sources enough to pay my note on the 17th.   On
the 29th, the mattress maker, a colored man, came for
one hundred dollars I owed him.   I did not have a dollar
in the bank, but I gave him a check, telling him, as it
was after bank hours, he could not present it until next
day.   I determined to put a note in the bank to meet it.
That night the choir boys were at my house, when Mr.
W. F. Winston, of New York, called to see me.   The next
day he went with me to see the colored children's school,
at the Marine Hospital, and then visited my academy.
When leaving he handed me a check for a hundred dollars.   I deposited it before my check to the colored man
came in.   These coincidences, and they have been numberless, are only things of chance to some minds, but
thank God, they help to strengthen my faith in the
providence of a personal, present Father.

said, ' My Lord and my God.'   You have been the means of giving me back my faith, and I have come to thank you for it."   I
was very grateful for this, even if the book never brought me a
dollar.

CHAPTER XXXIII

SERVICE WITH THE ANGELS

I am inopportunely seized with sudden sickness—A time of rest in which I hold service with the angels—My confidence in God is justified by convalescence—My financial troubles—Friendly help—The far-reaching results of my pamphlet.

MY story is now brought down to the 16th of May, 1875. Whit-Monday, the day before, we had a glorious service at the Church of the Holy Communion. The congregation was large, the school was full, the music was devotional, and unusually good. The Rev. Dr. DuBose, then Chaplain of the University of the South, preached on Whitsunday. The Sunday-schools of the different city parishes assembled at the church to practise for the anniversary service next day. I had been with them, practised all the tunes, and had returned home, and was preparing one of a series of lectures on the Prayer-Book, when about ten at night, I was called to see a man who was supposed to be dying. I remained until after twelve o'clock with him, and had resumed the writing of my lecture when, without warning, I was attacked with a hemorrhage. It was a great shock, for I had no cold or cough ; and although tired and wearied and worn had not the slightest suspicion of my condition. In the very midst of work, everything going on well save the finances, which were considerably in arrears, with two months and a half still before me, I, apparently the mainstay, was thus stricken down helpless. It did seem desperate, but I rallied, however, and seemed to have recovered. During the winter, Mr. Wm. A. Courtenay and Col. Thomas Simons, Major R. C. Gilchrist, and myself had been very busy inducing the Washington Light Infantry, of which I was, and still am, chaplain, to accept an invitation to take part in the Bunker Hill celebration ; for we had to create a public sentiment at home which would make it possible for them to go. At length it was all arranged, the day came, and I was to go with them. Nearly four weeks had passed since my attack of sickness and I felt quite well again. The company was on board the steamer for New York, my trunk was packed, Mr. F. A. Mitchell, one of my friends and vestrymen, had come to bid me good-bye, the carriage was at the door, and while talking to him, the hemorrhage returned, this time very much more severe than at first.

Of course this ended my trip to Boston. As soon as I could be moved I was taken to Aiken, and Doctor Ogier said I had not a month to live. Thank God, I did not lose my faith. Firmly convinced that my work was God's, I felt assured it would be carried on by Him through every difficulty. If He had used me as far as He wished, and was about to take me to Himself, He could raise up some other agent to do His will. His hand was laid heavily upon me. I was forbidden to write, even to speak, but I felt by some means God would sustain the work. The blow to me personally was a severe one, but I had no doubt He would make it conduce to His glory, and to the good of the work, and if what has gone before has excited any surprise and interest, that which is still to be told will show that this sickness was the instrumental means of far more wonderful results than any that have been as yet recorded. My not going with the company, and the cause of my absence, was of course published in the papers, and was copied in the New York *Churchman*. Letters of sympathy poured in on me. Mr. Howard Potter wrote, " I need not tell you how profoundly I feel for you and the cause you represent. Both you and it have my deepest sympathy and warmest admiration, but you know in Whose hands both you and your work are, and to Him and to His grace I commend you, in perfect confidence that your heart will be kept in the peace which is promised those whose minds are stayed on Him. I will send you in a few days what I can collect for you."

Mr. Potter very shortly afterwards sent me nine hundred dollars, Mr. A. A. Lawrence, of Boston, sent me money and a loving letter. Even from London, Mr. Junius S. Morgan, whom I had met at Mr. R. M. Mason's, when he gave me a check for five hundred dollars, wrote me, expressing his sympathy, and said of my work : " I do not doubt great good will come of it, and my prayer is, that you may be long spared to superintend and develop the good work." And he enclosed a check to help me. These are specimens of the letters and the character of those to whose kind feeling God had given me entrance. This sympathy was very soothing, and the pecuniary aid voluntarily sent to me greatly relieved the situation. Still there was a deficiency, for the school was going on, up to the first of August. I recuperated very slowly. Doctor Amory Coffin, of Aiken, was very kind, and Mr. Finlay, a Presbyterian friend, put his pony at my disposal, and I took a short ride in the pines daily. It was my habit to take my Bible, Prayer-Book, and Hymnal, and sit in the pine grove, and hold service with the angels. On the 14th of August, I came to the psalter for the day, the Seventy-first Psalm. I had then the same sensations I experienced at the grave of my child, on the 25th of October, 1867. I seemed to be enveloped in a Spiritual Presence, and the first words of the Psalm seemed to be my own. " In Thee, O Lord, have I put my trust, let me never be put to confusion, but rid me and deliver me in Thy righteousness, incline Thine ear unto and save me. Be Thou my stronghold whereunto I may always resort, Thou hast promised to help me, for Thou art my house of defence, and my castle."

I never before had felt all the comprehensiveness of these words. The feeling of devotion was so deep, that when I reached the fourth verse, " Thou Lord God art the thing that I long for, Thou art my hope even from my youth, through Thee have I been holden up ever since I was born, Thou art He that took me out of my mother's womb, my praise shall always be of Thee," I knelt on the ground and said, " Father, I can say this as truly as the Psalmist. I do not remember the time when I did not love Thee ; why, then, am I cast down ? " I read on, and when I came to the eighth verse, " Cast me not away in the time of age, forsake me not when my strength faileth me," again I knelt and prayed, that God would graciously hear this prayer. I read on to the sixteenth verse, " Forsake me not, O God, in mine old age, when I am gray-headed, until I have showed Thy strength to this generation, and Thy power to them that are yet to come." Had I been spoken to, and told directly that my prayer had been answered, the effect upon me could not have been greater. I knelt again alone in the quiet depths of the forest, the bright summer sky above me, that was looking up as it were in the face of God, and thanked Him that He had granted me this respite, that I might have more time to work for Him here, and that He was willing to use me, His most unworthy servant, to magnify His grace, and to manifest His power. I could scarcely keep still long enough to finish all the morning prayers. I did, however, and mounting my horse, I cantered back to the village of Aiken. Hitherto, I had not dared to ride faster than a walk. Going into my wife's room, I said to her: "Wife, I cannot explain it all now, but I have had a message from God, through the Seventy-first Psalm. I am not going to die, I will soon be well. I have to bear witness for God, as to His strength and power, in this unbelieving age. I do not know where the help is coming from which is so much needed, but come it will. Let us kneel and thank God for His great goodness."

My wife burst into tears of thankfulness at seeing me so cheerful and hopeful, for she, dear helpmate, had been bearing a heavy load to keep up her spirits in the presence of my depression and hopeless condition. And we knelt and thanked God for His goodness. Two days passed, and in the mail arrived a budget of letters. The first I opened was from Mrs. W. H. Aspinwall, of New York, dated Tarrytown, August 14th: "My dear Mr. Porter, I see by *The Churchman* that you are still sick at Aiken. I know you must be disturbed, and to help relieve your troubles, I beg to enclose a check, which I hope will be of some service to you. May God spare your valuable life, and soon restore you to health and strength."

Before opening the other letters (there were nine in all), I said to my wife, "Did I not tell you that relief was coming? Look at the date of that letter ; Mrs. Aspinwall must have been writing it at the very hour I was on my knees in the pine woods." I had not had one word of communication with Mrs. Aspinwall for a year. The other letters were all dated 14th of August, and contained checks unsolicited. Thus my pressing necessities were relieved. I thanked God for this manifestation of His loving care. My health continued to improve, and on the 9th of September I left Aiken for Charleston, and on the

17th took the steamer for New York, in charge of twenty-
nine of my boys, passed free by Mr. W. P. Clyde, on their
way to Union College, Schenectady.   On our way up the
Hudson, the river was low and the trip was long.   Whether
the change from the South brought it out, or what I do
not know, but when I reached Newport, with my youngest
son, Charles, then a little boy, I was stricken down with
a fever at the house of my kind friends, Mr. and Mrs.
Daniel Le Roy, and was desperately ill.   I knew I was
not to die ; the message in the pine woods was in my
heart, and under God, by the skilful treatment of good
Doctor King, and the tender nursing of my friends, I was
restored.   Mrs. J. W. Chanler, seeing how very miserable
I looked after getting about, insisted on my going to
Saratoga.   She paid my expenses there for a month.   A
few friends there gave me some money for my work, and
I returned home, preaching at the Church of the Holy
Communion on Advent Sunday, the first time in seven
months, with no sign of the two serious sicknesses I had
passed through.   It is now twenty-seven years since the
events above recorded, and the work that has been done
is before the Church and before the world.   It has not
been in a corner.   Some who read this book may know
about it ; many will not have heard of it: but if any
one doubts, I beg him to make inquiries, if these things
can be so ?   Come and see, and if this recital strengthens
the faith of anyone, I shall not know it, but God will, and
it will go on showing God's strength to this generation,
and His power to those that are yet to come.   Is it asked,
" Have these visitations been often granted you ? "   I
answer : " No ; I recall three—the night I gave myself up
to the ministry ; again, at the grave of my child; and this
in the pine woods near Aiken."   If I have failed to convince my readers, then they must account for this history
as best they can.

The visit of the Washington Light Infantry to Boston in 1875, has passed into history. Their enthusiastic reception as representatives of South Carolina, carrying their old historic flag, of Eutaw, which had waved at Eutaw Springs, and Cowpens, in the Revolutionary War, when Col. Wm. Washington gave Colonel Tarleton and his British forces such a merciless thrashing. This flag is of red damask, and had been the seat of a parlor chair, which Colonel Washington's sweetheart cut out of the chair, and gave to Colonel Washington, as he had no flag. In all that throng in Boston, this small command was the observed of all observers.

Mr. A. A. Lawrence wrote me from near Boston on the 17th June, 1875 : " I am sorry to hear that you have not recovered your strength so as to come here. But it would have been a great risk under any circumstances. The excitement would have been too great ; you can hardly estimate it, without seeing the expression in Boston to-day. Your friends will tell you about it. The revulsion of feeling is complete, and it goes to prove what I told you a year ago, namely, our people only have to know the trouble to range themselves on the side that is oppressed, and against the oppressors. What you have done to bring this about will be a lasting comfort and satisfaction to you, and it will come at the right time, when you most need cheering up. May God bless you in sickness and in health ! "

That visit of this small company did indeed revolutionize the feeling throughout New England and the North, and years after ex-President Hayes told Mr. Courtenay at a meeting of the trustees of the Peabody Fund, of which both were members, that the political influence of that visit had made it possible for him, when President, to recognize the government of South Carolina under General Hampton. As I have said, Mr. W. A. Courtenay,

Major Gilchrist, Col. T. Y. Simons, and myself were the moving spirits in that transaction. I still look back with much satisfaction to my share in the event.

While I was lying sick in Newport, at Mr. Daniel Le Roy's cottage, in the fall of 1875, I received a letter from Miss E. Waterman, of Providence, Rhode Island. It had been sent to Charleston and forwarded to me. " Dear sir, please find enclosed a check for one hundred dollars, for your Institute. [At that time it was known as the Holy Communion Church Institute, changed by the Board of Trustees some years later to the Porter Military Academy.] Although an Episcopalian, and trying to keep pretty well informed on what is done in the Church, I heard of your work for the first time about two months ago, through your report. On starting on a little excursion, with my friend, Miss B——, a Baptist, she said to me, ' I have a pamphlet which I wish you to read ; it was handed to me by my cousin, a Unitarian, for me to read, and give to another lady, but I thought it so wonderful and interest- ing, that I decided to take it with me, and see if I could not induce people to aid so excellent an object.' I read it, and shared her enthusiasm, and we took it to Lake Mohunk, a charming quiet watering-place, near the Hud- son River. Here we took pains to have it read by one and another, and as a number of wealthy people seemed interested in it, and asked many questions about it, I hope ere this you have had more than one contribution as the result. Rev. Wiliam Leonard, of Brooklyn [now Bishop of Ohio] told us that he was acquainted with you, and highly commended your efforts. Finally, he gathered a little circle round him, and read your pamphlet aloud. If you could send me two copies, or direct me where to get them, I shall be greatly obliged. I heard with great regret that your health was much impaired ; I hope that it is now restored, and that you may long be spared to labor in the noble cause for which you have done so much. I never heard of a work more evidently of God, nor one which was so eminently and wonderfully blessed of Him. May He still continue His favors, granting all needed spiritual and temporal blessing ! ''

I had never heard of the lady until this letter came. I afterwards found out she had relatives in South Carolina, the Thurston family. I have had several of her relatives in this school as beneficiaries ; I had one for three years, until his graduation, last year, and have one now, in 1897. Mr. Alex. Brown, that noble Christian gentleman of Philadelphia, was one of those who heard the pamphlet read. He said nothing, but went to his room, and wrote a warm letter, enclosing a check for two hundred and fifty dollars, and this he did on the 15th of May, from 1875 until he died. Nor was this all. Many kind letters I received, and whenever I was sorely pressed, a letter to him always brought a response, sometimes one thousand dollars, sometimes five hundred; but this intermediate giving never interrupted that annual two hundred and fifty, which came without a reminder every year until the day of his death. Some years after, during a visit at Mohunk, as the guest of Mr. Smiley, I addressed a large audience on Sunday afternoon. Mrs. Ed. Morgan gave me a check for five hundred dollars, and a large offering, o˙ ʒr a thousand dollars besides, was taken up that afternoon, and all of this came from the Unitarian lady giving my pamphlet to a Baptist friend, who gave it to Miss E. Waterman; and this was the pamphlet which I thought had fallen unappreciated. '' O ye of little faith, wherefore did ye doubt ? '' Miss Waterman, finding I was so near, sent my pamphlet to my reverend brethren in Providence. The Rev. Dr. David H. Greer was one of them, and the Rt. Rev. Bishop Clark, who extended me an invitation to visit Providence, which I did, receiving some thirteen hundred dollars, be-

20

sides making many friends. Now it is right to recount right here how all this sympathy and aid came of a five-dollar bill. It happened in this way. The Rev. Mr. Tustin, who had been a Baptist minister in Charleston, but in charge of the Huguenot congregation, had become very friendly with me, and was eventually ordained by Bishop Littlejohn, in Rome, to the priesthood of the Church. He had sent from Sweden his wife's annual contribution to my work to Miss B——, the Unitarian lady who had given the pamphlet to the Baptist, and she to Miss Waterman. When she sent the five dollars she did not know that I was a clergyman, or what the five dollars were for, but in acknowledging its receipt, I had sent her the pamphlet which did so much good work. Hence her efforts on my behalf. I pray God if this book ever sees the light, it may be used in the same way, whether I be alive or dead, for the work is the same great philanthropic work it was then, and needs all the help the generous will give.

CHAPTER XXXIV

MORE TRAVELS ABROAD

The admission of colored parishes into the Diocesan Conven-
tion—A burning question, on which I espouse the cause
of the blacks—A final compromise—I succumb to the toils
and anxieties of my work—I seek for renewed health in a
voyage to England—Thence I travel over the continent of
Europe—The kindness of English friends.

THE Convention of the Diocese of South Carolina met
at St. Philip's Church, on the 13th of May, 1875,
and in the journal of that date is this harmless-looking
entry : " The Bishop communicated the application of St.
Mark's Church, Charleston, for admission to the Convention." It was in the regular course of business, and there
was a standing committee on the admission of new parishes,
of which Rev. P. T. Shand, D.D., Mr. Jas. M. Davis, and
Mr. Wm. Parker were members. The regular course
was to refer the application to that committee. But St.
Mark's was a colored congregation, of which Rev. J. B.
Seabrook, an old white ex-planter and slave-holder, was
rector. Mr. Edw. McCrady rose immediately, and made
the following motion : " Resolved, that the application of
St. Mark's congregation for admission into union with this
Convention, be referred to a commission to be appointed
by the Bishop, to report to the next Convention upon the

same, and all its relations to the Church and constitution of this diocese.''

I did not know that the Bishop had received this petition of St. Mark's Church, nor that he proposed to offer it. I did know that Bishop Davis, in 1866, had received the vestry of this congregation at my house in Rutledge Avenue, when they asked if they then should apply for admission, and he had told them he thought not. They were made up of the colored members of St. Philip's, St. Michael's, Grace, St. Paul's, and the Church of the Holy Communion, in which parishes they had worshipped, as part of such congregations, before the war, but had since separated from the whites, and formed this congregation, and were worshipping at the Orphans' Chapel, under the rectorship of the Rev. J. B. Seabrook. The Bishop told them they were not yet established, they had no church building, and it was not clear that they could maintain their organization. It would, he added, be wiser to wait, and when the time came, he would be ready to welcome them into the Convention.* I was reading the morning paper, as it was only routine business, but as soon as Mr. McCrady offered his resolution, I dropped the paper, and looked around the church, to see if no one would meet it ; as no one moved, I rose, and said : " Mr. President, is not that an extraordinary resolution ? We have a committee appointed to consider all such applications ; have we lost confidence in that committee ? What does the gentleman from St. Philip's mean ? "

---

* The time never came in his administration. He was blind, and sick, and feeble, and was not equal to the emergency, and they waited for nine years. Then Bishop Howe thought the time had come, and took counsel only from the Canons and Constitution of the Church, from his own Catholic spirit, and from the Divine Master, who established His Church for all mankind.

This brought Mr. McCrady to his feet, and he gave a lawyer's intricate reasons for his motion. I replied, by saying: " Why should we dodge the question raised ? Sooner or later that petition had to come. It was the logical result of the surrender at Appomattox, and all this opposition springs from the fact that St. Mark's is a colored congregation. Let us here and now say, that if they have complied with all the requirements of the constitution, they be admitted into union. Or, like men, let us say at once they shall not be admitted because they are colored, and no colored delegates shall sit in this Convention.''

Mr. George A. Trenholm sustained me, so did Col. E. M. Seabrook and others ; while Judge H. D. Lessesne, Mr. Meminger, and others ranged themselves on Mr. McCrady's side. The discussion was very warm, but an adjournment was made before the vote was taken. The next day the discussion was resumed, motion after motion followed, but all were lost, and finally Mr. McCrady's resolution was adopted. That year was not unimproved by those in the opposition, and when the Convention met in Columbia, May 10, 1876, the whole diocese was in fever heat, and on the second day, Mr. McCrady read the report of the commission appointed under his resolution, which was signed but by three of the commission.

In the providence of God, the majority of the commission had dwindled away by sickness, removal, or death, and the minority, as appointed, became the majority, and had their first say. Among others I made a speech, which was published in the *News* and *Courier*, in full, and is therefore on record in the annals of the State, and I have never been ashamed of it, nor have ever doubted I was right. Of course I opposed Mr. McCrady's report with all the force I possessed. At the close of the debate, the Bishop addressed the Convention at length, and his speech, as recorded in the Journal of 1876, is instructive and interesting reading to-day.

This controversy went on for thirteen years, and shook the Church in the diocese to its centre. It was a sad and a miserable time. Friends and families were divided ; the Bishop was an intense sufferer, but he was unflinching in his convictions. His life was a martyrdom for the truth, and he went to his grave with the iron lodged in his soul. He was unfortunately a Northerner, a New Hampshire man by birth, but he had been in the diocese since he was twenty-one years old, and had been the idolized rector of St. Philip's Church. But all the love was forgotten in that bitter contest. As for myself, I stood by him through good and evil report, loving the people, working for them, educating and supporting their children, and being a Southerner, an ex-slaveholder and planter, the son and the grandson of slaveholders, it could not be attributed to me that it was my foreign birth, but rather that I was a traitor to my section. But as the Bishop stood on Catholic ground, so did I, and fought as long as it was possible to fight. It was only when Col. John Haskel and Mr. Robert Shand, in Anderson, rose in Convention and told us we knew they were with us, but they never would be permitted to meet with us again unless some way was found to pacify the diocese, that I came forward and offered resolutions which will be found in the Journal of 1888, of the Convention held in Anderson. These were unanimously carried, and paved the way for rehabilitation. It was a compromise, but it stilled the tempest, and in time brought back all the parishes which had seceded, save St. Paul's and St. Michael's,—the latter of which, under the judicious guidance of the Rev. John Kershaw, the present rector, will undoubtedly soon return to the Convention.

The ecclesiastical troubles of 1875–1876 had greatly

absorbed me. The political atmosphere was thick and gloomy. I had collected no money anywhere, and had been compelled to do exterior repairs, and make additions to buildings, and I saw that without some help I could but face a debt of fifteen thousand dollars at the close of the term, in July, 1876. So I wrote a letter to a very rich man in New York—he died leaving an estate to an only son, worth near one hundred millions of dollars. He knew me well ; I had dined at his house with the Rev. Dr. Dix, and he and his wife had been kind to my work, and yet, for no reason whatever that I could account for, save the political feeling about the time of General Grant's election to the presidency, which ran quite bitter against the South, I received from him the coldest kind of a letter, in which he stated that he had so many calls immediately around him that he had nothing to give to anything beyond. Well, I thought, if that be true of one of the richest men in America, what is the use of telling your needs to anyone else ? So I did not.

Thus matters went on, each day putting me deeper in debt for teachers' salaries, and daily expenses for this large school ; till without one cheering event to show that God's watchful care was over us, the anxiety to which I was constantly subjected began to tell upon my enfeebled constitution. It was about the time of my severe illness the year before, and my appearance excited alarm among my friends. One day in May, 1876, Mr. Charles T. Lowndes, whom I met in Broad Street, remarked, " You are looking very sick and feeble." I said, " I do not look worse than I feel." He went on, " You must go to Europe." " Why, Mr. Lowndes," I said, " I could as easily go to the moon." " No, sir," he replied, " you must go ; you have made yourself necessary to the Church and to the State. You must not die yet if it can be prevented."

I thanked him for his kindness, but saw no way

by which the visit could be accomplished, and so we parted.

About ten days afterwards Mr. Lowndes inquired if I had made any arrangements to go. I told him I had not thought of it, except to thank him for his kindness. '' I have thought of it,'' he answered, '' and have made arrangements for you to go. As I dare say your basket is empty at your school, I have already sent you my annual subscription '' (which, by the way, was a large one), '' and I can send you some more money, but if I do it will only go into the general fund and be consumed. If I send you abroad and you recover your health, I will be doing more for the school than merely paying its present baker's bill.''

Thus saying, he asked me to step into his counting-house. There he filled up a check, and said, '' Now, sir, when you get on the other side let me know and I will send you more.''

I was quite overwhelmed by this unexpected kindness, but feeling I had not in any way moved in the matter, I believed it was God's method of helping on my work. I frankly thanked Mr. Lowndes for his generous and thoughtful kindness, and expressed my willingness to go, provided my vestry consented, which they promptly did. Several friends hearing of this, notably Mr. Theo. D. Wagner, helped me with funds. Dear Mr. Trenholm was too ill to think of such matters ; he died while I was in Europe. As these friends thought that I was too feeble to go abroad alone, they arranged that as soon as my son Theodore graduated in Hartford from Trinity College, he must go to take care of me, and they provided the funds. I took my wife and child Charles, and Josephine, my adopted daughter, to Asheville, where I procured board for them. My mother preferred staying in Charleston, and on the 5th of July, 1876, I sailed in the *Abyssinia*, leaving the school in the charge of Mr. John Gadsden, and the church in the hands of the vestry, committing them all to God. I left behind a debt of fifteen thousand dollars, not knowing how it ever could be paid. But my creditors were all very considerate, and told me that they would wait, being sure they would be paid in time. Now, previous to sailing thirty-three of my boys were confirmed, and there were six graduates of colleges in course of preparation for the ministry. During the winter of 1876, I had frequently visited the United States arsenal grounds, as many of the officers attended the Church of the Holy Communion. It is a whole square of eight acres of land, with many buildings on it. I became impressed with the belief that in not a very long time, Charleston would be given up as a military post and the arsenal would be abandoned. The needs of my school had out-grown the capacity of my builidings and grounds, and I felt that this arsenal was the place I needed. How to get it was of course the question. I told my wife what was in my mind, and daily at our prayers together we asked that, if it were possible, when the Government had no further use for it, I might obtain it. It seemed a far-off hope, but I did a great deal of thinking about it, in our ten days' trip across the Atlantic.

We landed at Queenstown on the 15th of July, and went to Cork, Killarney, and Dublin, across to Glasgow and Edinburgh, Stirling, and the lakes of Scotland, and down to London, where we arrived on the 5th of August. I had left London on the 15th of October, 1858, with my wife. How much had happened in those eighteen years ! I had taken letters of introduction to Messrs. Brown, Shipley & Co., to the Lord Bishop of Winchester, to the Archbishop of Canterbury, to Dean Stanley, and to Doctor Tremlett, of St. Peter's, Hampstead. I called at the office of Messrs. Brown, Shipley & Co., and sent in my card, with Mr. Howard Potter's letter of introduction. Mr. William Collet met me with the words, " Where have you been ? We have been expecting you for three weeks. You are doing a very wonderful work in America, and no doubt you would like to get some help in England."

" Pardon me," I said ; " how do you know anything of my work ? "

" Oh," he said, " Mr. Howard Potter sent me your pamphlet. It reads like a novel, and if it did not come so endorsed is scarcely credible."

I said to him : " It is all true ; God's providence has sent me abroad, in search of health. I have become much shattered by my anxious life. I have come only for health. There is too much money in America, for me to come to England for help. It would be a reflection on the gener-osity of my fellow-citizens."

" Well," he said, " your work will touch the religious heart of the English people, and if we give you money without your asking for it, will you not take it ? "

" Of course," I answered, " on those conditions I would be grateful for any help."

He said : " You look like a sick man. Go to Switzer-land, and spend the summer there. Try to forget your responsibilities at home and get well. Come back in the autumn, when people return to London, and we will help you."

We remained a few days in London, where I met my friend, Mrs. Ogle Taylor, of Washington, D. C., with her niece, Miss Price, of Troy. She insisted on my seeing that celebrated physician, Sir Andrew Clark. I told her it was impossible ; I did not have the means to visit such a celebrity. She said she had arranged for all that, and had made an appointment for me. I called, and Doctor Clark was very kind. He gave me a searching examina-tion, and told me my lungs were perfectly sound, and that the hemorrhage had been from the heart's feeble action ; that the anxieties of an overtaxed life had told upon my nervous system, and that separation from my work was my only safety. I must try to forget America, the church and school, for had I remained much longer at my post my case would have been hopeless. Rest and a bracing air would bring me all right again. I felt better at once on hearing this opinion. My son Theodore was a young man fresh from college, and Miss Price,* a bright blooming young girl on her first outing. Mrs. Taylor was very glad for her to have an escort, and they had a good time together, at the theatres, drives, and general sight-seeing of London.

We went to Paris ; from there to Switzerland, visiting Geneva, Chamouni, Lausanne, Martigny, the Ghorner Grat, the Rhone Glacier, the Wengern Alp, Interlaken, Lucerne, Basle, Berne, Cologne, Antwerp, Brussels, and Paris, returning to London on the 29th of September. My son, with Colonel Simons, who was our companion in travel, left me that afternoon and sailed for America to enter the Berkeley Divinity School, at Middletown. My health was so far restored, that I too could have returned home, but there was that fifteen thousand dollars debt staring me in the face, and the promise of Mr. Collet to fall back on. I can never forget the awful loneliness of that moment, as the train rolled out of Euston Station, and I stood on the platform—alone—in London, knowing only Mr. Collet, of Brown, Shipley & Co. The school had been disbanded a month earlier in consequence of my absence, but the 1st of October was at hand, and how could I open again with that debt before me ? The Bank of Charleston had enabled me to tide over the summer, but notes would soon fall due, and not a dollar had come in. I felt as powerless as a child alone on a raft in the midst of the tempestuous sea. I was very much in the state

* Miss Price married Mr. Hammersley, then the Duke of Marl-borough, and is now Lady Berresford.

of mind in which I stood on Broadway, New York, in 1866, when Bishop Davis sent me on his mission. But I felt I was in London in the providence of God, and I cast myself on Him, who has said : " Cast thy care upon God, for He careth for thee." I believed it, and trusted Him. I went to Russell Square and engaged a room. The next day I took a hansom, and drove five miles to Doctor Tremlett's at Belsize Park. It is not easy to describe my reception there. The Doctor was engaged and could not see me, but he sent my letter to his mother and sister, who received me cordially, making me feel I was no longer a stranger in a strange land. I found that this hospitable house had been the headquarters of many Southerners during the civil war, all of whom were known to me. Bishop Quintard, an old friend who had visited England in the interest of the University of the South, had also been Doctor Tremlett's guest. Thus bound together by subjects of common interest, we soon became well acquainted, and a friendship began that night which strengthened with years and is one of the sweet memories of life. Hours rolled on and still the Doctor did not make his appearance. In the meanwhile, not having learned the ways of London, I had kept the cab, much to the satisfaction of the driver, but dearly to the cost of my not overfull purse. As I was leaving, the Doctor came in apologizing for his delay, but he said, " As a clergyman, you can easily understand." His first words were, " Where are you staying ? " I told him my address. " Stay where you are, and give me the number of your packages, and I will go and bring your luggage here." This I declined with many thanks, but he said : " You are a South Carolina clergyman, in London alone, with a letter from the Bishop of Alabama, and not staying in my house. I will not tolerate it. You must come here and make your home here while you stay in London."

He was so earnest that I yielded, but refusing his offer to get my effects, I went myself, and by ten o'clock I found myself the guest of a gentleman I had never seen before, and at whose house I remained four months and a half, only broken by occasional visits to others. I cannot convey an idea of the genial and generous hospitality of those months ; had I been a brother I could not have been treated with greater kindness. Just before retiring that night, I gave the Doctor one of my pamphlets which contained the records of my school to the close of 1875. Next morning he said to me : " You ought never to give that book to anyone late in the evening if you do not intend to take away his night's rest. I began to read it, not intending to spend much time over it, but I read on and on until I had read every word, and it was near morning when I finished it. I had no idea who you were when I asked you to stay with me. You must get some aid in England."

I told him that I had come to England for health, and would have returned with my son, but for the observation of Mr. Collet, which was similar to his, and it did seem that God was making a way for me, and therefore I had remained. He said there were many persons in England who would be interested in such a work ; the only trouble would be to reach them, but he would lend me his aid, which he did most royally.

CHAPTER XXXV

GENEROUS HELPERS

Account of my warm reception in England.

NOW, reader, do you see the hand of God in all this? My broken health alone put me where I was. If you do not yet understand, read on, and you soon will. That day I called on Mr. Collet. By this time Mr. Hamilton, the head of the firm of Brown, Shipley & Co., had returned, and I received from himself, his wife and daughter, most cordial and enjoyable hospitality, at Brent Lodge, Finchley, near London. Mrs. Hamilton had lost two dear boys in one week, and when my story was known it struck a responsive chord. Mr. Collet gave a dinner party to which he invited a number of gentlemen whom he had told that he wished to introduce me and desired them to hear the story I had to tell. After dinner Mr. Collet requested me to tell my story. I did not know at the time that those gentlemen had come to hear it, and I told it as succinctly as I could. They asked many questions and before we left the dinner-table, a day had been named by each, asking me to dinner. Next day I received a note from each containing a check for from five pounds up to fifty pounds. I dined with each of these gentlemen and met a different party each time, with the same results. I had twenty-five copies of my pamphlet with me and my friends requested me to cable the Messrs. Appleton, who had published it, for five hundred copies : these arrived and were soon distributed. My friends published in England an edition of one thousand, which they distributed, so that help came to me from many quarters. By the 1st of December I felt that I had been long enough in London, so I prepared to return. I had letters to Mr. Stephen Watson, from Mr. Wm. M. Lawton, of Charleston, and to Mr. A. H. Brown, M.P., from Mr. Howard Potter. I sent these to Liverpool, and soon received pressing invitations from both gentlemen to visit them. During my visit in London, I had presented my letter of introduction to the Lord Bishop of Winchester, Harold Browne, well known as the author of the work on the Thirty-nine Articles of Religion. He entertained me at his Episcopal palace, Fulham. He was a charming man, simple and unostentatious. Walking with him in his grounds, I two or three times addressed him as Bishop, when catching myself, I begged pardon by saying '' My Lord.'' He put his arm around my neck and said : '' I am only Bishop to you ; never mind about the ' My Lord.' ''

I also presented my letter to Archbishop Tait, of Canterbury, with whom I dined. He took me all over Lambeth Palace, and pointed out many historic places, and was genial and courteous. I also met Dean Stanley, but distinguished as he was, he did not interest me. He gave me a letter to his sister, Mrs. Vaughan, the wife of the Master of the Temple, and Mrs. Vaughan invited me to several receptions, and to dinner. She was rather given to assemble in her parlors everybody and anybody from all parts of the world who had been in any way distinguished for having done anything out of the ordinary life.

Quite an amusing circumstance occurred while I was in London. There were some persons from India, or from

Africa, I forget which, and she invited them to dinner, with guests to meet them. Of course they were of dark complexion. The day came, and the hour for dinner, and five minutes are allowed a guest for delay, after which the dinner is served. Ten minutes passed and the dinner was announced, but the special guests did not put in an appearance. The hour passed and still they did not come. At length Mrs. Vaughan asked the butler if no one had called during dinner. "No one," he said, "except some nigger minstrels, but they had been sent away." Mrs. Vaughan's consternation can be imagined, for they were not nigger minstrels, but her guests. I heard a good story in London of a certain merchant : There was a clergyman noted for good works, who had a ready *entrée* to the prominent offices in London. He called on this merchant and told his object. Of course the merchant assented and drew his check, put it in an envelope, and gave it to the minister. He was raising two thousand pounds and when he went out of the office he opened the envelope and found it was for one thousand pounds. Returning at once, he said : "Surely you have made a mistake, you meant to give me one hundred pounds and you gave me one thousand pounds." "No," the merchant answered ; "your time is too valuable to be going about much, and I wished to hasten the time when you would get what you need for your work. But I am glad that you have come back. Since you left I have opened my mail and find that things have changed with me. Two of my ships have gone down in the China Sea, and as we are our own insurers, they are a total loss. I will have to get you to return that check."

The clergyman of course gave it back and very much regretting his friend's loss as well as his own, he turned to go, but the merchant stopped him saying : "You cannot go from this office empty-handed." So he drew another check, put it in an envelope, and gave it to the clergyman, who again looked at it when he reached the street. He thought he could not read aright, as the check was written for two thousand pounds. So he hastened back, saying: " My friend, you certainly now have made a mistake. You meant twenty pounds and you have made it two thousand pounds." " No," was the reply; " I meant two thousand pounds, for if my fortune is going to the bottom of the sea, I wish to deposit some of it first where it cannot be lost."

Some years after this I was again in London and dining with my dear friend, Mr. Fred. A. White. I related the story and wondered if it was true. His uncle, the Rev. Edw. White, was at table, and said it was true ; he had known the merchant and the clergyman and the circumstance. But how many of us Christian people are like that merchant ?

I left London and went to Liverpool, to be the guest of Mr. Stephen Watson and Mr. Brown, by both of whom I was most hospitably entertained and generously helped. I noticed one evening that Mr. Watson, who was an old gentleman, was a little fidgety, and it occurred to me that whist was a habit with some old gentlemen, so I asked, " Mr. Watson, do you play whist ? " He said, " Yes, he was very fond of it."

" Why do you not play, then ? "

" We are only three, and the dummy would not be entertaining to you."

" Oh," I said, " I have not played a game of whist for twenty years, but I will be as good as dummy; if you will let me take a hand, I will do so with pleasure."

The old gentleman brightened up : " You will ? " he said. " Why, certainly."

The cards were ordered, and we played over five games. I soon found I was doubly welcome, and instead of a

2:

couple of days, he insisted on my staying a week.   Friday
came and I was to leave on the *Scythia.*   The next day a
budget of letters were forwarded from London; among
them was one which has had a great influence on the
shaping of many events of my after life.   It was very
short ; it was in these words :

" REV. AND DEAR SIR :
    " I have read your little book and would like to make
your acquaintance.   I am a very busy man, and therefore
if you will make an appointment, I will call and see you,
but if you will not stand on ceremony and will call on me,
I will be glad to see you.
                              " Yours truly,
                                 " GEORGE H. WILKINSON."

I had read Mr. Wilkinson's book, *The Devout Life*, and
had heard a great deal about the author in London, of
whom what Churchman in those days who entered the
church life in London did not hear ?   Such a man had
made himself felt even in such a mighty world as London.
He was then the vicar of St. Peter's Church, Eaton
Square, and afterwards Bishop of Truro, where he succeeded Doctor Benson.   Doctor Wilkinson became the
Bishop of St. Andrew's, Edinburgh, Scotland.   He was
the very centre of an immense church work.   To reach
him had never entered my head ; to interest him in my
work I had never presumed to hope ; I had not done or
said a thing to bring this about.   How he had got hold
of my pamphlet, I did not know, and yet, here was a letter from him asking me to call and see him.
    Here was another door which God had opened for me.
I was very much in the same state of mind in which I
think St. Peter was when the angel opened the prison

door and let him out. I telegraphed Doctor Tremlett that I would return on Saturday, for the Cunard Line agreed to extend my ticket for six months.

I therefore forwarded five thousand five hundred dollars to Charleston and went back to London. How different my frame of mind from what it had been two and a half months before, when I was left by my son and Colonel Simons alone ! I showed Mr. Wilkinson's note to Doctor Tremlett and he told me how Mr. Wilkinson had received my book—that he, Doctor Tremlett, had given it to the Rev. Dr. Cutts, the author of *Turning Points in Church History*, a most interesting book. Doctor Cutts had given my pamphlet to Mr. Wilkinson, and told Mr. Tremlett that he was sure if Mr. Wilkinson read it, he would be my friend and I would find his friendship valuable ; that the door was now open to me wider than it was before. I went to St. Peter's, Eaton Square, on Sunday morning, when Mr. Wilkinson preached from the text, St. Mark ii., 2 : "And Jesus entered into Jerusalem and into the Temple : and when He had looked round about upon all things, and now the eventide had come, He went out unto Bethany with the twelve." I thought I never heard such preaching. It was not learned or abstruse, nor what in general would be called eloquent, but it was eloquence of the sublimest kind. Every word came with power and the congregation seemed spellbound ; there was a deathlike stillness over the throng of worshippers, and when he came to the close, he said slowly and calmly: "And now, my brethren, this same Jesus has come into this Temple to-day, and is looking around upon all things. He is looking at you. Yes, He is looking through you (pointing to one portion of his flock), and through you (pointing to another quarter of the church), yes, through me, through everyone of us, and "—leaning on his pulpit, gazing with a fixed earnestness into the faces of his hearers, he added, slowly, '' and what does He see in us ? ''

He waited a moment, then rising, he turned and made the ascription to the Triune God.   I have never forgotten the moment; every countenance seemed to express the thought, '' What does He see in me ? ''   Over twenty years have passed, but my reverend brother's words have often been asked since then: '' What does He see in me ? ''   Mr. Wilkinson was a man, at that time, whom to know was a privilege.   If ever a man lived within the veil, it was himself.   He was nearly exhausted with hard work when he was made Bishop of Truro.   At Truro he built the Choir of the Cathedral, and an exquisite work it is, but the pressure was too great, and he broke down in health utterly.

In due time after the close of the service, I sent my card into the vestry-room.   Never will I forget that day.   Mr. Wilkinson came forward and extending both of his hands, took mine in them, saying: '' My brother, I am glad to see you ; I have read your book ; I know I am very full-handed, and thought I could not take hold of another thing, but you are doing a work that has upon it so mani-festly the impress of God, that I claim the privilege of sharing with you some of the blessing.   I can help you and I will.''

Then I was introduced to his dear wife and children. She has now gone to her Saviour, leaving a vacancy that only memory fills ; a memory that dwells fondly on her beautiful, loving presence, that made her home so attrac-tive and so enjoyable, for she was everything to that household, its sunlight and its joy.

In 1881, when we had moved from our old quarters in the building I had bought in 1868, I refitted the house and called it, in memory of her, The Caroline Wilkinson Home.   It was a refuge for ladies in reduced circumstances, with accommodàtion for fourteen, and it has been filled nearly ever since. Several widows and orphans of clergymen have there found shelter. It is the charge of my parish, and we do all we can to add to the comfort of its inmates. I wish I had a few thousand dollars invested to make it a more desirable home.

Mr. Wilkinson had invited me to preach for him the following Sunday night, which I did, but Mrs. Wilkinson said that was not the opportunity that I ought to have. It was the morning congregation I needed to address.

The Vicar looked over his engagements and found I could not have his pulpit until the 14th of February. This was the 18th of December. In the meantime Mr. Wilkinson undertook that home after home was thrown open to me, several pulpits were secured, friends were made in new circles, and offerings began to come in again.

My good friend, Doctor Tremlett, whose guest I still was, had introduced me to many of his flock, so that when I preached at his church, I addressed a number of persons whose acquaintance I had made. I preached morning and night to a large congregation and the offering was, next to St. Peter's, Eaton Square, the largest that I received in England. Indeed, it was much larger than I ever received after preaching in any church in America.

I had now been absent from home since the 1st of July and affairs there needed my presence.

Rev. Mr. Perry had broken down in health, had been called to Maryland, had gone, and I was needed in the school ; and my wife, whose health was so frail, had begun to feel the separation.

A frightful state of things had prevailed at home.

One of those horrors of the American system of government that occurs every four years, the election of a President, which always deranges finance and politics, had been held, the result having brought the country again to the verge of civil war.

South Carolina had been the scene of violent agitation, Charleston had been taken possession of by a desperate mob of negroes, and blood had been shed in the streets.

A young man who had been educated at my school, and was then a member of my choir, had been shot dead, while quietly walking with his father to his business, ignorant of the disturbance that was going on.

But for the firmness of General Hunt, who lived at the arsenal, and was in command of the United States forces in the city, and the cool courage and tact of General James Conner (the same man to whom I had offered the command of the Washington Light Infantry Volunteers in 1861 under St. Michael's porch), there would have been an awful massacre of negroes, and none can tell what might have been the consequence.

The negroes had been incited by some of the miserable carpet-baggers and scaliwags, as they were termed, renegade Southerners, to deeds of violence, and in this case they were the aggressors. Every white man flew to arms. The Rifle Clubs rendezvoused at their armories and five thousand armed, incensed men chafed that they were held in check. One word and the trouble would have been quelled, but thousands of blacks would have died. James Conner, however, rode from armory to armory and appealed for the obedience of the men, and for their trust in him. Such was the respect and confidence they had in him that they obeyed. Going to General Hunt, he reported a large body of citizen soldiery ready for duty, and General Hunt directed him to bring out his men, and to range them in the rear of his United States troops. So overwhelming a display of organized power soon quelled the mob, and so the bloodshed was stopped and a fearful massacre prevented. All honor to the memory of General Hunt and General James Conner, two names worthy of high place in American history, and to whom Charleston ought to be eternally grateful.

Under all these circumstances I determined my duty was to start home, although it was a risk to make the passage at that midwinter season, on the 17th of February.

On the 14th day of February, I preached to an immense congregation at St. Peter's, Eaton Square. Mr. Wilkinson had said, " Do not preach longer than twenty minutes, for I will announce that you will again preach at four o'clock, when I only have a hymn and a few collects and the sermon, and you can then preach as long as you desire.'' While the service was going on, he asked if my voice could fill the church. " Try me," I said, " with the first lesson." I read it, and as I came back he said, " You will do." I went into the pulpit, feeling that I had before me the very cream of the English aristocracy, titled people without number, but I did not feel one tenth the excitement I did the day, in 1865, I preached to Doctor Littlejohn's congregation in Brooklyn.

I went on very quietly for a quarter of an hour, when my mind suddenly failed me ; I could not have said another word for my life. So I turned and made the ascription and came down. Mr. Wilkinson said: " Just right, you have left off where you have made them wish to hear more." It was not premeditated ; memory had left me. The verger told Mr. Wilkinson that the Marquis of Westminster, as he went out of the church, said to him: " That gentleman evidently had more to tell," and he came back at four o'clock to hear what I had to say. The church was again crowded at four o'clock and Mr. Wilkinson told me he saw persons there he had never before seen at a second service.

I preached again at night to a wholly different class of people, but this time my effort was to help them, not they

to help me. After the service in the morning, a card was
sent into the vestry and a gentleman desired an introduction ; this was Mr. Frederick A. White, then of Kenross
House, Cromwell Road.

I had but one night unengaged before I was to leave
London, which he requested me to spend at his house,
as I did. An ever-memorable night it was, for then
began a friendship which I prize as one of the most precious of my life, and even up to January 1, 1897, I received a cable from him of love and greeting. He added
largely to the offering made at St. Peter's. On the 16th
I received a card from the Earl of Aberdeen, then quite
a young man, inviting me to luncheon, and to spend the
evening with him.

I was to leave at four o'clock in the morning, and had
bidden them good-bye at Doctor Tremlett's and at Mr.
White's, and so I stayed with the Earl. About ten
o'clock I proposed to go, for I had to get my luggage
from where I had left it, but he asked for the receipt
from the expressman, and begged me to stay and we
talked on until three in the morning. Perhaps he may
have forgotten that night ; I never shall. His landau
was at the door, and he told me his man would meet me
at the station with my trunk, and as he bade me good-
bye he handed me an envelope with a check for one hundred pounds, the same amount which he had previously
given me.

At the house of Mr. Wilkinson, I had met Mr. and Mrs.
Thomas Kinscote, he, the grandson of Lord Bloomfield,
and she, the daughter of Lord Gordon, both of whom are
still my warm friends.

I also met Hon. Edward Thesinger, son of Lord Chelms-
ford, who, with his wife, were warm friends.

Through the Earl of Aberdeen, I was introduced to
Lord High Chancellor of England, and Lady Shelborne,

at whose hands in after years, I received many acts of kindness, as I did from Mr. and Mrs. Hamilton, and Sir William Collet, from the Messrs. Gilliat of Crosby Square—yes, from a host of friends, I received kindness for which I have not language to express my gratitude.

My fellow countryman, Mr. J. S. Morgan, extended to me warm hospitality, renewed his donation, and continued until his death to do the same.

When I arrived at Liverpool I wrote to Mr. Wilkinson that I was going home with all my fifteen thousand dollars provided for, except seventy-one pounds, which I knew I could collect in New York. When I reached Queenstown a telegram met me, saying : " Go on your way rejoicing, as the Earl of Aberdeen has put seventy-one pounds to your credit."

CHAPTER XXXVI

A CHURCH FOR COLORED PEOPLE

The School is full—The colored question in the Church—The Bishop piles another burden on my willing shoulders—How I went to work to build up St. Mark's—I found the House of Rest.

WHEN I look back at that visit to England, whither I went a sick man, knowing no one, with a debt of fifteen thousand dollars on my shoulders, when I remember how I returned with health reëstablished, with a host of friends and the debt all paid, am I wrong in stating that God had His own way to accomplish His ends? Had I not been sick I would never have gone to England, and much of my after life had not been lived. On the 1st of March, 1877, I arrived in New York, after a long voyage, for the *Abyssinia* was a slow boat, but the ocean was as smooth as a mill-pond. I have crossed the ocean five times in summer, but have never had so calm a passage as this in midwinter. After a short visit to my boys at Union College, Schenectady, I returned home, where a warm welcome greeted me.

The Home and School were full of boys. Mr. Perry had been ordained priest ; Mr. P. H. Whaley had been ordained a deacon, in Connecticut. Both of them had been my boys, the latter had been a playmate of that sainted child at whose grave this institution arose, and he was the first boy who came into my mind, when God told me to rouse myself from my grief, and go and do something for Christ and His Church. Thus has He blessed me. My child is in Paradise, but his young companion, through my instrumentality, is doing His Master's work in the Church militant.

He is now rector of the church in Pensacola, and has a bright boy at my school. The generous treatment I had received in England stimulated our people at home, but though friends at the North aided me to some extent, we closed the school in July with a debt of three thousand five hundred dollars. In June, 1877, at St. Philip's Church, Rt. Rev. W. B. W. Howe had ordained Mr. C. J. La Roche to the diaconate. He was one of my boys, was educated at my school, went to the University of the South, and to the Theological Seminary at Nashotah, and is now rector at Thomasville, Georgia.

I have mentioned that my wife and I had daily prayed that whenever the arsenal was given up by the government we might get it.

I had told General Hunt, who was in command, my wishes, and he promised if ever the time came he would assist me. In the fall of 1877, the General Convention sat in Boston and I was the guest of Mr. Robert M. Mason, as was Rt. Rev. Horatio Potter, of New York, Bishop Whipple, of Minnesota, and others. It so happened that the delegations from Louisiana and South Carolina sat in adjoining pews. Next to me was General Auger, who was in command of the Southern Department, and was a delegate from Louisiana, who became my close friend, and when I told him what I had told General Hunt, he promised his aid also. This was in October, 1877.

We had reached the beginning of the eleventh year,

and the reader can form some faint idea of how full these
years were of joys and sorrows, hopes and fears, all of
which are known in Heaven.   But no one can tell what
such a work as this costs, but those who have the like
work to do.   Does my reader say, " Why do you perse-
vere in doing it, why not give it up ?   Enough has been
done and you are likely to weary your friends, and we
know all the work, the labor, the anxiety."   My only
answer is, " I do not dare to stop.   There is no cessation
for me until I lie down in the grave.   God sent me to do
a work, and this work He has carried on in a manner that
is miraculous."

An amount of good has been accomplished which never
can be estimated in this world, and unless it becomes apparent by the entire failure of means that the appointed
end has come, I simply must go on.   Woe would be to
me, and more, if I should stop because of weariness.   I
can no more cease my efforts than St. Paul could forego
to preach the Gospel ; like him, I must " forget the things
behind, and press for the mark."   If this is fanaticism, it
is a strong conviction.

The last words of my dying child were, " O Lord, save
Thy people and bless Thine heritage," and I feel his
prayer is being answered.

While we were in Boston at the Convention, the Rev.
J. B. Seabrook, the rector of St. Mark's (the colored congregation), died and they were left without a head.

They had bought an old building in Alexander Street
from St. Luke's Church, a building which Rev. C. P.
Gadsden had built while St. Luke's Church was in process of erection.   They had also bought a lot at the
corner of Thomas and Warren Streets, laid a brick foundation, and set the frame of a large church up, and after the
death of Rev. Mr. Seabrook had stopped work from October to May.   By very bad management some eleven thou-

sand dollars had been wasted and this exhausted their resources, and the congregation was fast disintegrating. One day in May, 1878, Bishop Howe came to see me. I was in my study and having just received several boxes of very superior claret as a present from my friend Mr. Thomas Kinscote, from England, I offered a glass to my guest. After refreshing, the Bishop said : " Porter, does not St. Mark's Church trouble your conscience ? "

" Well," I said, " it is a shame, Bishop, that they are not helped, and I never pass that frame building that I do not feel the Church at large should take hold of it and finish it."

" That is what I have come here for you to do."

" Bishop, I cannot do it, I am overwhelmed with work now."

" I know it," he said. " You have more to do than six men ordinarily have, and I think this will kill you, yet it is a good cause to die in; but," he added, " you have always taken an interest in the colored work, they are fond of you, and you are the only one of the clergy who knows anything about finance, and there will have to be a great deal of financial work done there, and you can do it."

" Is it W. B. W. Howe who says this to me, or the Rt. Rev. W. B. W. Howe ? If the former, I answer at once, 'No, I will not touch it '; if it is my Bishop, I am under orders and I will obey."

The Bishop laughed, and said, " Well, it is the Bishop."

" Very well," I replied, " you do not expect me to give up the Church of the Holy Communion or the School, do you ? "

" Oh, no, but you must take this too."

" Very well," I said ; " go and have me elected rector, and promise to give me, for one year, each of the deacons as they are ordained, and I will undertake it."

As he went out of my office, he added : "You have rolled away a weight that was on my heart."

He went and assembled the vestry of St. Mark's and told them their prospects. They were delighted, and at once unanimously elected me rector. On Sunday night the 7th of June, 1878, I held service for them and after the sermon said :

" Now, friends, your vestry have elected me your rector. I can only give you a service one Sunday morning a month, when I will have a Celebration, and also service every Sunday night and Wednesday night.

" I will visit your sick, bury your dead, and marry those who desire me to do so. The Bishop promises me Mr. La Roche, who will be ordained in a few days deacon, and he will minister at other times, but if there is a man among you who does not wish me to accept, now is the time to say it or forever after hold your peace.

" All who wish me to accept, rise."

Ninety-one men rose. "Now," I said, "those who do not wish me to accept, rise." None rose. "While," I said, " women do not vote in this church, yet all of you can express your wishes ; all the women who wish me to accept, rise." Over two hundred rose, being all the women present. " It is unanimous," I said, " and in the name of the Trinity I accept the rectorship and next Wednesday night I will be here, and after service I shall talk about money and nothing else. Those who do not wish to hear about that subject can stay away."

On Monday night I called a meeting of the younger members of the vestry, C. C. Leslie, Richard Birnie, Wm. Ingliss, and John Stoken, at Ingliss's house, and said : " You know your people better than I do. How can I best reach them next Wednesday night ? " Birnie suggested that I draw up two copies each of subscriptions for twenty-five, twenty, fifteen, ten, and five dollars, payable quarterly, and then for miscellaneous amounts, and send one after the other down the aisle.

I adopted his plan, and on Wednesday night the building was packed with the congregation.

I then told them I did not propose to stay long in this tumble-down shanty, nor let their church go unfinished ; that we must be in it in six months ; I would not go for help outside until we had raised our last dollar. That I would send these lists down among them, and none of them must sign one of them for an amount they would not pay. That I would place these lists on the altar as a gift to God, and they must not rob Him.

I then started the lists. I had no singing, no excitement, but calmly read the offertory, expounding each verse as I went along. As the lists were brought up, I reverently placed them on the altar, and started sending down another set. It took some time to do it; but when they were all in, I gave them to the vestry, and told them to add up the amount that I might announce it to them. The pledges footed up three thousand five hundred dollars, and I collected every dollar of it except one hundred and seventy-nine dollars, which failed from deaths; and this from a colored congregation in 1878. The vestry met, and voted me a salary of nine hundred dollars.

When Mr. La Roche was ordained and came to me, I gave him every cent of the nine hundred dollars ; indeed, I served those people for ten years, and never received, personally, one dollar for my work. They presented me with a horse and buggy to enable me to do my extra parish work ; with that exception, they had my labors without money and without price, as the deacons in charge received all the salary. I had in succession, C. J. La Roche; Theo. A. Porter, my son; Thaddeus Saltus, a colored man, first as deacon, then as priest ; and after his death, Rev. Mr.

Bishop; and then Rev. J. H. M. Pollard, into whose hands I resigned the work after ten years in 1888, leaving him with a communicant list of three hundred and fifty, a church built and paid for, all to some eleven hundred dollars contracted for repairs.

But I must go back to the first efforts. Next day after this free offering, on Wednesday night, June 10th, I went to Mr. Wm. C. Courtney, President of the Bank of Charleston. I told him I had set the contractor at work on the church that morning, and would need money from time to time, at ninety days, to be paid out of these pledges. He asked if I would give my note. " Yes, with the names already mentioned as endorsers." " Well," he said, " I shall look to you for the money." " Yes," I answered, " I will be responsible, but I will never pay one dollar of it beyond my subscription " ; and I never did. They paid it all themselves, and we never renewed without taking off a good slice of the debt. On the 7th of November, the church was consecrated, as the debt was all personal, being mine and three members of the congregation. We had not long occupied it before I induced them to buy an organ which cost sixteen hundred dollars, and we had just paid the last dollar we owed when the cyclone of 1885 unroofed the church and ruined the organ.

It was a terrible blow to these hard-working people, and they seemed ready to give up, but I called the vestry together, and invited the congregation through them to worship at St. Timothy's Chapel, which held fully five hundred persons. This chapel I had built on my grounds, at the old arsenal. There they worshipped for six months. About one thousand dollars came from the North to help them, and about one thousand dollars at home, but it cost them four thousand five hundred to repair and enlarge the chancel and restore the organ. Then the earthquake of 1886 again damaged them about fifteen hundred dollars, and it was from this cause I left them with that eleven hundred dollars debt.   It did not kill me as Bishop Howe thought it would.   I gave up my summer's holidays in 1878 to them, and worked very hard, but I look back with much gratitude to the work I did for Christ and His Church in that congregation.   When I left them they ranked second in numbers in the diocese, and fifth in the list of contributions for Church work.

St. Mark's Church has become historical, for it was about it that that dreadful contest waged in this diocese; it almost killed me, and it did kill the Bishop, for he died of a broken heart ; broken by his love for the Church which he ruled and loved so well.

When I came back from England, my blessed friend, Mr. George A. Trenholm, was dead—one of the noblest, greatest men this State has ever produced.   I missed him then ; I have missed him in all these long years ; I need him now, for our parish needs his wisdom and his aid.

But a new work was now opened up to me, for Miss Celia Campbell and Miss Jane Wagner came to me in the church, after a week-day service, in the seventies, and told me they had found in their visits to the City Hospital an unfortunate woman who wished to lead a better life. She had been ill, and was now convalescent and had to leave the hospital, and they did not know what to do with her.

I soon saw what was in their minds.   '' Go,'' I said, '' and hire a house and begin your work. I will be responsible for three months' rent.''   I did not have to pay the rent, for these blessed women themselves established The House of Rest, which has done a great work for fifteen years.

The school began again on the 1st of October, 1878, and I find nothing of note, save the consecration of St. Mark's Church, and the steady routine life of the two parishes, and the school.

22

My notes tell of the same trials, perplexities, and needs as we drifted along I scarcely know how ; but God was preparing a new movement in my behalf.

I had begun the year with a debt of thirty-five hundred dollars. I saw in the month of December that my debt at the end of the year would be nearly double that amount. I wrote several letters to persons whom I knew to be very rich and whom I regarded as my friends. From one I received a very curt reply; another, an immensely wealthy person, said he had nothing to spare. I concluded if such men could give me such answers, it was useless to apply to any others. About the 22d of December I wrote to my friend Canon Wilkinson, and told him of my distress, adding, in the then depressed condition of things in England, I could not think of turning to my friends there for help. A committee of gentlemen, after my first visit to England, had agreed to keep my memory green in the hearts of my English friends, and they had sent me each year, several hundreds of pounds.* Early in February, 1879, I received a letter from Fred. A. White, Secretary, stating that the committee had held a meeting and directed him to write me that they could not counsel me to come across the water, but that I had many friends in England, and although the times were very hard, still, if I determined to come they would ensure me a hearty welcome, and would render me all the assistance they could. The decision they must leave with the Bishop of my diocese and myself, but if I came not to do so until after Easter. I immediately went to the Bishop and laid the whole matter before him. He asked me if I went, what would I do with my two parishes, the Holy Communion and St. Mark's ? I told him the Rev. Mr. La Roche would fill one, and for the other, I proposed to get three or four of the brethren who were in small country parishes to take my place. " On what grounds ? " the

* For list of English Committee, see Appendix H.

Bishop asked. I said : " On the ground that this Academy was rearing laymen for every parish in the diocese. That from it, we had to look for most of the clergy of the future, and if it failed now, it would carry desolation into hundreds of households."

The Bishop remained thoughtful for some time, and then said : " I regard your work of so much value to the Church that it must not fail if human aid can prevent it. I will recall my appointments to the diocese for the Sundays, and I will myself take charge of your parish until you return."

I told the Bishop this endorsement of my work would be worth a trip to England if I did not bring back one dollar. I called the vestry and board of trustees together, and submitted to them the question—to go, or not? They deplored their inability to deny that it was my duty to go. After the cheering offer of the Bishop, and the unanimous advice of the vestry and trustees, there seemed nothing else to do. During all this while my wife had been desperately sick, and had been confined to her bed for weeks, and was so feeble she could not hold up her head. I shrank from leaving home under such circumstances. My wife very ill, my eldest son to be soon ordained to the diaconate, my other son in my confirmation class—from all of which I would be absent. How could I go ? I laid all this before my wife, who, hearing me through, said : " I have determined your duty long since ; you must go." " I 'm leaving you," I said, " in this condition." Her answer was worthy of the best age of the Church—" ' He that loveth father or mother, wife or children, houses or lands, more than Me, is not worthy of Me.' If your Master has given you a work to do, do it, whatever sacrifice it costs."

This determined me, and all my arrangements began to be made to leave, on the 2d of April, in the *Scythia*.

CHAPTER XXXVII

I APPLY FOR THE ARSENAL

Vague thoughts of obtaining the arsenal buildings for the Institute—I am well supported by friends in my application —General Sherman endorses it—Help in England for my school.

DURING the month of February, my friend General Auger had visited Charleston, and sent me a message by General Hunt that he was in the city and invited me to see him. I accordingly called, and in the presence of General Auger, General Hunt said, "I wish you to tell General Auger what you have told me." I did so, saying to the General I did not know what it meant, but I had done as General Hunt requested, though he had heard the same from me in Boston. The General smiled and replied, "I will remember this, and if in anything I can be of service to you, you may depend on my assistance. It is the best purpose the property can be put to."

I had thought no more of this matter and turned my attention to my duties, and to my preparations for leaving America in April. A few days before I was to leave for England, I received a letter from General Auger, from Newport Barracks, Kentucky, telling me that the authorities at Washington had determined to withdraw the troops

from Charleston, and if I would make proper application
he thought I could get the arsenal, and that he would
assist me. His letter nearly took my breath away. Were
the prayers of my wife and self so near fulfilment? We
never mentioned it to a soul, but I wrote to General
Auger of my contemplated trip to England, and asked
what steps I should take. He telegraphed me to get a
strong letter of endorsement from General Hunt, and that
I would find letters from him in New York.

In the goodness of God my wife's health improved, so
when I left Charleston on the 27th of March, 1879 for
New York, I took her with me, to go and be with my
adopted daughter, Mrs. De Witt, whose husband, a most
distinguished surgeon in the United States army, was
stationed in Montana. I thought the change would be
good for her, and with Doctor De Witt's care, would revive her, which it did. I took with me the following
paper :

" *To the Hon. G. W. McGrary, Secretary of War:*

" SIR : I have been informed that it is the purpose of the
Government to withdraw the troops from the arsenal
property in Charleston, South Carolina, and leave it practically vacant, for the present, at least. If such be the
case, I have the honor to make application for the lease
of the property upon such terms as will secure its preservation and protect the interests of the Government. My
purpose is to occupy the buildings and grounds with my
school, The Holy Communion Church Institute, an institution incorporatd under the laws of South Carolina
for educational purposes, and which has accomplished important results in the last twelve years, in the education
of a large number of boys and young men, almost entirely
by voluntary contribution from the North and England
and other sections of this country. I am anxious to ex-

tend and enlarge the scope of this work, and am encouraged to hope that the Government may help me by contracting with me for a lease of the vacant property, which is admirably adapted to the purposes of a school such as mine.   It is quite competent for the institution to contract for a lease, and I am prepared to guarantee the preservation and return of the property in such order as I find it, upon proper notice.   I invite your attention to the letters of General Auger and General Hunt, with General Sherman's endorsement, and I am prepared to furnish any information which may be desired as to the character and purposes and history of this institution, which I think commends itself to the sympathy and kind offices of every lover of education and progress.   It is perhaps proper that I should say that I derive no pecuniary benefit from this school, and have no compensation from it, more than the satisfaction of knowing that I am and have been instrumental, through it, in extending the blessings of a liberal education to numbers of boys who would not otherwise have enjoyed them.   In other words, I desire to impress upon you that I am not making application for speculative purposes.

" Very respectfully, etc.,

" A. TOOMER PORTER,

" Chairman Board of Trustees."

The above, in part, was the substance of the paper I prepared, which General Hunt refers to in the following letter :

"HEADQUARTERS FIFTH ARTILLERY,

"CHARLESTON, S. C., March 21, 1879.

" I have examined Rev. Dr. A. Toomer Porter's paper with respect to the acquisition of the arsenal grounds,

Charleston, for the school of which he has charge, and believe that all the statements found in it are correct. In all excavations made in these grounds human remains are found, a boggy creek originally ran through the Square, diagonally, and it is difficult to get good foundations for new buildings. The locality is entirely outside the business part of the town, and the existing quarters, barracks, storehouses, and hospital are unfitted for any private use. To tear them down and sell the old materials would probably be the most profitable money use they could be put to. If no longer needed for military purposes, the place, nearly as it stands, would be admirably adapted for the uses of such a school as Dr. Porter's. I know the school, it is all it is claimed to be, has done incalculable good, and the transfer of the grounds to it would greatly augment its value to the people of this State. No other grant of lands (of the same money value) for purposes of education, would, in my opinion, be so useful, at this time, as the transfer of this reservation to the school for its permanent establishment.

"HENRY J. HUNT, Bvt. Major-Genl., U. S. A.,
"Comdg. Post of Charleston."

In New York I met a long and warm letter from General Auger telling me how to proceed. I had but six days now to work in, as I was to leave on the 2d of April. I left Mrs. Porter in New York and hastened to Washington. I called immediately on General Sherman. He and I had frequently met in the intervening years, and he always spoke of that trip I made with McQueen, and what he thought of the act on my part; and again and again he had asked me what the Government had done for me in return for my saving that young man. I had always said the Government could do nothing. It certainly could not pay me money, for I had taken my life in my hand to manifest my gratitude to McQueen, and that the running of such a risk had no money value.

"Just like you South Carolina fools," he had said; "very pretty, but not business."

This time when I called I said, "General, now the Government can do something, not for me, but for the State;" and I unfolded my wishes.

The General had gone on writing while I was talking, and when I had finished, he put down his pen, and turning his chair round, he said: "Do you never mean to stop putting this Government under obligations to you?"

"What do you mean?" I asked.

"Why, you saved the life of a valuable officer at the risk of your own in the war, and now the Government has a piece of abandoned property that it does not know what to do with, and here you are with this noble use to put it to. You do not think a man like you can hide himself? I have watched your career. I know about your colored school, and how you have struggled to educate the children of the impoverished white people there in Charleston. You ought to have a vote of thanks for taking it. I could give it to you with a stroke of my pen, but just as you get fixed, some politician might come and take it from you. You go to General Hampton and General Butler, and get them to draw a bill, and let them go to the Democrats, and me to the Republicans, and we will see if we cannot get it done."

General Sherman then took the paper I had drawn in Charleston, with General Hunt's letter, and drafted himself the paper given above. He then endorsed it strongly, and himself went with it to the Secretary of War, who also favorably endorsed it and sent it to the Adjutant-General to find out who had the power in the matter. The Adjutant-General said it would be necessary to get an act of Congress authorizing the lease. I then saw

General M. C. Butler, who became very much interested, and drafted a joint resolution, and had it introduced into the Senate. There it was referred to the Military Committee, of which General Wade Hampton was a member, and the next day they brought in a report recommending the adoption of the resolution and it went on the calendar. The same process was observed in the House of Representatives, and General Butler told me that was as far as it likely would go this session, and I need not stay longer. So I returned to New York, having no doubt about ultimate success. I felt I had been led on by an unseen hand to undertake the work, and God's blessing would go with it, and committing it to our Heavenly Father, asked that His will, not mine, be done. I made arrangements for my wife to go out to my adopted daughter, and on the 2d of April, 1879, sailed in the *Scythia* for my third trip across the ocean. On this trip I made the acquaintance of Mr. and Mrs. James T. Swift, both of whom were warm and generous friends until they died.

I arrived in London on Easter Eve, April 12, 1879, and stayed at Kenrose House, Cromwell Road, London, the guest of the truest friend I have ever had on earth, Mr. Frederick A. White. I met with a warm reception from him, his wife, and his sister, and found a letter of kindly welcome from Canon Wilkinson, saying I had done right to come. On the table was a note from my host containing twenty pounds as an Easter offering for my own use. This was only a sample of the unbounded kindness I received at their hands. For three months I was the guest of these dear friends, who left nothing undone to make my visit agreeable to myself and profitable to my work. Through Mr. Wilkinson, Doctor Tremlett, Mr. White, and Mr. Thomas Kinscote, all the plans were laid out for me, and I preached in several churches, where offerings were made to my cause. Several dinner parties were given to me, and thus more friends were made for my work. The Archbishop of Canterbury, Doctor Tait, the Archbishop of Dublin, the celebrated Doctor Trench, the Primate of Scotland, Lord Cairns, then Lord High Chancellor of England, Lord and Lady Shelborne, and the Earl and Countess of Aberdeen all extended to me social hospitality and some of them generous contributions. Mr. John Welsh, the American Minister at the Court of St. James, Mr. Junius S. Morgan, Mr. Sturgis, of the firm of Baring Brothers, gave me liberal assistance. It would be almost impossible to tell of all the kindness manifested to me in word and act. I look back to this visit with great pleasure, and am filled with gratitude not only to those liberal and hospitable friends, but to the Giver of every good and perfect gift, who moved the hearts of His people to aid me so materially in sustaining an institution, the importance of which I know I do not overestimate. Oh, that I could impress my own countrymen, North and South, with an idea of the good such an institution is capable of doing ! Single-handed I have maintained the struggle. I have begged and prayed daily for an endowment which will secure its continuance and give me some little rest, but it has not been the will of God to grant either yet, and here I am, after thirty years, battling hard as ever, and not seeing how I can maintain it another month. The proposed transfer of the arsenal property by the United States Government gave increased interest in my work. Soon after I arrived in England, I received papers from home containing the introduction of the joint resolution by Senator Butler, and the favorable report of the Military Committee of the Senate. This gave publicity to my work, for I had hitherto studiously kept the whole matter a profound secret, and this publication was the first intimation, at home, of my movement, and for several days the papers published articles laudatory and congratulatory.

Of course all undertakings of a public character meet with a certain amount of opposition. In due time I received a letter from General Butler stating that a certain person in Charleston had employed a lawyer to defeat my object. The person intended, if he could, to purchase the arsenal, pull down the buildings and put up in the middle of the square a private residence. I was not alarmed, for I knew the Government would not sell ; but I foresaw some trouble. I knew, however, that if it was true that I had been led so far by God's hand, and if it was for His glory and the good of the Church, I would not be defeated in my efforts, and I was quite willing to leave it all to Him.

The Rev. John Morgan, of the American Protestant Episcopal Church in Paris, invited me to come to Paris and preach for him on the 15th of June. From a few Americans in Paris I collected nearly one thousand dollars. But there was an incident of my visit to Paris that is worth repeating.

I met there Miss Mason of Virginia, who told me that she was anxious for me to go and see a Virginia family who were stranded in Paris. I was very much pushed for time, but I hunted them up in an obscure part of Paris, and called at eleven o'clock at night. I found the family looking for me. The father, from Virginia, had been a buyer of silk, but the house he represented in New York had failed and left them in great destitution. I really did not know what I had gone for, except to express my sympathy, but a rather handsome boy of about twelve years of age came out of an adjoining room in his night dress. I inquired if they had other boys, and they took me into their sleeping apartment, where I found another little fellow of ten or eleven, asleep. I asked what prospects were ahead for these boys, and found there was really little hope for them so far as their education was concerned. I had prayers with them, and then said to the master of the house : " I do not know why Miss Mason asked me to come here, unless it was to interest me in these boys. Suppose I take them to America and place them in my institute."

Both father and mother said they had been praying for two years that some means would be found to send these boys home to be educated.

" Well," I replied, " perhaps I am to be the answer to your prayers. I have been, perhaps, sent for them, and I will take them on two conditions. First, that I can get them free passages to America, and next that they be not interfered with by any of the family." To these conditions they readily assented.

On my return to London I called on Mr. William Cunard and told him their story.

" Well," he said, " I will let them go for ten pounds each." I said I did not have the twenty pounds, but I would go and see if I could raise the amount.

" Well," he said, " if you have to get it from anyone else, I may as well give it myself, and if you will go home in the *Abyssinia* I will pass them free."

My ticket was for the *Gallia*, and the other boat was to leave before I was ready, but the way seemed so clear, that I sent for the boys, Fendall and Henry, and after furnishing them both with a full outfit of clothes, in which some friends in London helped me, we sailed in the *Abyssinia* on the 5th of July. I had collected seven thousand five hundred dollars. Here it is a good place to mention that my English friends, from first to last, have contributed forty-five thousand dollars towards the maintenance of this work.

As the school had closed, I took these two boys into my

family, and kept Fendall from 1879 to 1885, Henry from 1879 to 1886, and most faithfully did their family observe the conditions. I never received from them in all these years the value of a straw hat to assist in clothing them. In 1885 I sent Fendall to the University of the South. For his brother Henry, through the Rev. E. N. Potter's kindness, I got a scholarship at Hobart College. He graduated well, at the head of a small class. I let him teach for a while, and then sent for him to give him a position in my school.

During my absence in England, my son Theodore was ordained on the 4th of June, 1879, by the Rt. Rev. John Williams, to the order of deacon. He returned with me to Charleston, and was married on the 29th of July, 1879, to Kate Fuller, with whom he lived in happy wedlock for fourteen years. She died on the 18th of March, 1893, leaving five children. Mysterious are the orderings of Divine Providence! A devoted wife and mother, and to me all that a daughter could be! By her death a great shadow fell on my life, for she was the brightening of my declining days when the light went out. For three years my son and myself struggled along alone, with two faithful colored women-servants, in charge of this family of children, the youngest twelve days old when the mother died, the oldest only thirteen years. It was the Father's will and we accepted it. The day of my son's wedding a niece of mine had died, leaving two little children, a boy and a girl, who fell to our lot to care for. Some people are dripping-pans of fortune ; my fate has been to be a dripping-pan of penniless orphans. I first had my wife's brother Charles, who was killed in the civil war ; then a cousin, Thomas Ford, whom I educated, and he did gallant service as captain through the war ; then two daughters of one sister, then one daughter of another. In 1867, the only son of my friend, Joshua Ward, had inherited a

million dollars from his father.   It was all swept away by
the war, and when he died he left his only son, Samuel
Mortimer, to my wife and myself without a dollar.   Then
came these two children of my niece in 1879, and so on ;
all through my dear wife's life, she, in her wretched
health, took cheerfully the charge of one after another of
these orphans and was a mother to them.

CHAPTER XXXVIII

My efforts to obtain the Charleston arsenal as a home for my school—Obstructions and oppositions—The military committee treats me generously—The kindness of President Hayes—The arsenal is duly transferred to me—Newspaper reflections on the transfer—Warm support of my Philadelphia friends.

AS soon as Congress assembled in December, 1879, I went to Washington. Before going I called on the party who had tried to obstruct me in getting the arsenal and told him all my plans. " Now," I said, " would you try to defeat so great a public benefaction for your individual gratification ? " His answer was characteristic. " I do not care a snap for the public. I want that property and I mean to get it. Money can do anything in Washington." " Very well," I said ; " I shall use that speech in Washington." " I do not care if you do," was his reply. " Agreed," I said. " The longest pole will get the persimmon."

I did not tell him that I had every prominent official on record in its favor. I knew that I would not have to pay one dollar, and I knew his fortune, twice told, could not get the property. My only object in seeing him was to

get it through Congress without any opposition from
Charleston.   In any case I knew I would not come out
worsted.   I had taken with me to Washington very strong
letters from my staunch friend, Hon. Clarkson N. Potter
and others, some to Democrats and some to Republicans.

Day after day passed, and I sat on the Senate Chamber
floor beside General Hampton, who was to watch his
opportunity to call up the joint resolution from the calendar. Oh, what anxious days those were ! I had told
General Butler what had been said about money being
able to do anything in Washington, and with a term
more emphatic than I can repeat, the General replied :
" He said that ?   Well, I will show him."

On the 12th of December, there was a lull in business
in the Senate, when General Butler said to General
Hampton, " Now is the time to call for the resolution."
General Hampton answered, " I will do it."   Then General Butler asked consent to take it from the calendar.
How my heart did beat !   Consent was given and General
Butler read it.   When Senator Edmunds from Vermont
rose and said : " What does General Sherman say about
this transfer ? "   No better card could have been played
for General Butler, who said: " I will read General Sherman's endorsement, which is very strong."   " Does General Sherman say that ? " asked Mr. Edmunds, when the
endorsement had been read.   " If the gentleman wishes
to see, I will hand him the paper," said General Butler.
" Certainly not ; I am satisfied, and I will vote for it."

I had letters to Mr. Blaine, having spent an evening
with him at his house, and he had promised me his support, and had the next day crossed the floor of the Senate
to give General Butler the assurance of his support.   As
Senator Edmunds ceased speaking, the resolution was
offered, and passed the Senate unanimously.   General
Hampton, General M. C. Butler, Senator Bayard, Gover-

nor Randolph, and others shook my hand warmly, and congratulated me on the progress of the affair. Governor Baldwin of Michigan, a warm friend of mine, told me afterwards, no sooner had the action been taken, than Senator Logan came in from the cloak-room, into which he had gone only five minutes before, and asked, "What is that you have passed?" When he was told, he said, "Why I meant to have opposed that," but several Republican Senators said to him : "It is a good thing it is done, and we are glad you were not here, if you had any such intention."

Governor Baldwin once told me some years after, "Doctor Porter, God seems to watch over you with loving care. But for General Logan leaving the Chamber for those five minutes, there is no telling what might have been the fate of the paper"; and he added, "I never knew while I was in the Senate another moment when it could have been done in the manner it was." I was a happy man that night.

The news was flashed to Charleston, but there was one man there not happy next day.

The House of Representatives had to be faced. "Now," said General Butler, "we must get Mr. Evans of Spartansburg, South Carolina, to take charge of the resolution." Hon. M. P. O'Connor would cheerfully have done so, but it was thought expedient to bring in interest from the interior of the State. General Butler told Mr. Evans that he must, if possible, get me before the Military Committee of the House, to which the resolution went after it had passed the Senate. By great good fortune this was effected, and on its first meeting I was invited in. To my great joy I saw General Joseph E. Johnston was a member of the Committee. He recognized and saluted me, and I was politely invited to take a seat, when the Chairman of the Committee, who, with a majority of its members were

23

Republicans, asked me how I had managed to get such an endorsement as this from General Sherman. I said, "It is rather a long story, but if you have the time to hear I will tell." "Let us hear it," the Chairman answered. Then I related in full my adventure with McQueen, who was on General Howard's escort. This adventure had brought General Howard and myself together, and he had brought me to General Sherman, who became my warm friend. The Committee listened with intense interest. I had no sooner finished, than General Johnston arose, and said: "Gentlemen, every word of that story is true. I am the officer to whom Mr. Porter brought that young Federal officer. I thought it then, as I think it now, a noble deed on his part, and I gave the young man his parole without exchange, and told him to stay in Raleigh until General Sherman occupied it."

The whole Committee to a man rose. The Chairman came forward, took my hand, and said : "Such a man should get anything he asks from the Government. I am sure you will have the unanimous recommendation of this Committee." Everyone of them shook hands with me, and told me I should have it, and that afternoon their recommendation came in and was placed on the calendar. I went over to Mrs. Ogle Taylor, to tell her the good news, for the battle was half won. "But," I said, "if it passes the house, it will have to go to the President and pass that ordeal." She immediately wrote a note to Mrs. Hayes and sent it to the White House, and asked if the President and herself would be at home the next day as she wished to bring a friend to introduce to them. Mrs. Hayes replied, that the President and herself would be at home, and would be glad to see Mrs. Taylor with her friend. Friday evening we went over to the White House, and found our hosts alone. "Now," Mrs. Taylor said to me, "tell the President the story of your work." Which I did concisely, and found that I had interested my hearers, especially Mrs. Hayes, who said : " You must have it, you must have the arsenal, and your boys must be brought up under the old flag."

When leaving, I said, " Mr. President, nothing will be done until Monday. If the resolution passes the House, as it has passed the Senate, it will have to come to you. I am going to-night to Charleston. I have to preach a special sermon there on Sunday ; but I will be back by Tuesday. If the resolution reaches you before my return," I added, turning to Mrs. Hayes, and bowing, " I leave myself in the hands of Mrs. Hayes." The President laughed and said : " I cannot tell what influence Mrs. Hayes has with Congress, but she certainly has great influence over the President." " Then I am safe," I answered. We were all pleased with the graceful turn the President had given to the incident, and I left in very high spirits. I started that night for Charleston, discharged my duties there, and left for Washington on Sunday night. On my arrival on Tuesday morning, my friend Rev. Dr. Elliott told me a severe attack had been made on me in the New York *Times*. I hastened to the Capitol, and in the library of the Senate Chamber found the paper containing the attack. However, I went boldly to those who I heard would oppose me. Hon. Randolph Tucker introduced me to General Garfield, the leader of the Republican side of the House, and I called at his house that night, and told him my story in brief. He said the piece in the *Times* had had an effect, but he promised to correct it for me. Like Mr. Blaine in the Senate, he expressed much pleasure to hear of such a work, and pledged his assistance. I saw the reporter for the *Times*, and told him the facts. He expressed great regret at having written the article, and said he would correct it ; which he did, but it did not appear in his paper until its necessity had passed. General Hunt was in Washington, and he got General Fitz John Porter to use his influence. General Sherman was roused by the attack and he exerted himself in my behalf. General Butler gave himself up to seeing the members of the House. Two or three days passed, and no opportunity occurred to call it up, till at length General Butler came over from the Senate Chamber to the Speaker of the House, and begged him to recognize Mr. Dargan, and briefly told him what for. God must have opened the hearts of the people, for the Speaker consented. General Butler spoke to Mr. Dargan, and as I was in the gallery I saw him rise and the Speaker recognized him. The resolution was read. A member on the Republican side rose and began to speak against it, but Mr. Chittenden, a friend of mine, sitting by him, pulled his coat and whispered something to him, and he took his seat again, but I was in such a state of excitement that I could not stand any more. My nervous system for a week had been overtaxed, and I went down to Mr. Butler's room, thinking nothing could be done, but in those few moments the favorable report of the Military Committee was read, the vote taken—one hundred and eighteen ayes and thirty-six noes. As soon as it was declared passed, General Butler's son came rushing into his father's room, saying, " We have got it, we have got it." " Got what," I said. " Why, the arsenal. The resolution has passed five to one." It was then my turn to rush down to the lobby of the House, where I met the whole South Carolina delegation. The House had adjourned, but not until it had passed the resolution ; and if ever a man was congratulated, I was by every one of them. I felt sure now, for that morning the President had told me he would sign it if it passed, and I felt that this, which would give such an impetus to my work, was an accomplished fact. I thanked God, and prayed for wisdom and strength for the increased responsibility, and that the hearts of many would be opened to me. The members of Congress told me what to do, what course had to be pursued, and I went at it at once. I approached each person who had anything to do with it, and next day I followed the messenger from the Capitol to the White House, he having the resolution to submit to the President. I had no difficulty in getting it sent to the President, or to get admittance with it, and said : " Mr. President, here is the resolution." " Why," he answered, " you have been expeditious." He read it over, took up his pen, and signed it at once. It was then registered, and the paper delivered to me.

Thus, in seven days from the day that General Butler called up the Resolution, the whole transaction was completed. I was told that such expedition had never been known in Congress before. The Adjutant-General issued the following paper:

HEADQUARTERS OF THE ARMY
ADJUTANT GENERAL'S OFFICE.

A Joint Resolution of Congress, approved Dec. 19, 1879, entitled, Joint Resolution to transfer the arsenal property, in the City of Charleston, South Carolina, to the Trustees of the Holy Communion Church Institute, for the use and accommodation of said school required, —

" That the Secretary of War be and is hereby authorized and directed to lease and deliver possession upon such terms and conditions as to him may seem best, for the use of, or in the interests of, the Government, to the Trustees of the Holy Communion Church Institute, the property known as the arsenal, situated in the city of Charleston, State of South Carolina, together with all the buildings, rights, and appurtenances thereto belonging, to be had and held by said Trustees for the use and accommodation of said School for such time as said lease may run, if not theretofore required by the Secretary of War.

"Sec. 2. That the Secretary of War be, and is hereby authorized to make such terms and arrangements with said Trustees, for the care, and protection of said property during its occupancy by said School, and for the re-delivering of possession to the Government when thereto required, as will best subserve the interests of the Government, provided that the Government shall not be required to pay for any improvements that may be placed on said grounds during the continuance of the lease."

Accordingly the Secretary of War directs, that the United States property known as the arsenal (Charleston Barracks), situated in the city of Charleston, State of South Carolina, together with all the buildings, rights, and appurtenances, and the United States flag thereto belonging, be transferred to the Rev. A. Toomer Porter, D.D., to hold until a lease of said property is duly executed by the Secretary of War.

The Quartermaster's ordnance, and other property in store, at the arsenal, will be properly disposed of under the direction of the Department.

By command of General Sherman,

E. D. TOWNSEND,
Adjutant-General.

In due time this lease for ninety-nine years at one dollar a year was duly executed. The reader will find when he reaches the record of ten years after, how that lease was supplemented by an act of Congress, signed by the President, giving a fee simple title to this property to the Trustees, the only condition being that it shall always be used for educational purposes.

The article which appeared in the New York *Times*, attracted some attention, and what was meant to do me harm, in God's providence resulted in much good. I put it here on permanent record in the appendix. The Washington correspondent says :

" A very objectionable Joint Resolution was passed very quietly in the Senate, upon the motion of Mr. Butler of South Carolina, and in the absence of Messrs. Edmunds, Logan, and McMillan, who had been prepared to oppose it. The original Resolution, which was introduced May 6, 1879, authorized and directed the Secretary of War to transfer the United States arsenal property in Charleston, South Carolina, to the Trustees of the Holy Communion Church Institute, to be held by those Trustees for the use of the school as long as it is not wanted by the Government, etc.

" This arsenal is not now used by the Government, and like other unoccupied arsenals, is left to the care of an ordnance sergeant. The Rev. A. Toomer Porter is the rector of the Church of the Holy Communion in Charleston, and after the war he came to the North to raise subscriptions to aid his church. Attached to his church is a sectarian school, under his charge, and for some time he has desired to obtain possession of the United States arsenal, with its large buildings, for the use of his school, at a nominal rent, for a long period. Leading Republicans in Charleston have opposed this design on the ground that this school is sectarian, aristocratic, and exclusive, and one to which the children of no Union man or Republican can gain admission. They assert that the youths educated in it are taught the extreme doctrines which were held in the South before the war, and were powerful in causing the war, and they claim, if the Government has no use for the arsenal, and desires to leave it, it would be more equitable to the residents of the State, and more profitable to the Government, to allow competition for it, and lease it to the highest bidder. Some day, if it is no longer

of use, it should be sold, and the proceeds carried into the
Treasury; but all agree, that special privileges should not
be granted to this aristocratic school, in which they say
pupils and teachers are unfriendly to the Government.
Having no Representatives on the floor of Congress, the
Republicans of South Carolina depend for support upon
Republican Senators and Representatives from other
States, and think these gentlemen should guard their interests. It was stated by Mr. Butler in urging the passage
of the Resolution, that the transfer had been recommended
by the Secretary of War and General Sherman, but those
who oppose the transaction say that these officers could
not have fully understood the matter.''

It was not difficult to find who had inspired the article.
The agent from Charleston, finding he had failed to stop
the progress any other way, supposed he could instil into
these Republican Senators and Representatives views
which were absolutely false in every particular, save as
related to General Logan. If Mr. Edmunds had intended
to oppose, he was not absent, but his few words secured
the unanimous vote of the Republican Senators. At the
very time two sons of a prominent Republican official
were members of the school, and as soon as the article
was seen a number of Republicans, white and colored,
united in writing to me a paper in which they denied
their opposition. So far from opposing me, they would
do anything they could for me, if I needed their assistance ;
and so false statements ran through the whole paper. My
record at home and abroad had been for fourteen years so
pronounced as to my views with regard to the duties of
citizens who in good faith had laid down arms, that the
charge that my pupils were taught the extreme doctrines
held in the South before the war was so extremely
absurd it was easy to confute, and as I have said, the
writer retracted the whole article and apologized. It was

so unjust, however, and my friends at the North were so much afraid it would do me harm, that some of them wrote a special article and published it in several of the Philadelphia papers, sent it to New York, and had it published there.*

I was entirely ignorant of their act of kindness, as I had heard nothing of it, nor had seen the paper. I forget now what induced me, but after getting the resolution approved by the President, I ran up to Philadelphia for a little rest, and was the guest of Rev. Mr. McVickar, who read to me this communication, which of course was very grateful to me. The signers of it did not know I was coming to Philadelphia, as no communication had passed between us. Their action had been dictated by Christian love and justice towards an absent brother. The week after this there appeared in the *Episcopal Register*, an editorial under the heading, "The Charleston Arsenal turned to the Uses of Peace and Education." It detailed the circumstances I have just related and ended thus :

"The liberal contributions already made in this city for his work show how unjust assaults are mercifully turned into benefits, and it is only proper to add, that no man in the South has done more to allay sectional bitterness, and further good-will to men throughout the country, than the Rev. Dr. Porter." †

This editorial was an immense help to me in the com-

* See Appendix D.

† I see, in looking over these papers, I am called Doctor. It had escaped my mind to say that in the year 1876 I was at one of the Commencement exercises of Union College, Schenectady. I was astounded by hearing my name called out with some distinguished gentlemen—Rev. C. Vedder of Charleston, and others—as having the degree of D.D. conferred on me by the Trustees. I had to laugh, for never was the honor bestowed on one more utterly unworthy to receive it. My life has been too exacting, too active, too much employed with affairs, to enable me to be a student. I

passing of my great undertaking. As I recount all these wonderful deliverances that have come to me in time of the greatest needs, I reproach myself most earnestly when this poor heart fails me in emergencies. God has not changed, and if it be in accord with his Divine will, He will in His own way raise up some means for the necessities of His work. If I have been faithful to my trust, I want it to go on record that if ever this work fails, it is not that prayer and faith are absolutely ineffectual, but simply because the poor, weak, earthen vessel has failed. To God be all the glory, to me be all the blame.

have to do a great deal of reading, but study very little, and I protested that while I appreciated the compliment, it was too undeserved ; but my protest was unheeded, and so through the kind feeling of Rev. Dr. E. N. Potter I have borne this title ever since.

CHAPTER XXXIX

SCHOOL OPENS IN THE ARSENAL

Ceremonies attending the opening of the arsenal as our new home—Points of my parochial work—Mr. E. R. Mudge of Boston—His soldier son—Progress of our school.

I RETURNED to Charleston on the 24th of December, 1879, having had all the papers for the transference of the arsenal properly made out in Washington. Before service on Christmas morning I went to the arsenal with the workman, a very intelligent colored man named Bell, and pointed out the work necessary to be done at once. A kitchen and pantry had to be built, the store-room converted into a dining-room and study hall, the second and third stories to be converted into dormitories, and other changes absolutely necessary to be made. I had no funds with which to carry on the work, but I felt after such an achievement friends would now come forward and help me. On the 8th of January, 1854, as a young man not twenty-five years old, I had held my first service in one of these buildings, and it occurred to me that day would be the proper time for a grand ceremonial. I accordingly prepared a programme which I submitted to the Bishop, and on the 8th of January, 1880, just twenty-six years from the day I came on one cloudy Sunday morning to minister there to eight people, I took formal possession

of the whole property.   Manifold have been Thy mercies
to me, O God, and wonderfully hast Thou used one of the
most unworthy of Thy servants to manifest Thy power to
the people with whom I have lived !

We had sent invitations far and wide, and I received
congratulatory letters from Mr. John Eaton, Commissioner
of Education, Mr. James S. Amory, of Boston, Gen. Henry
J. Hunt, U. S. A., Mr. C. T. Lowndes, Dr. Manning
Simons, Gen. Joseph E. Johnston, Gen. W. T. Sherman,
Judge A. G. Magrath, and many others.   These letters
have all been published and preserved in my little volume
of the *History of a Work of Faith and Love,* so they need
not be presented here.   The ceremonies as reported next
day in the daily papers were as follows :

" The celebration of the formal occupation of the grounds
and buildings hitherto used as the United States arsenal
by the Trustees of the Holy Communion Church Institute
was an impressive event.   The ceremonies were simple,
but conveyed, as they were meant to do, an expression of
the warm sympathy of the community with the work, and
the general satisfaction at the success that has so far attended it.   A short service consisting of the Creed, some
Collects, and the Lord's Prayer was held at the Church of
the Holy Communion.   Promptly at five o'clock the procession moved from the Church in the following order :

St. Patrick's Helicon Band, the Washington Light Infantry, Capt. G. D. Bryan ; Charleston Riflemen, Capt.
R. J. Magill ; carriages containing the Bishop in his robes
and the clergy in surplices ; officers of the Army and Navy
of the United States ; Judge of the United States Court,
and other officers ; Mr. James G. Holmes and Mr. W. M.
Lawton, two venerable and prominent citizens ; the Mayor
and City Council ; Honorary Members of the Washington
Light Infantry; President and Faculty of Charleston College ; Teachers of Schools ; Board of Trustees, Holy Com-

munion Church Institute, Principal and Teachers of the
Institute, Alumni Students and Residents of the Institute,
with a long procession of citizens on foot.   In this order
the procession moved down Ashley Street to Doughty, to
President, up President to Bee, and back through Ashley
to the gate.   Here those who were in carriages alighted,
and all passed in on foot.   Three large flags were sus-
pended at intervals ; the United States flag, the State
flag, and a large white banner with a red cross, and
H. C. C. I., 1867, in large red letters on it.   The Bishop
preceded, reading a remarkably appropriate selection of
verses from the Psalter, the clergy responding immediately
behind him, followed by the choir-boys in their cassocks
and cottas.   The procession had encompassed the grounds
when the Bishop finished, and the choir-boys sang the
hymn,

'Glorious things of Thee are spoken,
Zion City of our God.'

which was taken up by the crowd assembled, among
whom were very many ladies.   The national flag, which
had been given by the order of General Sherman,
floated from the flagstaff.   The two military companies
presented arms, as the Bishop and clergy and guests
filed into the very building Doctor Porter had held
his first service in twenty-six years ago on this day.''
Then, and now, the choir sang, ''The Church's one
foundation,'' the Bishop repeated the Creed and a Collect,
and Rev. A. Toomer Porter rose and said, '' ——.'' It
was a long oration, too long for this work, but it is printed
in a book for preservation.   The Hon. W. D. Porter,
known as the silver-tongued orator, then delivered an
address as only he could do.   Mayor W. A. Courtenay,
my friend from boyhood, then addressed the audience
with words which came from his heart.   Mr. S. Y. Tupper,
the President of the Chamber of Commerce, then ad-

dressed the audience in a most noteworthy speech. Mr.
Tupper was a Baptist, and his pastor had made a violent
attack upon the whole transaction, and Mr. Tupper's
speech was a pointed rebuke. The Bishop, Rt. Rev. W.
B. W. Howe, made the closing address. Nothing ever
fell from Bishop Howe's lips that was not good, and
now he declared that he was grateful that God had so
blessed the labors of one of the presbyters of his diocese.
All these addresses are also published in my little book ;
therefore, they are not here repeated. A warm editorial
of the *News and Courier* concluded with the words, " The
transfer of the arsenal to the Church Institute was the
joint work of the President, the Cabinet, and Congress.
Both Democrats and Republicans supported the proposition. This is, as Doctor Porter says, ' Practical Reconstruction,' honorable alike to both parties, to North and
South, to President and people. The ambition of Doctor
Porter's life bids fair to be realized, and the greater his
success the broader and deeper the benefit to the people
of the State."

The improvements and alterations had so far progressed
that on the 11th of February, 1880, Mr. Gadsden, the
principal, and Miss Seabrook, the matron, moved with
all the boys into quarters in the arsenal. I had to use the
old schoolhouse for some months until I could convert the
foundry, which the Confederate Government had built
during the war, into a schoolhouse, changing its use from
moulding bullets into moulding brains and hearts and
characters. It cost the Government twelve thousand
dollars to remove the old cannon and shot and shell, etc.,
a work which General Sherman had done as expeditiously
as possible. I was then living at the corner of Rutledge
Avenue and Spring Street, and one day General Sherman
asked me if I was not going to move into the arsenal ? I
told him, No. " How ever can you manage such a work

if you are not on the spot?"   I soon saw that he was right, and with my wife's consent we left the house endeared to us by many associations and moved into these grounds.   Thrown more immediately in contact with the work, I very soon found it necessary to take the reins into my own hands and apply myself to the remodelling and development of that which had been but a large private school, into what had become a great public institution. My friends had cheered me with their presence and their words.   They little knew the mighty burden I had assumed, but I did not fear that God, who had given me the work, would fail to give also the strength to carry it on.

Up to the time that we had been in my private buildings two thousand boys had been under my charge, and I had sent sixty-three to college.   In all those years there had been but one death in the institution.   The sum necessary to fit up the buildings for our use amounted to sixteen thousand dollars, and I had not a dollar to do it with, but from one source and another the money came.   Miss E. F. Mason and Miss Ida Mason, of Boston, Massachusetts, were in Cannes, France, when they heard of my success, and each sent me one thousand dollars, and from then until now they have been my steadfast friends.   I have never needed to ask their aid.   Yearly they have munificently helped me, and as I have said before, but for their systematic annual aid, I do not see how this institution could have lived a year.   God bless them !

Our thirteenth year closed with a debt of two thousand five hundred dollars for current expenses, and eight thousand due on the improvements of buildings and grounds.   The property could not have been available without these improvements and adaptations, and I felt that I had been carried on by the felt but unseen power of God ; and I knew that He would not forsake me.   It is a wonderful record, that I, single-handed, with no counsellor except my wife, should have gone unheralded to Washington, with a long line of preparatory Providences stretching through a series of years, each apparently independent of the other, but all preparing the way; should have come from Charleston, the hotbed of secession, and gone to a Republican General of the armies, a Republican President and Cabinet, to a Republican Congress, either, or any one of whom, could have put an insurmountable obstacle in my way, and yet, step by step, each became my friend, coöperated with me, and delivered to me without money or price that which no money could have bought. Reader, go back with me to the grave of my child, on that 25th of October, 1867, and stand with me in those grounds this 8th of January, 1880, knowing all the facts—was it infatuation, enthusiasm, delusion ; or was it inspiration, the finger and the voice of God that had driven me forward ? Whatever you may think, my conviction is as strong this night, 23d February, 1897, as it was thirty years ago—yes, stronger, for I did not know then what experience has taught me now, " If thou hast faith as a grain of mustard seed,"—you know the rest.

Some reader may think that the church of which I am rector seems all these years to have been lost sight of. It was not, but is not often referred to, because the regular ministrations were carried on, for I had two hundred and fifty-nine communicants, to whom I ministered, and a congregation of some five hundred souls. We raised in the parish during the year some four thousand dollars for parish expenses and Church purposes. I baptized twenty-three, presented for confirmation forty persons, so there was no neglect of that work ; but there is nothing of general interest in the usual clerical life which needs to be recorded.

After giving up my house in Ashley Street for the use of the school for twelve years, I now rented it out, and

the house I had bought I deeded to the vestry, in trust
for the Caroline Wilkinson Home, a refuge for indigent
ladies which is still in existence, and has been a sweet
refuge for many in these seventeen years.   From 1867 to
1880 one hundred and thirty-eight of my boys had been
confirmed, of whom eleven had been ordained to the sacred
ministry, and one of my graduates is Vice-Chancellor of
the University of the South.   I find in the closing para-
graphs of the book which was written up to the occupation of the arsenal, " I know not what is before us, in the
unwritten future ; God's eye alone can penetrate that
darkness.   We propose, by God's grace, to try to do our
duty faithfully.   We shall endeavor to give our boys the
best education in our power, and shall try to bring them
up as loyal citizens of the government under the flag of
which they live.   Ours is not a political nor a partisan
school, but an educational institution governed by the
laws of religion and morality.   We give our boys the
training of Christian gentlemen, brought up in the fear
and admonition of the Lord, and neither political party
nor religious sect need fear the result.   We have so far
had over two thousand boys in our charge, and I have
sent sixty-three to college.   Has this been God's work ?
We ask the prayers of the faithful that God will continue
to bless us, and that in all our cares, necessities and
anxieties, and disappointments, we may keep a single eye
to His glory, and the welfare of our fellowmen.''

I must now show what use I have made of the property
committed to my care.   When October 1, 1880, had come,
the usual stir began, and every train and steamer brought
the new and old boys to the Institute.   The General Convention of the Protestant Episcopal Church was about to
meet in New York, and I was a deputy to it from the Diocese of South Carolina, so I received a few of the incoming
boys, but had to leave the organization of the school to the

24

principal, Mr. John Gadsden. The school year closed with a debt of ten thousand five hundred dollars, which had been increased by some fifteen hundred dollars for furniture and repairs, and when I reached New York, knowing the large gathering of boys which was taking place at home, and the daily expense of it all, with this large debt before me, my heart was anxious, but not despairing. The year of the meeting of the General Convention is a very bad year to collect money for private charities. The cost of the Convention is so great, the Missions of the Church in the organized channels have the field, and the presence of Missionary Bishops who, from their official station, have *entrée* everywhere, and reach those whom a simple presbyter cannot, add greatly to the difficulties in the way. I approached an old and true friend, Mr. E. R. Mudge, of Boston, and told him my needs. I never can forget the blank look he gave me, and the ominous shake of the head, as he said, " You never can carry on that work ; it is too much for any man."

I told him the Government had given me the opportunity to do a good work for the country and the Church, and I felt bound, as fast as I could, to develop it to its utmost capacity ; that I did not believe I would be in the position I then was, had it not been the will of God for me to hold it, and I would work and pray, and wait and trust, as I had been doing all these years ; that now the work had been brought prominently before the public, and those extraordinary events which marked the earlier years did not now so often occur, but God seemed to purpose that the ordinary agencies should work. It is like the establishment of the Christian faith ; at first miracles were common, but as years went on the Church was left to grow by natural processes.

Mr. Mudge seemed to think it hopeless, and was not reassuring. Indeed, were I to put in print all of my experience, the days and nights of anxious suspense, the disappointments and rebuffs, the mortifications and trials which every year of the life of this institute has entailed upon me, there is no reader of these pages who would not feel as intensely as I do, that I can account for my perseverance only by the indwelling presence and power of the Spirit of God, who gave me the work to do and has not suffered me to withdraw my hand, even though it has cost, and still costs, an amount of self-abnegation of which, unaided by Divine grace, I am utterly incapable. I now called on another friend, Mr. Robert Lenox Kennedy, and told him my needs. He at once drew his check for five hundred dollars, and gave it to me. He told me to cheer up and keep on, for if I was doing God's work, of which he had no doubt, the ways and means would come ; and come they did, I scarcely know how.

Having mentioned Mr. Mudge's name, I relate an incident of 1866, when I first went to Boston and was his guest. As we walked upstairs from the dining-room, there was hanging in the hall a life-size portrait of a handsome young officer in the United States uniform. "This," Mr. Mudge said, "is the portrait of my son, who laid down his life for his country."

We all stood for a few moments in silence before the picture, when I said : " Mr. Mudge, what an illustration this is of the triumph of the Christian religion. Here is the likeness of your dead boy, killed in fighting against those I represent. Here am I, an ex-officer of that opposing army, in the presence of that picture, a welcome guest of his father and mother and sisters." Mr. Mudge put out both his hands and with much emotion said, "And none more welcome ; he gave his life for what he thought was right; you risked yours for what you thought to be right; you were each as conscientious the one as the other. The God of Battles settled it as He saw fit, but that does not convict you of wrong, nor does it prove him right. You have accepted the decision in the spirit of a Christian patriot, and my son would rejoice to know that we have welcomed you to our home and to our hearts." *

Mr. S. G. Wyman had given me a letter of introduction to the Mr. Robert Lenox Kennedy mentioned above ; he was a prominent Presbyterian who from time to time had given me a little help. One winter he was visiting the South with his wife. She was taken sick in Savannah, and he hastened towards home, but she was so ill that they had to stop in Charleston, and one Sunday morning Mr. Kennedy wrote for me to come to him at the Charleston Hotel. There I found his wife desperately ill with diphtheria, and Mr. Kennedy at a loss what to do. I immediately summoned Dr. T. L. Ogier, the most distinguished physician of that day in Charleston, and I hunted the town for a nurse. Between the services of the day I stayed with Mr. Kennedy and remained all night and all Monday. On Tuesday, Mrs. Kennedy died, and I closed her eyes. Of course this made Mr. Kennedy a warm friend and a generous helper until he died.

I was in New York in the Spring of 1881, and one evening I went with a very heavy heart to visit my friend, Mrs. Samuel G. Wyman of Baltimore, who was then in New York. She had always taken a lively interest in the work. She said to me, " There is to be a meeting at Doctor Barker's of the friends of Mrs. Buford, who is engaged in a great work among the negroes in Virginia ; I wish you to go there." It was useless for me to remonstrate and urge that I did not know the people, nor had I

---

* Death has since severed Mr. Mudge and myself as friends. But has it ? I remember him with love and gratitude, and has he forgotten where he is that he knew, and loved, and helped me here ? Will we not meet again and talk it all over in the land beyond ? I believe it.

been invited. "Nevertheless, go," she insisted; "I feel that good will come of it."

With great reluctance I went, feeling, as all my readers may imagine, very much out of place. I was, however, greeted by host and hostess with a very courteous welcome. They both knew of me, and there I was introduced by Mr. F. Winston to two gentlemen whom I had long wished to know, but never before had been brought in contact with, Mr. Cornelius Vanderbilt and Mr. R. Fulton Cutting. We had some pleasant conversation, and from then until 1896 they have been anually large contributors. Had I not gone, I do not know a time or place when and where I could have met either of them, for all our subsequent interviews have come through our past acqaintance, and not by an accidental meeting. I find strength in believing that we are led by an unseen hand.

Friends in New York that year gave me $4698 ; in Boston, $3580 ; and a few friends in Philadelphia, Baltimore, Hartford, Providence, Newport, Ellicott City, Md., Albany, Brookline, Brooklyn, added their aid ; and altogether, I collected $10,532.41, and friends in England sent me $4,716.76. I collected in Charleston and South Carolina, $12,207.86—a total of $27,457.03. The cost of the year was $20,535.57; I had to meet a debt of $12,000 —a total of $32,535.57, and I received $27,457.03; leaving a deficit of $4978.54 to carry over to the next year. Although the burden still was very heavy, to have paid off $7000, and still carry on the work, proved to me that I was not forsaken by the gracious Providence which had so long provided for me.

CHAPTER XL

IMPORTANT ADDITIONS TO OUR CURRICULUM

Death amongst my teachers—I am enabled to build a gymnasium—I make an important addition to the curriculum in the shape of linear drawing for machine shops—The powder magazine is flooded for a reason—Typewriting and stenography added to our course—The beginning of an endowment.

JUST after the close of the last term, Miss Emma Rhett, who for nearly fourteen years had served this institution as one of the teachers with a zeal and devotion beyond her strength, died on the 15th of August. Mr. Wm. Benjamin Roper, one of our pupils who had graduated from Union College, Schenectady, and had been our assistant in the classical department, sickened and died on the 27th of July. These teachers were much beloved and deeply mourned. Nine of those who have been teachers here have passed to their final account, and the principal was the only one left, in 1881, of those who were first engaged on December 9, 1867. Only one death has so far occurred at the Home in all these eighteen years. The scarlet-fever prevailed during the year, and was in every street around these grounds, and though one boy, who had just come in, was taken sick with the fever, it did not spread, and not another case occurred ; so graciously has

God taken care of us. During the year I had many loads of sand brought in to fill up the low places, and the whole square has been thoroughly drained with subsoil tile draining.

Mr. James T. Swift, of New York, one day in going over the premises, asked why we had no gymnasium, since we had a building suited for it ? I told him we found it so hard to provide for necessaries, that I had not felt authorized to use any money given for other purposes. He kindly told me to fit up the gymnasium, and to send the bill to him. He subsequently added to the gymnasium.

One day in 1881, I chanced to be in a machine-shop of Messrs. Smith & Valk, when, observing that one of the youths seemed to be doing clumsy work, I asked if he could draw the piece of machinery he was making. Finding that he could not, and learning after careful inquiry that this was the case in all of the machine-shops, I invited all the leading mechanics to my house to supper, and from them learned that there was no teacher of linear drawing in the city. Failing to get a teacher at home, I went to Boston in February where Mr. Mudge took me to his house, and the next day gave me a fifteen mile sleigh-ride, the first and last of my life. When we reached home I told him it was magnificent, but I had not come to enjoy myself, but on business, and he gave me a letter of introduction to Mr. Rogers, the President of the School of Technology. This, with letters from Mr. A. A. Lawrence and Mr. R. C. Winthrop, secured the president's attention, and he sent for Mr. C. S. Gooding, a young man whom he highly recommended. I told him that while I knew nothing at all about linear drawing, I had discovered a great need, and had boys whom I wished to be taught linear drawing ; if he felt himself man enough to undertake it, I wanted him to do so. He said he would take the situation for twelve hundred dollars. This seemed a good deal of money, but as he was a specialist, said to be an expert, and I knew to make my place a success I must have a good man, I engaged him. Mr. Wm. P. Clyde gave me a ticket for him, and I authorized him to purchase instruments. I went out among my friends in Boston, and they gave me money enough to cover the first year's expenses, for they seemed pleased at this practical development of my educational scheme. Mr. Gooding stayed two years, married, and returned North, but I have kept up this branch of instruction, always having a good teacher, for the past sixteen years. At first it was not understood, for it was a new thing in the South, and I had to take a firm stand and insist upon its being taught. It has since grown to large proportions, is a popular branch, and has turned out a large number of young men who, with no further education than that received in this school, have obtained places as draughtsmen and engineers. There were two boys who were as good as boys are ever made, but they were very slow at books. I took these two to Mr. Gooding, and begged him to try and make something of them. In about a month he told me those boys had a wonderful talent in this line, and as they improved, their capacity for mathematics seemed to develop, and when they graduated one became the head draughtsman in the shop in which the idea came to me, and the other went to the Baldwin Locomotive Works, where he is occupying a responsible position. If I had not started that branch of education they would probably be to-day in some country store, poor and unknown. These are illustrations only, for several hundred have been taught mechanical drawing. One is now with the Cramps in Philadelphia, and I find in my report to the Trustees of that year, these words :

" The needs of this fast-developing republic, on this

vast continent, with its shops and manufactories, demand an immense corps of draughtsmen. Thus a new avenue is opened to our boys to earn a lucrative and an honorable support. I shall save some from seeking situations in small country stores, or following laborers in our cotton and rice fields, or flocking to every opening in the city where a vacancy occurs, to receive a small compensation. These places must be filled, but it is sad to see much good material comparatively wasted in such limited spheres, sadder to know how many are pining in enforced idleness, so that every additional means of earning a livelihood is a benefaction.''

In the spring of the year the boys were permitted to go in swimming in the river. Two of these came near drowning ; so that it is needless to say this was the last swim my scholars had in the river. I at once converted the powder-magazine into two large swimming pools. The water I brought into the ponds from the city artesian well, and thus I have carried out General Sherman's suggestion to get as far from the military associations of the place as possible. I knew not how to do so more effectually than to turn water into a powder magazine. It will be noticed that my friends in England continue to remember us. They sent some four thousand seven hundred dollars this year to help at a time of very pressing need. But still we closed the twelve months with a debt of five thousand dollars.

As I was going backwards and forwards to the North, and coming in contact with many minds, I endeavored to keep my eyes open to the march of events and to fit myself for greater usefulness to my fellow-citizens, and perceiving that stenography was becoming fast a factor in modern life, I determined to introduce this into my school. I obtained the services of a young lady, through the Cooper Institute, and brought her to Charleston, where I tried for three years to incorporate the study into my curriculum. But the boys were so overloaded with work that I found it impracticable. They would have had to give up studies which they could not do without, if I pressed this in. I did induce some young ladies of my congregation to take lessons. One of these became a proficient and then a teacher, and has found it a source of income. At that time, save in the daily press, there were no stenographers in Charleston, but I foresaw the time would come when they would become a necessity in all our prominent offices.

One young lady, singularly bright, began to take lessons from Miss Lee, the young lady who had first perfected herself, and her uncle, General James Conner, was quite put out at this useless waste of time. He actually remonstrated with her father, then a bank president, who replied that as she had the time, and it was her pleasure to so employ it, he had no objection. In time her uncle and father both died, the father leaving a very insufficient estate to support his daughter and her mother. This daughter applied herself, became an adept, in time became as she still is, the stenographer of the United States District Court, and is comfortably supporting herself. She would scarcely have thought of it if I had not brought Miss Scott here.

The year 1882 brought to me a sore affliction. My wife, who had been so feeble and sick for so many years, was stricken with paralysis, from which she never recovered, but bore her incessant sufferings with that same gentle submission which characterized a life of thirty years' of ill-health. She lingered thus for nine long years ; it was another burden our dear Lord required us both to bear. Why, we know not now ; we shall know hereafter. The only time she ever broke down would be on Sunday morning, when I would go to her room to have a short service for her, before I went to church. Then at times, it would seem so hard, for she loved the church, but for fourteen years she had never been able to go to it. This was not a refreshing preparation with which to go to my public duties, but God gave me grace to hide deep down with Him the sorrow that was there, that the public eye never saw. I hope it drew us both nearer to Him.

Some years ago, long before there were any railroads going to Asheville, in casting about for some place where life would be more bearable to my wife, we had chanced to think of Asheville, North Carolina, and there she seemed to be more at her ease. Though boarding-houses were uncomfortable, property was cheap; so I borrowed some money and bought some land with a house on it. My second son, Charles, was in business, and devoted the half of his salary to help me pay for it. My dear friend, Fred. A. White, from London, for many years every January and July sent me a munificent personal gift which I put on this debt, and so I got a summer home for this dear wife, where I took her every year till the year she died. It was a great struggle to pay for it, but I look back thankfully that I did my best to give her comfort.

My purchase turned out a good investment, for with the arrival of railroads, property enhanced in value, and by renting out the house in winter, and throwing in every dollar I could spare, I have improved the property and it is improving itself, and in time I trust my children may have some little estate from that which was started only to give their mother a home where she could have some rest.

This year, at the suggestion of Mr. W. Bayard Cutting, I began to try to gather an endowment for the Institute, and little by little I have accumulated a beginning. I have an abundance of land on these premises, and have with the consent of the trustees so far erected seven houses,

on the streets surrounding the grounds. All of these are
rented and yield a little income. I have room for about
fourteen, and I hope to use the rents to build on, until the
ground is all taken up.*

I have prayed daily three times a day, at my stated
prayers, and always at the celebration of the Holy Communion, that God would put it in the heart of someone,
or in the hearts of many, to give or to bequeath to the
academy a sum sufficient to insure its permanence, and
to relieve me from this annual torture of nervous anxiety.
I have known very many men and women who in life
were very generous to me, but none of them have bequeathed anything to the work. I do not doubt my
prayers are heard, and even if it be not the will of God
that I may live to see it, yet the promise stands, " Ask
and ye shall receive ! "

Some two months before my wife was stricken with
paralysis, I had been very much run down from overstrained nerves, and the doctor advised a trip to Florida. I
went to Palatka, not knowing who was there, and met at
the hotel my old friend, Mr. John H. Shoenberger, who
told me there was an old lady in the house, Mrs. Robert T.
Stuart, whom he would like me to know. He sent her
his card, with mine, and we were invited to her parlor.
She became interested in my work, gave me one thousand dollars for that year and repeated the gift several
other years. Afterwards she increased her donation to
two thousand dollars annually, until she died. She was

* One of the houses was built by funds supplied by Mrs. Ed.
King and children, of Newport, and is a memorial of her son
Alexander. Another home was erected by Miss Mary LeRoy
King, in memoriam of her brother, LeRoy King, a noble man, cut
down in the flower of his manhood. The decrees of Divine
Providence are an inexplicable mystery. He had so much to live
for, and filled so well his life. They received their bereavement
with Christian submission.

a Presbyterian, and I said to her one day, at her palatial home in Fifth Avenue, New York, that I hoped she knew I was an Episcopal minister. "I do," she said, "but what of that. I have been down there in the South, and I know the need of the work, and how well you are doing it. You are doing the work of Christ, and I am glad to help you. I am only sorry for all who can and yet will not help such a work." It was a dreadful loss when she died a few years ago. And so one after another has gone and no new friends come. Still God does not pass away. He is the same yesterday, to-day and forever, and there I rest.

Mr. James H. La Roche and John E. Bold, two graduates of this school, were ordained to the diaconate this year. We closed with a debt of near six thousand dollars.

CHAPTER XLI

THE PORTER ACADEMY

" My grace is sufficient for Thee"—Honor among boys—
Improvements in the building – General Lee's most dan-
gerous antagonist—A risky bridge—I see McQueen at
his home—Death of a wise and good physician—A strange
dream — The Institute becomes the Porter Academy—
Friends in need.

IT will be seen how this school had been developing and
extending ; ever growing larger, needing greater
efforts, requiring more money, and yet by the goodness
of God, meeting its obligations, or tiding them over until
they were met. I often ask myself, "What am I that
God should so honor me?" for the whole responsibility
had been concentrated in my hands, and my poor head
had to do all the planning and devising. My one stay is
the promise, "My Grace is sufficient for thee." There
will be no greater burden than He will give strength to
bear. I cannot help it, but if I see what ought to be done
I feel that I ought to try to do it. I am aware that there
must be kindred spirits who will say that man must and
shall be helped to do his Master's work.

During the year 1883, I was forced to expel two youths
who were incapable of living up to the high standard of

honor and self-control which has been established in the Institute. One incident will illustrate my system of internal government. I have a rule that every boy is on his honor not to leave the premises, day or night, without permission. One night I was called out to see a sick parishioner, and did not get back until half-past one. Seeing a bright light in one of the alcoves, I feared some boy was sick, and therefore went to learn what was the matter. I was astounded to find one of the students was not in the dormitory, and on inquiring, found a second boy absent. Both of these were over twenty-one years old. I gave orders that they should report to me in the morning.

Both came to me next day and one of them said, " Doctor Porter, had you not found us out, we intended to tell you we had gone out, where we were, and how we came to do it ; we left the light on purpose, thinking it would attract attention."

I heard their statement quietly, and answered, " Young gentlemen, you know the rule of this institution. You have forfeited your word, and violated your honor. There is nothing left for me to do, but to express my sincere regrets, and to tell you both, to——"

But before I could get out the fatal word, they both exclaimed : " Doctor Porter, on the honor of gentlemen, it is the first time, and it happened just as we have told you. We did what we have said and nothing else. We felt we had betrayed ourselves, and feel miserable, and throw ourselves on your mercy."

" But," I said, " when a man violates his plighted word, how can he be again trusted ? "

The elder of the two, threw himself on his knees, clasped me round my waist, and burst into tears, saying, " Doctor Porter, I have nothing on earth to depend upon but my character. Do not brand me for this. Forgive me, and take my word. This incident shall be a lesson to me through life, and you shall never have reason to regret your clemency.''

I accepted their pledge, and retained them, and they gave me no cause to regret my decision.

In the year of 1883, I erected a large four-story building for a dining-room, and dormitories ; this had become a necessity. We needed a chapel, so I removed the roof from a large artillery shed, raised the walls four feet, and put a Gothic roof upon it ; I also inserted some stained-glass windows. The chancel window I placed in memoriam of my dear boy at whose grave the idea of the institution rose. In September I went to Bar Harbor, the White Mountains, and to Newport. At one of the hotels in the White Mountains I met General George B. McClellan. I told him that General Lee had regarded him as his most dangerous antagonist, and had said of him, that he had done what he believed no other man in the United States could have done, gathered the débris of Pope's shattered armies, and with raw recruits organized his force in eleven days, met General Lee's victorious army at Antietam, fought, and checked him, with a success resulting in a drawn battle. The General was much pleased, and remarked that General Robert E. Lee was the most knightly man who had ever drawn sword in battle. In December I went to Boston ; thence, at the invitation of Bishop Harris, the Bishop of Michigan, I went to Detroit, in the month of February. The change of climate at that season made me very sick, and I lost my voice entirely. Returning by way of Cincinnati, I encountered that great flood memorable in history. I had waited at Toledo for two days, and then took an experimental train with a half-dozen other men, and remember coming to a submerged town—I think it was Lima—where the water was up to the window-sills of the church, and the people could only get out of their houses by boats. We dragged along until we came within three hundred yards of a long covered bridge. The track was under water, and the fire in the engine was nearly reached when we stopped. The water was rushing past us, so that we could neither advance nor recede. The report was that the bridge was some inches out of plumb, and was expected to go over every instant. At last the conductor determined to try to get over the bridge, and we began to crawl along, and when the bridge was reached, the few men on board crowded on the rear platform to save themselves if the bridge went over. Through this covered vault we pulled ; it could not have been for over five minutes, and though we went as cautiously as possible, it seemed an hour. I do not think I ever spent so long a time in so few moments in my life. When we cleared the bridge, and reached higher land on the other side, we felt we had escaped from the jaws of death, as the bridge went over in a very few moments afterwards. I went to Florida, as far as Palatka, in April. The fourth Sunday in May, I preached at Grace Church, New York, at the invitation of the Rev. H. C. Potter, D.D., then rector ; and at Christ Church, New York, at the invitation of Rev. Hugh Miller Thompson, rector, and afterwards at Christ Church, Hartford. Having been invited by Rev. Dr. Clinton Locke, to go to Chicago, I there visited my friend, Lieutenant John A. McQueen, at his home in Elgin. It was our first meeting for eighteen years. We had parted in Raleigh, North Carolina, where I left him with General Jos. E. Johnston's pass to go back to his army. It was a very happy meeting. I returned to Hartford to meet the Washington Light Infantry of Charleston, who had gone there as the guests of some of the military companies, and then returned home. I think I can say I have been in journeyings often, and sometimes in peril, to prosecute my work. The Duke of Newcastle,

25

England, visited Charleston, and called on me, and left a
check for the school of $300.

In the year 1884, as Chairman of a committee in our
Diocesan Convention, I presented a preamble and resolutions expressing our sympathy with the movement in the
general Church, in the organization of sisterhoods and
deaconesses. It was warmly supported by some and as
warmly opposed by others. After much discussion, a
milk and water resolution was passed, which meant
nothing, and has resulted in nothing. This staid,
ultra-conservative old diocese was not ready then, but
the world has moved since then, and were I a younger
man I would press the subject, for I think the day has
come.

During the winter of 1885, I lost a warm friend, Mr.
Charles T. Lowndes. To the day of his death he was a
supporter of the institution and of myself. It was he
who sent me to Europe in 1876, and thereby my life was
prolonged. Mr. Lowndes understood that my work was
hard, and I needed sympathy and aid, and he gave me
both. Dr. Wm. T. Wragg, who had been my physician
from my boyhood, and of this institution from its foundation, five days before he took to his bed told me that he
knew his hours were numbered, his work was done, and
he added that I was the first person to whom he had
mentioned his condition.

" I wish you to remember," he added, " that I told you
I know in whom I have believed, and I am now ready and
willing to go. I have no regrets that the end of the
journey is in view." We were seated in the office of the
hospital after his visit to the wards, and he seemed so calm
and composed that no one would have supposed he was
speaking of his own case. Suddenly a paroxysm of pain
seized him while we were talking, and when it passed, he
remarked: " This is it, angina pectoris, and there is no

cure.'' It was his last visit to the hospital. His last words to me from his sick bed were: '' No one shall ever speak against you in my presence.'' He was a true friend, and his death left a blank in my life.

Elias D. H. Ball, a grandson of Bishop Odenheimer, of New Jersey, had the same year died of heart disease. This was the second death in the institution in seventeen years, and Doctor Wragg remarked when standing by his corpse, '' He was as perfect a specimen of a gentlemen as I have ever known.'' The following incident was told me by his grandmother, Mrs. Odenheimer.

Just before he came to me he dreamed he found himself in a great throng with others in the presence of a high seat, veiled from sight, but in which they understood God was seated. Each one was to pass singly before that throne, and to receive whatsoever was appointed to be borne for God's sake, and to accept it, if willing. One who preceded him was offered '' consumption '' and it was refused. To the next, '' heart disease,'' and it was refused. He determined to accept whatever was offered to him, and as he in his turn passed, he received a paper containing the words: '' Be good and faithful, true, and kind, and just ; be brave and benevolent, and you shall enter the Kingdom of Heaven.'' His life was an application of this dream. He lived in the faith and fear of God, and died in the Communion of the Church.

Mr. Henry E. Pellew, of New York, presented me this year with 166 volumes of the Latin Classics, handsomely bound, which since have found their place in the Hoffman Library. There were 226 boys in the institution this year, and yet I refused with much pain over one hundred applications to be received as beneficiaries. Six boys went to Hobart College this year, during which I carried 108 total beneficiaries. I received from South Carolina, that year, $14,527.63 ; from other States, $12,756.46, and from England, $340. I began the year with a debt of $8435, and closed with a deficit of $6450.

Two of the trustees, Mr. W. C. Courtney and Mr. John Hanckel, died within a month of each other, during the year 1885 and 1886. They were lifelong friends, and are greatly missed. Mr. John Gadsden, the Principal of the Institution for eighteen years, accepted another position, and my son, Rev. Theo. A. Porter, came to my assistance. The Board of Trustees, during my absence, on the 28th of January, 1886, changed the name of the institution from the Holy Communion Church Institute, to the Porter Academy, and took measures to have the same legalized by act of the Legislature. This is the resolution that was passed at the meeting of the Trustees. The Hon. Henry Buist offered the following preamble and resolutions, which were unanimously adopted :

" The trustees of the Holy Communion Church Institute, of Charleston, think that the time has arrived for the change of its corporate name to that of the Porter Academy. They deem this a just tribute to a great Christian philanthropist, who from its origin, and amid all its trials and struggles, has borne the burden and heat of the day. His name should in the coming years be indissolubly connected with it, for he has devoted to it the best years of a long and honorable life ; in its darkest days his faith never wavered, his heroic courage never failed.

" *Resolved*, therefore, that the Institute hereafter be known as the Porter Academy, and that application be presented to the next General Assembly for change of its corporate name."

Of course this procedure was gratifying to me, and being the act of the unanimous board, save myself, there was nothing for me to do. It was a mistake at the first in attaching the name of a parish church to the work, and had I conceived that it would have grown to the extent it has, it would not have been done. If regarded only as an Episcopal school, the prospect of general aid and patronage is diminished. Hence it is necessary to put the work on a broader basis, and while it will ever, as far as I can control the future, be under the influence of Episcopal ministration, it is now dissevered from all official connection therewith, and stands upon the broad platform of a school, the aim of which is to afford the best facilities for training mind and heart and body for the duties and obligations and privileges of life here and hereafter. At the same meeting of the trustees, Mr. R. Fulton Cutting, of New York, was elected a member of the Board, which he accepted, and is still a trustee. Mr. Cutting was a generous friend for many years and has continued to be so. I was very glad at this latter action of the Board. Surely it is an evidence of a genuine reunion of the country, when a Southern board voluntarily elects a Northern friend to be a trustee of a Southern school, and he generously accepts the place.*

While speaking of the trustees, it is proper to say here, that but for the kindness of Trustee E. Horry Frost,† I would often have been at a standstill. Frequently, at the close of a term, he has endorsed my private note for two thousand dollars to meet our obligations. He endorsed not as a trustee but as a friend, feeling confident that if I lived I would pay, but if I died, he would have to make the deficit good. They were always paid, but it does not make me the less grateful to him. I began this year with a debt of $6456. I supplied students at college with clothes to the amount of $509, and we had been visited by a cyclone, in August, 1885, which damaged the buildings to the amount of $1500, so that it was a hard, hard

* The Board, on April 5, 1897, unanimously elected Mr. Charles Frederick Hoffman, Jr., of New York, a member of the Board, and he, too, has generously accepted the position.

† Mr. E. Horry Frost died in the summer of 1897.

year, but I came to the end with a debt of but $2116. Can anyone doubt that God's watchful and loving care has been over it all?

The change in head masters caused me to throw myself more entirely into the administration, and from that year we began to rise in efficiency. There were several changes, but in 1890, I made Mr. Charles J. Colcock head master. He was a graduate of the school, and afterwards of Union College, Schenectady, and from his appointment our progress has been steadily on and upward.

CHAPTER XLII

THE CHARLESTON EARTHQUAKE

*I introduce a department of carpentering into the Institute—
The Charleston earthquake—Strange and terrible scenes
—The ludicrous side of the situation.*

DURING the year 1887, my steadfast friend, Miss Ida
Mason, gave me a sufficient sum of money to purchase a Harris-Corliss engine, twenty-five horse-power,
and a boiler of forty-horse power, and to equip a first-class
carpenter machine shop. Since then all the boys of the
first, second, and third classes, have worked one hour a
day in the carpenter shop, and some of them have learned
to make really excellent furniture. It is worthy of note,
that boys who stand highest in their classes generally
stand highest in this department, which supplements that
of mechanical drawing. This gift of Miss Mason has
been of inestimable value, for the engine not only propels
the machinery of the machine shop, but it also operates
the steam laundry, and pumps the water from my artesian
well, and supplies the dormitories with water and steam
heat in winter. A swimming pool, which is thirty feet
long, twenty wide, and ten feet deep, receives the water
and steam from the boiler in cold weather, thus heating
the room, and enabling the boys to swim all winter.

On the 31st of August, 1886, I was seated in my parlor
in Asheville, North Carolina, about a quarter to ten at
night, when I heard strange noises in my wife's chamber
above. They continued so long, I went to the foot of the
stairs and called to her nurse, for, as I have stated, my
wife had been a confirmed invalid for many years. I asked
the nurse why she was moving the furniture about in my
wife's chamber. She replied: "We thought you were
moving the drawing-room furniture, for we heard the
same noise ; I thought it strange." Next I heard the
wheels of many vehicles, apparently driving up the mountain very fast. Next the sound of many trains of cars,
and immediately after one corner of the house seemed to
be lifted up, and came down with a thud.

I then realized that it was an earthquake ; and as my
summer cottage is built on the side of a mountain, I did
not know whether it was over a cave, and something had
not given away. I rushed upstairs to take Mrs. Porter
out, and directed the rest of the family to get ready to
leave the house, but as the disturbance subsided, we all
remained quiet. After awhile I went over to some neighbors, and found them all quite wild with excitement. The
earthquake had been felt down in the valley much more
distinctly than on the mountain, and the vibration of the
turret on the City Hall had caused the bell to toll. We
imagined it was local, and as it seemed to be over, soon
settled down.

Next day about noon, a telegram was received from
Columbia, by someone, saying : "We are all safe, but
poor Charleston," and nothing more. We all began at
once to telegraph to Charleston, but received no response.

It was not until eleven o'clock at night that we began to
get news. A half sentence, and then a break. After three
or four hours incessant telegraphing, we patched together
sufficient to show that Charleston had been destroyed by

an earthquake. The Rev. Theodore A. Porter had gone down on the 31st, and we could hear nothing from him. My aged mother, an aunt, and a niece were in my house in Charleston. The Church, the school, and the little property I owned was there, and no tidings could be had. My other son, Charles, returned home with me from the telegraph office at four o'clock A.M., when we determined to take the train next morning, and get as near to Charleston as we could. But in taking the horse out of the buggy he put his foot down on mine, and in a few seconds I could scarcely move. It was impossible for me to leave next morning as my foot was terribly swollen. Charles, however, by constant telegraphing, at last learned that the members of my family were uninjured, but the city was in ruins.

On the following Friday, all bandaged and bundled up, I determined to go to Charleston, as I felt I must be needed; and as we neared Summerville, we met a sad sight, for everyone had left their houses, and were camping in their yards. We learned that the train on which my son and a large excursion party had been on Friday night, near Summerville, had a fearful experience. The cars had been swayed from side to side, throwing people from their seats, and had suddenly been stopped, with the rails in front and rear twisted into the letter S. Summerville, indeed, seemed to be the centre of the disturbance. We reached Charleston about ten at night, and it was pitiable to see the distracted people all in the streets, afraid to enter their houses. I hastened with my son Charles to the Academy, and such a sight met my eyes. Over six hundred men, women, and children were camped out on the grounds where there was every conceivable kind of extemporized tent. Blankets and even shawls had been stretched over poles, and sick and well, men, women, and children were all gathered there. I found my aged mother

had been taken out of bed, carried on to the grounds
and laid on a bed over which they had rigged up some
kind of shelter. I at once went into my house, which is
of brick, and found the chimney-tops gone; but saving
some cracks here and there, no damage sufficient to en-
danger the house was apparent. It was the month of
September, when it is not safe in this climate to sleep in
the open air, and I insisted in moving my mother back
into the house. There had been a constant rumbling
under the earth, but no shock since Tuesday night, so I
had beds brought into the lower story, and had just made
them all comfortable, when someone exclaimed: " There
it is again ! " and an awful roaring, rushing sound swept
under us. The large brick house swayed and swung like
a ship at sea, and as it settled down, every brick in it
seemed to grate one on another. This shock was almost
equal to the first. All were so much alarmed, that we
beat a hasty retreat back on to the open ground, which
rose and swelled like waves at sea. As soon as mother
was made comfortable, and was protected as far as she
could be from the weather, I went through the crowd;
some of them were bearing it very heroically, others were
totally unnerved. I found an aged relative, who had been
an invalid since she was fifteen, among the refugees.
Poor old lady, her spirit took its flight in the midst of it,
and she was at rest. I found cases of typhoid fever, and
there had been one or two births from fright. It was a
heart-sickening sight. The air was filled with many
sounds. The negroes were terrified, and took to vociferous praying, loud shouting, and weird singing. Sleep
was impossible. All night the rumbling underneath and
the quivering of the earth told us that all was not over.
Indeed, during the year there were seventy-nine shocks
in all before it ceased.

Early on Saturday I received a cablegram from London,

from my friend, Hon. Fred. A. White, which said: " Are you safe ? What damage ? " I replied, " Safe. About $20,000, as far as I can now estimate." Immediately I received another cable; it ran: " Brown Bros. will send you $3800." I devoted Saturday to going over the field. Not a house had escaped ; not one hundred chimney-tops were left ; many houses had crumbled, the fronts had fallen from some, the sides from others. St. Michael's Church seemed a hopeless ruin ; it eventually cost $40,000 to repair it. Grace Church was in the same plight. Indeed all the churches and large buildings were in ruins. The Church of the Holy Communion, having an open wood roof, seemed to have swayed and given way, with less damage, than almost any of the large brick churches. Early Sunday morning, I received a telegram from Mr. J. Pierrpont Morgan : " Intense sympathy ; draw on me for $5000."

I could not induce anyone to go into the church, so I gathered the crowd on the green, and held a full service, and preached an *ex tempore* sermon out in the open air, and had a celebration of the Holy Communion. It was a solemn occasion and a devout congregation. On Saturday night I was exhausted, for I had not slept since Thursday night, and I threw myself on the floor of a small wooden house which was on my grounds and tried to sleep. I could hear a whirling sound, and ever and again a violent shock, as if the ground beneath me had been struck with a tremendous sledge-hammer, which was not soothing ; but added to this, a large crowd of negroes had assembled just outside my wall, in the street, and they were indulging in howls and yells, screaming, praying, and singing. It was a very pandemonium. I could not stand it, so I went out to them. I soon singled out the ringleader. He was an old gray-headed man, and was praying at the top of his stentorian lungs, and informing the Lord how very wicked he and all of them had been, that hell was open, and that they were all going down into its burning jaws. I let him go on until, while he did not mean it, he was bordering on profanity, and was stirring the crowd round him to frenzy.

I put my hand gently on his head, and said : " My friend, look at me ; you know who I am, and that I am a preacher, too. I believe in prayer, but you can't fool the Lord. If you have been doing all those things you say, He knows it is fright, not conversion, that is bringing out all this excitement. Now you are not going to hell just now ; the earth has not opened and it is not going to open. The most religious thing you can do now is to keep quiet and go to sleep and let everybody else do the same. Just over that wall is a lady not two weeks out of the lunatic asylum, and you have nearly made her wild again, and you must stop."

He remonstrated, and said the negroes were having meetings all over the city. " It must stop," I said; " Mr. Courtenay, the Mayor, is on the sea, but Mr. W. E. Huger is Mayor *pro tem*, and I have seen him, and arranged to have all this noise stopped by ten o'clock. It is now eleven. Go to the Citadel Square where the largest crowd is, and you will find it all quiet."

He went, and soon came back, saying it was so, and it should be stopped. He had scarcely gone, when a negro woman came at me in a rage.

" Yes," she said ; " just like you buckra. Here we is all going down to hell, and you won't let us even say a prayer ! "

I saw a row was imminent; so I went up to her, and raising a small cane I had in my hand, I said : " Look here, I never struck a woman, but if you do not hush up, this instant, I will wear this out on you."

The threat took effect; silence followed ; but I had not

gone ten feet, when she, and the crowd who wanted to pray, broke out with a song. " Oh, pretty yaller gal, can't you come out to-night." I turned back, and told her, not that, any more than her hymns ; silence was what I had come for.

The old man came back by this time, and we had silence and I got some sleep. The Sunday-school house which had such a history, the first industrial school of the South, the place where all the uniforms of the soldiers of the State for some time were made, the Confederate States Post Office, where the first twelve years of the school had been held, were all shaken into ruins. The Church, School, Wilkinson Home, House of Rest, The Academy, and my own private property, were damaged to the amount of $21,000; but kind friends at the North, and in England, enabled me to restore them. My gymnasium was so unsafe I had to take it down. As I had the bricks, Mr. Cornelius Vanderbilt gave me $1500 to replace it. The earthquake cost the city six millions of dollars to repair damages.

The great generosity of the whole land sent some $900,000 to help us, which was a splendid exhibition of philanthropy. The North forgot there had been a war which had separated us, and gave us freely, as if we were on the other side of Mason and Dixon's line. Our people should never forget this, and when hungry politicians seek to stir up strife, they should answer: " Remember the earthquake !" Much of the remaining five million dollars was borrowed, and added to other causes, has helped to keep us down and poor. Ever since that, six millions to Charleston is more than six hundred millions to New York.

I must put on record some of the funny doings that happened during the earthquake. It is told of a young man, that he had been visiting a young woman a long while,

but had never had the courage to come to the point.
They were upstairs in the parlor when the shock came,
and as the house was on the battery, with the bay just in
front of it, and was much exposed—for everyone supposed
a tidal-wave would accompany the earthquake—the young
man rushed to the front window, and putting his arms
out, sure enough, he thrust them to the shoulder into
water.   Running back, and throwing his arms round the
young lady, he exclaimed: " Come, O my darling, let us
die together." And so they stood, dying together; but the
water also stood, for it did not come in at the windows.
After awhile the mother and father came upstairs and
caught the pair in this fond, if alarmed embrace. They
wished to know the meaning of it, and the wet arms were
the explanation.   The young man was, however, informed, that he only plunged into the aquarium which
was outside the window.   He felt bad, but it did the business; and they have not died, but lived together.

It was an awfully hot, still night, and nearly everyone
was in the bath-tub at the time of the first shock.   This
resulted in many ludicrous scenes.   One young man
seized his gauze undervest and put it on, and rushing
out, jumped a fence, and of course there was a nail that
caught the garment in the rear.   He had gotten over, but
the nail was on the other side, and do what he would, he
could not tear the garment.   There he hung with his toes
just touching the ground, when a party of young ladies
came by, and not recognizing his condition, said: " Mr.
——, where, oh where shall we go ? " " Go," he answered;
" for Heaven's sake, go anywhere, but don't come here."

A staid old gentleman who had married late in life but
had two young children, jumped out of the bath, seized
his beaver hat, put it on his head, caught up the two little
ones, and rushed out into the street with one in each arm.
As he was hurrying along, he knew not whither, someone

met him, and said; " Why, Mr. ——, do you know you have no clothes on, save your beaver ? " " Oh ! " he cried, and dropping both children, ran off. There is a ludicrous side to almost everything in life.

This was the 31st of August; but I worked like a beaver all September to get everything in order, and promptly on the 1st of October opened the Academy. It was the only school opened in town, for all the free school buildings had been so much injured that it was impossible to open them; so I placed my large schoolhouse at the disposal of the Commissioners of the Meminger School for girls, and they occupied it for over a month. I utilized other buildings for my own until the girls left, much to the regret of the boys, very naturally. A great deal has passed from memory, but I wrote a full account, and published it in the *Churchman* of November, 1886.

CHAPTER XLIII

Travels in the East

DURING the summer of 1888, I met Hon. M. C. Butler, Senator from South Carolina, at the Battery
Park Hotel, in Asheville, and talking over the school, he
remarked: "That work, sooner or later, will have to get
an endowment, and if you had the property on better
terms, I think people would be willing to give you an endowment. Come to Washington next term and see what
we can do." At Washington I went, with General Butler, to see the President. It was Mr. Cleveland's first
term, and when General Butler introduced me, I told the
President that we were going to try and get a bill through
Congress giving to the trustees the title of the arsenal, in
fee, on the condition that it be always used for educational
purposes. I gave Mr. Cleveland a hasty sketch of the
origin and history of the work, and how I had the ninety-
nine year lease of the property. He asked, "Why have
you come to me?" "What is the use," I answered,
"of our taking the trouble to go through Congress, if,
after passing the bill, it is met with your veto. We wish
to know, first, what you think about the matter?" He
laughed, and said: "You are a diplomatist." "No," I
answered; "only a man with a little plain, hard, common

sense." He then asked me to tell him all about the event, which I did. I gave him the family name of many of my boys, and he said: " Do you tell me that boys bearing those names are using a jack-plane and handsaw ? " " Yes," I answered. " Do you have any difficulty in making them ? " " None whatever," I said. " It is part of my curriculum and if any boy is socially too good to do this, he is too good socially to stay there ; but I have never dismissed any boy for this cause."

The President was very much interested and asked a great many pertinent questions; at last he was satisfied, and he said: " Have you any particular friend here ? " I said, " Yes, your Assistant-Treasurer, ex-Governor Hugh Thompson, is a very great friend of mine." " Well," he said, " you tell Thompson to keep his eye on this bill, and if it passes to come and tell me and I will sign it."

In due time the bill was passed. Governor Thompson took it to the President, who not only signed it at once, but wrote an autograph letter to General Wade Hampton, and wished him to telegraph me that he had signed my bill with much pleasure. So that now this property is held in fee by the Board of Trustees, and the only condition is that it be used for educational purposes. It is somewhat of a white elephant without an endowment; but I have the hope that the hard struggle of my life, and the marvellous success of the work, will touch some generous hearts, and cause somebody to take it up, and by their own gifts, and those of their friends, place its future, humanly speaking, beyond a peradventure, if it is the will of God.

On the 12th of January, 1889, I went to New York, and delivered an address to the Missionary Association of the General Theological Seminary, at Calvary Church, New York. I had been invited in October to deliver this address. I gave up much time to put my best thoughts into
26

it, and read it to Mr. Julian Mitchell, a distinguished
lawyer of Charleston.   He then read it over himself, and
when he sent it back he wrote me that old Southern ex-
slaveholder as he was, I had taught him things he did not
know.   He regarded my lecture as a most valuable contribution to the subject of the colored question.   It is a long
journey from Charleston to New York, and costs some
money.   Of course I supposed I was to deliver the address
of the evening, when to my surprise, I found that three
speakers were to speak on general missionary subjects.
At the end of the evening, when everyone was tired, I was
to come in for a five or ten minutes' talk on a subject so
great as the Church's relation to seven millions of people,
conditioned as are the negroes in the United States.   I
frankly confess I was a little put out.   When, at a quarter
to ten o'clock, I was introduced, I very deliberately walked
into the pulpit, and said: " I have come one thousand
miles to read an address to which I have given much
thought and time after a three months' invitation to deliver it.   It is here," and I held up the paper.   " It will
take all of an hour to deliver it, for I cannot relegate so
great a subject to a few minutes' off-hand speech, and I
must either decline to address you or deliver this."   When
intimations were given to go on, I told the audience that
if any of them desired to leave, they had better do so at
once but no one left and I delivered it.   It was published
afterwards in three issues of the *Churchman*.   The publication brought me many letters of commendation and
thanks from many sections of the country.   I took a violent cold that night and left the next day for home.   I
had to stop at Sumter to meet the Bishop of South Carolina and a committee of clergymen and laymen—such
men as the present Bishop Ellison Capers, and ex-
Governor Manning, and General J. B. Kershaw, to formu-
late a report to be submitted to the Diocesan Convention

on this same negro question. It was a cold, rainy night, and I had to remain on the platform at Florence, South Carolina, four hours, not under shelter, until another train came along. Of course my cold was increased, and when I reached Charleston I had to go to bed a very sick man. I was confined to my bed for nine weeks with a severe attack of bronchitis, and when I was able to sit up there was not much left of me. Again a Divine Providence turned my sickness into a great blessing. My good friend, Mrs. Daniel Le Roy, hearing of my illness, wrote me a letter saying that she, with her daughter, Mrs. Edw. King, and the Misses Mason had heard of my state of health, and that my life was too valuable not to do everything to preserve it. They had made up a purse, and she would send me the check, provided I would use it, and go abroad for the summer. I had repeatedly been urged by my friends in England to visit them, but my wife's health had deterred me. Now, she insisted on my going, so I accepted the kindness of my friends, and determined to go. My son Charles had been in business as a cotton buyer for some years, and he had saved up some of his salary, and he determined to go with me to take care of me. So we sailed on the 17th of June and duly arrived at Liverpool, this making the fourth time I have crossed the ocean. We travelled through England and Scotland, and went to Paris; thence to Italy, through Switzerland and Germany, up the Rhine, and on to Antwerp; back to Paris, and then to London. Two young Charlestonians were with us, Wm. Gregg Chisholm and E. H. Cain. Having gone over all this ground before, I was of some use to these young gentlemen. We were about to return to America, when Doctor McKenzie, who had attended me, assured me that although I was better, if I returned and attended the General Convention which was to meet in October, and joined in a debate, especially upon this negro question in which I was much interested, I ran the risk of throwing myself back where I had been the year before.

So I wrote to Bishop Howe that I would not be present, and asked him to supply my place. My friend, Mr. Fred. A. White, insisted on my staying with him, when my son had left me and returned home. There I determined to wait until the middle of the month. I had just gone down to pass a few days with my friend Mr. Thomas Kinscote, at the Trench, near Tunbridge Wells, in Kent, forty miles from London, when I received a telegram from Bishop Wilkinson, of Truro, from Florence, Italy, saying he had been ordered to Egypt for the benefit of his health, and asking me to come and go with him. Mr. Kinscote sent this telegram to Mr. White, who telegraphed me from London asking whether I would go? If so, he would pay all my expenses. I cabled home to ask what I should do. My wife and vestry cabled: " Go." So on the 14th of October I joined Bishop Wilkinson at Florence. We remained there a few days and went over to Venice, where we took ship and went to Brindisi, and from thence to Alexandria. It may be well imagined the intense interest of that visit to the land of so much history. We did not stay long at Alexandria, but went on to Cairo, where we remained until the 14th of December. The Bishop's health was very bad. He was in a distressingly nervous condition, broken down from overwork as Vicar of St. Peter's, Eaton Square, and then as Bishop of Truro, where he took up the task left by his predecessor, who had been made Archbishop of Canterbury—the sainted Bishop Benson. Bishop Wilkinson had continued the task of completing the first, and I think only cathedral erected since the Reformation in England, and a magnificent cathedral it is, as far as it has been built. It cost the Bishop years of much suffering, and nearly his life. The delta ot the Nile is nearly one hundred and sixty-five miles wide, and the English have reclaimed much of this fertile land, but our sea-island planters, who plant long staple cotton, have to regret it, for Egyptian cotton is a sore menace to them. At Cairo, the fertile land of Egypt narrows down to about nine miles, which is about the average width to the first cataract where the Nile runs between two ranges of hills, covered with sand, with this nine miles of alluvial deposit on either side. There is much to interest one in Cairo, the old city, and the new. During the French occupation, they built a miniature Paris where all the modern hotels are; but old Cairo remains. There is a fine carriage drive to the Pyramids nine miles off. This road was built by order of the Sultan of Turkey for the Empress Eugenie of France to get there comfortably. I frequently visited these great and wonderful works, ascended the largest, and was amused when I found a friend who put a United States flag in my hand as I stood on the summit of the Pyramid, took a snap-shot with his camera, and presented me with my picture. So, though an ex-Confederate, I held, and held cheerfully, the United States flag, and waved it over this monument of the ages. The ascent of the Pyramids is tiresome ; there are very long steps, from stone to stone, but by the pushing and pulling of the guides, who demand Bakshish at every other step, one gets there at last. When I came down, I went into the Pyramids—a very senseless undertaking. You go down a narrow passage, and then stooping very low, you are pulled and pushed by a set of fellaheens, chanting the Koran, and each with a lighted tallow candle in his hand. At length you reach a large square room as dark as pitch, only lighted by these candles, and full of smoke and smells. There before you stands a large empty porphyry sarcophagus, with the lid laid back, and the mummy of the King who built it gone. They tried to induce me to go up into the Queen's chamber, but I was nearly smothered, and demanded to get out of the place in double-quick time. I have been in the Pyramids, but I think I was an idiot for going there. The Sphinx interested me as much as anything I saw there. That patient, waiting, expectant look upon the face, I can never forget— looking, as it were, for someone coming. I think it is the best type of the Jews looking for the coming Messiah that I can think of. The mummy of Rameses II., said to be the father of the princess who rescued Moses, is in the Boulak Museum. It is of intense interest, for the expression of the face gives you an idea of the character of the man, and one can well imagine that such a man would have been the persecutor of the Jews.

Finding that the Bishop with his two daughters and a lady friend who had joined the party in England were going to stay some time in Cairo, and I wished to make a trip to Jerusalem, and finding that it would not cost much, and could be done in twelve days, with the Bishop's ready consent, I left the party, and went by rail over the land of Goshen, to Ismalia, on the Suez Canal, and through the Canal to Port Said. There I took steamer to Joppa, and after a night's trip, was in this ancient city of Joppa. I had really gone to the Holy Land. It seemed a dream, for it had never entered my mind that I would have had such a privilege.

CHAPTER XLIV

I visit the Far East—Palestine, Egypt, Damascus, all pass before me—My emotions at Jerusalem in Holy Week—I return safe home.

MY good friend, Mr. John Cook, from whom I purchased my tourist ticket, and from whom I received many acts of kindness during my sojourn in Egypt, has secured for me a dragoman who was a Coptic Christian, a native of Palestine. He took charge of me as soon as I landed, and made all arrangements for me. It is not my purpose to lengthen out this book with very many details; so many books are written purposely to describe the Holy Land, that I shall confine myself to merely stating where I went, and my general impressions. Of course, we visited the few places of Biblical interest in this ancient city of Joppa, the traditional site of the house of Simon the tanner, and the location where it is said Dorcas, whom St. Peter restored to life, lived. A small mosque stands there now. Of course I thought of the prophet Jonah, and his flight from hence. Somehow, notwithstanding the learned critics of the latter part of the nineteenth century, I find I cannot help believing that our Lord knew what He was talking about when He referred to Jonah as a type of

407

His Resurrection, and that the prophet did have the un-
usual experience of being swallowed by a big fish. When
passing through its narrow streets, I realized I was on the
spot, if not surrounded by the same houses, where the calling of the Gentiles was revealed to St. Peter. Roman
history and the time of the Crusades, and the diabolical
massacre of its garrison by Napoleon, gave interest to a
place in its present condition absolutely uninteresting.

· My dragoman having secured a seat for me in a most
uncomfortable wagon, we started for Jerusalem. Some
Englishmen have extensive vineyards and orchards of
limes, lemons, and oranges on the outskirts, through
which we passed into the Vale of Sharon. The soil, in
general appearance, reminded me of the sea island cotton-
fields on Edisto Island, near my home in South Carolina;
but as there was little vegetation save an abundance of
red poppies, I wondered if these were the Rose of Sharon.
We stopped some twenty miles from Joppa, and passed the
night at Ramleh on our left ; some five miles off from
Ramleh we saw Lydda. The next day we left Ramleh
and were soon in the hill country of Judea. There is a
magnificent macadamized road winding through these
hills, and as you enter and look up, it appears like an
unbroken mass of rock, the very personification of desolation; but as you travel along, you see these hills are all
detached, and stand separate in mounds, and as you
ascend, and look down from the second tier of hills, you
see that those circular hills seem to be terraced from bottom to top with a low natural wall, having a yard or two
of earth between the front wall and the one next above,
and so on to the top ; and this seemed to be the nature of
each. In these terraces a few fig and olive trees were
growing. When I again went over the same ground in
the spring, wheat or rye or barley was growing there, and
the desolation had passed away. After riding some

twenty miles we came in sight of Jerusalem. A long line of modern houses outside the walls obstructs the view of the city, and I found it difficult to persuade myself that it was a fact that I was looking at that place around which so much history, sacred and profane, centres. We passed through the Jaffa Gate, with camels, and donkeys, and a motley throng apparently of many nations. Jerusalem having been destroyed some eighteen times, of course the surface is not the same as was trod by the feet of our blessed Lord; but the locality is the same, and notwithstanding the dirty, narrow streets, the mixed population, the trading and traffic of the everyday life of its present inhabitants, I felt all the week I was there a constant sense of awe and reverence, as we went from place to place, traditional scenes in our blessed Lord's life. The site of the Temple, now occupied by the Mosque of Omar, Mt. Sion, and the tomb of David, the Church of the Holy Sepulchre, the pools of Bethesda and Siloam made very real the Bible record. I strongly felt the hill outside the Damascus Gate, first pointed out by Chinese Gordon, the English martyr, was most probably the hill of the Crucifixion, but the learned Bishop of Jerusalem told me, that after careful study of the whole subject, he felt satisfied the Church was the true location. He must be a very poor Christian who is not moved by such surroundings.

Jerusalem as it is, is a disappointing place, for the filth and odors make one willing to shorten one's stay. This was in 1890. Since then, a railroad has been built from Joppa. I am glad I went before it was built, for it seems to me almost profane to ride into Jerusalem in a Pullman car, to stop at a station, and hear: " All out for Emmaus." I think it would send a shudder through me, but we soon get used to everything. I went to all the traditional places in Jerusalem, but there is the Mount of Olives, and there is the same stony path over the mountain to Bethany

which our Lord must often have trod. There is Gethsemane and the Brook Kidron. The valley of Jehosaphat
and of Hinnom no change of time has effaced, and he
must be slow of heart whose emotions are not deeply
stirred when he is in the midst of such surroundings.

I went down the same path that our Lord must have
travelled over when He went down to Jericho, a descent
of over two thousand feet in twenty miles. We had a
guard, an Arab, marvellously gotten up, and a perfect
arsenal of arms which he had not the slightest occasion to
use.

My dragoman and I lunched at an inn, and soon after
entered a tortuous ravine. In the middle of it the dragoman made the cheerful remark that this had been the most
dangerous spot in Palestine, as robbery and murder had
frequently taken place in it. Being a Christian, he asked
me if I remembered the parable of the Good Samaritan, for
this was the only road between Jerusalem and Jericho,
and this spot must have suggested it to our Lord. It was
very wild ; I am glad I saw it. The next time I went
over that road, in the spring, a wide straight road had
been cut through that ravine, and a macadamized road
runs there now ; it is possible to drive over this magnificent road from Jerusalem to Jericho in two hours,
such is the march of modern improvement, but at the
sacrifice of sentiment, and of landmarks. I stopped at
New Jericho, and visited the old site of Jericho, built on
one of these mound-like hills. The foundations of the
wall are still there, and a valley surrounds the site, so that
the march of the Israelites around was perfectly practicable. Elisha's fountain is at the base, and the water flowing from it, makes fertile all its banks as it meanders
through the plain. There stand bananas, figs, grapes,
oranges, oleanders in profusion, while all else is sterile;
but where the water is, it is fertility itself. If the Jordan

were dammed up, as it might be, and the valley irrigated through canals, an immense population could be supported on the products of that valley. I saw one grapevine whose stem three men could scarcely encompass.

On our way down we passed along the brook Cherith, and the cave of Elijah, where he was miraculously fed. We rode down over the six-mile-wide plain to the Jordan and the Dead Sea, and I went to the spot where the Jordan enters the sea. In my left hand I took water from the Jordan, with my right from the Dead Sea. The one was fresh, the other was so intensely salt I was glad to get rid of it.

Marvellous, that even when this fresh water has passed in for so many ages, it does not affect the salt sea one foot from the point of entrance. From the conformation of the land, the children of Israel must have crossed over from the land of Moab, very near the mouth of the Jordan. The place where twenty-four thousand perished for their sin is just beyond, and the mountains of Moab rise nearby four thousand feet over against you. In going down to the Jordan, we passed several flocks of goats and sheep with their shepherds. Palestine is the only part of the world I ever saw sheep and goats flock together.

On our return, I noticed one of these shepherds carrying a new-born lamb very tenderly in his arms. A little while after I observed another shepherd dragging two new-born lambs by their hind legs in a very cruel manner, and I remarked on it to the dragoman, who very innocently said : '' Oh ! the first owned that flock; this last was an hireling.'' It was all very suggestive. On my return to Jerusalem, I visited Bethlehem, and the reputed cave where the Saviour was born. It is fitted up as a chapel, and many handsome silver lamps hang from the ceiling, the gifts of kings, and emperors, and rich men ; and there is an altar on the reputed spot of the

Nativity, and a silver star, with the legend in Latin :
" Here the Saviour was born." (*Hic de Virgine Maria
Jesus Christus natus est.*)   It might have been superstition,
but the impulse was irresistible to kneel down and kiss
the spot.

I went to Hebron, some fifteen miles off from Jerusalem;
by the roadside passed Rachel's tomb as I went to visit
the cave of Machpelah, where we know Abraham, Isaac,
and Jacob, and Sarah and Leah were buried.   A great
mosque now covers the area.   I went all round it; of
course could not get in, not being as fortunate as the
Prince of Wales and Dean Stanley, and not having one
thousand soldiers to guard me against the inhabitants of
Hebron, the most fanatical people in Judea.

I visited the site of Gibeon and Mizpah, where Samuel
lived and was buried.   But I find I am entering too much
into detail, which I promised not to do, though the temptation is very great.   I returned from the various trips
around Jerusalem, and after twelve days returned by the
Suez Canal and went back to Cairo.   I found on my return that Canon Scott Holland, of St. Paul's, London, was
to join the party.   The Holy Land is no place for a
tourist to visit who is not thoroughly acquainted with its
history, and with his Bible, as it offers nothing to the
sight-seer but desolate limestone hills.

I met two men from Chicago who seemed to be dreadfully bored and pronounced it all a fraud.   I tried to interest them, but found I was casting pearls before swine,
and suggested that the fraud was not in Palestine but it
was in such men visiting it.   We remained in Cairo
until the 14th of December, when the whole party, consisting of Bishop Wilkinson, his two daughters, a lady
from London, Canon Holland, and myself entered a
dahabiyeh, which is a long, flat-bottom boat, with a
cabin at the stern, one huge mast and trisail.   To have

this costs a little fortune per month, and it is the most wearisome mode of locomotion, though charming to people who have plenty of money to throw away, and any quantity of time that they do not know how to make use of. In our trip we once made twenty miles in five days. The monotony was intense. A trip by rail, or better still by the great Cook steamer *Rameses II.*, gives you more comfort, and more opportunity for observation by far. This is not the right thing to say, but I would not take the trip up the Nile in a dahabiyeh again with my expenses paid three times over.

We did not reach the first cataract until somewhere in March. Of course there was much to interest, but I will not allow myself to go over what has been so often said, and better than I can say it. At Luxor, I met with Mr. Clarence Wadsworth, a young man from New York, travelling in a dahabiyeh with a tutor, Rev. Mr. Craig, of New York. Mr. Wadsworth told me he was going to Mt. Sinai, and through the Holy Land to Damascus, Palmyra, and across to Antioch, and kindly invited me to be his guest. On my return from the first cataract to Luxor, I bade my friends of the Bishop's party good-bye, as he was in the good hands of Canon Holland. In going up the Nile I had not been very long on the boat before I had complete control over the seventeen black hands from Libya. I did not understand them, but when at a loss, the dragoman interpreted for me. They had a few words of English, and I picked up a few of their words, and by degrees I could communicate with them, and they soon dubbed me Pasha. I could make them do anything I wished. The Bishop and Canon Holland were quite amused at the relationship so soon established, and asked how I had managed to get control of them so soon, as they themselves absolutely had nothing to do with them. " Oh ! " I said, " I was born among the black race, and had them under me from my boyhood. I understand them pretty well, and these people soon discovered that I was not a stranger to their race.'' One of them seemed quite sick one day, and I went up to him, and put my hand on his head, and by signs found out he had a bad headache. I made up some mustard plasters and put them on his temples, telling the dragoman to warn him not to keep them on too long. He, however, tied them on, and went down into the hole of the boat, and closed the hatch after him. He did not come out till morning, when the headache was gone, but so, too, the skin on his temples, for he had kept the plasters on all night, and two large, raw, white patches were on each side of his head. As he was cured, I gained quite a reputation, and had to prescribe for every ailment of all the crew the rest of the trip. It was noised abroad, and when I returned to Cairo and went out again to the Pyramids, I could not get off from going to a village to see a man with paralysis. I prescribed very earnestly, but did not cure that man.

From Luxor, I took the steamer to Assyout, from there by rail to Cairo, returning in two days from a trip which had taken three months, when I met Mr. Wadsworth and Mr. Craig, and became their guest. In a week we went over to Suez, and took a boat a few miles down the Red Sea, where we met our camels and started on our journey, following the track of the Children of Israel, through the wilderness of Sin, and then through the different wadys or valleys of Mt. Sinai. The fountain of Moses, the well of Marah, the wells of Elim, and the place where manna was first given, and the quails were sent, were the points of interest, before we turned off from the sea to make towards Mt. Sinai. The sandy plain through which we travelled on the camels is about three miles wide, with the Red Sea on the right, and a range of sand-covered hills on the left. These hills are almost entirely of alabaster, large and handsome pieces of which lie scattered over the plain. I wonder some syndicate does not get the privilege of mining these hills, in which there is a fortune for somebody.

As we turned to the left, at right angles from the sea, the ground gradually ascends to a few hundred yards from the mouth of the valley. I looked back and do not remember to have seen a more magnificent sight. The marvellous blueness of the sea, the Libyan Mountains in the background, and the walls of the mountains on either side of the valley of bare, solid rock, and of divers colors, make it a gorgeous gateway. I never saw such rocks or mountains before ; they were separate ; one was white, one black, one red, one purple, one variegated, and then some of them gray and disintegrating with age ; and this continues for some miles. I believe we were in the very track of the children of Israel, but, instead of a dreary desert, it was a magnificent highway leading up to Mt. Sinai. By the third day on the camels I wished I had no back, and did as much walking as I could. As the ascent to the foot of Mt. Sinai is very gradual, we had to use our instruments each night to find out how many miles we had ascended, but the slope of the winding valleys is so gradual, we scarcely noticed it.

Of course, there was much of interest in the ten days' journey, for we did not travel long each day, and laid over Sunday at the Wady Feiran, which is well watered and fertile. We camped outside the wall of the Convent of St. Catherine, on Mt. Sinai. The group of peaks forming Mt. Sinai, as you approach, gives the impression of an immense cathedral, with four high and pointed towers, one of which is the mountain of the Law. From its top, and winding somewhat in the rear, there is a stream of water which, flowing down and winding near to the base, loses itself in the sand. This is the stream into which Moses threw the particles of the brazen calf which the people had made. All is there now, as it must have been then. I could not help thinking, " This is the water that with others rises to the surface at Feiran and at the wells of Elim," and thought if Moses had known anything about artesian wells he need not have been troubled about watering his host. This group of peaks seems to be the culminating point of this peninsula which lies between the Red Sea and the gulf of Akabah. Entirely encircling the group is a wide valley. The Mount of the Law rises with a straight wall from the plain which stretches some two miles away and a mile wide. Here the Israelites were encamped for two years. The floor of the plain rises from the base of Sinai, back like the floor of a theatre, so that those who were encamped on the further outskirt could see the mount, from its base to its summit. My two friends started to ascend the peak, and I went with them ; but they had youth on their side, and I gave out at the Chapel of Elijah, the traditional spot where God, in the still, small voice, spoke to the prophet. The others went some miles farther on, but returned without reaching the summit. We paid many visits to the Convent, and I could fill many pages with descriptions, but so much is written on the subject that I hurry on.

We stayed a week here and experienced a great variety of weather. We had thunder-storms, hail and snow, and warm, clear days. Returning by a shorter way, we reached Suez in some four days, where we bade not an affectionate farewell to our camels. The next day we went to Port Said, via the Suez Canal, and from there to Joppa, and arrived at the Mount of Olives on the 29th of March, 1890. The 30th was Palm Sunday, and we camped on the Mount of Olives, walked over to Jerusalem, and attended service at the English Chapel. We spent Holy Week in Jerusalem, and Maundy Thursday night I was at the celebration at the chapel, a night never to be forgotten.   After service, I mounted my horse, and rode around the walls of Jerusalem, across the brook Kidron, and by the Garden of Gethsemane.   The moon was very bright, and as I reached the wall I heard the old familiar tune, Hebron, which was being sung by a large congregation in the Garden.   It seems it was the custom for the congregation to go in a body from the church, after the celebration, to Gethsemane, and there to sing and pray.   I did not know it, or would have been with them ; but I rode near to the wall, and leaned against it, and my emotional nature gave vent in tears of gratitude to Him who there had sweated great drops of blood for me.

It was quite cold, and when I reached the tent I found the dragoman had a nice fire of coals, where I warmed my hands and thought of poor Peter, and prayed I might never deny my Lord.   We went to the Church of the Holy Sepulchre on Easter Sunday, and there, in a chapel loaned to the English priest, we partook of the Holy Eucharist.   On Monday we left for the Jordan.   We took a more circuitous route, going by the Vale of Ajalon, and by Beth Horon, and so crossed, by a bridge, beyond Jordan, into the land of Moab, when we crossed the Jordan and ascended the steep side of what seemed to be a mountain. We reached the top, and found ourselves upon a wide-extended, undulating plain, and as far as the eye could see it was one vast green field, and here and there camps of Arabs, who locate for a time and plant and then go on to other fields until they cover a large area, and in harvest time repeat their nomadic life.   I did not wonder that Reuben and Gad wished to stay there, after their weary journey in the wilderness, for there was abundant pasturage for their cattle, and the barren hills over the Jordan were less inviting.   Our first objective point was Heshbon, of which we read in the second chapter of Deuteron-

27

omy. This was the city of Sihon, King of the Amorites, who refused to let Moses pass through, and God gave him and his cities into the hands of Moses. It is all a ruin now, but there must have been very large buildings there once. Mt. Nebo, or Pisgah, is not far off, and thither we prepared to go, as we were under the protection of the sheik of that district, to whom quite a sum had been paid.

As we were riding on very quietly, suddenly our sheik stopped and said his jurisdiction there ended, and an Arab took hold of the bridle of our dragoman, and refused to allow us to proceed. Mt. Nebo was not a half-mile distant, and we insisted on going on. The Bedouin became furious, and our dragoman lost his temper and drew his pistol. I was riding beside him, and as he threw it over to take aim at the man I looked down the barrel, caught his arm, and threw it up, and told him very peremptorily not to shoot. Should he kill that man, our lives would not be worth a penny. The man tore himself off, and rushed down the side of the mountain, towards the Dead Sea. We rode on, and soon stood on the top of Pisgah, where Moses stood. We had not been there long when we saw a great crowd of dark figures coming up out of the valley, headed by the man who had tried to stop us. They were coming up very fast, and in great numbers, so we concluded we had better return to the protection of our sheik, which we did in a hurry. Mt. Nebo is only a rocky mound, rising some two or three hundred feet from the plain, on the edge of the precipice overlooking the Dead Sea. The view must have been more attractive in Moses' day than it was to us, for as far as we could see the whole country had a most desolate appearance. We could see the tower of Ascension, on Mt. Olivet, some twenty miles away, but up the Jordan Valley, and over the hill country of Judea, we saw only barren limestone rocks.

Our next journey was to Rabbah-Ammon, a few miles off. Here Og, the King of Basan, with his iron bedstead, nine cubits the length and four cubits the breadth, of course came to our minds. It was here the events recorded in the second chapter of Second Samuel took place, the scene of David's awful sin in the murder of Uriah the Hittite. From thence we went to Ramoth Gilead, now called Salt, then over the brook Jabbok, where Jacob wrestled with the Angel, and on to Jerash. The foundations of the gates where David heard of the death of Absalom are still there. We then crossed back over the Jordan, and made our way to Shechem, now called Nablous, a somewhat populous town, a place that recalls Abraham and Jacob. Here is the grave of Joseph, and the well of Jacob, where our Lord met the woman of Samaria and revealed to her His Divine nature. The grave is there and the well is there, and Mount Ebal is on one side of the valley and Mount Gerizim on the other. Those who are familiar with the Bible will remember how much history is connected with this locality. We passed on to Samaria, a few miles distant, where Naaman the leper and the Prophet Elisha of course came to our minds, with all the rest of the interesting history connected with the place.

We passed through Dothan, and saw many of the pits which are there, into one of which Joseph was cast by his jealous brothers. We left Mount Carmel a few miles to the left, and descended to the valley of Esdraelon ; skirting along the river Kishon, we went to Gilboa, where Saul and Jonathan were slain, and to Jezreel, where Jezebel was thrown to the dogs, and to Shunem, and Endor, and Nain. There, the widow's dead son and our Lord came vividly to memory. In this small area, a vast deal of history has been enacted. This is the scene which reveals Jabin and Sisera and Jael, and where in later times great battles have been fought. The river Kishon, which rises through the valley, may be at times a stream of some dimensions ; when we saw it, in the month of May, it was a very small creek, with very little water in it. We crossed over, and ascended the hills of Galilee, and went to Nazareth, the home of the blessed Virgin, the scene of the boyhood and early manhood of Him who rules our hearts, and from whom the joy of earth and the hope of heaven are derived. I could have lingered longer there than we did, but time was beginning to press, and we went on down to the Sea of Galilee, where we stayed some days. It escaped my memory when writing of Jerash that, as we made our way through the woods of Gilead, I felt very homesick ; we seemed to be so far from home, so out of the world. I was riding alone, some little distance from my friends, when I happened to look up, and there, hanging in the air, was a telegraph wire. On inquiry, I found that at Jerash I could have sent a message to the dear ones at home. At once the feeling of isolation left me. Thanks to the science of this wonderful age, away off, on the other side of the Jordan, surrounded by wild Bedouins, I could in a few moments have told them at home where I was.

We camped beside the sea of Galilee, near a very hot spring, where there is a bath-house ; visited Tiberias, and Magdala, and Bethsaida, Capernaum, and Chorazin, or rather the sites, for all else is ruin and desolation. There are some very fine broken columns at Capernaum, with the tracery of a vine, and with a plate with something, thought to represent manna, carved on the lintel, and the ruin is held to be that of the synagogue built by the pious centurion. We crossed the sea in one of those little ships, or boats, exactly similar to those in which our Lord crossed the lake. We went to the reputed scene of the herd of swine, and the field where there is much grass, and where the five thousand were fed. It was on one of the small hills just back of the site of Capernaum that our Lord delivered His great Sermon on the Mount. It was very calm, and very hot, when we rowed over in the morning, but we had a stiff breeze against us, and it was somewhat rough on our return. Leaving the sea, we followed the course of the Jordan, by the waters of Merom, and reached Dan, now called Banias, the site of Cæsarea Philippi, the farthest point north that our Lord went, near which He was transfigured on one of the spurs of Mount Hermon. Though Mount Tabor is the traditional place, it could not have been there ; it does not topographically fit in with the history. From here our Lord took His way back to Jerusalem, to be crucified. From under the mountain at Dan a considerable stream gushes out, and this is one of the sources of the Jordan.

We crossed over a part of Mount Hermon, and the little stream of Pharpar, and entered the plain, somewhere in which Saul of Tarsus was travelling on his way to Damascus. It was intensely hot, and the water had disagreed with me, and I was pretty well used up by the time we reached Damascus. This is the most unchanged Oriental city I had visited. As I looked into the clear waters of the Abana, which flows through the city, I did not wonder that Naaman looked contemptuously on the muddy waters of Jordan, and rather resented that he was to go and wash in it. There is a hospital for lepers on the reputed site of his house. There I saw a horrible sight and cut my visit to the hospital very short. The street which is called Straight, with the other points of interest, we visited. My friends were going on to Palmyra, but this meant six days more each way, through a desert, and I had been on horseback every day, save Sunday, since the 27th of March, and was two weeks before on a camel. This was now the last of May, and I was tired out ; so I thanked them for their kindness and turned my face homeward.

I took passage in a very comfortable wagon, and went over to Baalbeck ; saw seven wonderful columns, and the ruins of the great Temple of Baal; was charmed with that trip, but next day took stage, over the splendid macadamized road, and before dark was at Beyrout. I could very easily have written a volume of descriptions and impressions, but I must bring this biography to a close, and refer my readers to the books of those whose writings would be more interesting. Beyrout is a charming seaport town on the Mediterranean Sea, and I stayed there a few days waiting for a ship ; then sailed to Smyrna, and Ephesus by rail some sixty-four miles from Smyrna. The foundations of the great Temple of Diana are still there, and there are some most magnificent columns prostrate and broken. I thought the carvings superior to anything I saw in Greece. St. Paul and the Beloved Disciple were in the mind all the while ; Ignatius and Polycarp, the second chapter of the Revelation of St. John I was reading while in those places. I was amazed at the beauty, and extent of the present Smyrna, and the handsome buildings and grand harbor. I saw more ocean steamers in the three days I was there than I see in a winter in my own home in Charleston. The effete East quite vanished from my mind ; for signs of life, enterprise, and progress were all around. I sailed next for Athens, passed the isle of Patmos, and stopped at Cyprus ; enjoyed my visit and stay of three days at Athens immensely; then sailed for Brindisi, thence to Naples, Rome, Paris, London, where my dear friend, Mr. Fred. A. White, and his family, received me with loving hospitality. I spent a week in London, bade them good-bye, I fear forever; went on to Liverpool, thence to New York, where my sons Theodore and Charles met me, and then for home, Charleston, where I arrived on the 17th of June, 1890, having been gone just one year and one day.

This extended tour, which I believe has prolonged my life, cost neither myself nor my school one penny. It was enjoyed through the generosity of Mrs. Daniel Le Roy, Mrs. Edward King, the Misses Mason, Mr. Fred. A. White, Bishop Wilkinson, and Mr. Clarence Wadsworth. I was thus enabled to visit countries which I never dreamed I should see. My benefactors, each and all, have my profoundest gratitude. I found my son Theodore had successfully carried the parish and the school through the year; but he was so broken down by the strain that I made arrangements for him and sent him abroad to spend three or four months.

CHAPTER XLV

END OF A BEAUTIFUL LIFE

I suffer a sad bereavement in the death of my wife—Her great power in helping and guiding my life's work—Summary of some years' toil.

DURING my absence in Europe, the Diocesan Council held its annual session at the Church of the Holy Communion, and from many sources I learned that the service held at the opening of the Council was very fine. My son, who is my assistant, received many congratulations for his successful effort, and it afforded to very many the first opportunity of knowing the capabilities of the liturgy of the Church. It removed many misapprehensions and prejudices, and has enabled many clergymen to introduce a more elaborate and reverential service, without arousing antagonisms and unfavorable comment. Our surpliced choir, with our most excellent organist, Mr. Huguelet, accompanied by a full orchestra, enabled my son to render such a service as was never before held in South Carolina.

I omitted in the record of 1888 to mention the death of my aged mother, who entered into rest on the 30th of January, in her eighty-sixth year, having been a great invalid for some seven years. She was buried on the sixtieth anniversary of my birth, and had lived to see her children's children to the third generation. She was buried by the side of her husband, to whose memory she had been so faithful.

After the close of the school, the last of June, I took my wife to Asheville, where in her suffering life she had enjoyed most comfort during the past few summers. She had borne up cheerfully under our long separation, but when I returned home the tension was removed, and she declined rapidly. We returned to Charleston in the fall, the school opened as usual, and there is nothing of particular interest to relate.

In February, my wife was attacked with that disease which has afflicted the country for many years, the grippe, and she continued very feeble all the winter and spring. Then my son Charles was to be married in Opelika, Alabama, to Miss Nellie Driver, on the 12th of May. My wife was not able to go, but my son Theodore and his wife and I had to go, of course. We left my wife apparently no worse than she had been for months, but on our return on the 13th we found her in bed and very sick. Gradually she grew worse, and on the 19th of June, 1891, her pure and saintly spirit entered into the paradise of God, and her poor suffering body was at rest. We had been married thirty-nine years, and thirty of those years she had been a patient sufferer, unable to engage in any of the activities of the parish life ; but such was the strength of her spotless character, that she wielded an influence through all my parish. Often have ladies gone into her sick-room with sad countenance and heavy heart, and after telling to her their trouble, and listening to her wise and gentle counsel, and often being convinced by her that their sorrows were self-made, I have seen them leave that room of pain with bright smiles, saying it was a privilege to have a few moments with her. In all my acquaintance with men and women, I have never known a person of such wonderful judgment and discretion. She never took sides, but always weighed every grievance, and invariably acted as peacemaker. In all our married life, I never did a thing that was contrary to her advice or opinion without having reason to regret it. Impulsive myself by nature, she was ever my corrective. I have been alone now for eight years, and I have mourned her, and miss her now, more than I can express. In the weary years of my incessant struggle to maintain this work, she was always hopeful and encouraging. How often have I gone to her sick-bed feeling I had to give up, for there was nothing in the treasury, and months to get to the end of the term, and again and again she would say: " Husband, did God give you that work to do ? Have you done your best ? Has He not signally blessed it ? Is it right to doubt His providential care ? Help will come. Do your duty and trust." And help always did come, sometimes most unexpectedly and unsought.

Her life was a benediction to all around her, and though seldom free from pain, her calm and cheerful temper made it a privilege to minister to her. A conversation held with her during her illness illustrates her life. I thought she must die, and sitting by her I said : " My wife, what will I do without you ? I dread the loneliness."

Turning her eyes, beaming with love and faith, upon me, she said: " Alone ; oh, no, my dear, not alone. You by faith will be with Jesus, I, by sight, will be with Him, and in and through Him we will still be together."

I recollect that on one occasion since her death I was much perplexed as to what I ought to do about opening the school again in view of the financial tempest, the wild silver craze, the depression everywhere : I was asleep, and I thought my wife stood at the head of my bed. I felt her hand on my forehead and stroking my hair. I did not seem to be asleep, nor was she at all spiritual in appearance ; she had her old-time sweet, natural look, and she said, " My dear, your life is guided by a Providence you know not of." I turned and told her, " Yes, my wife, I believe it," and as I looked at her, she vanished. Was it a dream or was it a visitation ? I believe the latter.

I live now on those words of cheer and comfort. She has not forgotten, and in the presence of our blessed Lord I have no doubt that through her intercession, the help has come that has enabled me to go on. But for her this work had never been done. It was she who cheerfully gave up the rent of the house which was our only income in 1867. It was she who said: " If God has given you a work to do go and do it ; we will not starve. Weak as I am, we will take boarders to enable you to give up our rented house for an Orphanage." And never did she once repent of it, nor ever once suggest that I had done enough, but rather urged me to go on. She was a model daughter, a wife and mother as perfect as it is possible for poor humanity to be, and I wait the time when we shall be reunited in the life where there is no more parting.

I closed the school two weeks after my wife's death, for the summer holidays, and began again in October. There is now nothing of importance to relate ; the usual hard struggle to get through, but somehow in the Providence of God we closed the school the last of June and went to Asheville. Early in September our coast was visited by the most terrific cyclone ever experienced here, accompanied by a tidal wave, which swept over our sea islands and drowned over one thousand persons, principally negro laborers. Here was a dilemma for me. Not a single person in all that section applied for the admission of a boy into the school, and I was greatly perplexed. What was I to do? I had been praying very earnestly for light and guidance, one evening, when the thought came to me, If your treasury is full, where is your faith? If you go on with your work, with nothing in view, but only trust in God, that is faith. I took it as an answer to my prayers, and rose from my knees, and wrote a circular to the desolate parents of my boys, and told them to send their sons, pay if they could, if not, God would help me in some way. I took ninety-eight boys, without the promise of a cent. I wrote an appeal in the *Churchman* and received a few dollars in reply, but, later in the fall, Miss Ellen and Miss Ida Mason sent me their annual large donation, and somehow or other I pulled through; and so we have gone on, and now I am at the close of my thirtieth year, in the year 1897, having been sustained through all these years by the merciful providence of God, and the generosity of friends at the North, and in England.

And what are the results of this varied life? I am now in the forty-fourth year of my rectorship of the Church of the Holy Communion, having built the church from the foundation. I have married 267 couples; baptized 1113 persons; there have been confirmed under my ministry, 887; and I have buried 651 persons. I have seen my congregation scattered to the winds by a four years' war. I have been a rector of a church in which there was much wealth, but have lived to see that wealth take wings and fly away. I have a congregation of earnest, loving people, all poor, and we find the greatest difficulty to sustain ourselves on the most economical basis. Through this congregation, in forty years I have been instrumental in raising and distributing for church purposes four hundred thousand dollars. I served St.

Mark's Church, a colored congregation, for ten years, and finished their church. I have been permitted to carry on this great school for thirty years, have given a more or less finished education to over three thousand boys, fully twenty-five hundred of these gratuitously or for a mere pittance, have sent over two hundred boys to college, and have educated one hundred and fifty sons of clergymen gratuitously; have furnished twenty-two men to the ministry, with several candidates for Holy Orders at this moment preparing for the ministry; have acquired a whole block of property from the United States Government; have erected seven houses on the grounds, and have rented them out, as the investment of a small permanent endowment fund; have raised and expended in Christian education nearly one million of dollars; have labored and suffered, had disappointments and sorrows, met with ingratitude, and with the warmest love and gratitude of others, and close up after thirty years with a deficiency of five thousand dollars staring me in the face. But, blessed be God, though perplexed, yet not in despair, for I believe there are loving hearts beating in some breasts which shall be moved to help me through.

CHAPTER XLVI

THE LATE DR. CHARLES FREDERICK HOFFMAN

The inauguration of McKinley—I meet an old friend at Washington—Death of my dear friend and benefactor, the Rev. Charles Frederick Hoffman—His life and character, and an account of his obsequies.

LIEUT. JOHN McQUEEN wrote me on the 8th of February, 1897, that he was to meet Gen. O. O. Howard in Washington, at the inauguration of President McKinley, and, as we were all growing old, it was not likely that we three would ever meet again, as he lived in Elgin, Illinois, General Howard in Burlington, Vermont, and I in Charleston. The events following the burning of Columbia had intertwined the current of our lives, he said, and he asked me to meet him in Washington. Accordingly I went, and it was a joyful meeting between the three. It is now thirty-two years since the events of 1865, recorded in these pages. McQueen was then twenty-seven, General Howard thirty-three, I was thirty-seven ; we are now three gray-haired old men of fifty-nine, sixty-five, and sixty-nine, but neither of us has forgotten those days. McQueen is writing the story from his standpoint ; I wish I could insert it here. Many details I was unacquainted with, and it will not be unintersting to read the record, of the same event, by the two men engaged in it. McQueen told me he felt that his work was done, but it had come over him that he might still be of use, and he intended to devote much time to try to interest persons in this work, and thus show his gratitude to the man who had saved his life, by striving to ease the burden which is now pressing so heavily on me. General Howard told McQueen how, in 1893, he had started out with me, in New York, to try to raise a large sum of money, as he wanted to be instrumental in endowing the work of the man for whom he had such regard. He related how we went to three rich men, and one of them was so rude to him that he had shed tears, and I had said : " General, we must stop this. I see distinctly these men are frightened ; we are at the beginning of a financial panic; this is no time for our work."

And it was true. The panic of 1893 had begun, and the effects we feel in 1897. "But," added General Howard, " I have not given up my wish and purpose. I mean yet to help in that work. Now," he said, " you wish to do the same, McQueen ? Give me your hand."

" Where two of you agree in any matter, ask, and it shall be done unto you." I trust in God it may be given to these two friends to further that which is so on my heart—the endowment of this institute.

The whole story of McQueen and myself seems like a romance. He is a Northern man, I am a Southerner ; he was a Federal officer, I a Confederate; he is a Republican, I a Democrat, although not of the Bryan stripe ; he is a Western farmer, I a clergyman ; he is a Presbyterian, I an Episcopalian; and yet, while differing at every point, there are no two men whose lives have been more blended together by no design, or purpose, or volition. Strange are the ways of Providence.

The Inauguration ceremonies were all over. It was an ideal day, and a very magnificent pageant, and I was preparing to return to Charleston, by the night's train, when I received a telegram from my dear friend, Mr. Charles Frederick Hoffman, Jr., from Jekyl Island, Georgia, informing me of the sudden death, on the 4th of March, of his revered father, the Rev. Charles Frederick Hoffman, D.D., LL.D., D.C.L. In speaking of the late Dr. Hoffman, I must go back to the year 1892, when I was in New York, and had met with much to discourage me, so that I had actually come to a standstill. In that great city, so full of wealth, with so many members of my own Church, yet I did not know to whom I could go, to ask for aid. So I went up to my room at the Everett House, and prayed very earnestly for direction, and after a while, I went down to the sitting-room, and while there it had occurred to me that I must go and call on the Rev. Charles Frederick Hoffman, D.D., of whom I had often heard, but to whom I had never been introduced. I knew his brother, the Dean, well, but I had never had the opportunity of meeting his brother, the rector. I had no letter of introduction, and I hesitated a long while, for it is not my habit to call on anyone without an introduction. Still I thought perhaps he might have heard of me, and I would venture to call. I did not know where he lived, and so had to look up his residence in the Directory. Finding it was 31 West 72d Street, New York, I boarded a Columbus Avenue car, and went with anxious heart.

Reaching his house, I sent in my card, and was invited into his handsome study. He asked me to be seated, and finished with a couple of men, who seemed to be engaged in some kind of work for him. Having dismissed them, he took his seat, and the first thing he said was, " I know what you have come for."

" Yes," I replied ; " Dr. Hoffman, I suppose you are

so frequently intruded upon that you can readily imagine the object of my visit.''

I found out afterwards that the Doctor, when interested, often sat with his elbow on the table, and his cheek in the palm of his hand. He was in that position, and said :

'' Before you go on, I will say to you, in my judgment, considering your surroundings, you have done the largest and most important single-handed work which has been done by any man in the Church since the war. You wish me to help you ; of course I will, as every man in the Church ought to do.''

This, of course, relieved me of anxiety and embarrassment, as he evidently meant it should. I thanked him for his good opinion, but did not flatter myself that he knew what my work had been, but he told me he knew all about it, and asked me to tell him what I wanted. We then went very fully into the work, and he asked me if I had a library building. I told him no ; I had some books, but only in a room. '' Such an institution,'' he said, '' ought to have a library building.''

I told him that the struggle for bread and for teachers' salaries had been so great that while I hoped some time a library would come, my hope was far in the distant future.

'' No,'' he said; '' go to Messrs. J. B. Snooks & Co., 12 Chambers Street, and tell them what you wish, and direct them to furnish plans, and I will pay for it.''

My joy may be imagined. The architects furnished plans, but they did not meet with the Doctor's approval. He asked if I had any idea of the kind of building I needed. I told him I could draw a ground plan, but not the elevations. He handed me a pencil and some paper. I drew the plan. He smiled when he looked at it, and taking a paper from his drawer which he had sketched, he said, '' Which is yours and which is mine ? '' We had made the same design without consultation ; the only

28

difference was, that I had placed the four reading-rooms on the four sides, and he had put them on the angles of the octagon. I liked his best. He accordingly gave general directions to the architects as to the elevations, and they prepared the design, which he accepted, and authorized me to advertise for bids for its erection. On the 19th of October, 1893, the corner-stone was laid, with appropriate ceremonies, and on the 26th of June, 1894, it was formally opened. At the laying of the corner-stone, Mr. J. P. Kennedy Bryan, a distinguished member of the Charleston bar, delivered a chaste, thoughtful, and eloquent address. The Citadel Cadets, escorted by the Porter Military Academy Cadets, were in the chapel. Mr. Bryan's address was partly written and partly *ex tempore*, and his tribute to the broad-minded and noble generosity of Rev. Dr. Hoffman was worthy of preservation ; it was at the time a source of regret that it could not be reproduced. *Now* I would give a great deal if I had it on permanent record.

At the opening exercises, Rev. Dr. Pinckney, Hon. John F. Ficken, the Mayor of Charleston, the Hon. W. A. Courtenay, ex-Mayor, who is also one of the trustees of the Academy, with Hon. Augustine F. Smythe, State Senator, made addresses ; and each offered a warm tribute to the generous donor. This building cost $7500, and Doctor Hoffman gave me his check for it. It has been much used by the cadets, and has been a great benefaction to this Academy. In the winter of 1895, the Doctor and Mrs. Hoffman, and their daughter, Mrs. Rhodewald, and her husband, paid us a visit. Doctor Hoffman expressed great pleasure at all he saw here, and kindly gave me one thousand dollars to help in current expenses. During the winter of 1896, Doctor Hoffman invited me to visit him at the Jekyl Island Club, and introduced me to many persons of wealth, some few of whom were kind enough to take an interest in the school. Mrs. Wm. Rockefeller gave me $500, Mr. and Mrs. Frederick Baker $225, Mrs. Larz Anderson $100, Mr. Scrymser $100, Miss Lake $50. Doctor Hoffman had also in the summer of 1895, invited me to visit him at Elberon, where the Rev. Dr. Bodine, rector, invited me to tell my story, and $660 was the result.

In August, 1896, Doctor Hoffman was to preach the Commencement sermon at the University of the South, at Sewanee, and he kindly invited me to go with his party in his private car. It was a fearfully hot spell, and I fear he never fully recovered from the fatigue of that journey. It was at his suggestion that this biography is written, and he saw all the sheets to the year 1882, and it met with his approval. He took my manuscript with him to Jekyl Island, where it was found in his trunk. Thus, from the day of my acquaintance with him until his death he was my friend, helping me himself, and trying to put me in the way of making friends. The telegram announcing his death gave me a great shock. Of course I went on to New York to be with my dear friends in their sorrow, and on my return, wrote the following article, which was published in the Charleston *News and Courier*, on the 16th of March, 1897 :

" The Rev. Charles Frederick Hoffman, D.D., LL.D., D.C.L., rector of All Angels Church, New York, died suddenly at Jekyl Island, Georgia, on the 4th of March, and the funeral services were held at All Angels Church, on the 8th. It has been my good fortune to witness many high ecclesiastical functions at Rome, in Cologne, in Paris, and in London, but I have never been so impressed by a service as I was on this occasion. Forty-eight clergymen, including a Bishop, with all the professors of the General Theological Seminary, proceeded from the vestry, the choir singing a hymn, down the north aisle to the front door, where the casket was met, borne on the shoulders of eight men, preceded by the full vestry, and followed by the family and friends. The choir passed on to their stalls, while Dr. E. N. Potter read the introductory sentences. The casket was placed in the choir between the stalls, the head to the altar. There was a large cross presented by the vestry, of most expensive white rosebuds, placed at the head of the casket. The Easter hangings were in place, and the whole chancel was a magnificent display of costly flowers, all the special offerings of friends. The service then began. It seemed a great Easter festival. It was more like a marriage-feast than a funeral. I read the lesson, and this was followed by the office of the Holy Communion, Bishop Doane being the celebrant, and the thought that the spirit of the departed must be there I found was common to many. A gentleman remarked afterwards : ' Is that what you Episcopalians call sadness ? Why, it is triumphant. I was taken nearer Heaven than I ever was before.' I mention this to show the teaching power of a ritual, intelligently and effectively rendered. From first to last it proclaimed that Christians believe what they profess, and that they do not sorrow as those without hope. The students of the Theological Seminary attended in a body. Some forty clergy were in the body of the church, and the very large and splendid building was filled to its utmost capacity. No bishop, prince, or potentate was ever buried with more evidence of respect and regard, and with a more general manifestation of intense feeling, than was the revered rector of All Angels Church. There was nothing perfunctory about it, but all a heart service. The tenor, Mr. Williams, who sings in opera (and such a voice as he has !) voluntarily cancelled engagements in Pittsburg to come and sing at the funeral of one who had been a friend and benefactor. I know nothing of Doctor

Hoffman's fortune; he was accounted a man of very great wealth, but it was for the man, not his money, that this tribute was given. He possessed a singularly sensitive nature, with warm and tender sympathies, and though his public benefactions were large, it was in the daily and private ministrations to the poor and suffering that he won and kept many warm hearts near him. While a man of extraordinary business capacity, his heart was in the welfare of the Church. Keenly alive to the necessity of education, his larger gifts, outside of building All Angels Church, were connected with colleges and schools. He had a natural gift and great fondness for architecture, and had much to do with the designs of all the buildings he erected.

" The reason why I ask the publication of this tribute to a clergyman of New York in your paper, is this. His politics were not in accord with the South, but his religion extended over the whole land. Broad and catholic in his feelings, his generosity was not confined to the institutions at the North, and in this city there stands, in the grounds of the Porter Military Academy, a unique library building as a perpetual monument to his generosity. The erection of that building was a voluntary act ; it was not suggested or asked for by me. In talking about the work here, with which he was familiar, he remarked: ' Such an institution ought to have a library building, and if you wish one, I will pay for it.' Nor was this all. The papers have published, and it has not been contradicted, that just previous to his death, he gave to the University of the South, at Sewanee, forty thousand dollars, for the erection of a large dormitory. But Doctor Hoffman's largeness of heart did not stop there ; he fully realized that the South had to deal with a difficult, and as yet unsolved, problem ; and that the great mass of negroes within the borders of the Southern land, unless fitted for citizenship by a Christian

education, are a perpetual menace ; and to do his share
towards elevating them in the scale of being, he built at
Nashville, Tennessee, a hall for colored theological students, and at Lexington, Virginia, a large schoolhouse
and home for colored children. Thus he has shown his
interest in and regard for whites and blacks, for the North
and for the South. He was an omnivorous reader, and
one of the most laborious workers I ever met with. For
many years, conscious of a weakness of his heart, he did
not spare himself by night nor by day. When those who
are the stewards of wealth use it so wisely and well, it is a
blessing to the world that some have riches. The sweetest
memory treasured by those he has left behind, is the un-
failing benevolence and generosity of his unselfish life.
The record of such a life is an incentive to all to do what
they can while they live for their Saviour's honor, and
the welfare of those for whom He died.

" A. TOOMER PORTER."

It is all over now, and only memory is left. We shall
meet again on the other shore, and I know that the joys
of Paradise are intensified by the memory of the good use
we made of time and its opportunities. I trust my dear
friend has not found that his interest in me and my work
was misplaced. On my return from New York, I found
a kind note from Mr. Frederick Baker inviting me to
preach at Jekyl Island. I went, and he and his wife and
Miss Lake again assisted me; Mr. Anderson, Mr. Scrymser,
and Mr. Charles F. Stickney, to the amount, in all, of six
hundred dollars. The Very Rev. E. A. Hoffman, the
Dean of the Seminary, sent me from New York one thousand dollars, and all of this has been an immense help in
a time of desperate extremity.

CHAPTER XLVII

TESTIMONIES TO MY LIFE'S WORK

This chapter contains letters from ex-Governor Chamber-
lain and Mr. Charles Cowley, testifying to the value of
my life's work—I receive also a kind note containing an
invitation from McQueen—I hear also from his daughter.

I AM sometimes afraid that the readers of this book will feel some hesitancy in accepting many of its incidents, for they are very marvellous, even to myself. The accidental finding of my diary, kept from 1862 to 1875, which confirmed all that I had written from memory ; and from manuscripts, has within a few days had added to its testimony the following letters. I have now been rector of the Church of the Holy Communion for forty-three years, and on the 8th of January, 1897, preached an anniversary sermon which was published in the Charleston *News and Courier*, was seen by Governor Chamberlain, and was sent to Mr. Charles Cowley by someone in this city. Ex-Governor Chamberlain is himself a distinguished historical character. I always admired his undoubted ability. I was one of those who gave him every credit for honesty of purpose during the trying days in which he figured in the history of South Carolina. I always treated him with courtesy, but our intercourse was only casual. All of which makes his letter the more gratifying, while I do not feel in anywise worthy of the high encomium.

"LAW OFFICE OF DANIEL H. CHAMBERLAIN,
"40 AND 42 WALL ST., NEW YORK, January 11, 1897.

" DEAR DR. PORTER :

" I have read—I could not find time to do it sooner—your address on the coming of the forty-third anniversary of your work in Charleston. Will you permit an absentee, and mere looker-on, by his recognition of your great work, to help make up for the short-comings of some of those whom you describe as so unsympathetic, in Charleston ? I heard an eminent Charlestonian, known to good fame far outside of Charleston, say in 1885, and I will give his remarks verbatim : ' Toomer Porter is a statesman, yes, sir, a statesman, as well as a clergyman, and if the care of all South Carolina could have been given to him in 1867, her political, educational, industrial, and racial interests would have been advanced three hundred per cent. above what they are now.' I venture to use a slang phrase to one of your cloth, and say, ' Put that in your pipe, and smoke it !' Seriously, my dear Doctor, when despondency overtakes you, or ingratitude and indifference afflict you, comfort yourself with the knowledge that this man said, what very many others have thought, and now think. I must not preach to a preacher, but if I could, I would say : Be sure no good work you have done in Charleston will perish without bearing good fruit. The moral world is so constituted, that goodness is blessed, like charity in Shakespeare, ' twice blessed,' blessing him that does and him that receives. I have profound respect for your achievements, and I sincerely hope this word will be pleasant to you to read.

" Sincerely yours,
" D. H. CHAMBERLAIN."

Ten days after this I received the following letter :

'LOWELL, MASS., January 22, 1897.

" DEAR SIR :

" Thirty-two years ago, while in Charleston, attached to the staff of Rear-Admiral Dahlgren, I read with much satisfaction the Charleston *Courier's* report of your sermon, on your return to Charleston. It was a genuine *sursum corda.* I am sorry I saved no copy of that report. In 1881, midway between that especial sermon and now, I had the pleasure to meet you at the arsenal, and I cherish the recollection of that visit very much. Is the Institute still at the arsenal ? Recently, while recovering from *la grippe,* I found among the newspapers which a friend brought in to me, the copies of the *News and Courier* containing your appeal in behalf of the Porter Military Academy, and your forty-third anniversary sermon, and I read them both with very great interest. You have indeed fought a good fight, and I hope you will continue until you are fourscore. I am very sorry that you should have cause for discouragement ; you cannot fail to be recognized as one of the benefactors of the Africans, and of your country. I wish I had the means to aid in endowing your Institute. Please send me a copy of your forty-third anniversary sermon ; if you send me a half-dozen copies of that sermon, I will place them well. I am still at work on the *Siege of Charleston.*

" Sincerely yours,

" CHARLES COWLEY."

Of course I sent the sermons. Perhaps, in God's providence, they may bring some fruit, like Miss Waterman's pamphlet. I have no recollection of Mr. Cowley's visit, nor can I trace any acquaintance with him. The sermon he refers to of thirty-two years ago was the one I preached on the 4th June, 1865: "Set your house in order." In reply to my letter to him I received the following :

"LOWELL, MASS., February 4, 1897.

" MY DEAR SIR :

" Yours of the 25th ulto. was duly received. I am glad you are writing your autobiography ; it will be valuable now, and still more valuable half a century hence. What a host of memories it will preserve; what a multitude of topics will sweep within your ken ! Let your readers know how, in the case of the Federal officers imprisoned within range of the Federal artillery, you remembered who said, ' I was in prison, and you came to Me.' Let them know, too, how, instead of wasting your life in vain regrets for the lost cause, you returned to Charleston, took the oath of allegiance, and set your house in order, and urged others to do likewise. I recall the joy with which I read the *Courier's* report of that sermon. I said at once, though I had never heard of you before : ' Here is a Southern man, a clergyman of the Episcopal Church, capable of rising above his party and above sectional prejudice, and of seeing, and saying, there is a great future before the South. Men who would not come to Fort Sumter to hear Beecher, will hear him, and adjust themselves to the new situation.' The first Sunday in June, 1865, was the 4th day of the month, a day never to be forgotten in any history of Charleston. May you live to see many returns of that day; although you have lost that sermon, you have not lost the great message which it contained. It was in advance of the times, and might have been unheeded, if it had not come from a Southern man. Your autobiography will afford you a fine opportunity to relate the story of the earthquake, and of the cyclone, and of the generous aid supplied from the North. Sincerely yours,

" CHARLES COWLEY."

With this evidence will anyone think I have exaggerated ? This letter is from one who was on the staff of Rear-Admiral Dahlgren in 1865. The following was a cheering incident of the day 10th February, 1897 : I had written to my dear friend, Charles Frederick Hoffman, Jr., how worried I was, and received a telegram to-day from him, telling me to draw on him for one hundred dollars. God bless him ! There are some striking instances right now, which encourage me to hope that the good and gracious Father is working some agencies to help me in my declining days. I finished the above last night, February 10, 1897, at eleven o'clock, and to-day, the 11th, the mail brought me a kind letter from Mr. Robert Treat Paine, of Boston, with a check for one hundred dollars, which amount he has been sending, unreminded, every February for many years; and by same mail also a letter from Lieut. John A. McQueen, from Elgin, Kane County, Illinois. I have not heard of him, or from him, in ten years. I feared he was dead. Here is the letter :

" ELGIN, February 8, 1897.

" MY DEAR FRIEND :

" Can you come to Washington, D. C., about March 2 to 4 ? General Howard will be there. I would be delighted to see you. My address will be, to the care of D. P. McCormack, First Auditor's Office, Treasury Department, Washington, D. C.

" Yours faithfully,

" JOHN A. McQUEEN."

But stranger still, the same mail brought me a postal card from his daughter, whom I had never seen since she was a little girl, when I went to Elgin to see her father, sometime in the early seventies. The card is as follows :

"BELOIT, WISCONSIN, February 8, 1897.

" MY VERY DEAR DR. PORTER :

" Some people in Beloit have been reading your book, *A Work of Faith and Love* (which I have loaned them) and have been asking me regarding your institution. I was ashamed to confess that I did not know what your school was doing now, so I would be much pleased if you would send me a copy of your catalogue (or several if you will), in order that I may bring the story up to date. My father, Lieut. J. A. McQueen, would send his kindest regards if he were here, as he often speaks lovingly of you.

" Very sincerely,

" ALICE F. McQUEEN,

" 918 Bushnell Street."

Let anyone put these four letters, Governor Chamberlain's, Mr. Cowley's, Lieutenant McQueen's, and his daughter's, from New York ; Lowell, Massachusetts ; Elgin, Illinois ; Beloit, Wisconsin ; neither of which writers knew each other, save the father and daughter, neither of whom have I communicated with,—and candidly say, Is it all coincidence or chance, or is it not sent to animate my faith, and cheer my heart ? Will anyone say, " But you need money, and there is no money in any of these " ? That is so, but who knows how God is working ? I wait, and watch, and pray.

CHAPTER XLVIII

THE ACADEMY'S THIRTY-FIRST YEAR

Twenty-five of our cadets graduated—I am stricken with sickness—A parish rectorship of forty-four years is closed —This book intended to magnify the grace of God— Farewell.

THE thirtieth term of the Porter Military Academy closed on the 24th of June, 1897, and twenty-five cadets were graduated. Five of them, through the generosity of the Rev. Dr. Jones of Hobart College, were received in September, and are now there with three who are not far from graduation. One was admitted on a scholarship at Union College, Schenectady, and one of my boys is at St. Stephen's, through the generosity of the late Dr. Hoffman ; one went to Sewanee and two to the South Carolina College. I have sent to West Point, to Annapolis, and to various colleges, two hundred and eighty young men, during these years, principally to colleges at the North, where scholarships have been generously given me. I think it an advantage that our Southern youths shall come in contact with broader views, than they would if they live, and are educated in the surroundings of their birthplace. I wish that Northern youths would change about, and some of them come South : each would find that all virtue, and all wisdom, was not confined

445

to either section. The summer of 1897 passed with the usual large application to me to admit many beneficiaries, while as usual, the pay-roll was comparatively small. I consented to take as many as I thought it prudent, but refused the applications of over one hundred. With all this work done, with this great plant in possession, and no certain income, I only owe for all the past six hundred dollars. I was in Asheville, North Carolina, and every preparation made to return to Charleston on the 28th of September, when, on the 27th, without one indication, or a moment's warning, I was suddenly seized with a severe hemorrhage. An attack precisely similar to the one I had twenty-two years ago, and the doctors said, just as Dr. Sir Andrew Clark had done, it was from imperfect action of the heart. I was brought to Charleston on the 6th of October and was for a month extremely sick. The school was opened on the first of October and in full operation ; my son, Rev. Theodore A. Porter, with able assistants, doing the duties of the school, and he carried on the services of the church. For a long while my physicians have been telling me I was overworked, and overstrained, so now they emphatically said, if I desired to live and still to work, I must give up some of my duties, either the church, or the school, and after consultation with the Bishop, and much prayer, I determined that of the two, the parish could spare me best. I therefore sent my letter of resignation to the vestry, to take effect on the 8th of January, 1898, and on Sunday the 9th, preached my farewell sermon, after a rectorship of forty-four years, during which I built the church and enlarged it three times, finished St. Mark's Church for colored people, and St. Timothy's Chapel on the grounds of the Academy.

So my autobiography ends with the closing of that chapter of my life. God in gracious mercy has raised me up again, and has restored my strength, so that I am now enabled to give my time and thoughts to this great educational work. In writing this book, and presuming to tell to the public the story of my life, listening to the suggestions, and complying with the wish of that good friend Dr. C. F. Hoffman, the motive has been to magnify the grace of God ; to show " His strength to this generation, and His power to them that are yet to come." I will attain to seventy years, 31st January, 1898.

Of course I do not know what the future has in store, or what use God may still have for me, what I will be permitted to do. That which is now upon me is, as it has been for thirty years, one of faith, and struggle, and anxiety. I earnestly pray that it may commend itself to the generous hearts of many: that it may be sustained by willing contributions, and that it may please God to put in the hearts of some of His people to so endow it, that its future may be secured.

And now I say farewell to my readers, praying that each may know the comfort, and peace, that come from a loving trust in God, and a firm faith in His providential care.

APPENDIX A

To the Editor of the " News and Courier" :

On the morning of the 7th of November, 1860, I was
informed by Corporal Finley of my squad, that I was detailed as one of twenty picked men to capture the Charleston Arsenal. Not feeling particularly warlike at that
time, and fully believing what our leaders told us, that
there would be no war because it was unconstitutional,
and that it would be merely a peaceable secession, I suggested that it might be taken as an overt act, and might
lead to unpleasant consequences ; besides, I had an engagement to walk with a young lady that afternoon, and
it would be awkward for me to get off, and begged to get
the Captain to pick over. But my appeals were in vain.
" Duty," said the Corporal, " calls you to do or die," and
I did. Rushing to my friends I informed them of the
compliment paid to my desperate courage, and my sol-
dierly qualities. I borrowed from them everything they
had in the way of weapons, and a pocket-flask. I was
presented with a beautiful scarf as a tribute from " virtue
to valor " by the " girl I left behind me," and by my
mother with an umbrella, in case of rain—for the night
looked threatening. Then bidding farewell to my sisters,
and my cousins, and my aunts, who were not as much distressed as I thought they should be under the circumstances, I buckled on my armor, composed of three large
and one small revolver, State rifle, bowie-knife, and

bayonet, over the majestic uniform of the Washington Light Infantry. I thought of the *Leopard* and *Chesapeake*; the winter at Valley Forge. I repeated "The Soldier's Grave," " 'Tis sweet to die for one's country" (as those who have never tried it say), " Freedom's battle once begun" (was there use in beginning it?), " What perils do environ"; I felt the force of every line and they weighed upon my spirits as heavily as my armament on my spine.

Thus dressed to kill I repaired to the rendezvous, Mr. Porter's church, Ashley Street, stopping on the way two or three times to bid good-bye, and realize that drinking is the " soldier's pleasure." There we met under the pale light of the moon a little before the last bell rang. Never shall I forget the solemnity of the scene ; the awful stillness so unlike a Fourth of July parade ; the church— the place for a graveyard, perhaps for us—no music, no toasts, no health-drinking, nothing but the suppressed breathing of the twenty picked men as they sat upon Mr. Porter's church doorsteps, waiting for the order, "Fall in." Soon this was given, " according to height." Now this amendment put me uncomfortably near the front line, so I moved that we go " left in front," if I could not be left behind. This motion, with a few very appropriate remarks by the tallest man of the picked twenty, was feelingly put by the Lieutenant in command of the squad. The short ones were too many for us, and I stood as " I was," thinking of home and the vacant chair, and of Her; and so I was wondering if she was thinking of me, and if she would like to be a man, and, if she were a man, if she would exchange places with me; and so I was thinking, when the Lieutenant said, " Soldiers ! in obedience to the call of our country, our duty, and our Captain, we meet, ready, I see by your countenances, to rush through the imminent breach, or mount the tottering wall. Remember Leonidas and his Spartan few. Remember to preserve—1. Silence in ranks!'' he abruptly said, to stop one of the picked, who was telling the squad how his grandfather had told him how soldiers had been shot crossing the streets in Mexico, which was having a demoralizing effect. '' Reinforcements,'' the Lieutenant continued, '' if required, will be sent to us. They are, or are supposed to be, holding themselves in readiness at the Military Hall.''

One of us asked, how many men were there at the arsenal? '' Twenty,'' he replied; '' counting the women.'' I could no longer keep quiet, and falling back on the reserved right of every citizen of this great and glorious country, viz., the right of speech, I asked if our country and our Captain thought it a fair fight, and if our duty compelled us, in our present state of training, to meet the forces of the United States. Why not bring up the reinforcements and make victory certain? why not let me go for the Fourth Brigade? I was willing to volunteer to go on that volunteer hope. Here the fellow who told what his grandfather had told him about shooting soldiers in the streets of Mexico said, his grandfather told him that when he was in the Florida war, they always sent two men or more to carry despatches, in the case one got killed, and he volunteered to go with me, and so did all of them. As this would have broken up the storming party, the Lieutenant determined not to send for reinforcements. Another fellow proposed that we send to the arsenal to see if they were at home before we called, but the Lieutenant said that was not military; and off to the arsenal gate we marched, and there we halted, pinked, ordered arms, and rested; and there the Lieutenant congratulated us on our steadiness in marching, and the quickness of the march. '' For,'' said he, '' we reached here before the gate was shut for the night, otherwise we would have been

forced to escalade the fence,'' which is very dangerous over
sharp-pointed fences, and he did not know whether there
was a dog inside or not. Then, for the first time, we
marched in through the gateway, with heads erect ; up to
this time the picked had been hanging their heads down,
to reduce their height, and dodge shot if necessary, and
with no foeman's steel to bar our way, I felt now "*Dulce et
decorum est pro patria mori.*" Marching up the pathway
a brother soldier said to me, "You see anything your
side ? " Looking ahead, I saw a field-piece with three
men near it. "One on my right saw two," he said,
"pointing right at us." *Dulce et decorum* left me. "Have
they arms ? " "Two of them have," I replied ; "but
the third has but one." I have since heard he lost an
arm in Mexico.

He whispered to me, "It is an ambush "; and while ex-
plaining to me—he was an ex-officer of the Beat—what an
ambush was, we marched past the guns and the men up
into the very centre of the arsenal, and stacked our guns
in the barracks of the arsenal, in the building once used
as a church by our chaplain, the Rev. Dr. Porter. We
heard afterwards that this good man had asked the officer
in charge to take good care of us. How much pleasanter
it would have been if we had known this when we were
attacking! For the truth of history, I must mention
casualties. My breeches, either from the weight of my
armament or from my taking too long a breath, broke
down behind. I stuck my bayonet through the upper
portion of the seat and held them up. What might have
been had I no bayonet I would not like to tell. The
other was the repulse of a sentinel by a United States
cow, which the garrison drove off, crying, "Remember
Cowpens," and re-established the Post.

And thus on the 7th of November, 1860, was the Charleston Arsenal captured.   ONE WHO WAS THERE.

APPENDIX B

REPORT

Resolved, That a Board of Missions to the colored people and freedmen of the Diocese, to consist of three clergymen and three laymen, the Bishop being *ex-officio* Chairman, be elected annually. To whom the whole subject of their instruction shall be intrusted.

2. *Resolved,* That this Board be requested to take early action to revive and sustain such missions to colored people exclusively as existed before their emancipation.

3. *Resolved,* That this Board do consider the expediency of organizing churches and congregations, consisting in whole, or part, of colored people, under such regulations as to them may seem advisable and consistent with the Constitution and Canons of the Church in this diocese.

4. *Resolved,* That this Board be urged to take early action to establish and maintain parochial schools for the secular and religious instruction of the colored people in our cities, towns, and parishes, to be conducted by teachers, male and female, of our own communion, and under the supervision of the clergy within whose cures they may be established. The industrial features being engrafted thereon, whenever practicable.

5. *Resolved,* That this Board be authorized, and requested, to search out and take by the hand any of their class who may be desirous of preparing for the sacred ministry of our Church, to whose capacity and moral fitness their pastor may testify, and to provide for their education and training at school or seminary, and with the sanction and approval of their Bishop.

6. *Resolved,* That whenever churches or parsonages, glebes, or other Church property, in the several parishes, are no longer occupied, or needed by the white members

29

of our Church, and can be made available for any of the aforesaid objects, the duty and expediency of so applying the same be respectfully urged upon the legal representatives of such churches or property.

7. *Resolved*, That this Board be, and are, hereby constituted trustees, to receive and disburse any funds contributed for the objects herein recommended from within or beyond the limits of the diocese.

8. *Resolved*, That the expediency be submitted to the Board, of appointing forthwith a missionary agent to visit the several parishes and other precincts of the diocese where the colored people may be congregated, to ascertain their general condition, wants and wishes, to collect all information pertaining to the work, to report from time to time to the Board or through some Church periodical, and to solicit pecuniary aid within, and if found necessary beyond the diocese.

(Signed)

J. STUART HANCKEL,
P. F. STEVENS,
A. GLENNIE,
G. A. TRENHOLM,
WM. C. BEE,
THOS. W. PORCHER,
Committee.

On motion of Rev. C. P. Gadsden the Resolutions were taken up *seriatim*, and severally agreed to. The question recurring on the adoption of the whole, the Report was unanimously adopted.

APPENDIX C

DR. PORTER'S APPEAL

The Rev. A. Toomer Porter, rector of the Holy Communion Church, whom all Charleston knows, has made an appeal to the people of our city in behalf of his life-work, the Porter Academy. As Doctor Porter has labored among many of our colored people, and as they love and esteem him therefor, and as many white citizens read our paper, and as Doctor Porter's paper should reach both races, the *Messenger* takes pleasure in reproducing the Doctor's article from the *News and Courier*, with the hope that our readers will give it every consideration and contribute largely to the support of this good man in his most noble undertaking. The Doctor's institution is a worthy one, and he has labored hard to keep it alive and up to its established standard of excellence. Doctor Porter is a man who entertains very broad and liberal views on the subject of Christian education and Christian charity. It was through his influence that the building now used for the Jenkins' Orphanage Institute was tendered the Rev. D. J. Jenkins, which has been the means of furthering the work of caring for orphans and destitute children of this city. We hope, therefore, that our citizens will sustain their reputation for advancing their educational interests by responding unstintedly to Doctor Porter's appeal.

APPENDIX D

I hereby place on record the names of those benefactors since 1888, living and dead, who for many years have assisted me. Supplementing what has been paid by the pupils of the school, their aid has enabled me to do this work. I here place on record my grateful thanks, while I pray that God, who loves a cheerful giver, may restore to the living fourfold for all they have done for the education of this host of boys. I feel sure that the joys of Paradise have been intensified to those who are dead by the recollection of every good and faithful work they did while still in the flesh.

The following are the names. Those marked with a star are dead ; those previous to the year 1888 have already been recorded :

*COLONEL AUCHMUTY	New York
MRS. AUCHMUTY	New York
MRS. WILLIAM APPLETON	Boston
MRS. JULIA W. ANDERSON	Cincinnati
MR. W. BAYARD BROWN	New York
MRS. W. E. BAYLIES	New York
*REV. J. BUFORD	New York
*MRS. DR. BUCKLER	Baltimore
MR. N. G. BOURNE	New York
*MR. ALEX. BROWN	Philadelphia
MRS. JANE D. BARNUM	Boston
*MR. J. M. BROWN	New York
MRS. N. A. BALDWIN	New Haven
*MR. H. P. BALDWIN	Detroit, Mich.
MRS. H. P. BALDWIN	Detroit, Mich.
MR. W. H. BALDWIN	Baltimore
MRS. EMILY A. BEEBE	Boston
MR. J. PIERSON BEEBE	Boston
MR. J. ARTHUR BEEBE	Boston
MR. SAMUEL D. BABCOCK	Boston
DR. BLAKE	Boston
MR. EDMUND H. BENNETT	Taunton, Mass.
MISS ANNA BLANCHARD	Philadelphia
MRS. ALEX. BROWN	Philadelphia
MRS. FRANCIS BAKER	New York
MR. FREDERICK BAKER	New York
MR. E. F. BURKE	Orange, N. J.
MR. R. FULTON CUTTING	New York
MRS. V. CLARK	New York
MR. WILLIAM BAYARD CUTTING	New York
MR. WILLIAM P. CLYDE	New York
MR. C. H. CONTOIT	New York
MR. J. M. COMSTOCK	New York
MR. GEORGE F. CROCKER	New York
*DR. J. J. CRANE	New Haven
MRS. E. A. COXE	Philadelphia

MISS REBECCA COXE	Philadelphia
MR. J. W. COATS	Pawtucket
MRS. H. F. CUNNINGHAM	Boston
MR. WILLIAM C. COMSTOCK	Chicago
MR. DAVID CLARKSON	New York
MRS. W. F. COCKRAN	New York
MR. WILLIAM E. DODGE	New York
*MR. CHARLES D. DICKEY	New York
MRS. A. F. DAMON	New York
MR. WILLIAM B. DOUGLAS	Rochester, N. Y.
MR. W. S. EATON	Boston
MR. WILLIAM ENDICOTT, JR.	Boston
MRS. M. M. ELLISON	Boston
*MRS. EGGLESTON	Baltimore
MRS. EDGAR	New York
MRS. M. EDGERTON	New York
*MR. JOS. S. FAY	Boston
MRS. CHARLES FAY	Boston
MRS. GEORGE S. FISKE	Boston
MRS. CHARLOTTE M. FISKE	Boston
MR. J. C. FARGO	New York
MR. H. C. FAHNESTOCK	New York
MR. F. MORTON FOX	Philadelphia
MISS ELIZABETH S. FISKE	Boston
MRS. K. F. GREY	New York
REV. MR. GROSVENOR	New York
MR. JAMES GOODWIN	New York
MRS. E. A. GAMMELL	Providence, R. I.
*MR. FRED. HUBBARD	New York
*MR. W. H. HUSTED	New York
VERY REV. E. A. HOFFMAN, D.D.	New York
*REV. CHARLES F. HOFFMAN, D.D.	New York
MR. C. F. HOFFMAN, JR.	New York
MR. F. W. HUNNEWELL	Boston
REV. W. R. HUNTINGTON, D.D.	New York
MRS. H. P. HEMMENWAY	Boston
MR. CHARLES HEBARD	Philadelphia
MR. JOHN HOGG	Boston
MRS. HANNAH M. HEBARD	Chestnut Hill
*MR. R. J. INGERSOLL	New York
MR. MORRIS K. JESUP	New York

Mrs. Florence M. Jamison	New York
*Mr. John D. Jones	New York
Mr. George Gordon King	New York
Mr. John A. King	New York
Mrs. Edward King	New York
*Mrs. M. Ketellas	New York
Miss Alice Ketellas	New York
*Mr. LeRoy King.	Newport
Mrs. Mary A. King	Newport
Miss M. LeRoy King	Newport
Miss Edith E. Kinc	Newport
*Mrs. Susan LeRoy	Newport
*Mr. A. A. Low, Sr.	New York
Mr. A. A. Low, Jr.	New York
Hon. Seth Low, LL.D.	New York
Mr. W. G. Low	New York
*Mr. Robert J. Livingston	New York
Mr. Lounder	New York
*Mr. W. B. Leonard	New York
Mr. Charles Laneau	New York
Mrs. Sarah E. Lawrence	Newport
Rt. Rev. William Lawrence, D.D	Boston
Mr. Amory A. Lawrence	Boston
Mrs. W. R. Lawrence	Boston
Miss Susan Lovering	Boston
Miss Frances E. Lake	New York
Miss Ida M. Mason	Newport
Miss Ellen F. Mason	Newport
Mr. J. Pierpont Morgan	New York
*Mr. J. S. Morgan	London, Eng.
Mrs. John D. Martin	New York
Capt. Henry Metcalfe	New York
Mrs. Edith Edgar McCags	Newport
Mrs. Julia Merrett	Rochester, N. Y.
Mr. E. D. Morgan	Newport
Mr. Gordon Norris	New York
Mr. Charles A. Peabody	New York
Mr. Robert Treat Paine	Boston
*Mrs. W. H. Powers	Philadelphia
Mr. H. E. Pellew	Washington
Rev. Dr. Quinn	Iowa

Mr. John C. Ropes	Boston
Mr. F. W. Rhinelander	New York
Dr. William C. Rieves	New York
Mr. William Rockefeller	New York
Miss Hannah F. Randolph	Philadelphia
Mrs. Shephard	Providence, R. I.
Mrs. W. D. Sloane	New York
Through Rev. Dr. Shipman	New York
Mr. Charles F. Stickney	New York
Mr. A. Scrymser	New York
*Mr. W. E. Sheldon	New York
*Mrs. Robert L. Stuart	New York
Mr. W. C. Schermerhorn	New York
Mr. T. A. Schermerhorn	New York
*Mr. J. H. Shoenberger	New York
*Dr. George C. Shattuck	Boston
Mr. A. F. Stuyvesant	New York
Mrs. Emily G. Stule	Connecticut
Messrs. Smith, Hogg, and Gardner	Boston
Rev. Alex. Mackay Smith	Washington
Mr. George S. St. Arnaud	Paris
Mr. John J. Thompson	New York
Mrs. S. F. Thompson	New York
Col. William L. Trenholm	New York
Miss A. G. Thayer	Boston
Mrs. C. M. Titus	Hartford
Mr. Cornelius Vanderbilt	New York
*Mrs. William H. Vanderbilt	New York
Mrs. M. L. Vanderbilt	New York
Rev. M. Van Rensselaer	New York
Mrs. Mary J. Winthrop	New York
*Mrs. R. C. Winthrop	Boston
Mr. Charles B. Witherell	Boston
Mr. A. G. Weeks	Boston
Mr. Henry White	New York
*Miss H. A. Wood	Philadelphia
Mr. C. A. Williams	New London, Conn.
Mr Fred. A. White	London, Eng.

APPENDIX E

PHILADELPHIA, December 15, 1879.

Such unjust public criticisms having been elicited by the passage by the United States Senate of a Resolution to lease the Charleston arsenal to the Holy Communion Church Institute, it gives us pleasure as Northern men, differing in political opinion from the rector of that Institute, but personally acquainted with him, and with his noble work, carried on by him in Charleston, to testify in his behalf. A more unselfish, devoted, and tolerant clergyman than the Rev. A. Toomer Porter it has never been our lot to meet. He has devoted all of his private means, and the whole of his life and matchless energy to bring in and board and educate the poverty-stricken sons of South Carolina without charge; he is training for useful positions in life boys who would otherwise grow up in ignorance. It can hardly be a reproach that many of these boys are of Revolutionary lineage. The assertion that his school is a '' rebel school '' is amply met by the fact that when his more advanced scholars have needed collegiate education they have been sent to Schenectady, New York, and Hartford, Connecticut. One of his largest contributors was a colored man in Charleston. If to be an Episcopal Institute is sectarian, it is of that kind which instructs and feeds the poor, clothes the naked, and builds hospitals and infirmaries. The more of such sectarianism the better. No American can read the roll of the Holy Communion Church Institute without feeling pride and thankfulness that the young Francis Marions and Isaac Haynes of to-day are receiving from the United States Government even so small a boon as the use of a dilapidated United States arsenal.

JOHN WELCH,	JAMES W. ROBINS,	NELSON McVICAR,
THOMAS ROBINS,	THOMAS CLYDE,	EDW. T. BUCKLEY,
LEMUEL COFFIN,	M. RUSSEL THAYER,	GEO. N. CONARROE,
J. ANDREWS HARRIS,	ALEX. BROWN,	GEO. H. KIRKHAM.

APPENDIX F

So many of those friends of thirty, yes, of twenty, years ago are dead. While they were living I often told them of my gratitude, and now in Paradise, I trust they are reaping a rich reward. Near the close of the second year of the Institution, I received a letter from the Rev. Mr. Huntington, then Professor of Greek in Trinity College, Hartford, offering tuition, room-rent, and one hundred dollars towards expenses of any boy I would send there. I had never looked so far as that. I only hoped to fit boys with some education to go out into life, but here was expansion. It was unsought, and I felt that God was leading me on. Of course it gave great impetus to the school. I sent one boy, Josiah B. Perry, on in September, Mr. W. P. Clyde giving me a free pass for him. And here I will state that all my boys who have since gone to Trinity, to Union, and to Hobart Colleges—and they number more than two hundred—Mr. Clyde passed free on his steamers until within the past two years, and now he still passes them at reduced rates. I made a calculation some time since and found in the item of transportation alone, he had given me in furtherance of this work nearly seven thousand dollars.

APPENDIX G

I find, in my mission in 1866, I preached in its interest at Holy Trinity, Grace, Brooklyn ; at Newton, Long Island ; at St. Bartholomew, Transfiguration, St. Luke's, Grace, Ascension, Christ Churches, New York; Emmanuel Advent, St. Paul's, Boston ; St. Peter's and St. Mary's, Brooklyn ; Christ Church, New Rochelle ; St. John's, Hartford ; Christ Church, Hartford ; Christ Church, Rye; St. John's, Grace Church, Buffalo. Strange how many of these facts have passed out of my mind, but the record made at the time has brought back many recollections. When it is remembered that when I landed in New York, on April 6, 1866, I was a total stranger, and all this was done by the last of August, it shows with what a generous welcome I was met, and I think it was the groundwork for my attachment for the North.

APPENDIX H

THE ENGLISH COMMITTEE

THE EARL OF ABERDEEN, *Chairman.*
FRED A. WHITE, ESQ., *Secretary,*   170 Queens Gate, London
A. H. BROWN, M. P. . . . . Liverpool
REV. CANON FLEMMING, Vicar of St. Michael's,   Chester Square
REV. CANON WILKINSON, Vicar of St. Peter's .   Eaton Square
THE HON. AND REV. E. CARR GLYN, Vicar of St. Mary's,
                     Kensington
REV. C. GREEN . . . . St. Paul's near Beckenham
REV. T. TEIGNMOUTH SHORE, Chaplain to the Queen.
REV. DR. TREMLETT, Vicar of St. Peter's . . Belsize Park
HOWARD GILLIAT, ESQ. . . . . . 4 Crosby Square
LEIDHAM WHITE, ESQ.
THOS. KINGSCOTE, ESQ., *Treasurer.*

THE END.

INDEX

INDEX

INDEX

INDEX

INDEX

INDEX